LITERATURE AND GENDER

Elizabeth Primamore

Borough of Manhattan Community College
City University of New York
New York, NY

Dolores DeLuise

Borough of Manhattan Community College
City University of New York
New York, NY

Longman

Boston   Columbus   Indianapolis   New York   San Francisco
Upper Saddle River   Amsterdam   Cape Town   Dubai   London   Madrid
Milan   Munich   Paris   Montreal   Toronto   Delhi   Mexico City   Sao Paulo
Sydney   Hong Kong   Seoul   Singapore   Taipei   Tokyo

Senior Acquisitions Editor: Vivian Garcia
Executive Marketing Manager: Joyce Nilsen
Editorial Assistant: Heather Vomero
Production Manager: Meghan DeMaio
Creative Director: Jayne Conte
Cover Designer: Bruce Kenselaar
Cover Illustration/Photo: © musicorso/Fotolia
Project Coordination, Text Design, and Electronic Page Makeup: Niraj Bhatt/Aptara®, Inc.
Printer/Binder/Cover Printer: R. R. Donnelley & Sons

Credits and acknowledgments borrowed from other sources and reproduced, with permission, in this textbook appear on the appropriate page within the text or on page 333.

Library of Congress Cataloging-in-Publication Data

Literature and gender / [edited by] Elizabeth Primamore, Dolores DeLuise.
   p. cm.
  An anthology.
  Summary: This book introduces students to gender by having them read, discuss, and write about gender-related topics. It features contemporary as well as classic literature with a global perspective. Each section is introduced by broad overviews of the subject, authors' biographies, short introductions to each work, the works themselves, and selections of study questions.
  ISBN-13: 978-0-205-74487-9
  ISBN-10: 0-205-74487-7
  1. College readers. 2. Readers—Sex role. 3. Readers—Women. 4. Sex role—Literary collections. 5. Women—Literary collections. 6. Sex role—Problems, exercises, etc. 7. Report writing—Problems, exercises, etc. 8. English language—Rhetoric—Problems, exercises, etc. 9. English language—Composition and exercises. I. Primamore, Elizabeth. II. DeLuise, Dolores.
  PE1127.S4L57 2011
  808'.0427—dc20

2010041068

1 2 3 4 5 6 7 8 9 10—DOH—13 12 11 10

Longman
is an imprint of

www.pearsonhighered.com

ISBN-13: 978-0-205-74487-9
ISBN-10: 0-205-74487-7

THEMATIC TABLE OF CONTENTS

GENRE TABLE OF CONTENTS

SHORT STORY BY AUTHOR

CREATIVE NONFICTION BY AUTHOR

ESSAYS BY AUTHOR

POETRY BY AUTHOR

DRAMA BY AUTHOR

MYTHS AND FAIRY TALE

PREFACE

Literature and Gender is part of a series that is designed to offer short, affordable, self-contained anthologies for use in introductory courses or as a supplement to primary works in advanced courses. The selections in this anthology are thematically presented and designed to optimize students' ability to locate issues of gender in our culture. Composed of poetry, fiction, drama, essays and creative nonfiction, the literature addresses the topic of gender in both traditional and innovative ways.

The anthology is distinguished by a global perspective and includes, among others, texts by African American, Chinese, Korean, Egyptian American, Iranian American, Italian American, lesbian and gay American, Hispanic, and Irish authors. While the majority of the works are contemporary, the anthology also contains myths, a fairy tale, and nineteenth-century American poetry. The wide range of poets and writers and of periods provides students with a strong overview of the possibilities opened up by discussions of gender. Specific questions ask students to research literary terms and historic events in order to grow in knowledge and enhance their understanding of the texts; when appropriate, we invite students to refer to widely available outside sources.

The literature is arranged according to five primary themes: Femininities with subheadings of women as art, women as artists, the body, women and nature, and girlhood; Masculinities with subheadings of fatherhood, boyhood, and male identities; Sexualities; Ethnicities and Identities; and The Changing Roles of Women and Men in Society. We have included a separate subsection on fatherhood, but not motherhood, for two reasons. The role of the father in the life of the family has changed dramatically over the years, which has broadened and redefined cultural meanings of male parentage. We thought that a separate category for fatherhood would be an effective way to bring attention to this major cultural shift. Motherhood, on the other hand, has been a woman's primary traditional role, if not the defining characteristic of her being, which is why we have included works on representations of motherhood in "The Changing Roles of Women and Men in Society." Each section is introduced by broad overviews of the subject, authors' biographies, short introductions to each work, the works themselves, and questions for study and writing. We have included footnotes to explain specific concepts, terms, and people, and we encourage students to enhance their own knowledge of these specifics by researching them in appropriate databases and on the World Wide Web.

The overall purpose of *Literature and Gender* is to direct students of diverse backgrounds, at both two-and four-year colleges, through a study of gender by having them read, discuss, and write about gender-related topics, which are often connected to issues of race, ethnicity, and class. This anthology also will help students increase their ability to read critically and thoughtfully, and to experience the readings in relation to their own lives and personal issues; it will, as well, help students establish their own psychological and social awareness of gender.

A NOTE TO THE INSTRUCTOR

This text has been designed not only with students in mind but with instructors as well. This text will provide you with a great deal of flexibility because it does not over-define literary terms, but gives you, instead, an opportunity to introduce and develop, or not, literary definitions and issues of genre and style at your own discretion so that it remains your course and not someone else's. Included in the questions for study and writing are the briefest of definitions of literary terms pertinent to the interpretation of particular readings, thus allowing a great deal of space for you to pursue, or not, an avenue of study. This anthology invites you to design your own course in literature and gender, while providing you with the essential materials you require.

ACKNOWLEDGMENTS

This anthology has benefited from invaluable guidance and assistance from a number of people. We would like to thank our reviewers: Dr. Patricia R. Campbell, Lake Sumter Community College; Kate Waites, Farquhar College of Nova Southeastern University; Ericka A. Hoagland, Stephen F. Austin State University; Anne Brannen, Duquesne University; Jeffrey Santa Ana, Stony Brook University; Ed Madden, University of South Carolina; Susan E. Gunter, Westminster College; Jeffrey Smitten, Utah State University; Leigh Bennett, Fitchburg State College; and Kate Falvey, New York City College of Technology. We would also like to thank the editorial staff at Pearson: Editor-in-Chief Joseph Terry and Senior Literature Editor Vivian Garcia for understanding the need for this book. The considerable computer skills and patience of editorial assistant Heather Vomero proved invaluable as we were constantly changing the table of contents. A special thank you to Wesley Hall for his diligence and persever-ance in securing permissions, and to Brigeth Rivera for her initial enthusiasm and support. A particular thank you to our management and production team: Joanne Riker, Meghan DeMaio, Susan Wales and Niraj Bhatt. And thanks to Carl Pellman.

Thanks goes to Joyce Harte, Chair of the Department of English at the Borough of Manhattan Community College. A special thank-you especially goes to colleagues Robert Zweig for his guidance throughout the entire process and Joyce Zonana for her suggestions with regard to global authors and texts. Finally, we would like to thank all of the wonderful poets and writers who have contributed their work to help make *Literature and Gender* innovative, excit-ing, and diverse.

ABOUT THE AUTHORS

Elizabeth Primamore is an Associate Professor of English at BMCC-CUNY. She was born in New Jersey where she grew up in an Italian American family. Moving to New York to attend college, she quickly became part of the downtown New York arts and music scene of the 1980s and 1990s. She wrote, performed, and recorded original music with her own bands, including Run Girl Run, Angel and the Drunken Gods, and Presents of Mind. She earned a BA from Hunter College in 1980, an MA from the University of London in 1996 and a PhD from the CUNY Graduate Center in 2005. Her scholarly work focuses on Virginia Woolf and "Michael Field." Her most recent work is a full length solo play, *questioning,* which is in development with notable American playwright/director Craig Lucas in New York City. She is currently working on a screenplay, a bio-drama, titled *Michael Field.*

Dolores DeLuise received a PhD in English Literature and a Certificate in Women's Studies from the Graduate Center of the City University of New York in 1992. She is Associate Professor of English at BMCC/CUNY, where she teaches both writing and literature. A writer of creative nonfiction, her areas of scholarship and publication are writing pedagogy, literature written by women, and women's spirituality. She has played folk guitar for many years and is currently studying Southern Italian-style singing and tambourine. She is the married mother of a twenty-four old daughter, Ariel. In 1997, she searched for and recovered a large number of close maternal relatives in Sicily, and is now a member of this loving extended family. She is currently working on a book about Sicily and women's spirituality, and is publishing a chapter on the goddess Tanit in Sicily in the forthcoming *Goddesses in World Culture* (ABC-Clio).

PART I

FEMININITIES

At this moment of late modernity, western femininities are associated with women's release from the bonds of tradition, a shift that intersects with race, ethnicity, and class. This broadening of possibilities for the gendered lives of women is rooted in the enormous historical impact of the second-wave feminism[1] of Betty Friedan and Gloria Steinem in the 1960s and 1970s.[2] It is useful to offer a brief, generic definition of feminism, which covers a broad range of topics from activism to gender and sexuality to theory. Feminism also refers to various political, cultural, economic, and social factions geared toward the empowerment of women. Feminists do share certain beliefs, which generally concern working against the gender (and racial) oppression historically prevalent in western culture by fighting for equal rights and equal pay for women. Since the major cultural shift effected by second-wave feminism, feminist theories have transformed higher education across disciplines for the past three decades, affecting the continually changing society, political parity, innovation, and reform.

---

[1]There are three waves of feminism. The first wave emerged during the late nineteenth and early twentieth centuries in England and the United States. While the movement made significant advances with the opening of higher education for women, wider access to the professions, and married women's property rights, the movement's primary gain was women's suffrage, or the right to vote, which was won in 1920 in the United States with the passage of the Nineteenth Amendment to the United States Constitution. Second-wave feminism refers to the increase in feminist agitation beginning in the late 1960s to about the late 1970s. The Women's Liberation Movement, as it was known, arose out of the Civil Rights and Anti-Vietnam War Movements. The third wave is thought to have emerged in the 1990s and continues to the present day. This latest form of feminism focuses more on the individual empowerment of women and less on political and social activism.

[2]Leading figures of the second-wave movement, among others, were Betty Friedan and Gloria Steinem. Friedan's landmark text, *The Feminine Mystique* (1963) challenged the belief that the only way a woman could achieve fulfillment was through marriage and children. Gloria Steinem began her career as a journalist and became an important political figure as spokesperson for the women's movement. With the slogan, "The personal is political," second-wave feminism sought to effect radical changes in both the public and private lives of women. While its achievements are wide, varied, and many, one of the most significant is *Roe v. Wade*, the U.S. Supreme Court landmark decision to legalize abortion.

In attempting to de-traditionalize western culture, feminism has disrupted the structured processes of the political, the economic, the social, and the cultural with global implications. Yet, with all of this apparent progress, gender, including gender relations, remains one of the most contested sites of negotiation across sociocultural lines. Consider the disfranchisement of Anita Hill, Hillary Clinton, or a female screenwriter in Hollywood or elsewhere trying to sell a script.[3]

Ironically enough, as feminism moved into the 1980s and 1990s, the dispute over shifting notions of femininity and masculinity reflected a generation gap within feminism itself, as much as, if not more than, the gender gap between the sexes. As the daughters of feminist mothers (and fathers), this new generation benefitted from the gains of feminism—access to sports programs, open doors to higher education, and access to reproductive health care—at the same time rejecting the label "feminist." Many younger women, however, felt caught in the dilemma of wanting those freedoms and opportunities and feeling penalized by men who might find them sexually unattractive. Those women who did identify as "feminists," such as Katie Roiphe, Naomi Wolf, and Camille Paglia[4] exploited this ambivalence by demonizing the second-wave movement, which they believed promoted what they called "victim feminism" to posit "power feminism," a perspective in which women are thought to be responsible for their own oppression. Moreover, inside the movement, women of color argued for the need for a women's movement that demanded a more thorough understanding of the intersections of race, class, and gender injustices. This revolt began with the publication of *This Bridge Called My Back: Writings by Radical Women of Color* (1981), edited by Cherrie Moraga and Gloria Anzaldua.

While such infighting might suggest that feminism will finally destroy itself, a significant social movement needs tension to evolve and progress.

---

[3]Law professor Anita Hill was a colleague of U.S. Supreme Court Justice Clarence Thomas when he was head of the Equal Employment Opportunity Commission. She alleged that Thomas had sexually harassed her, and Hill's charges were heard in a widely publicized public forum in 1991 when she testified against Thomas at his Senate Confirmation hearings and was severely ridiculed in the press. Hillary Clinton was a serious contender for the Democratic Primary in 2008, but lost to Barack Obama, who was less well known at the time. She could have been the first woman president of the United States. She also suffered a barrage of sexist slurs and attacks from the media. According to the Writers Guild of America, as recently as 2005, women made up only 27% of television writers and 19% of feature film writers.

[4]Katie Roiphe (b. 1968), the daughter of feminist writer Anne Roiphe, is an American journalist and writer who entered the feminist debate with the publication of *The Morning After: Sex, Fear, and Feminism* (1994) in which she criticizes feminists for their agitated response to the issue of date rape on college campuses. Naomi Wolf (b. 1962) became a prominent figure in the third-wave feminist movement with the publication of *The Beauty Myth* (1991) in which she argues that beauty is the "last belief system that keeps male dominance intact." After the publication of her best seller, *Sexual Personae: Art and Decadence from Nefertiti to Emily Dickinson* (1990), author Camille Paglia (b. 1947) made countless media and campus appearances in which she harshly criticized leaders of the second-wave feminist movement. Notably, Paglia accused them of creating a cult of victimhood for young women.

The resolution of this Hegelian dialectic[5] is the ongoing negotiation of third-wave feminism.

In a culture that would like to believe that gender equality has been achieved, thereby rendering feminism irrelevant, Rebecca Walker, daughter of author Alice Walker[6] and goddaughter of Gloria Steinem, gave voice to third-wave feminism when she declared in "Becoming the Third Wave" (1992), a *Ms. Magazine* article on the Anita Hill hearings, "I am not a post feminist. I am the Third Wave." As in the two prior phases, third-wave feminism is not a monolith—there are many different ways of being "female." Influenced by popular culture, much of third-wave feminism seems to exhibit reverse discourses by embracing the contradictory—including reclamation of the word *girl*, knitting, and cooking. What was once considered sexually exploitive for women is now seen as "pro-sex." This brand of feminism refuses to adhere to the fixed categories of gender and sexuality, exemplified by a belief in transgenderism, which has almost eliminated the theoretical construction of "woman" or "man" altogether. In an act of resistance, many young African American women prefer the term "hip-hop feminist" to "third-wave." In a postmodern world, it makes sense that third-wave feminism resists labels and categories, and that the idea of freedom of choice for its own sake continues to occupy the movement's center.

As the evolution of feminism has provided a way to open up new interpretations of what it means to be a woman, Femininities will explore women's ideas and experiences in the context of gender implications in the process of identity formations.

---

[5]The Hegelian dialectic is a model of logical thought ascribed to German philosopher Georg Wilhelm Friedrich Hegel (1770–1831). In the simplest terms, the dialectic is a process of change that develops through three stages: thesis, antithesis, and synthesis. The tension between the thesis (argument) and antithesis (counterargument) results in the creation of something new, or synthesis.

[6]Alice Walker (b. 1944) is an African American poet and novelist. She won the Pulitzer Prize for her novel *The Color Purple* (1982), which was made into a film in 1985.

Chapter 1

Women as Art

Throughout the centuries of western culture, images of women have figured preeminently in all of the arts—literature, music, sculpture, and painting. The female figure has been perfected and idealized by men, the chief practitioners of art until very recently, into two major tropes—the saint and the whore—to the extent that such representations have come to stand for the reality of femininity in real life and have served as models for women themselves. In our own time, women have come to view themselves as substandard if their appearances do not match those seen in the media: thin and svelte. The deep-seated extent of such polarization has given rise to emotional disorders such as bulimia and anorexia in women and girls as young as ten years of age whose attempts to conform to the current standard of beauty harms their bodies and may result in death.

This section presents work that demonstrates the uneasy, sometimes morbid, relationship between women and the masculine enterprise of representing women, explaining and illustrating the problematic relationship between women and art.

Edgar Allan Poe
(1809–1849)

The death of a beautiful woman is "the most poetical topic in the world."

An American icon, Edgar Allan Poe is best known for his tales of mystery, balladic poetry, and the macabre. Losing both parents to early deaths, the Boston native's life and career suffered from relentless financial hardships. In 1835, he married Virginia Clemm, his thirteen-year-old cousin. Coming of age during the American Romantic movement, his early success focused mostly on literary criticism. Poe's brilliant command of language, provocative subject matter, and dark perspective reflect his unique style as an architect of the modern short story, as well as initiator of both the modern detective story and the tradition of Gothic literature. Poe died at forty years of age under mysterious circumstances, recently considered to be rabies. His major works include two volumes of short stories, *Tales of the Grotesque and Arabesque* (1840), and a volume of poetry, *The Raven and Other Poems* (1845).

"The Oval Portrait" (1842)

In this story, Poe writes about an artist wishing to "capture" a woman's beauty on canvas. It points out the single-mindedness involved in representing women in a culture that can no longer perceive the value of a woman's actual presence, but rather redirects the measurements of a woman's value onto the male project of recreating only her ideal aspects. This proves literally fatal to the woman in the story while suggesting the metaphoric fatality to women themselves. This story parallels the prevalence of eating disorders among women who are unable to discern the worth of their own lives; the desire to be perceived as idealized works of art in contemporary society may be stronger than the desire to live in a less-than-ideal state.

The chateau into which my valet had ventured to make forcible entrance, rather than permit me, in my desperately wounded condition, to pass a night in the open air, was one of those piles of commingled gloom and grandeur which have so long frowned among the Apennines, not less in fact than in the fancy of Mrs. Radcliffe. To all appearance it had been temporarily and very lately abandoned. We established ourselves in one of the smallest and least sumptuously furnished apartments. It lay in a remote turret of the building. Its decorations were rich, yet tattered and antique. Its walls were hung with tapestry and bedecked with manifold and multiform armorial trophies, together with an unusually great number of very spirited modern paintings in frames of rich golden arabesque. In these paintings, which depended from the walls not only in their main surfaces, but in very many nooks which the bizarre architecture of the chateau rendered necessary—in these paintings my incipient delirium, perhaps, had caused me to take deep interest; so that I bade Pedro to close the heavy shutters of the room—since it was already night—to light the tongues of a tall candelabrum which stood by the head of my bed—and to throw open far and wide the fringed curtains of black velvet which enveloped the bed itself. I wished all this done that I might resign myself, if not to sleep, at least alternately to the contemplation of these pictures, and the perusal of a small volume which had been found upon the pillow, and which purported to criticize and describe them.

Long—long I read—and devoutly, devotedly I gazed. Rapidly and gloriously the hours flew by, and the deep midnight came. The position of the candelabrum displeased me, and outreaching my hand with difficulty, rather than disturb my slumbering valet, I placed it so as to throw its rays more fully upon the book.

But the action produced an effect altogether unanticipated. The rays of the numerous candles (for there were many) now fell within a niche of the room which had hitherto been thrown into deep shade by one of the bed-posts. I thus saw in vivid light a picture all unnoticed before. It was the portrait of a young girl just ripening into womanhood. I glanced at the painting hurriedly, and then closed my eyes. Why I did this was not at first apparent even to my own perception. But while my lids remained thus shut, I ran over in mind my reason for so shutting them. It was an impulsive movement to gain time for thought—to make sure that my vision had not deceived me—to calm and subdue my fancy for a more sober and more certain gaze. In a very few moments I again looked fixedly at the painting.

That I now saw aright I could not and would not doubt; for the first flashing of the candles upon that canvas had seemed to dissipate the dreamy stupor which was stealing over my senses, and to startle me at once into waking life.

The portrait, I have already said, was that of a young girl. It was a mere head and shoulders, done in what is technically termed a vignette manner; much in the style of the favorite heads of Sully. The arms, the bosom and even the ends of the radiant hair, melted imperceptibly into the vague yet deep shadow which formed the background of the whole. The frame was oval, richly gilded and filigreed in Moresque. As a thing of art nothing could be more admirable than the painting itself. But it could have been neither the execution of the work, nor the immortal beauty of the countenance, which had so suddenly and so vehemently moved me. Least of all, could it have been that my fancy, shaken from its half slumber, had mistaken the head for that of a living person.

I saw at once that the peculiarities of the design, of the vignetting, and of the frame, must have instantly dispelled such idea—must have prevented even its momentary entertainment. Thinking earnestly upon these points, I remained, for an hour perhaps, half sitting, half reclining, with my vision riveted upon the portrait. At length, satisfied with the true secret of its effect, I fell back within the bed. I had found the spell of the picture in an absolute life-likeliness of expression, which at first startling, finally confounded, subdued and appalled me. With deep and reverent awe I replaced the candelabrum in its former position. The cause of my deep agitation being thus shut from view, I sought eagerly the volume which discussed the paintings and their histories. Turning to the number which designated the oval portrait, I there read the vague and quaint words which follow:

"She was a maiden of rarest beauty, and not more lovely than full of glee. And evil was the hour when she saw, and loved, and wedded the painter. He, passionate, studious, austere, and having already a bride in his Art; she a maiden of rarest beauty, and not more lovely than full of glee: all light and smiles, and frolicsome as the young fawn: loving and cherishing all things: hating only the Art which was her rival: dreading only the pallet and brushes and other untoward instruments which deprived her of the countenance of her lover. It was thus a terrible thing for this lady to hear the painter speak of his desire to portray even his young bride. But she was humble and obedient, and sat meekly for many weeks in the dark high turret-chamber where the light dripped upon the pale canvas only from overhead. But he, the painter, took glory in his work, which went on from hour to hour and from day to day. And he was a passionate, and wild and moody man, who became lost in reveries; so that he would not see that the light which fell so ghastlily in that lone turret withered the health and the spirits of his bride, who pined visibly to all but him. Yet she smiled on and still on, uncomplainingly, because she saw that the painter (who had high renown) took a fervid and burning pleasure in his task, and wrought day and night to depict her who so loved him, yet who grew daily more dispirited and weak. And in sooth some who beheld the portrait spoke of its resemblance in low words, as of a mighty marvel, and a proof not less of the power of the painter than of his deep love for her whom he depicted so surpassingly well. But at length, as the labor drew nearer to its conclusion, there were admitted none into the turret; for the painter had grown wild with the ardor of his work, and turned his eyes from the canvas rarely, even to regard the countenance of his wife. And he would not see that the tints which he spread upon the canvas were drawn from the cheeks of her who sate beside him. And when many weeks had passed, and but little remained to do, save one brush upon the mouth and one tint upon the eye, the spirit of the lady again flickered up as the flame within the socket of the lamp. And then the brush was given, and then the tint was placed; and, for one moment, the painter stood entranced before the work which he had wrought; but in the next, while he yet gazed he grew tremulous and very pallid, and aghast and crying with a loud voice, 'This is indeed Life itself!' turned suddenly to regard his beloved:—She was dead!"

Questions and Ideas for Journaling and Discussion

1. Consider the narrator's role. What happens to him? What interferes with his reliability as a narrator?
2. In his essay "The Philosophy of Composition," Poe states that the death of a beautiful woman is "the most poetical topic in the world." How does "The Oval Portrait" engage that aesthetic?
3. "The Oval Portrait" may be classified as Gothic fiction, a genre rising out of the Romantic movement of the nineteenth century. It is associated with a kind of pleasurable terror and usually involves a mansion, a terrifying masculine figure, and a helpless woman. Sandra M. Gilbert and Susan Gubar[7] have suggested that the Gothic is a feminine genre, wherein the metaphoric becomes literal. Explain how this works in the story.

Writing to Explore and Learn

1. Explore Poe's use of the vampire myth in "The Oval Portrait" as a model for love.
2. Write your own Gothic horror tale in which gender relations are expressed through the creation of art.

As he painted his wife & the painting was more alife his wife was dying.
Both couldn't simultaneously subsist for long without one defeating the other

---

[7] *Madwoman in the Attic: The Woman Writer and the Literary Imagination*, 2nd ed., Cambridge, MA: Yale University Press, 2000.

Robert Browning
(1812–1889)

Love is energy of life.

Victorian poet Robert Browning was born into a well-to-do family in Camberwell, a suburb of London. His erudite father took delight in providing his son with a first-rate education; his mother was a staunch Evangelical and accomplished pianist. Mostly educated at home, with the exception of a short stint at the University of London in 1828, Browning was an exceedingly bright, voracious reader. Having a flair for creating a single character in long orations, he perfected the genre of the dramatic monologue, a poetic form in which the character of the speaker may be assessed through his or her opinions and not through ideas that are generally held by society. In 1845, Browning read poems by Elizabeth Barrett and was determined to meet her; she was, at the time, the more famous poet. In 1846, they eloped to Italy together where they lived and wrote companionably until her death in 1861. Browning continued to write until the end of his life. His major works include *Men and Women* (1855) and *The Ring and the Book* (1868).

"My Last Duchess" (1842)

In this dramatic monologue, Browning creates the character of an Italian Renaissance duke who unveils the treasured portrait of his deceased wife. It is the portrait, the idealized representation, that has value and not the woman herself.

Ferrara

That's my last Duchess painted on the wall,
Looking as if she were alive; I call
That piece a wonder, now: Frà Pandolf's hands
Worked busily a day, and there she stands.
Will't please you sit and look at her? I said   5
"Frà Pandolf" by design, for never read
Strangers like you that pictured countenance,
The depth and passion of its earnest glance,
But to myself they turned (since none puts by
The curtain I have drawn for you, but I)   10

And seemed as they would ask me, if they durst,
How such a glance came there; so, not the first
Are you to turn and ask thus. Sir, 'twas not
Her husband's presence only, called that spot
Of joy into the Duchess' cheek: perhaps   15
Frà Pandolf chanced to say "Her mantle laps
Over my Lady's wrist too much," or "Paint
Must never hope to reproduce the faint
Half-flush that dies along her throat": such stuff
Was courtesy, she thought, and cause enough   20
For calling up that spot of joy. She had
A heart—how shall I say?—too soon made glad,
Too easily impressed; she liked whate'er
She looked on, and her looks went everywhere.
Sir, 'twas all one! My favor at her breast,   25
The dropping of the daylight in the west,
The bough of cherries some officious fool
Broke in the orchard for her, the white mule
She rode with round the terrace—all and each
Would draw from her alike the approving speech,   30
Or blush, at least. She thanked men,—good; but thanked
Somehow—I know not how—as if she ranked
My gift of a nine-hundred-years-old name
With anybody's gift. Who'd stoop to blame
This sort of trifling? Even had you skill   35
In speech—(which I have not)—to make your will
Quite clear to such a one, and say, "Just this
Or that in you disgusts me; here you miss,
Or there exceed the mark"—and if she let
Herself be lessoned so, nor plainly set   40
Her wits to yours, forsooth, and made excuse,
—E'en then would be some stooping, and I choose
Never to stoop. Oh, Sir, she smiled, no doubt,
Whene'er I passed her; but who passed without
Much the same smile? This grew; I gave commands;   45
Then all smiles stopped together. There she stands
As if alive. Will't please you rise? We'll meet
The company below, then. I repeat,
The Count your Master's known munificence
Is ample warrant that no just pretense   50
Of mine for dowry will be disallowed;
Though his fair daughter's self, as I avowed
At starting, is my object. Nay, we'll go
Together down, Sir! Notice Neptune, though,
Taming a sea-horse, thought a rarity,   55
Which Claus of Innsbruck cast in bronze for me.

Questions and Ideas for Journaling and Discussion

1. Research the proper names with which you are unfamiliar and discuss how they enhance your understanding of the poem.
2. In this poem, Browning's most popular and well-developed dramatic monologue, the duke speaks to an emissary of a foreign state. He reveals a great deal about his character, his life, and his suitability as a bridegroom. Write about some of the things that he tells us about himself and explain whether or not you think he is aware of the significance of his revelations.
3. A speaker is the literary entity who relates a poem to a reader. In poetry, speakers must be regarded as separate from poets. Speakers created by poets may be reliable or unreliable, deliberately lying or unable to perceive truths that are obvious to readers. Is the duke a reliable speaker with respect to his representation of the duchess? How about with regard to other matters?

Writing to Explore and Learn

1. Discuss how Browning achieves irony using the genre of the dramatic monologue.
2. Write your own dramatic monologue in which you reveal the personality of someone you know or of a fictional character from a book, TV program, or movie.

-The Duke is the speaker (16th century)

(- He gave commands to the Duche that killed her.)

- Duke murdered his wife (so she wouldn't flirt with anybody else) to save her happy glances solely for him.

Elizabeth Barrett Browning (1806–1861)

How do I love thee? Let me count the ways.

Born into a wealthy family in Herefordshire, England, Elizabeth Barrett Browning was the oldest of eleven children. She was a precocious child who was educated at home and began writing poetry at the age of four, mastering the classics as a teenager. Her formidable father encouraged her literary pursuits, but forbade her (and all of his children) to marry. As a result of various maladies, Elizabeth became a semi-invalid and recluse, writing poetry from confinement in the family home on Wimpole Street in London. She became one of the most respected poets in Victorian England. The publication of her 1844 *Poems* inspired Robert Browning to write to her, saying, "I love your verses with all my heart, dear Miss Barrett," adding, "I love you, too." In 1846, they eloped to Italy, and Elizabeth was promptly disinherited by her father. In 1849, the couple had a son. She rests in the English Cemetery, Florence, Italy. Notable works include *Sonnets from the Portuguese* (1850) and *Aurora Leigh* (1857).

"A Musical Instrument" (1860)

In this poem, Barrett Browning takes exception to the notion of the creation of art at the expense of women. She returns to the mythical beginning of music, which reveals that the god Pan picked a reed from the water, sucked out its inner core, and fashioned it into a flute, pleased with his work and his subsequent ability to create music. What Barrett Browning also points out, in an intent, unrelenting manner, is that the reed contained a feminine entity, the nymph Syrinx, whose life was sacrificed to the male project of the creation of art.

I.

WHAT was he doing, the great god Pan.
    Down in the reeds by the river?
Spreading ruin and scattering ban,
Splashing and paddling with hoofs of a goat,
And breaking the golden lilies afloat
    With the dragon-fly on the river?

II.

He tore out a reed, the great god Pan,
    From the deep cool bed of the river.
The limpid water turbidly ran,
And the broken lilies a-dying lay,
And the dragon-fly had fled away,
    Ere he brought it out of the river.

III.

High on the shore sate the great god Pan,
    While turbidly flowed the river,
And hacked and hewed as a great god can,
With his hard bleak steel at the patient reed,
Till there was not a sign of a leaf indeed
    To prove it fresh from the river.

IV.

He cut it short, did the great god Pan,
    (How tall it stood in the river!)
Then drew the pith, like the heart of a man,
Steadily from the outside ring,
Then notched the poor dry empty thing
    In holes as he sate by the river.

V.

'This is the way,' laughed the great god Pan,
    (Laughed while he sate by the river!)
'The only way since gods began
To make sweet music they could succeed.'
Then, dropping his mouth to a hole in the reed,
    He blew in power by the river.

VI.

Sweet, sweet, sweet, O Pan,
    Piercing sweet by the river!
Blinding sweet, O great god Pan!
The sun on the hill forgot to die,
And the lilies revived, and the dragon-fly
    Came back to dream on the river.

[Handwritten margin notes: "Pan is causing destruction to make something beautiful"; "reed (woman) is innocent."; "Pan is guilty"]

VII.

Yet half a beast, is the great god Pan
　　To laugh, as he sits by the river,
Making a poet out of a man.
The true gods sigh for the cost and pain,—
For the reed that grows nevermore again
　　As a reed with the reeds in the river.

Questions and Ideas for Journaling and Discussion

1. It is not explicitly mentioned in the poem, but the reed was the nymph, Syrinx, a female entity. How does this knowledge change your reading of the poem?
2. Pan's animal nature is emphasized in the poem. Point out words and phrases that demonstrate this. Why do you think Barrett Browning wanted this animal nature highlighted?
3. The last stanza tells us that Pan sat by the river, laughing, as he made a "poet out of a man." What does this imply about Pan's actions?
4. Repetition is an important feature of poetry. Poets use such repetition in alliteration, the repetition of consonant sounds; assonance, the repetition of vowel sounds; and rime riche, the repetition of the same word in the rhyming position. Note that the first line of every stanza (or poetic paragraph) ends in "the great god Pan." How does this repetition change the meaning by the end of the poem?

Writing to Explore and Learn

1. Write an imaginative essay in the voice of Elizabeth Barrett Browning, explaining what the poem means with respect to male creativity at the expense of women. As Elizabeth, describe how you hoped the poem would work and what audience you hoped to influence by your words.

Wherever there is beauty, there may also be pain.
destruction.
We all have the potential to create beauty
or destruction.

Young-ha Kim (b. 1968)

Many of my works have been inspired by a single sentence, but often they are driven by a compelling story.

The sensation of twenty-first century Korean literature, Young-ha Kim views himself as a sufferer of attention deficit hyperactivity disorder (ADHD). He is an artist with many interests, a radio disc jockey, and an actor. Kim is a professor of drama at the Korean National University of the Arts and has been the recipient of many prestigious literary awards. His father was in the military, so the family was itinerant. Two events mark his early years: When he was ten years old, he was poisoned by inhaling the fumes from coal gas, causing him to forget early memories, and when he was a teenager, his father volunteered to fight in Vietnam, causing him great consternation. Because television was usually unavailable on the front line, Kim turned to books. He was a natural storyteller and began writing for publication in 1996, emerging as a prolific writer of short stories, novels, essays, and a screenplay. His most recent work is a novel titled *Black Flower*.

"Their Last Visitor" Trans. Dafna Zur (2008)

Kim tells the tale of a set designer who lives with his wife, a graphic artist, as they await the arrival on New Year's Eve of a Hollywood film director who is to view his work: a lifelike corpse of a teenage girl, created for a crime film. Although there is some overlapping of gender identities, the story suggests a traditional attitude toward gender in which a man occupies the space of artistic genius while a woman is merely a helpmeet. The subtext provides a way in which to understand the sway of gender in social regulation by portraying a contemporary version of the Victorian obsession with rendering dead young virgins into aesthetic objects in paintings and literature as a means to control women's sexuality and titillate male viewers.[8]

---

[8]See Elizabeth Bronfen, *Over Her Dead Body: Death, Femininity and the Aesthetic*, New York: Routledge, 1992, for a discussion on the prevalence of representations of the beautiful, dead young woman as a site of visual pleasure in western culture.

"Shouldn't I prepare some kind of dinner?" Yŏngsŏn called out from the kitchen, peeling off her pink rubber gloves. Between the kitchen and the living room was a walnut-colored table that barely seated two. Chŏngsu was bent over his work, his back to her.

"Don't bother. He won't stay long."

Chŏngsu wiped the back of his gloved hand across his sweaty forehead. Yŏngsŏn dried the kitchen counter with a dishcloth. She looked over the sink out the window. Stray cats sometimes prowled along the windowsill and stared into their basement apartment. Yŏngsŏn liked to toss them scraps of leftover fish. For some reason, though, their visits had become less frequent.

Chŏngsu rinsed his fine paintbrush in a bowl of water. Yŏngsŏn picked up the container, emptied it into the toilet, and refilled it with fresh water. "But why the hell does he have to come today? And at this hour?"

The television in the living room showed masses of curious spectators. They were swarming toward Chongno to watch the ceremonial striking of the bell in the Poshin Pavilion that rings in the New Year.

"He just wants to see it."

"Real night owls, both of you. It's the year of the monkey, isn't it?"

Yŏngsŏn brought him the container of water and rested her hand lightly on his shoulder. He was mixing colors, trying to come up with the blend he was looking for.

"Hey, aren't you a monkey?" he said.

"Um . . . I guess."

Yŏngsŏn was twenty-four. She had majored in sculpture at a prestigious art school, then married Chŏngsu, a graduate of the same school, before the ink was dry on her diploma. It happened so quickly that most of their friends thought the wedding invitation was a practical joke. She was already working as a graphic designer for an internet firm, and a friend had gotten Chŏngsu a job as a set designer for a movie producer. Yŏngsŏn's small-scale start-up company kept her busy, but Chŏngsu was even busier. He usually worked through the night. Movies were always produced on a tight schedule. Chŏngsu basically lived with his tool belt on. He'd pound away for days constructing an elaborate set only to bash it to pieces within hours. That was life: good work went completely unnoticed while carelessness was criticized ruthlessly. He had to put up with a lot of crap. Yŏngsŏn tended to think her husband's talents were going to waste, but she kept her opinion to herself.

And then, a week earlier, Chŏngsu had brought home some materials from the art supply store.

"What's all this?" she had asked.

"They need a corpse. The director told me it was time for me to live up to my reputation."

The company had started production on a movie about a serial killer. The screenplay called for five bodies, four of which would be actors in makeup. The remaining corpse was the responsibility of Chŏngsu's unit. They were to fix up a mannequin so it looked real. Chŏngsu slaved away. He mustered his five years of art school and the skills he'd picked up on the job, and put together a dead high school girl who looked so real it was creepy. Yŏngsŏn, of course, helped when she could. The high school uniform hugging the mannequin was her own. Yŏngsŏn and Chŏngsu still felt like newlyweds, and she was grateful for the time they spent together the way they used to when they were students. Even if it *was* time spent over the mannequin of a dead girl.

"When's the director coming?"

"He just called—he'll be here any minute."

"Is he coming alone?"

"Yes."

"Isn't he married?"

"Used to be. His wife took off for New Zealand a few months ago with their teenage daughter."

Yŏngsŏn watched her husband's hands. His brush was tracing a thick scarlet stream from the girl's mouth down to her neck. He was alert—this part of her face would require the most delicate touch. There would surely be close-ups in the movie. Under the bright living room lights, the black lines along the throat—marks of decomposition—looked truly putrid, Yŏngsŏn chuckled—if a thief were to break in and trip over the mannequin, he'd have a heart attack.

"What's so funny?"

"Nothing. It looks almost done!"

"Look, I know this hasn't been easy for you. If it's okay with the director, how about we take a few days off? Check out the hot springs?"

"Hot springs? That's for old people."

"C'mon. For the New Year."

Yŏngsŏn looked at the clock hanging on the wall. It was almost eleven. Chŏngsu examined his mannequin.

"Could you fix her right leg? It's way too straight. She's supposed to have twisted her ankle trying to escape the killer."

She bent over the mannequin and gave it a twist. It didn't bend as much as she expected. She grabbed the ankle and yanked. It twisted with a crack. She felt awful doing it. Just then the doorbell rang. Chŏngsu paused while his wife went to the front door. She opened it and found herself face-to-face with a man in glasses. She recognized him from the tabloids.

"Please come in. Cold out there, isn't it?"

"I brought a little something for the two of you." The director held up the typical housewarming gift of laundry detergent.

"Really, you shouldn't have . . ."

"I couldn't show up at a love nest empty-handed, could I?"

Yŏngsŏn set the gift down beside the table. Without bothering to take off his coat, the director went straight to where Chŏngsu was working. They exchanged nods and he proceeded to examine the body as if he were a detective.

"So this is it?"

"Yes."

Yŏngsŏn caught a glimpse of Chŏngsu, who suddenly blushed like a child who'd been caught with his hand in the cookie jar. It was the same expression he wore every time he completed a piece that was to go on display. She was used to that expression. But the director clearly didn't appreciate the emotions involved.

"Not bad." The director smacked his lips.

Yŏngsŏn peeked at her husband to see if the timing was right, and turned to the director.

"Would you care for a cup of coffee?"

"That would be nice."

Yŏngsŏn led him to the small table where she and her husband shared breakfast each morning. The dead body continued to draw the director's gaze. Finally he removed his coat and sat. Chŏngsu joined him across the table.

"Unbelievable. Another year gone," the director commented, looking at the calendar hanging on the wall.

"Amazing, isn't it?" Chŏngsu stood and tore the December page off of the calendar. The wall behind it was left blank. But it was a brighter blank, shielded from months of dust.

"It looks like it wasn't easy."

"It was nothing."

"It must be your first corpse."

Chŏngsu scratched his head. "Yes, it is. It was harder than I expected."

"I'm sure it was."

"I've heard it's your first thriller."

Instead of answering, the director straightened his suit and rubbed his face. He looked exhausted. Yŏngsŏn took the pot from the coffeemaker and poured a cup for the director and her husband. The director added a sugar cube and stirred. She hesitated for a moment, and then perched on a stool between the two men.

"So . . . when's the release?" she asked awkwardly, reaching for the sugar bowl. The director's open stare was making her feel uncomfortable.

"We have to finish filming first." The director shrugged, brought the coffee mug to his lips and sipped. Yŏngsŏn immediately understood the kind of man he was: the kind who always put on an air of bravado and mystery because he thought it was "cool." She considered his divorce. There was probably another woman . . . She tried momentarily, without success, to come up with a convincing scenario. In the meantime, the director's eyes had returned to the mannequin lying on the living room floor. Chŏngsu and Yŏngsŏn followed his gaze, all three staring down at the bleeding girl in her high school uniform.

"It's pretty much done . . . When would you like to pick it up?" Yŏngsŏn asked.

The director turned to her; he took his time answering.

"Can't she stay here for a few days?"

"Excuse me?"

"We don't have anywhere to put her. And we won't shoot her scene for a few days. The office is so small . . ."

She felt herself frown. The problem wasn't just that they had a body that was bleeding from the mouth. Rather, her husband would fuss over it as long as it stayed there—he wouldn't rest. But what choice did they have? No room, he'd said.

The director emptied his cup and got up. He threw one last glance at the dead girl lying on her side, went to the front door, and picked up his shoes. He looked around briefly for a shoehorn, then wedged his feet in.

"Leaving so soon?" Yŏngsŏn asked.

"Yes, Happy New Year. You too, Chŏngsu."

Yŏngsŏn opened the door for him. "Goodbye."

"I'll be in touch."

They heard him walk up the steps to the street, slowly and deliberately. They locked the door behind him gently, so as not to make a sound. Back in the living room they stood over the mannequin. Yŏngsŏn stared at her high school uniform clinging to the doll's body. Chŏngsu returned to water down the hardening paint, preparing to get back to work.

"Oh, shit! Did you see her eyes open just now?!" Chŏngsu pointed at the corpse's face. He was always playing tricks on Yŏngsŏn, but this time the corpse's glassy stare gave her a real fright and she shuddered.

"Cut it out, will you? You're scaring me!" She scowled at him, lightly slapping his arm. Then they heard a mournful yowl. A white-striped stray was lurking on their windowsill. She walked towards the cat, looking it in the eye. She'd never seen this one before. She reached out and slammed the window shut with such force she thought the glass might shatter. At the same, moment they heard the TV announcer start the countdown to the New Year.

Dong . . . dong . . . dong . . . Thirty-three dull, weighty rings ushered in the New Year. Hundreds of thousands of people were shouting. Fireworks exploded into the city sky. Only then did Chŏngsu turn to the television. His face was blank, expressionless. Yŏngsŏn picked up the remote from the floor and turned the television off. And with that a sticky silence blanketed the newlyweds' apartment. A new year had begun.

Questions and Ideas for Journaling and Discussion

1. Setting refers to the time and place of a story. What is the significance of the New Year's Eve setting in "Their Last Visitor"?
2. Discuss the relationship between the husband and wife with regard to gender roles.

Writing to Explore and Learn

1. Compare and contrast the Gothic elements in "The Oval Portrait" and "Their Last Visitor."
2. Write your own short story in which the protagonist creates a young male corpse as a work of art.

Chapter 2

Women as Artists

Since the beginning of recorded history, female creativity has been deliberately suppressed. European philosophical thought constructs a split that associates the mind with masculinity and the body with femininity, thus defining women solely by their reproductive capacities. We can trace such suppression in literature to Ovid's bowdlerization of Sappho's lyrics. Since that time, literary women have been immobilized in the aesthetic position of muse, or inspiration. In almost all annals of culture, moreover, men have written, painted and/or sculpted women into being, thereby denying them agency in their own creative lives. By creating art, women have been seen as taunting the dominant thinking, which is why, consciously or unconsciously, women's art has been considered inferior and even transgressive. It has been difficult for women to cross this line and have their art held in the same esteem in which men's art is—serious, significant and universal.

This iniquity is reflected in today's world. While gender equality in the professions has made significant progress, the same cannot be said for the arts. In fact, the numbers are so disproportionate that we have to ask ourselves, "What will it take to achieve equality for women in the creative arts?" Playwright Marsha Norman in the magazine *American Theater* (November 2009) rails against the glaring underrepresentation of women in theater, claiming that 83 percent of produced plays today are written by men. "We have a fairness problem, and we have to fix it now," she says. In the art world, in 1995, a group of women called the Guerilla Girls plastered posters across New York that read, "Do women have to be naked to get into the Met?" At the time, 5 percent of the artists in the Metropolitan Museum of Art were women, compared with 85 percent of the nudes. Queen Latifah on CNN.com (October 14, 2009) lamented, "There are not enough female rappers at all right now. It's almost non-existent." While there is much more to be said and done, it is obvious that measures should be taken to ensure fair representation for women in all areas of the arts.

The following writers invite us to think critically about literary discourses by women in various cultural contexts.

Adrienne Rich
(b. 1929)

Adrienne Rich's most recent books of poetry are *Telephone Ringing in the Labyrinth: Poems 2004–2006* and *The School Among the Ruins: 2000–2004*. A selection of her essays, *Arts of the Possible: Essays and Conversations*, appeared in 2001. She edited Muriel Rukeyser's *Selected Poems* for the Library of America. In spring 2010, Norton published *A Human Eye: Essays on Art in Society*. She is a recipient of the National Book Foundation's 2006 Medal for Distinguished Contribution to American Letters, among other honors. She lives in California.

"Diving into the Wreck" (1973)

In this poem, Rich challenges dominant worldviews and offers a liberating vision with wide cultural implications.

First having read the book of myths,
and loaded the camera,
and checked the edge of the knife-blade,
I put on
the body-armor of black rubber   5
the absurd flippers
the grave and awkward mask.
I am having to do this
not like Cousteau[1] with his
assiduous team   10
aboard the sun-flooded schooner
but here alone.

There is a ladder.
The ladder is always there
hanging innocently   15
close to the side of the schooner.
We know what it is for,
we who have used it.

---

[1] Jacques-Yves Cousteau (1910–1997), French underwater explorer and writer.

Otherwise
it's a piece of maritime floss
some sundry equipment.   20

I go down.
Rung after rung and still
the oxygen immerses me
the blue light   25
the clear atoms
of our human air.
I go down.
My flippers cripple me,
I crawl like an insect down the ladder   30
and there is no one
to tell me when the ocean
will begin.

First the air is blue and then
it is bluer and then green and then   35
black I am blacking out and yet
my mask is powerful
it pumps my blood with power
the sea is another story
the sea is not a question of power   40
I have to learn alone
to turn my body without force
in the deep element.

And now: it is easy to forget
what I came for   45
among so many who have always
lived here
swaying their crenellated fans
between the reefs
and besides   50
you breathe differently down here.

I came to explore the wreck.
The words are purposes.
The words are maps.
I came to see the damage that was done   55
and the treasures that prevail.
I stroke the beam of my lamp
slowly along the flank
of something more permanent
than fish or weed   60

the thing I came for:
the wreck and not the story of the wreck
the thing itself and not the myth
the drowned face always staring
toward the sun   65
the evidence of damage
worn by salt and sway into this threadbare beauty
the ribs of the disaster
curving their assertion
among the tentative haunters.   70

This is the place.
And I am here, the mermaid whose dark hair
streams black, the merman in his armored body
We circle silently
about the wreck   75
we dive into the hold.

I am she I am he
whose drowned face sleeps with open eyes
whose breasts still bear the stress
whose silver, copper, vermeil cargo lies   80
obscurely inside barrels
half-wedged and left to rot
we are the half-destroyed instruments
that once held to a course
the water-eaten log   85
the fouled compass
We are, I am, you are
by cowardice or courage
the one who find our way
back to this scene   90
carrying a knife, a camera
a book of myths
in which
our names do not appear.

Questions and Ideas for Journaling and Discussion

1. How does the speaker prepare for her deep-sea project? What can we read into her description of this preparation?
2. Research Jacques Cousteau; throughout the 1960s and 1970s, his undersea expeditions were widely broadcast on TV. What pieces of equipment are named in the poem, and how do these concrete images add to our understanding of the speaker's quest?
3. The figurative construction of traveling down into the water on a quest suggests both plumbing the depths of the unconscious mind and journeying to a strange destination

using unfamiliar equipment. In what ways are these two activities relevant to the working lives of women?

4. What might the poet mean by "wreck"?
5. Explore the significance of the dual-sexed personality.
6. What is the meaning of the "book of myths"?

Writing to Explore and Learn

1. Examine the extended metaphor of the poem and discuss its importance to the theme of the female quest.

Lois Elaine Griffith
(b. 1947)

Theater captures life's intent from moments when we confront our motives into action.

Born and raised in Brooklyn, New York, poet, writer, and playwright Lois Elaine Griffith is one of the founding members of the Nuyorican Poets Cafe, an influential avant-garde performance space in lower Manhattan. She is at the cutting edge of new writing and performance by people of color. Among her numerous publications in a range of genres is a novel, *Among Others* (1998). Currently, Griffith teaches at the Borough of Manhattan Community College/City University of New York.

"Sin Título" (2011)

This lyric poem challenges western privileging of the male poet as the sole creator of works of art. The speaker could be female or male, suggesting that "Sin Título" is a testament to the interchangeability of gender roles in love and relationships.

> Every time you go away
> I write you a poem
> on the breeze of early morning
> where my finger traces
> longing in the dark
> as a keepsake for your heart
> so you won't forget me
> in the storm of each new dawn
> that may not reflect
> the flower's glory
> in the summer of affection.

Questions and Ideas for Journaling and Discussion

1. The setting refers to the time and place of the poem. Discuss the significance of the summer setting in the poem.
2. Discuss the nature of the conflict between the two lovers and/or the lovers and the world as seen through the eyes of the speaker.

Michael Field (Katherine Bradley, 1846–1914; Edith Cooper, 1862–1913)

"We have many things to say that the world will not tolerate from a woman's lips," said Katherine Bradley, one half of the "male" literary enterprise known as "Michael Field," whose other half was her niece, Edith Cooper. Michael Field was the pseudonym under which Bradley and Cooper wrote volumes of poetry, plays, and prose in late nineteenth-century in England. Sixteen years apart in age, the two women poets grew up in the West Midlands in a traditional Victorian middle-class family. Using the discourse of aestheticism, the poets produced many works about a variety of subjects—historical figures and paintings of Sappho, for example.[2] A large part of Field's oeuvre was a body of love poetry written to and about each other. Their major works include *Long Ago*, a revisioning of Sappho's lyrics, and *Works and Days*, a collection of journal entries.

"A Girl" (1893)

"A Girl" is a love poem, most likely written by Katherine Bradley for her niece, Edith Cooper. In the poem, Field sets the stage for the connectedness of literary art to their personal relationship as a way to contest the dominant cultural beliefs about gender, sexuality, and creativity. Echoing Sappho by drawing on the literary conventions of love poems to young women, the poem provides the restoration of a female homosexual context that was previously denied or lost. This strategy produces, in stimulating ways, a struggle and rehabilitation over the significance of the recognition of a female literary tradition.

A Girl,

    Her soul a deep-wave pearl
    Dim, lucent of all lovely mysteries;
    A face flowered for heart's ease,

---

[2]The aesthetic movement, spearheaded by Walter Pater and his disciple, Oscar Wilde, was an avant-garde arts movement in late-nineteenth-century England. Its slogan was "Art for art's sake," which suggests that art is separate from morality and exists on its own terms, without an obligation to a moral purpose, as was previously believed.

A brow's grace soft as seas
Seen through faint forest-trees:
A mouth, the lips apart,
Like aspen-leaflets trembling in the breeze
From her tempestuous heart.
Such: and our souls so knit,
I leave a page half-writ—
The work begun
Will be to heaven's conception done,
If she come to it.

Questions and Ideas for Journaling and Discussion

1. What is the speaker's attitude toward the girl?
2. Discuss the way that sensuality is tied to creativity in the poem.

Writing to Explore and Learn

1. Compare and contrast how Field treats the theme of gender and art in "A Girl" with Rich's "Diving into the Wreck" or Griffith's "Sin Título."

Ruthann Robson
(b. 1956)

Ruthann Robson has published novels, short fiction, poetry, and, most recently, creative nonfiction in which she writes about her experiences with cancer, lesbianism, and her working-class background.

"Striving to Be Selfish" (2000)

Robson posits a theory of selfishness that opens up new interpretations of sexuality and creativity in the life of the queer writer. Robson's choice of the word selfish *to describe living a life of one's own design has added significance when placed in the context of reproduction, male domination, and power. The act of striving to be selfish suggests a move to reclaim one's power and independence from the dominant ideologies of gender and sexuality as a means to live a more genuine, and, ultimately, satisfying life.*

KEYWORDS. Self-writing, selfish, sex, dyke, writer

Being a writer, like being a dyke, is essentially selfish.

It takes a tremendous amount of selfishness to become a writer or a dyke. In both instances, one must put oneself first and foremost. A writer must write, which is a solitary activity requiring the forestalling of those who would claim one's time and attention. A dyke must disappoint others who had expectations that she would be heterosexual.

Selfishness has a bad reputation, of course. It's an accusation we level at others when we feel as if we're not getting our due. It's something we may worry over if we suspect it in ourselves. But, the selfishness I think of as negative is displayed by a narrow anxious self, what Freudians would call the ego. A writer's selfishness in those instances might be displayed when she worries over the placement of her work in an anthology or the misspelling of her name. A dyke's selfishness could be apparent when she finds herself resenting her lover's stories of a former lover. The self's anxiety—its "ishness" —concerns its felt necessity of proving its own importance.

But I want to argue for the significance of another kind of selfishness, call it capital "S" Selfishness. For the Self involved in this instance is the capital "S" Self. Forgetting the Freudians and their super-ego, I would prefer to think of this Self as being the drive to connect with something higher and more grandiose than daily life. Some call it Soul, or Spirit, or Goddess, or even God. And some do not name it at all. But practicing this kind of Selfishness paradoxically takes one out of that crabbed and insecure self which is prone to the kind of grasping selfishness we rightly abhor.

Too mystical for many, I suppose. Certainly not trendy in these postmodern times, when it is fashionable to reject any claims to truth or authenticity. Yet as a writer and a dyke, I feel I connect with something higher and more powerful when I engage in those selfish practices that make me a writer and a dyke. Meditation or ballet or pottery or tantric heterosexuality may work for others, but for me it's writing and sex. I like to think of these practices in broad senses; writing is not just pen to paper (or fingers to keyboard), just as sex is not just a finger on a clitoris. It's the idea scribbled and then crossed out; it's the flirtation; it's the car pulled over and pen pulled out to write a phrase; it's the kiss at the door goodbye and the smile hello. I might even call it a discipline. Working on a stanza because one word sounds wrong; looking at one's own body with love despite its scars. These practices forge a connection between the daily self and the expansive Self.

Not that I always connect. The struggle is to make that connection and to sustain it. This is not always easy, especially since the writer and the dyke are always in danger of being colonized—or in the term that I prefer, domesticated—by two other identities, that of the author and the lesbian.

Resisting the Author's domestication of the Writer is often difficult. It requires one to be Selfish. I strive to be Selfish by not allowing the Author much influence. It is the Author who looks at sales figures, who reads reviews, who gives readings and signs books and carefully considers the electronics rights clause in publishing contracts. These things may be necessary, but the Writer's Self must be protected against them lest they masquerade as the reasons the Writer writes. For I don't think the Writer writes to be an Author, she writes to explore some core of life that is otherwise inaccessible. Once the Writer concerns herself with sales figures or reviews of her last published effort, then the Writer's practice of her new work is affected. She might think of a reviewer's critique that a book did not have a happy ending, for example, and decide to have her new novel have a happy ending. When the impetus for writing comes from a desire to please others, the Writer is paradoxically locked inside her most parochial self.

Being Selfish as a Writer means writing for one's highest most expansive Self and exiling the Author. I have been heavily counseled to write about subjects and in genres other than the ones I am choosing. Replace poetry with a lesbian mystery, I've been told, by persons who believed they had my best interests at heart. Make my characters more likable, it's been suggested. Write shorter, write longer, take out the sex, pen erotica. The advice is often contradictory, but it consistently ignores the Self in favor of the market driven concerns that would interest the Author.

I try to write for my highest Self, but I often start my writing process with the ideas that interest my embodied lower case "s" self. I write things I want to know, but don't yet know when I start the writing. I write to solve a problem or explore an issue, even if that "issue" is one that I construct as a character, a plot, or a setting. For example, in the series of linked stories that is *Cecile,* I was occupied by the daily lives of two lesbians who were in love and stayed that way throughout the book. Until that time, I had not read a book involving a lesbian relationship that did not involve either a getting together love story or a breaking up/death tragedy. In the novel *Another Mother,* the situation I set for myself was a lesbian who was admired and cool and a professional role model on the outside and totally messed up on the inside. And in the novel *a/k/a,* I worried over whether there were such things as an essential core of identity and love at first sight.

Although fueled by lowercase "s" self-concerns, the actual practice of writing can lead to the concerns of this higher Self. For example, in *a/k/a,* my interest in the phenomenon of love at first sight led me to places that I could never have anticipated. In a novella entitled *Close to Utopia,* which will be part of my forthcoming collection of fiction, *The Struggle for Happiness,* I started with the issue of animal rights and found myself contemplating communication between animals and humans. Often, however, there is nothing in the content of the writing that reveals connection with the higher Self. For it is not really a matter of subject as much as it is a matter of the process, the practice, the craft. It's the juxtaposition of images, alliteration imagined or abandoned, a structural problem solved. It's listening to the chant-like sound of a line that no one else may hear or building the abstract scaffolding of a novel that will be invisible to most. It's sniffing out a word until it leaps out from behind the most unlikely bush, startling and almost scary.

Creative writing is most likely to manifest the epiphanies that mark connections with the higher Self, but I also try to practice Selfish Scholarship. Again, I strive to write about things that I want to know. What are the connections between the ways lesbians are treated in law and literature? How are lesbians treated when they are criminal defendants? How do critiques of narrative implicate lesbian narratives? What would happen if Sappho went to law school? Is it true that lesbians were never prosecuted for their sexual acts? In exploring these questions, I accessed what I thought were acceptable answers through the process of writing, supported by research and theorizing. As in fiction and poetry, however, I did not know what I wanted to say before I started the struggle to articulate it. Thus, I do not write to persuade or inform. I write because I want to know, even if what I want to know is only what I think about something.

I cannot always be Selfish, however, or even selfish. Like many others, writing is a part of the ways in which I earn a living. In my many years of working, as an attorney and a professor, I have written countless letters, more memos than I would like, a file cabinet full of exam hypotheticals and multiple choice questions, and probably hundreds of persuasive legal documents of all sorts. This type of writing is "work." Further, when asked, I do agree to do things that do not contribute to earning a living that I would classify as "service" rather than work or writing, such as encyclopedia entries, book reviews, and manuscript assessments. The Author rather than the Writer is asked to do these things and the

Author rather than the Writer performs them. Nevertheless, I try to limit these activities and never allow the Author to write creatively. So when I am asked to submit a piece of erotica or a memoir or some science fiction, my possibility of submission is limited by pieces I have already written, even if only in draft.

My best writing—which may not be my most popular work or my most critically acclaimed work—occurs when my Self is caught making love with something higher than its self. Which brings me to the Selfishness of being a dyke.

Like the Writer in danger of being domesticated by the Author, the Dyke lives in danger of being domesticated by the Lesbian. The Lesbian is the softer, more socially acceptable version, who struggles for the status of sexual subject in the context of political rights and who argues that her relationships are commensurate with heterosexual ones. The Lesbian is necessary, as is the Author, for she is the public figure whose goal is often to protect the private reality. Yet again, the inner Dyke needs to be protected from the outer Lesbian. The Lesbian would convince the Dyke that her reality is "equal" to heterosexuality. She would say that it's ludicrous to believe that the practices of dykedom— whatever one believes them to be—come from some higher Self or connect with some higher Spirit.

I am not advocating that Writers or Dykes abandon the sensory or intellectual worlds in favor of some shapeless spirituality. In fact, I believe Writers and Dykes must live fully in these realms. The smell of ink and my lover's sweat. The logical structure of a paragraph and a discussion in bed with my lover. But these are not the only realms that are accessible to me as a Dyke and as a Writer. Not the only realms that surface in conversations with other Dykes and other Writers. Not the realms which cause me to be Selfish.

To be a Dyke Writer is to be Selfish. Being a Dyke is attempting to communicate with this capital "S" Self through the body. Being a Writer is attempting to communicate with this capital "S" Self through language. Yet both the body and language are ultimately inadequate. It's the fate—and the joy—of the Dyke Writer that we keep trying, in our Selfish determination and ambition, to get it right.

Questions and Ideas for Journaling and Discussion

1. Define Robson's conception of "selfish."
2. Discuss how Robson defines the terms *dyke*, *lesbian*, *writer*, and *author*. How are they the same? How are they different?

Writing to Explore and Learn

1. Write an essay in which you discuss the significance of art and sex in light of Robson's thesis.

Charlotte Perkins Gilman (1860–1935)

"My own mistress at last. No one on earth had a right to ask obedience of me," declared feminist writer Charlotte Perkins Gilman on her twenty-first birthday. Born in Connecticut to educated parents, Gilman grew up in genteel poverty. In 1884, she married Charles Walter Stetson, an artist, and gave birth to a daughter a year later. This event precipitated what would today be called postpartum depression, which gave rise to her most notable work, "The Yellow Wallpaper." Divorcing her husband and sending their daughter to live with him and his new wife, Gilman's career as an author, public speaker, and reformer began to flourish. During her second marriage to an attorney, she wrote an important sociological treatise, *Women and Economics* (1898). She was brilliant thinker on gender who published short stories, an autobiography, and a feminist utopia, *Herland*, among many other works of fiction and nonfiction.

"The Yellow Wallpaper" (1892)

Gilman writes directly from her own experience in the short story, "The Yellow Wallpaper." After having lapsed into a serious depression after her marriage to Walter Stetson and upon the birth of their daughter, she was told by nerve specialist Dr. S.W. Mitchell, "Live as domestic a life as possible. Have your child with you all the time . . . Lie down an hour after each meal. Have but two hours' intellectual life a day. And never touch pen, brush or pencil as long as you live." In the story, the unnamed narrator, her physician husband John, and the child rent a colonial mansion where the narrator was to rest, according to John, to cure her hysterical illness. The story suggests that adherence to gender constraints denies women their full humanity; the effects are devastating not only for them, but for the family and larger culture as well.

It is very seldom that mere ordinary people like John and myself secure ancestral halls for the summer.

    A colonial mansion, a hereditary estate, I would say a haunted house and reach the height of romantic felicity—but that would be asking too much of fate!

Still I will proudly declare that there is something queer about it.

Else, why should it be let so cheaply? And why have stood so long untenanted?

John laughs at me, of course, but one expects that in marriage.

John is practical in the extreme. He has no patience with faith, an intense horror of superstition, and he scoffs openly at any talk of things not to be felt and seen and put down in figures.

John is a physician, and *perhaps*—(I would not say it to a living soul, of course, but this is dead paper and a great relief to my mind)—*perhaps* that is one reason I do not get well faster.

You see, he does not believe I am sick!

And what can one do?

If a physician of high standing, and one's own husband, assures friends and relatives that there is really nothing the matter with one but temporary nervous depression—a slight hysterical tendency—what is one to do?

My brother is also a physician, and also of high standing, and he says the same thing.

So I take phosphates or phosphites—whichever it is, and tonics, and journeys, and air, and exercise, and am absolutely forbidden to "work" until I am well again.

Personally, I disagree with their ideas.

Personally, I believe that congenial work, with excitement and change, would do me good.

But what is one to do?

I did write for a while in spite of them: but it *does* exhaust me a good deal—having to be so sly about it, or else meet with heavy opposition.

I sometimes fancy that in my condition, if I had less opposition and more society and stimulus—but John says the very worst thing I can do is to think about my condition, and I confess it always makes me feel bad.

So I will let it alone and talk about the house.

The most beautiful place! It is quite alone, standing well back from the road, quite three miles from the village. It makes me think of English places that you read about, for there are hedges and walls and gates that lock, and lots of separate little houses for the gardeners and people.

There is a *delicious* garden! I never saw such a garden—large and shady, full of box-bordered paths, and lined with long grape covered arbors with seats under them.

There were greenhouses, too, but they are all broken now. There was some legal trouble, I believe, something about the heirs and co heirs: anyhow, the place has been empty for years.

That spoils my ghostliness, I am afraid, but I don't care—there is something strange about the house—I can feel it.

I even said so to John one moonlight evening, but he said what I felt was a *draught*, and shut the window.

I get unreasonably angry with John sometimes. I'm sure I never used to be so sensitive. I think it is due to this nervous condition.

But John says if I feel so, I shall neglect proper self-control: so I take pains to control myself—before him, at least, and that makes me very tired.

I don't like our room a bit. I wanted one downstairs that opened onto the piazza and had roses all over the window, and such pretty old-fashioned chintz hangings! But John would not hear of it.

He said there was only one window and not room for two beds, and no near room for him if he took another.

He is very careful and loving, and hardly lets me stir without special direction.

I have a schedule prescription for each hour in the day: he takes all care from me, and so I feel basely ungrateful not to value it more.

He said he came here solely on my account, that I was to have perfect rest and all the air I could get. "Your exercise depends on your strength, my dear," said he, "and your food somewhat on your appetite; but air you can absorb all the time." So we took the nursery at the top of the house.

It is a big, airy room, the whole floor nearly, with windows that look all ways, and air and sunshine galore. It was nursery first, and then playroom and gymnasium, I should judge; for the windows are barred for little children, and there are rings and things in the walls.

The paint and paper look as if a boys' school had used it. It is stripped off—the paper—in great patches all around the head of my bed, about as far as I can reach, and in a great place on the other side of the room low down. I never saw a worse paper in my life.

One of those sprawling flamboyant patterns committing every artistic sin.

It is dull enough to confuse the eye in following, pronounced enough constantly to irritate and provoke study, and when you follow the lame uncertain curves for a little distance they suddenly commit suicide—plunge off at outrageous angles, destroy themselves in unheard of contradictions.

The color is repellent, almost revolting: a smouldering unclean yellow, strangely faded by the slow-turning sunlight.

It is a dull yet lurid orange in some places, a sickly sulphur tint in others.

No wonder the children hated it! I should hate it myself if I had to live in this room long.

There comes John, and I must put this away,—he hates to have me write a word.

We have been here two weeks, and I haven't felt like writing before, since that first day.

I am sitting by the window now, up in this atrocious nursery, and there is nothing to hinder my writing as much as I please, save lack of strength.

John is away all day, and even some nights when his cases are serious.

I am glad my case is not serious!

But these nervous troubles are dreadfully depressing.

John does not know how much I really suffer. He knows there is no *reason* to suffer, and that satisfies him.

Of course it is only nervousness. It does weigh on me so not to do my duty in any way!

I meant to be such a help to John, such a real rest and comfort, and here I am a comparative burden already!

Nobody would believe what an effort it is to do what little I am able,—to dress and entertain, and order things.

It is fortunate Mary is so good with the baby. Such a dear baby!

And yet I *cannot* be with him, it makes me so nervous.

I suppose John never was nervous in his life. He laughs at me so about this wallpaper!

At first he meant to repaper the room, but afterward he said that I was letting it get the better of me, and that nothing was worse for a nervous patient than to give way to such fancies.

He said that after the wallpaper was changed it would be the heavy bedstead, and then the barred windows, and then that gate at the head of the stairs, and so on.

"You know the place is doing you good," he said, "and really, dear, I don't care to renovate the house just for a three months' rental."

"Then do let us go downstairs," I said. "There are such pretty rooms there."

Then he took me in his arms and called me a blessed little goose, and said he would go down to the cellar, if I wished, and have it whitewashed into the bargain.

But he is right enough about the beds and windows and things.

It is as airy and comfortable a room as any one need wish, and, of course, I would not be so silly as to make him uncomfortable just for a whim.

I'm really getting quite fond of the big room, all but that horrid paper.

Out of one window I can see the garden, those mysterious deep-shaded arbors, the riotous old-fashioned flowers, and bushes and gnarly trees.

Out of another I get a lovely view of the bay and a little private wharf belonging to the estate. There is a beautiful shaded lane that runs down there from the house. I always fancy I see people walking in these numerous paths and arbors, but John has cautioned me not to give way to fancy in the least. He says that with my imaginative power and habit of story-making, a nervous weakness like mine is sure to lead to all manner of excited fancies, and that I ought to use my will and good sense to check the tendency. So I try.

I think sometimes that if I were only well enough to write a little it would relieve the press of ideas and rest me.

But I find I get pretty tired when I try.

It is so discouraging not to have any advice and companionship about my work. When I get really well, John says we will ask Cousin Henry and Julia down for a long visit; but he says he would as soon put fireworks in my pillow-case as to let me have those stimulating people about now.

I wish I could get well faster.

But I must not think about that. This paper looks to me as if it *knew* what a vicious influence it had!

There is a recurrent spot where the pattern lolls like a broken neck and two bulbous eyes stare at you upside down.

I get positively angry with the impertinence of it and the everlastingness. Up and down and sideways they crawl, and those absurd unblinking eyes are everywhere. There is one place where two breadths didn't match, and the eyes go all up and down the line, one a little higher than the other.

I never saw so much expression in an inanimate thing before, and we all know how much expression they have! I used to lie awake as a child and get more entertainment and terror out of blank walls and plain furniture than most children could find in a toy store.

I remember what a kindly wink the knobs of our big old bureau used to have, and there was one chair that always seemed like a strong friend.

I used to feel that if any of the other things looked too fierce I could always hop into that chair and be safe.

The furniture in this room is no worse than inharmonious, however, for we had to bring it all from downstairs. I suppose when this was used as a play-room they had to take the nursery things out, and no wonder! I never saw such ravages as the children have made here.

The wallpaper, as I said before, is torn off in spots, and it sticketh closer than a brother—they must have had perseverance as well as hatred.

Then the floor is scratched and gouged and splintered, the plaster itself is dug out here and there, and this great heavy bed which is all we found in the room, looks as if it had been through the wars.

But I don't mind it a bit—only the paper.

There comes John's sister. Such a dear girl as she is, and so careful of me! I must not let her find me writing.

She is a perfect and enthusiastic housekeeper, and hopes for no better profession. I verily believe she thinks it is the writing which made me sick!

But I can write when she is out, and see her a long way off from these windows.

There is one that commands the road, a lovely shaded winding road, and one that just looks off over the country. A lovely country, too, full of great elms and velvet meadows.

This wallpaper has a kind of sub-pattern in a different shade, a particularly irritating one, for you can only see it in certain lights, and not clearly then.

But in the places where it isn't faded and where the sun is just so—I can see a strange, provoking, formless sort of figure, that seems to skulk about behind that silly and conspicuous front design.

There's sister on the stairs!

Well, the Fourth of July is over! The people are all gone and I am tired out. John thought it might do me good to see a little company, so we just had Mother and Nellie and the children down for a week.

Of course I didn't do a thing. Jennie sees to everything now. But it tired me all the same.

John says if I don't pick up faster he shall send me to Weir Mitchell in the fall.

But I don't want to go there at all. I had a friend who was in his hands once, and she says he is just like John and my brother, only more so!

Besides, it is such an undertaking to go so far.

I don't feel as if it was worth while to turn my hand over for anything, and I'm getting dreadfully fretful and querulous.

I cry at nothing, and cry most of the time.

Of course I don't when John is here, or anybody else, but when I am alone.

And I am alone a good deal just now. John is kept in town very often by serious cases, and Jennie is good and lets me alone when I want her to.

So I walk a little in the garden or down that lovely lane, sit on the porch under the roses, and lie down up here a good deal.

I'm getting really fond of the room in spite of the wallpaper. Perhaps *because* of the wallpaper.

It dwells in my mind so!

I lie here on this great immovable bed—it is nailed down, I believe—and follow that pattern about by the hour. It is as good as gymnastics, I assure you. I start, we'll say, at the bottom, down in the corner over there where it has not been touched, and I determine for the thousandth time that I *will* follow that pointless pattern to some sort of a conclusion.

I know a little of the principle of design, and I know this thing was not arranged on any laws of radiation, or alternation, or repetition, or symmetry, or anything else that I ever heard of.

It is repeated, of course, by the breadths, but not otherwise.

Looked at in one way each breadth stands alone, the bloated curves and flourishes—a kind of "debased Romanesque" with *delirium tremens*—go waddling up and down in isolated columns of fatuity.

But, on the other hand, they connect diagonally, and the sprawling outlines run off in great slanting waves of optic horror, like a lot of wallowing seaweeds in full chase.

The whole thing goes horizontally, too, at least it seems so, and I exhaust myself trying to distinguish the order of its going in that direction.

They have used a horizontal breadth for a frieze, and that adds wonderfully to the confusion.

There is one end of the room where it is almost intact, and there, when the crosslights fade and the low sun shines directly upon it, I can almost fancy radiation after all,—the interminable grotesque seems to form around a common center and rush off in headlong plunges of equal distraction.

It makes me tired to follow it. I will take a nap I guess.

I don't know why I should write this.

I don't want to.

I don't feel able.

And I know John would think it absurd. But I *must* say what I feel and think in some way—it is such a relief.

But the effort is getting to be greater than the relief!

Half the time now I am awfully lazy, and lie down ever so much.

John says I mustn't lose my strength, and has me take cod liver oil and lots of tonics and things, to say nothing of ale and wine and rare meat.

Dear John! He loves me very dearly, and hates to have me sick. I tried to have a real earnest reasonable talk with him the other day, and tell him how I wish he would let me go and make a visit to Cousin Henry and Julia.

But he said I wasn't able to go, nor able to stand it after I got there: and I did not make out a very good case for myself, for I was crying before I had finished.

It is getting to be a great effort for me to think straight. Just this nervous weakness I suppose.

And dear John gathered me up in his arms, and just carried me upstairs and laid me on the bed, and sat by me and read to me till it tired my head.

He said I was his darling and his comfort and all he had, and that I must take care of myself for his sake, and keep well.

He says no one but myself can help me out of it, that I must use my will and self-control and not let any silly fancies run away with me.

There's one comfort, the baby is well and happy, and does not have to occupy this nursery with the horrid wallpaper.

If we had not used it, that blessed child would have! What a fortunate escape! Why, I wouldn't have a child of mine, an impressionable little thing, live in such a room for worlds.

I never thought of it before, but it is lucky that John kept me here after all. I can stand it so much easier than a baby, you see.

Of course I never mention it to them any more—I am too wise,—but I keep watch for it all the same.

There are things in that paper that nobody knows but me, or ever will.

Behind that outside pattern the dim shapes get clearer every day.

It is always the same shape, only very numerous.

And it is like a woman stooping down and creeping about behind that pattern. I don't like it a bit. I wonder—I begin to think—I wish John would take me away from here!

It is so hard to talk with John about my case, because he is so wise, and because he loves me so.

But I tried last night.

It was moonlight. The moon shines in all around just as the sun does.

I hate to see it sometimes, it creeps so slowly, and always comes in by one window or another.

John was asleep and I hated to waken him, so I kept still and watched the moonlight on that undulating wallpaper till I felt creepy.

The faint figure behind seemed to shake the pattern, just as if she wanted to get out.

I got up softly and went to feel and see if the paper *did* move, and when I came back John was awake.

"What is it, little girl?" he said. "Don't go walking about like that—you'll get cold."

I thought it was a good time to talk, so I told him that I really was not gaining here, and that I wished he would take me away.

"Why, darling!" said he, "our lease will be up in three weeks, and I can't see how to leave before."

"The repairs are not done at home, and I cannot possibly leave town just now. Of course, if you were in any danger, I could and would, but you really are better, dear, whether you can see it or not. I am a doctor, dear, and I know. You are gaining flesh and color, your appetite is better, I feel really much easier about you."

"I don't weigh a bit more," said I, "nor as much: and my appetite may be better in the evening when you are here, but it is worse in the morning when you are away!"

"Bless her little heart!" said he with a big hug. "She shall be as sick as she pleases! But now let's improve the shining hours by going to sleep, and talk about it in the morning!"

"And you won't go away?" I asked gloomily.

"Why, how can I, dear? It is only three weeks more and then we will take a nice little trip of a few days while Jennie is getting the house ready. Really dear you are better!"

"Better in body perhaps—" I began, and stopped short, for he sat up straight and looked at me with such a stern, reproachful look that I could not say another word.

"My darling," said he, "I beg of you, for my sake and for our child's sake, as well as for your own, that you will never for one instant let that idea enter your mind! There is nothing so dangerous, so fascinating, to a temperament like yours. It is a false and foolish fancy. Can you not trust me as a physician when I tell you so?"

So of course I said no more on that score, and we went to sleep before long. He thought I was asleep first, but I wasn't, and lay there for hours trying to decide whether that front pattern and the back pattern really did move together or separately.

On a pattern like this, by daylight, there is a lack of sequence, a defiance of law, that is a constant irritant to a normal mind.

The color is hideous enough, and unreliable enough, and infuriating enough, but the pattern is torturing.

You think you have mastered it, but just as you get well underway in following, it turns a back-somersault and there you are. It slaps you in the face, knocks you down, and tramples upon you. It is like a bad dream.

The outside pattern is a florid arabesque, reminding one of a fungus. If you can imagine a toadstool in joints an interminable string of toadstools, budding and sprouting in endless convolutions—why, that is something like it.

That is, sometimes!

There is one marked peculiarity about this paper, a thing nobody seems to notice but myself, and that is that it changes as the light changes.

When the sun shoots in through the east window—I always watch for that first long, straight ray—it changes so quickly than I never can quite believe it.

That is why I watch it always.

By moonlight—the moon shines in all night when there is a moon—I wouldn't know it was the same paper.

At night in any kind of light, in twilight, candle light, lamplight, and worst of all by moonlight, it becomes bars! The outside pattern, I mean, and the woman behind it is as plain as can be.

I didn't realize for a long time what the thing was that showed behind, that dim sub-pattern, but now I am quite sure it is a woman.

By daylight she is subdued, quiet. I fancy it is the pattern that keeps her so still. It is so puzzling. It keeps me quiet by the hour.

I lie down ever so much now. John says it is good for me, and to sleep all I can.

Indeed he started the habit by making me lie down for an hour after each meal.

It is a very bad habit I am convinced, for you see I don't sleep.

And that cultivates deceit, for I don't tell them I'm awake—O no!

The fact is I am getting a little afraid of John.

He seems very queer sometimes, and even Jennie has an inexplicable look.

It strikes me occasionally, just as a scientific hypothesis—that perhaps it is the paper!

I have watched John when he did not know I was looking, and come into the room suddenly on the most innocent excuses, and I've caught him several times *looking at the paper!* And Jennie too. I caught Jennie with her hand on it once.

She didn't know I was in the room, and when I asked her in a quiet, a very quiet voice, with the most restrained manner possible, what she was doing with the paper—she turned around as if she had been caught stealing, and looked quite angry—asked me why I should frighten her so!

Then she said that the paper stained everything it touched, that she had found yellow smooches on all my clothes and John's, and she wished we would be more careful!

Did not that sound innocent? But I know she was studying that pattern, and I am determined that nobody shall find it out but myself!

Life is very much more exciting now than it used to be. You see I have something more to expect, to look forward to, to watch. I really do eat better, and am more quiet than I was.

John is so pleased to see me improve! He laughed a little the other day, and said I seemed to be flourishing in spite of my wallpaper.

I turned it off with a laugh. I had no intention of telling him it was *because* of the wallpaper—he would make fun of me. He might even want to take me away.

I don't want to leave now until I have found it out. There is a week more, and I think that will be enough.

I'm feeling ever so much better! I don't sleep much at night, for it is so interesting to watch developments, but sleep a good deal in the daytime.

In the daytime it is tiresome and perplexing.

There are always new shoots on the fungus, and new shades of yellow all over it. I cannot keep count of them, though I have tried conscientiously.

It is the strangest yellow, that wallpaper! It makes me think of all the yellow things I ever saw—not beautiful ones like buttercups, but old foul, bad yellow things.

But there is something else about that paper—the smell! I noticed it the moment we came into the room, but with so much air and sun it was not bad. Now we have had a week of fog and rain, and whether the windows are open or not, the smell is here.

It creeps all over the house.

I find it hovering in the dining-room, skulking in the parlor, hiding in the hall, lying in wait for me on the stairs.

It gets into my hair.

Even when I go to ride, if I turn my head suddenly and surprise it—there is that smell!

Such a peculiar odor, too! I have spent hours in trying to analyze it, to find what it smelled like.

It is not bad—at first, and very gentle, but quite the subtlest, most enduring odor I ever met.

In this damp weather it is awful, I wake up in the night and find it hanging over me.

It used to disturb me at first. I thought seriously of burning the house—to reach the smell.

But now I am used to it. The only thing I can think of that it is like is the *color* of the paper! A yellow smell.

There is a very funny mark on this wall, low down, near the mopboard. A streak that runs round the room. It goes behind every piece of furniture, except the bed, a long, straight, even *smooch,* as if it had been rubbed over and over.

I wonder how it was done and who did it, and what they did it for. Round and round and round—round and round and round—it makes me dizzy!

I really have discovered something at last.

Through watching so much at night, when it changes so, I have finally found out.

The front pattern *does* move—and no wonder! The woman behind shakes it!

Sometimes I think there are a great many women behind, and sometimes only one, and she crawls around fast, and her crawling shakes it all over.

Then in the very bright spots she keeps still, and in the very shady spots she just takes hold of the bars and shakes them hard.

And she is all the time trying to climb through. But nobody could climb through that pattern—it strangles so: I think that is why it has so many heads.

They get through, and then the pattern strangles them off and turns them upside down, and makes their eyes white!

If those heads were covered or taken off it would not be half so bad.

I think that woman gets out in the daytime!

And I'll tell you why—privately—I've seen her!

I can see her out of every one of my windows!

It is the same woman, I know, for she is always creeping, and most women do not creep by daylight.

I see her on that long road under the trees, creeping along, and when a carriage comes she hides under the blackberry vines.

I don't blame her a bit. It must be very humiliating to be caught creeping by daylight!

I always lock the door when I creep by daylight. I can't do it at night, for I know John would suspect something at once.

And John is so queer now that I don't want to irritate him. I wish he would take another room! Besides, I don't want anybody to get that woman out at night but myself.

I often wonder if I could see her out of all the windows at once.

But, turn as fast as I can, I can only see out of one at a time. And though I always see her, she *may* be able to creep faster than I can turn!

I have watched her sometimes away off in the open country, creeping as fast as a cloud shadow in a wind.

If only that top pattern could be gotten off from the under one! I mean to try it, little by little.

I have found out another funny thing, but I shan't tell it this time! It does not do to trust people too much.

There are only two more days to get this paper off, and I believe John is beginning to notice. I don't like the look in his eyes.

And I heard him ask Jennie a lot of professional questions about me. She had a very good report to give.

She said I slept a good deal in the daytime.

John knows I don't sleep very well at night, for all I'm so quiet!

He asked me all sorts of questions, too, and pretended to be very loving and kind.

As if I couldn't see through him!

Still, I don't wonder he acts so, sleeping under this paper for three months.

It only interests me, but I feel sure John and Jennie are secretly affected by it.

Hurrah! This is the last day, but it is enough. John is to stay in town over night, and won't be out until this evening.

Jennie wanted to sleep with me—the sly thing! but I told her I should undoubtedly rest better for a night all alone.

That was clever, for really I wasn't alone a bit! As soon as it was moonlight and that poor thing began to crawl and shake the pattern, I got up and ran to help her.

I pulled and she shook. I shook and she pulled, and before morning we had peeled off yards of that paper.

A strip about as high as my head and half round the room. And then when the sun came and that awful pattern began to laugh at me, I declared I would finish it to-day!

We go away to-morrow, and they are moving all my furniture down again to leave things as they were before.

Jennie looked at the wall in amazement, but I told her merrily that I did it out of pure spite at the vicious thing.

She laughed and said she wouldn't mind doing it herself, but I must not get tired.

How she betrayed herself that time!

But I am here, and no person touches this paper but me—not *alive!*

She tried to get me out of the room—it was too patent! But I said it was so quiet and empty and clean now that I believed I would lie down again and sleep all I could; and not to wake me even for dinner—I would call when I woke.

So now she is gone, and the servants are gone, and the things are gone, and there is nothing left but that great bedstead nailed down, with the canvas mattress we found on it.

We shall sleep downstairs tonight, and take the boat home to-morrow.

I quite enjoy the room, now it is bare again.

How those children did tear about here!

This bedstead is fairly gnawed!

But I must get to work.

I have locked the door and thrown the key down into the front path.

I don't want to go out, and I don't want to have anybody come in, till John comes.

I want to astonish him.

I've got a rope up here that even Jennie did not find. If that woman does get out, and tries to get away, I can tie her!

But I forgot I could not reach far without anything to stand on! This bed will *not* move!

I tried to lift and push it until I was lame, and then I got so angry I bit off a little piece at one corner—but it hurt my teeth.

Then I peeled off all the paper I could reach standing on the floor. It sticks horribly and the pattern just enjoys it! All those strangled heads and bulbous eyes and waddling fungus growths just shriek with derision!

I am getting angry enough to do something desperate. To jump out of the window would be admirable exercise, but the bars are too strong even to try.

Besides I wouldn't do it. Of course not. I know well enough that a step like that is improper and might be misconstrued.

I don't like to *look* out of the windows even—there are so many of those creeping women, and they creep so fast.

I wonder if they all came out of that wallpaper as I did?

But I am securely fastened now by my well-hidden rope—you don't get *me* out in the road there!

I suppose I shall have to get back behind the pattern when it comes night, and that is hard!

It is so pleasant to be out in this great room and creep around as I please!

I don't want to go outside. I won't, even if Jennie asks me to.

For outside you have to creep on the ground, and everything is green instead of yellow.

But here I can creep smoothly on the floor, and my shoulder just fits in that long smooch around the wall, so I cannot lose my way.

Why there's John at the door!

It is no use, young man, you can't open it!

How he does call and pound!

Now he's crying to Jennie for an axe.

It would be a shame to break down that beautiful door!

"John, dear!" said I in the gentlest voice. "the key is down by the front steps, under a plantain leaf!"

That silenced him for a few moments.

Then he said—very quietly indeed, "Open the door, my darling!"

"I can't," said I. "The key is down by the front door under a plantain leaf!"

And then I said it again, several times, very gently and slowly, and said it so often that he had to go and see, and he got it of course, and came in. He stopped short by the door.

"What is the matter?" he cried. "For God's sake, what are you doing!"

I kept on creeping just the same, but I looked at him over my shoulder.

"I've got out at last," said I, "in spite of you and Jane. And I've pulled off most of the paper, so you can't put me back!"

Now why should that man have fainted? But he did, and right across my path by the wall, so that I had to creep over him every time!

Questions and Ideas for Journaling and Discussion

1. Trace the significance of the wallpaper in the life of the narrator.
2. Discuss gender relations in the story.
3. Why do you think the narrator does not have a name? How does this information add to your perception of her situation?

Writing to Explore and Learn

1. Research "the rest cure." How does this treatment compare with today's approach to postpartum depression? What purpose does this "cure" serve in the life of the narrator and her family?
2. What is the main irony in the story?
3. Discuss the theme of women and art by making connections among the protagonist, her family, and "the rest cure."

Chapter 3

The Body

It was the recognition of Sigmund Freud's psychosexual theory in the late nineteenth century that foregrounded the significance of the body in human lives.[1] Through granting the body status as a topic of discourse, we are able to understand the importance of how we function, through our bodies, in the world. Western philosophical tradition has constructed a mind–body dichotomy that privileges the rational, objective, intellectual "male" mind over the chaotic, subjective, emotional "female" body. Through the gendered body, masculinity is associated with the public realm of work, which means power and knowledge, while femininity is relegated to the private realm of domesticity, frivolousness, weakness, and feelings. For women, historically, the body is treated as a site of entrapment. To rethink the female body as a desiring subject rather than a vessel for reproduction challenges the margins to which women have been assigned. Taking into account the individuality of every woman and viewing motherhood as a by-product of choice that results from desire are moves to free the female body from the essentialism of oppressive, dominant discourses, social practices, and institutions.

---

[1]Sigmund Freud (1856–1939) was a nineteenth-century Viennese physician who invented the school and practice of psychoanalysis, which initiated a keen interest in this "talking" treatment in the west. Psychoanalysis, a method of investigation in which human mental processes and behaviors are explored through an examination of the unconscious, has evolved ideologically throughout the decades and is still relevant today. Freud's groundbreaking text, *The Interpretation of Dreams* (1900), develops the theory of the unconscious through the exploration of the significance of dreams.

Ovid (43 BCE–c. 18 CE)

The Story of Dryope, from *Metamorphoses*

In this myth, Dryope was seduced by the beauty and sensuousness of the lotus flower, picking it with disastrous consequences; the stem began to bleed, and she became transformed, as did Daphne. As a tree, she lost her beauty; her body became dried up and wooden, and her life as she knew it was over.

Bk IX:324-393 Iole tells the story of her half-sister Dryope

Alcmena finished speaking, and sighed . . . while she grieved, her daughter-in-law, Iole, said: 'Mother, what if I were to relate to you my sister's strange fate? Though sadness and tears hold me back, and hinder me from talking, Dryope was her mother's only child—I was my father's by another wife—and she was known as the most beautiful girl in Oechalia. Suffering the assault of Apollo,[2] that god who holds Delphi and Delos; her virginity lost; Andraemon[3] married her; and was considered fortunate to have her as his wife.

There is a lake, whose sloping shoreline is formed by steep banks, their summits crowned with myrtle. Dryope went there, unaware of any restrictions, and, to make what happened more unacceptable, bringing garlands for the nymphs. At her breast she carried a sweet burden, her son, not yet a year old, whom she was suckling with her warm milk. Not far away, a water-loving lotus tree flowered from the swamp, with the promise of fruits to come, its colors imitating Tyrian purples. Dryope picked some of these blossoms, to offer the child as playthings, and I was looking to do the same—I was with her—when I saw drops of blood fall from the flowers, and the branches move with a shiver of fear. It appears, as the locals now tell us, at last, but too late, that Lotis, a nymph, running from obscene Priapus,[4] turned into the tree, altering her features, keeping her name.

---

[2]The Sun God.

[3]Aetolian King.

[4]Represented with a huge phallus, he presided over the fecundity of fields, flocks, beehives, fishing and vineyards. He became part of the retinue of Dionysus, at whose revels he had pursued Lotis.

My sister had known nothing of this. When she wished to retreat, in fear, from the place, and escape by praying to the nymphs, her feet clung like roots. She struggled to tear them away, but nothing moved except her torso. Slowly, thick bark grew upward from her feet, hiding all her groin. When she saw this, and tried to tear at her hair, with her hands, her hands filled with leaves: leaves covered her whole head. But the child, Amphissos . . . felt his mother's breast harden, and the milky liquid failed when he sucked. I was there, a spectator of your cruel destiny, sister, and could bring you no help at all. Only, as far as I could, I held back the developing trunk and branches with my embrace, and I bear witness that I longed to be sheathed in that same bark.

Then her husband, Andraemon, and her luckless father, Eurytus, came, asking for Dryope: the Dryope they searched for I revealed as the lotus. They kissed the living wood, and prostrate on the ground clung to the roots of their tree. You, my dear sister, displayed nothing but your face that was not already tree. Your tears rained on the leaves of your poor body, and while your mouth left a path for your voice, while you still could, you poured out your lament like this into the air: "If there is truth in suffering, I swear by the gods I do not deserve this wrong. I am being punished without guilt. I lived in innocence. If I lie, let me lose the leaves I have through drought, be leveled with the axe, and burned. Take this child from these maternal branches, and find him a nurse, and have him often drink his milk under this tree of mine, and play under this tree. And when he learns to talk, have him greet his mother and say, sadly, 'My mother is revealed in this tree.' Let him still fear lakes, and pick no flowers from the trees, and think all shrubs are the body of the goddess.

Dear husband, farewell, and you, sister; father! If you love me, defend me from the sharp knife, and my leaves from the browsing herd. And since I am not allowed to bend to you, reach up with your arms, and find my lips, while I can still feel, and lift my little son up to me! I can speak no more. Now the soft sapwood spreads slowly over my white neck: I am imprisoned in its highest reaches. Take your hands from my eyes. Without trying to help me, allow the enveloping bark to mask the fading light!" At the moment her mouth ceased speaking, at that moment it ceased to be. For a long time, the freshly created branches glowed with warmth, from her altered body.'

Questions and Ideas for Journaling and Discussion

1. Research the story of the nymph Lotis and compare her situation with that of Dryope.
2. Explore the role of blood in a woman's reproductive life. What might be the significance of the blood in this story?
3. What are the properties of a tree that make it important in this story?

Writing to Explore and Learn

1. Write a short essay in which you compare and contrast the story of how Dryope turned into a tree and how the girl in Kimberly Gorall's story, "The End of Summer," reached the end of childhood.

Angela Costa
(1953–2008)

Words are expression, revealing existence, forming the everlasting experience of the world we're living in.

Poet, playwright, writer, and singer/songwriter Angela (Joann) Costa grew up in an Italian American family in Paterson, New Jersey. When she was a child, the family moved to nearby Haledon, and she began to write poetry at the age of nine. Upon graduation from William Paterson University, Costa emerged as a pioneer of performance poetry in the 1970s with her group, the Silk City Poets. Her life in poetry then became a life in music. Soon she began to split her time between London and New York, and released a solo album titled *Soul Disease* (1997). Her literary awards include the William Carlos Williams Poetry Award (1975) and the Paterson Poetry Prize (1977); she was short-listed for the London Writer's Award and the Beehive Poetry Award. Costa's work has appeared in publications as diverse as *Black Creation*, *Diversitas*, *Howling Dog*, and *The Femme Mystique*. Short plays include *New Year's Resolution* (2007) and *And They Call It Puppy Love* (2006), both of which were produced at HB Theatre in New York. Other works are *1,000 Reasons You Might Think She's My Lover* (1994) and *Soul Disease and Other Poems* (2012).

"and all she ever wanted" (1995)

Costa represents the female body as a site of power in subverting the established ideologies of gender and sexuality. By celebrating female sexuality, desire, and pleasure, the poet thinks through the body, hoping to find in the emotion of love a way to heal psychic wounds.

> and all she ever wanted
> was to be femme to your butch
> and she would dress the part
> and her skirt would climb easily
> so that fingers could find their way

she liked strong arms around her
she liked the whole hand inside her
she liked that you would work
hard enough to please her

she wanted to be wanted
to even feel a little pain
she wanted your hunger
to stir her need to writhe

she wanted to play games
to smell her flesh against your leather
she wanted you to do
what she needed to have done

she wanted to reach deep
into that place within your mind
to touch that single nerve
that would light your darkest room

she wanted your will to power
to ache for her surrender
she wanted your mouth
to romance her open wound

Questions and Ideas for Journaling and Discussion

1. Tone is the attitude of the speaker as perceived by the reader. The tone of a poem can be formal, informal, intimate, sad, happy, desperate, playful, serious, ironic, angry, condescending, among others. What is the tone of "and all she ever wanted"? Considering the tone, how are we to interpret the poet's take on the woman's expectations of sex?
2. What are the meanings of the terms *femme* and *butch* in the poem?
3. Discuss the significance of clothes, sex, and gender and its relationship to the construction of the body.

Writing to Explore and Learn

1. What is the meaning of desire? Discuss this aspect of the poem and its relationship to the larger themes of the female body and the speaker's conception of sex, healing, and emotion in human relationships.
2. Research the concept of "the will to power." Analyze the poet's interpretation of this concept in the poem.

Kimberly Gorall (b. 1957)[5]

Kimberly Gorall grew up in a large family in western New York, where she still lives. She is a full-time writer and an activist for progressive causes.

"The End of Summer" (1999)

Gorall's short piece of creative nonfiction relates the story of how a girl approaching adolescence learns about some unwelcome new rules that would govern her future manner of dress and behavior as she questions traditional gender constructs.

It was one of those sticky August days. Supper was over, and I'd hurried through the dishes to pursue my backyard passion. During those long school-free months, my father, brother, and I played baseball with the neighbor boys every evening till the sun slipped behind our willow tree.

I was in the outfield when my father called out that my mother wanted me in the house. I felt a pang of apprehension. In our family, you could be in trouble and not even know it.

I walked cautiously into the kitchen. As usual, my mother sat cross-legged at the table, a booklet of prayers and a mug of instant coffee in front of her, a tendril of cigarette smoke ascending from her hand. My older sister Donna was there too.

"Sit down. I want to talk to you," my mother said, not looking up. I sat.

"You're almost in the fifth grade," she began. "You can't walk around like that without a shirt any more."

"But it's *hot* outside," I protested. "I'm dyin'!"

"Girls have to wear shirts."

"But boys don't!"

"That's boys. You're a girl."

"But it's not fair!" I argued, feeling the familiar sting of a double standard. Girls couldn't have footballs, slingshots or pitcher's mitts.

---

[5]Kimberly Gorall requested that her biographical note be kept brief.

Boys didn't have to cook or baby-sit or do the dishes. Girls couldn't wear pants to school, even in the winter. Boys could be secret agents and astronauts. Girls had children. Boys had fun.

"You have to wear a shirt, and I don't want any arguments."

"All the time?"

"That's right."

My mother shifted uncomfortably in her chair. I sensed there was more.

"Pretty soon you'll become a woman," she said, sounding cheerful, rehearsed.

Who cares, I thought, cringing. What was her point? I was missing the game.

I stared at her impatiently.

Finally she said weakly, "You'll bleed in here," pointing down to her lap.

Horrified, I began to cry.

"Good one, Mom," my sister chided, rolling her eyes.

"Oh . . . ," my mother moaned, her voice trailing off. Then she, too, started crying.

I stood up, grabbed my glove, and headed for the door.

"You'll be a *woman*," she called after me.

"I don't wanna be a woman," I said through tears, letting the door slam behind me.

Questions and Ideas for Journaling and Discussion

1. What is the point of view of the mother in the story? Do you think that she could have handled her conversation with her daughter differently?

2. Think about the "double standard" that exists in the way that we treat male and female children. If you were a parent, would you impose these rules on your daughter? Explain why or why not.

3. The genre of this short piece is creative nonfiction—an essay enhanced by the techniques of novel writing. Note the places where dialogue, scene, and description are used and write about what they add to the story. What might the story have been like without these novelistic elements?

Writing to Explore and Learn

1. Write a short essay on the relationship between the title of the story and the events and details of the story.

Shahrnush Parsipur (b. 1946)

"Middle Eastern people have always been under attack and in wars and conflict, and this has made them take on a role of guardians of sex and sexuality of women," explains Shahrnush Parsipur on the banning of her books in Iran because of their sexual content. Born in Tehran, Parsipur began writing short stories and journalistic pieces when she was sixteen years old, later earning a BA in sociology from the University of Tehran. Most of her writing, which is in a style that combines realist prose and magical realism, focuses on the lives of women, including her own life and sexual experiences. Because of her work, she has been jailed twice, under the Shah's regime and that of the Islamic Republic. Currently, she lives in the United States as a political refugee.

"Mahdokht" from *Women Without Men* (2004)

In her novel Women Without Men, *Parsipur explores the lives of five women—among them a woman who is both a housewife and a prostitute—living in Iran today. Mahdokht, a school teacher, accidently witnesses an act of licentious sex, possibly rape, in which a young servant girl loses her virginity. To take control of her own body, Mahdokht longs to turn into a tree in the garden, a place of refuge for the five women. Parsipur combines the supernatural, symbolic, and realistic to show how, in Iranian culture, the female body is a contested site of negotiation between religious and contemporary thinking.*

The deep green garden, its walls plastered with mud and hay, faced the river, with the village behind it. The side by the river had no wall; the river was the border. It was a garden of sour and sweet cherries. In the garden was a house, half village house, half city house, with three rooms and a pool in front that was full of scum and frogs. The area around the pool was paved with pebbles, with a few willows nearby. In the afternoon, the light green reflection of the willows was in a silent battle with the dark green of the pool. This always troubled Mahdokht, for she could not tolerate any conflict. She was a simple woman, and wished that everyone could get along, even the myriad greens of the world.

"Such a tranquil color, but still . . . ," she thought.

A long bench sat under one of the trees at the edge of the pool. Because of the slime, there was always the possibility that it would slide and fall completely into the pool. On this bench Mahdokht would sit and watch the conflicts among the water and the willow's reflection, and the blue of the sky, which in the afternoon more than at any other time imposed itself on this gathering of shades of green, and which seemed to Mahdokht to be the divine judge between them.

In the winter, Mahdokht knit or thought about studying French or taking a trip, because in the winter one could breathe the clear, chill air, whereas in the summer, everything seemed to be finished. For summer was full of smoke and swirling clouds of dust from passing cars and pedestrians, and the sadness of windows in the burning sun.

"Damn these people, why don't they understand that the windows can't cure the pain of this country," she thought.

She had been forced to accept her older brother Hoshang's invitation to come to the garden and endure the noise of the children, who shouted and ate cherries all day, and then had the runs and ate yoghurt all night.

"The yoghurt is from the village."

"Yes, it's excellent."

The children were always cold and pale, even though they ate more than they needed, so that they could sprout up, as their mother would say.

Before, when she was a teacher, Mr. Ehteshami would say, "Miss Parhani, please put this notebook over there . . . Miss Parhani, ring the bell . . . Miss Parhani, say something to this Soghra, I have no idea what she wants . . . " Mr. Ehteshami liked for her to be the disciplinarian. It wasn't so bad. But one day Mr. Ehteshami said, "Miss Parhani, would you like to go to the movies with me tonight? There's a good movie showing."

Mahdokht turned pale. She did not know how to respond to this insult. What was this guy thinking? Who did he think she was? What did he really want? Now she understood why the other female teachers would stop smiling when Mr. Ehteshami spoke to her. They were assuming something, but they were wrong to think anything. Now she would show them all who she was. Mahdokht didn't go to school. The following year, when she heard that Mr. Ehteshami had married Miss Ata'i, the history teacher, she felt her heart contract.

"The problem is that dear father has left a lot of money."

That's the way it was. The following year, she spent the whole winter knitting. She knitted for Hoshang's first two children, who had just begun to walk. Ten years later, she was knitting for five children. "It's not clear why they have so many kids."

Hoshang would say, "It's out of my control. I like children, what can I do."

"Well, what can he do, really," she thought.

She had recently seen a movie with Julie Andrews. Her fiancé was an Austrian with seven children that he sent running this way and that with his whistle. In the end he married Julie. Of course, at first, Julie was going to go home and become a nun, but then she decided to marry the Austrian, since she was carrying his eighth child. That seemed like the best thing to do, especially because the Germans were coming and everything was happening fast.

"I am just like Julie," she thought.

She was right. She was like Julie. If she saw an ant with a broken leg, she would cry her eyes out. She had fed the starving stray dogs four times, and had given her new overcoat to the school custodian. When she was a teacher, she had participated in a charitable program by bringing several kilos of sweets to an orphanage.

"Such nice children," she thought.

She wouldn't have minded having some of them as her own. What was wrong with that? They would always have clean clothes to wear, and the snot would not run down their faces, and they would never pronounce the word "toilet" in such a crude way.

"What would become of them?"

Her question was a hard one. The government would sometimes announce on the radio or on television that something must be done about the orphans.

Both the government and Mahdokht were worried about the children. If only Mahdokht had a thousand hands and could knit five hundred sweaters a week. Every two hands could knit one sweater, so that would make five hundred sweaters.

But a person cannot have a thousand hands, especially Mahdokht, who liked the winter and liked to go for walks in the afternoon. Besides, it would take at least five hours just to put a thousand gloves on.

"No, with five hundred of my hands I could put gloves on the other five hundred. Three minutes at the most."

These are not the problems. They will eventually be solved. It's the government's responsibility, they should open a factory to knit sweaters.

Mahdokht wiggled her feet in the water of the pool.

The first day that she came to the garden she went to the riverbank and stood in the water. The icy water froze her feet so that she had to step out quickly. She could have caught cold. After she put her shoes back on, she went over to the greenhouse. The door to the greenhouse was open, and the humid air inside was warmer than summer air. Years ago Mr. Ehteshami had said that breathing the humid air of the greenhouse during the day was the best thing you could do, because all the flowers produce oxygen. He said this even though at that time they had taken all the flowers from the greenhouse and put them in the garden. Mahdokht walked along the narrow aisle in the greenhouse looking at the dusty windows. She heard the sound of breathing and struggling, something burning and hot, the smell of bodies.

Mahdokht's heart stopped. The girl, Fatemeh, at fifteen like a worldly woman, was at the end of the greenhouse with Yadallah, the gardener. With his bald head and oozing eyes, it was difficult to look at him.

The world around her went dark, and her legs began to tremble. She involuntarily clutched the edge of a table. But she could not take her eyes off them. She looked and looked until they saw her. The guy had begun to whimper. He wanted to escape but he couldn't. He was mindlessly beating the girl. The girl extended her hand toward Mahdokht. Mahdokht ran out of the greenhouse. She didn't know what to do. She headed for the pool in a daze, and wanted to throw up. She washed her hands and sat on the bench.

"What can I do?"

She thought about going to Hoshang and his wife and telling all. The girl was under their supervision.

"A little girl of fifteen—how awful . . . "

Hoshang would certainly give the girl a severe beating. Then they would let her go. Fatemeh's brothers would surely kill her.

"What can I do?"

She would quickly pack her bags and return to Tehran. At least that would be better than this anxiety.

"So what to do?"

She was paralyzed, but she felt compelled to return fearfully to the greenhouse. The girl stumbled out with her chador on inside out. Her face was red and scratched.

"Madam," she said, throwing herself at Mahdokht's feet.

"She is whimpering like a dog," Mahdokht thought.

"Go away, you filthy thing."

"No, madam, in the name of God, may I die for you. May I be your sacrifice."

"Shut up, step aside."

"In the name of God, may I be your sacrifice. If you tell my mother she'll kill me."

"Who said I wanted to tell?"

"By God, he wants to marry me. Tomorrow he's supposed to tell the master."

Mahdokht had to promise not to tell just to get the girl to leave her alone. When the girl's hands touched Mahdokht's feet, she felt disgusted. The girl walked back to the greenhouse, crestfallen. Mahdokht drew a deep breath. She felt an urge to cry.

Now three months had passed and the summer would be over in a few days. That day they would all go back to the city and no one would ever find out why Yadallah the gardener left so abruptly. Hoshang said, "It's strange, he himself said a hundred times that he wouldn't leave."

They had to hire another caretaker for the garden so that it wouldn't be vandalized during the winter. Without a caretaker, anyone could put four benches by the river and rent them out for thirty tomans a day to groups of men who wanted to hang out. Hoshang said this and everyone believed him.

The sound of Fatemeh's shrill laughter came from the end of the garden. She had taken the children out to play, and God only knew what kind of games she was teaching them. Mahdokht paced back and forth in her room, beating the door and walls with her fists. She was worried about the children.

"I hope she's pregnant so that they kill her," she thought.

It would be good if she were pregnant. All her brothers would descend on her and beat her to death. How good that would be. Then the children would not be corrupted.

"My virginity is like a tree," she thought suddenly.

She had to look in a mirror. She had to see her face.

"Maybe that's why I am green."

Her face was yellowish green. There were shadows under her eyes and the veins showed on her forehead.

Mr. Ehteshami had said, "How cold you are, like ice."

Now she thought, "Not like ice. I am a tree."

She could plant herself in the ground.

"I'm not a seed, I'm a tree. I must plant myself."

How could she tell this to Hoshang? She wanted to say, dear brother, let's sit down and have a friendly talk. As you know, the factories knit sweaters. But if she said this, she would have to explain about the thousand hands. She couldn't explain about the hands. It was impossible for Hoshang to understand this.

How could she say, when thousands of factories knit sweaters, there was no need for her to knit. Well, there was no alternative. Mahdokht decided to stay in the garden and plant herself at the beginning of winter. She had to ask the gardeners what was the best time for planting. She didn't know, but it wasn't important. She would stay and plant herself. Perhaps she would turn into a tree. She wanted to grow on the riverbank with leaves greener than the slime, and fight the battle of shades of green in the pool. If she became a tree, she would sprout new leaves. She would be covered with new leaves. She would give her new leaves to the wind, a garden full of Mahdokhts. They would have to cut down all the sour and sweet cherry trees so that Mahdokht could grow. Mahdokht would grow.

She would become thousands and thousands of branches. She would cover the entire world. Americans would buy her shoots and take them to California. They would call the forest of Mahdokht the forest of Mahdekat. Gradually they would pronounce her name so many times until it would become Maduk in some places and Maaduk in others. Then four hundred years later the linguists, with their veins standing out in their foreheads like twigs, would debate over her and prove that the two words come from the root Madeek which is of African origin. Then the biologists would object that a tree that grows in cold climates could not grow in Africa.

Mahdokht banged her head on the wall again and again until she broke into tears. Between sobs she thought that this year she would definitely take a trip to Africa. She would go to Africa so that she could grow. She wanted to be a tree in a warm climate. She wanted to, and it is always desire that drives one to madness.

Questions and Ideas for Journaling and Discussion

1. What is the meaning of virtue in Iranian culture?
2. Discuss the relationship among women, nature, and the body in the story.

Writing to Explore and Learn

1. Explore Parsipur's treatment of the theme of female sexuality as a way to understand gender relations in Iranian culture.
2. Write about the relationship between "Mahdokht" and the story of Dryope.

Chapter 4

Women and Nature

Women have a strong relationship to nature; consider, for example, that Mother Nature, Mother Earth, and the Goddess Natura are all female. These archetypes suggest that women *are* nature. Figures depicting women as the earth goddess, such as the Venus of Willendorf,[1] approximately 24,000 years old, possess exaggerated female characteristics—huge breasts and hips—inferring that these physical elements of femininity are those that are most important.

It was felt that women, like nature, needed to be controlled. They have been represented as irrational and willful, words that one might use to describe a violent thunderstorm, landslide, or hurricane. The comparison of women to nature also points to animal behavior, as evidenced by the literary trope that women are insatiable and must be carefully guarded. In addition, with the advent of scientific inquiry in the seventeenth century, male scientists took on the role of investigators of natural phenomena, and women easily fit into this category of investigation because they had traditionally occupied the role of object, not subject. One readily visible consequence of this role distribution can be seen in modern approaches to childbirth. From the inception of objective scientific study up until the 1960s, supervision and standards of childbirth were appropriated by the male medical establishment. Not only had male physicians replaced midwives as the repositories of obstetrical knowledge, but they carried out procedures that humiliated women and literally silenced their participation in the birth of their own children by using arm restraints and anesthetic and tranquilizing drugs, among them the amnesia-inducing scopolamine. Today, women have the option of actively participating in midwife-supervised, normal childbirth, which has been de-medicalized, and restored to its place as a memorable event in a woman's life.

It had been difficult for women to step out of the traditional role of natural object of scrutiny and into the role of subject or scientific investigator, but much recent progress has been made.[2]

---

[1]See this image online.

[2]See Sandra Harding, *The Science Question in Feminism*, Ithaca, NY: Cornell University Press, 1986.

Ovid (43 BCE–c.18 CE)

The Story of Daphne from *Metamorphoses*

In her quest to protect her virginity, Daphne suffers the unforeseen consequences of silence and immobility when she is turned into a laurel tree.

Bk I:438-472

. . . Phoebus's[3] first love was Daphne, daughter of Peneus,[4] and not through chance but because of Cupid's fierce anger. Recently the Delian[5] god . . . had seen him bending his tightly strung bow and said 'Impudent boy, what are you doing with a man's weapons? That one is suited to my shoulders, since I can hit wild beasts of a certainty, and wound my enemies, and not long ago destroyed with countless arrows the swollen Python that covered many acres with its plague-ridden belly. You should be intent on stirring the concealed fires of love with your burning brand, not laying claim to my glories!' Venus's son replied 'You may hit every other thing Phoebus, but my bow will strike you: to the degree that all living creatures are less than gods, by that degree is your glory less than mine.' He spoke, and striking the air fiercely with beating wings, he landed on the shady peak of Parnassus,[6] and took two arrows with opposite effects from his full quiver: one kindles love, the other dispels it. The one that kindles is golden with a sharp glistening point, the one that dispels is blunt with lead beneath its shaft. With the second he transfixed Peneus's daughter, but with the first he wounded Apollo piercing him to the marrow of his bones.

Bk I:473-503 Phoebus pursues Daphne

Now the one loved, and the other fled from love's name, taking delight in the depths of the woods, and the skins of the wild beasts she caught,

---

[3]The God Apollo.
[4]The River God.
[5]Apollo, born in Delos.
[6]Mountain in Greece, home of poetry and literature.

emulating virgin Phoebe,[7] a careless ribbon holding back her hair. Many courted her, but she, averse to being wooed, free from men and unable to endure them, roamed the pathless woods, careless of Hymen[8] or Amor,[9] or whatever marriage might be. Her father often said 'Girl you owe me a son-in-law', and again often 'Daughter, you owe me grandsons.' But, hating the wedding torch as if it smacked of crime she would blush red with shame all over her beautiful face, and clinging to her father's neck with coaxing arms, she would say 'Dearest father, let me be a virgin for ever! Diana's[10] father granted it to her.' He yields to that plea, but your beauty itself, Daphne, prevents your wish, and your loveliness opposes your prayer.

Phoebus loves her at first sight, and desires to wed her, and hopes for what he desires, but his own oracular powers fail him. As the light stubble of an empty cornfield blazes; as sparks fire a hedge when a traveler, by mischance, lets them get too close, or forgets them in the morning; so the god was altered by the flames, and all his heart burned, feeding his useless desire with hope. He sees her disordered hair hanging about her neck and sighs 'What if it were properly dressed?' He gazes at her eyes sparkling with the brightness of starlight. He gazes on her lips, where mere gazing does not satisfy. He praises her wrists and hands and fingers, and her arms bare to the shoulder: whatever is hidden, he imagines more beautiful. But she flees swifter than the lightest breath of air, and resists his words calling her back again.

Bk I:504-524 Phoebus begs Daphne to yield to him

'Wait nymph, daughter of Peneus, I beg you! I who am chasing you am not your enemy. Nymph, Wait! This is the way a sheep runs from the wolf, a deer from the mountain lion, and a dove with fluttering wings flies from the eagle: everything flies from its foes, but it is love that is driving me to follow you! Pity me! I am afraid you might fall headlong or thorns undeservedly scar your legs and I be a cause of grief to you! These are rough places you run through. Slow down, I ask you, check your flight, and I too will slow. At least enquire whom it is you have charmed. I am no mountain man, no shepherd, no rough guardian of the herds and flocks. Rash girl, you do not know, you cannot realize, who you run from, and so you run. Delphi's lands are mine, Claros and Tenedos, and Patara acknowledges me king. Jupiter is my father. Through me what was, what is, and what will be, are revealed. Through me strings sound in harmony, to song. My aim is certain, but an arrow truer than mine, has wounded my free heart! The whole world calls me the bringer of aid; medicine is my invention; my power is in herbs. But love cannot be healed by any herb, nor can the arts that cure others cure their lord!'

---

[7]The Goddess Diana, virgin huntress.

[8]God of Marriage.

[9]God of Love.

[10]The Goddess Diana, the virgin huntress.

Bk I:525-552 Daphne becomes the laurel bough

He would have said more as timid Peneïs ran, still lovely to see, leaving him with his words unfinished. The winds bared her body, the opposing breezes in her way fluttered her clothes, and the light airs threw her streaming hair behind her, her beauty enhanced by flight. But the young god could no longer waste time on further blandishments, urged on by Amor, he ran on at full speed. Like a hound of Gaul starting a hare in an empty field, that heads for its prey, she for safety: he, seeming about to clutch her, thinks now, or now, he has her fast, grazing her heels with his outstretched jaws, while she uncertain whether she is already caught, escaping his bite, spurts from the muzzle touching her. So the virgin and the god: he driven by desire, she by fear. He ran faster, Amor giving him wings, and allowed her no rest, hung on her fleeing shoulders, breathed on the hair flying round her neck. Her strength was gone, she grew pale, overcome by the effort of her rapid flight, and seeing Peneus's waters near cried out 'Help me father! If your streams have divine powers change me, destroy this beauty that pleases too well!' Her prayer was scarcely done when a heavy numbness seized her limbs, thin bark closed over her breast, her hair turned into leaves, her arms into branches, her feet so swift a moment ago stuck fast in slow-growing roots, her face was lost in the canopy. Only her shining beauty was left.

Bk I:553-567

Even like this Phoebus loved her and, placing his hand against the trunk, he felt her heart still quivering under the new bark. He clasped the branches as if they were parts of human arms, and kissed the wood. But even the wood shrank from his kisses, and the god said 'Since you cannot be my bride, you must be my tree! Laurel, with you my hair will be wreathed, with you my lyre, with you my quiver. You will go with the Roman generals when joyful voices acclaim their triumph, and the Capitol witnesses their long processions. You will stand outside Augustus's doorposts, a faithful guardian, and keep watch over the crown of oak between them. And just as my head with its un-cropped hair is always young, so you also will wear the beauty of undying leaves.' Paean had done: the laurel bowed her newly made branches, and seemed to shake her leafy crown like a head giving consent.

Questions and Ideas for Journaling and Discussion

1. Theme is an important idea conveyed in a piece of literature. It may be stated explicitly or drawn from the details. What are some common themes in the stories of Daphne, Dryope, and Mahdokht?

Grimms' Folktale

"Sleeping Beauty" or "Briar Rose" (1884)

In this fairy tale, a princess, her castle, and all within fall asleep for one hundred years. After one hundred years have passed, she and all the castle come back to life, as she is awakened by the kiss of a prince.

A long time ago there were a King and Queen, and one time when the Queen was bathing, a frog crept out of the water on to the land, and said to her, "Your wish shall be fulfilled; before a year has gone by, you shall have a daughter."

What the frog had said came true, and the Queen had a little girl who was so pretty that the King could not contain himself for joy, and ordered a great feast. He invited not only his kindred, friends and acquaintance, but also the Wise Women, in order that they might be kind and well-disposed towards the child. There were thirteen of them in his kingdom, but, as he had only twelve golden plates for them to eat out of, one of them had to be left at home.

The feast was held with all manner of splendor and when it came to an end, the Wise Women bestowed their magic gifts upon the baby: one gave virtue, another beauty, a third riches, and so on with everything in the world that one can wish for.

When eleven of them had made their promises, suddenly the thirteenth came in. She wished to avenge herself for not having been invited, and without greeting, or even looking at any one, she cried with a loud voice, "The King's daughter shall in her fifteenth year prick herself with a spindle, and fall down dead." And, without saying a word more, she turned round and left the room.

They were all shocked; but the twelfth, whose good wish still remained unspoken, came forward, and as she could not undo the evil sentence, but only soften it, she said, "It shall not be death, but a deep sleep of a hundred years, into which the princess shall fall."

The King, who would fain keep his dear child from the misfortune, gave orders that every spindle in the whole kingdom should be burnt. Meanwhile the gifts of the Wise Women were plenteously fulfilled on the young girl, for she was so beautiful, modest, good-natured, and wise, that everyone who saw her was bound to love her.

It happened that on the very day when she was fifteen years old, the King and Queen were not at home, and the maiden was left in the palace quite alone. So she went round into all sorts of places, looked into rooms and bed-chambers just as she liked, and at last came to an old tower. She climbed up the narrow winding-staircase, and reached a little door. A rusty key was in the lock, and when she turned it the door sprang open, and there in a little room sat an old woman with a spindle, busily spinning her flax.

"Good day, old dame," said the King's daughter; "what are you doing there?" "I am spinning," said the old woman, and nodded her head. "What sort of thing is that, that rattles round so merrily?" said the girl, and she took the spindle and wanted to spin too. But scarcely had she touched the spindle when the magic decree was fulfilled, and she pricked her finger with it.

And, in the very moment when she felt the prick, she fell down upon the bed that stood there, and lay in a deep sleep. And this sleep extended over the whole palace; the King and Queen who had just come home, and had entered the great hall, began to go to sleep, and the whole of the court with them. The horses, too, went to sleep in the stable, the dogs in the yard, the pigeons upon the roof, the flies on the wall; even the fire that was flaming on the hearth became quiet and slept, the roast meat left off frizzling, and the cook, who was just going to pull the hair of the scullery boy, because he had forgotten something, let him go, and went to sleep. And the wind fell, and on the trees before the castle not a leaf moved again.

But round about the castle there began to grow a hedge of thorns, which every year became higher, and at last grew close up round the castle and all over it, so that there was nothing of it to be seen, not even the flag upon the roof. But the story of the beautiful sleeping "Briar-rose," for so the princess was named, went about the country, so that from time to time kings' sons came and tried to get through the thorny hedge into the castle.

But they found it impossible, for the thorns held fast together, as if they had hands, and the youths were caught in them, could not get loose again, and died a miserable death.

After long, long years a King's son came again to that country, and heard an old man talking about the thorn hedge, and that a castle was said to stand behind it in which a wonderfully beautiful princess, named Briar-rose, had been asleep for a hundred years; and that the King and Queen and the whole court were asleep likewise. He had heard, too, from his grandfather, that many kings' sons had already come, and had tried to get through the thorny hedge, but they had remained sticking fast in it, and had died a pitiful death. Then the youth said, "I am not afraid, I will go and see the beautiful Briar-rose." The good old man might dissuade him as he would, he did not listen to his words.

But by this time the hundred years had just passed, and the day had come when Briar-rose was to awake again. When the King's son came near to the thorn hedge, it was nothing but large and beautiful flowers, which parted from each other of their own accord, and let him pass unhurt, then they closed again behind him like a hedge. In the castle-yard he saw the horses and the spotted hounds lying asleep; on the roof sat the pigeons with their heads under their wings. And when he entered the house, the flies were asleep upon the wall, the cook in the kitchen was still holding out his hand to seize the boy, and the maid was sitting by the black hen that she was going to pluck.

He went on farther, and in the great hall he saw the whole of the court lying asleep, and up by the throne lay the King and Queen.

Then he went on still farther, and all was so quiet that a breath could be heard, and at last he came to the tower, and opened the door into the little room where Briar-rose was sleeping. There she lay, so beautiful that he could not turn his eyes away; and he stooped down and gave her a kiss. But as soon as he kissed her, Briar-rose opened her eyes and awoke, and looked at him quite sweetly.

Then they went down together, and the King awoke, and the Queen, and the whole court, and looked at each other in great astonishment. And the horses in the court-yard stood up and shook themselves; the hounds jumped up and wagged their tails; the pigeons upon the roof pulled out their heads from under their wings, looked round, and flew into the open country; the flies on the wall crept again; the fire in the kitchen burned up and flickered and cooked the meat; the joint began to turn and frizzle again, and the cook gave the boy such a box on the ear that he screamed, and the maid plucked the fowl ready for the spit.

And then the marriage of the King's son with Briar-rose was celebrated with all splendor, and they lived contented to the end of their days.

Questions and Ideas for Journaling and Discussion

1. What is the role played by nature in the stories of Daphne and "Sleeping Beauty"?
2. What is the metaphoric meaning of Briar-rose's awakening to the prince's kiss in "Sleeping Beauty"?
3. How is "Sleeping Beauty" an idealized version of the heterosexual romance?

Writing to Explore and Learn

1. Compare and contrast the stories of the hero, the heroine, and the plant surrounding the heroines in the story of Daphne and "Sleeping Beauty." Is it possible that "Sleeping Beauty" is a later, evolved version of the story of Daphne, wherein the hero is successful? Write an essay in which you compare and contrast these stories.

Chapter 5

Girlhood

Young girls are often introduced to womanhood and the cultural ideal of feminine beauty with a Mattel's Barbie® doll. She originally had European features, a tiny waist, ample breasts, long legs, and a flawless, smooth face; in 1981, the first African American "Black Barbie" was released. The Barbie image is reminiscent of a woman in Victorian dress, which accented a small waist and "feminine" body; the way women dressed reflected their roles in society as men's decorative accessories. Some feminists are fearful that such images of a misguided feminine ideal are being incorporated into the ways that girls construct their own identities; failure to reach such goals may result in depression, anorexia, bulimia, and low self-esteem.

Even today, many girls, from an early age, are still taught to dress for male satisfaction. The area of education, fortunately, is more progressive when it comes to girls; girls and boys are taught the same subjects in school, and girls are generally encouraged to pursue careers. In many cultures, however, sons are preferred to daughters because males are thought to be superior beings. Hopefully, as the upbringing of girls evolves, young women across cultures will move beyond the societal expectations of beauty and the received notions of femininity.

Jamaica Kincaid
(b. 1949)

Everything in my work is autobiography—down to the punctuation.

Born in Antigua, Jamaica Kincaid, an intellectual child with an interest in books, left the island for New York in 1965. There she found success writing for *The New Yorker*, in which she published early fictional works. Many of her narratives explore extensively the themes of the mother/daughter relationship, female identity, sexuality, and power within the legacy of colonialism. Currently, she lives and teaches in Vermont. Notable texts include *Annie John* (1985), *A Small Place* (1988), and *The Autobiography of My Mother* (1996).

"Girl" (1978)

Kincaid's story is about a mother/daughter relationship in the context of Afro-Caribbean culture. A notable feature is the distinctive use of language; grammatically, the whole story is a single sentence with complete thoughts separated by semicolons, giving the piece a unique sense of rhythm, repetition, and sway. Out of this litany, a narrative of the meaning of girlhood and womanhood, daughter and mother emerges, which reflects a set of values and expectations of dominant notions of gender as it relates to both race and class.

Wash the white clothes on Monday and put them on the stone heap; wash the color clothes on Tuesday and put them on the clothesline to dry; don't walk barehead in the hot sun; cook pumpkin fritters in very hot sweet oil; soak your little clothes right after you take them off; when buying cotton to make yourself a nice blouse, be sure that it doesn't have gum on it, because that way it won't hold up well after a wash; soak salt fish overnight before you cook it; is it true that you sing benna in Sunday school?; always eat your food in such a way that it won't turn someone else's stomach; on Sundays try to walk like a lady and not like the slut you are so bent on becoming; don't sing benna in Sunday school; you mustn't speak to wharf-rat boys, not even to give directions; don't eat fruits on the street—flies will follow you; *but I don't sing benna on Sundays at all and never in Sunday school;* this is how to sew on a button; this is how to make a buttonhole for the button you have just sewed on; this is how to hem a dress when you see the hem coming down and so to prevent yourself from looking like the slut I know you are so bent on becoming; this is how you iron your father's khaki shirt so that it doesn't have a crease; this is how you iron your fathers' khaki pants so that they don't have a crease; this is how you grow okra—far from the house, because okra tree harbors red ants; when you are growing dasheen, make sure it gets plenty of water or else it makes your throat itch when you are eating it; this is how you sweep a corner; this is how you sweep a whole house; this is how you sweep a yard; this is how you smile to someone you don't like too much; this is how you smile at someone you don't like at all; this is how you smile to someone you like completely; this is how you set a table for tea; this is how you set a table for dinner; this is how you set a table for dinner with an important guest; this is how you set a table for lunch; this is how you set a table for breakfast; this is how to behave in the presence of men who don't know you very well, and this way they won't recognize immediately the slut I have warned you against becoming; be sure to wash every day, even if it is with your own spit; don't squat down to play marbles—you are not a boy, you know; don't pick people's flowers—you might catch something; don't throw stones at blackbirds, because it might not be a blackbird at all; this is how to make a bread pudding; this is how to make doukona; this is how to make pepper pot; this is how to make a good medicine for a cold; this is how to make a good medicine to throw away a child before it even becomes a child; this is how to catch a fish; this is how to throw back a fish you don't like, and that way something bad won't fall on you; this is how to bully a man; this is how a man bullies you; this is how to love a man, and if this doesn't work there are other ways, and if they don't work don't feel too bad about giving up; this is how to spit up in the air if you feel like it, and this is how to move quick so that it doesn't fall on you; this is how to make ends meet; always squeeze bread to make sure it's fresh; *but what if the baker won't let me feel the bread?* you mean to say that after all you are really going to be the kind of woman who the baker won't let near the bread?

Questions and Ideas for Journaling and Discussion

1. Who is the speaker? Is there evidence of another speaker?
2. Consider the mother's role. What is the intention of her advice? How does the girl respond?
3. Kincaid chose to write this story in one sentence. What are some of the effects of this decision?
4. What are the differences between this "monologue" and others that we have read?

Writing to Explore and Learn

1. Write your own version of the story "Girl" in which you are the recipient or giver of advice.
2. What does the narrative of girlhood/womanhood that Kincaid constructs in the story tell us about gender relations?

Audre Lorde
(1934–1992)

The question of social protest and art is inseparable for me.

Audre Lorde was born in Harlem to West Indian parents. In 1961, she graduated from Hunter College and then earned a master's degree in library science from Columbia University. She worked as a librarian and teacher, and was also a poet-in-residence at Tougaloo College, Mississippi. In 1954, a trip to Mexico confirmed her identity as both a lesbian and a poet. Politically committed, Lorde addresses a range of themes in her work: African history, myth, and social criticism, as well as sexual, gender, and racial politics, often within the context of her own personal experiences. One of the most radical poets of our time, she has written such notable works as *The Black Unicorn* (1978), *The Cancer Journals* (1980), and *Zami: A New Spelling of My Name* (1982).

"Hanging Fire" (1978)

For the fourteen-year-old speaker in Lorde's poem, the anxieties and pressures that are typical of adolescence serve as a pretext for exploring how gender shapes her experiences both at school and at home. That the teenager is African American is insignificant compared with the consequences of the rules of gender, particularly at school, which have a far greater impact on her life than race. The speaker's preoccupation with death and longing for communication with an absent mother reveal the isolation and loneliness that she feels in a world that is too limited to accommodate her spirit, abilities, and desires.

> I am fourteen
> and my skin has betrayed me
> the boy I cannot live without
> still sucks his thumb
> in secret   5
> how come my knees are
> always so ashy
> what if I die
> before morning

and momma's in the bedroom   10
with the door closed.

I have to learn how to dance
in time for the next party
my room is too small for me
suppose I die before graduation   15
they will sing sad melodies
but finally
tell the truth about me
There is nothing I want to do
and too much   20
that has to be done
and momma's in the bedroom
with the door closed.

Nobody even stops to think
about my side of it   25
I should have been on Math Team
my marks were better than his
why do I have to be
the one
wearing braces   30
I have nothing to wear tomorrow
will I live long enough
to grow up
and momma's in the bedroom
with the door closed.   35

Questions and Ideas for Journaling and Discussion

1. Discuss the girl's dilemma in terms of school and dating.
2. Free verse is poetry that is written without any formal pattern in meter or rhyme. The poem achieves much of its impact through the use of lyrical free verse and repetition. Think about the meaning of the line that closes each stanza: "and momma's in the bedroom/with the door closed."

Writing to Explore and Learn

1. Explore Lorde's treatment of the themes of gender and academic achievement.

Julia Órtiz Cofer
(b. 1952)

Literature excites me; it makes me feel that, as a writer, I can also create realities and move people.

Judith Órtiz Cofer was born in Puerto Rico; her family moved to Paterson, New Jersey, where she grew up. Writing in a range of genres, Cofer has a dual audience—teens and adults. Often she uses her writing to negotiate liminal spaces between Puerto Rican and American culture. The recipient of national fellowships and grants, Cofer lives and teaches in Georgia. Her most recent works include *Call Me Maria* (2004) and *A Love Story Beginning in Spanish* (2005).

"The Changeling" (1992)

In this poem, Cofer portrays a young girl who attempts to substitute her gender for that of her brother's as a way to understand gender as a force of social training and control within the confines of the family.

As a young girl
vying for my father's attention,
I invented a game that made him look up
from his reading and shake his head
as if both baffled and amused.

In my brother's closet, I'd change
into his dungarees—the rough material
molding me into boy shape; hide
my long hair under an army helmet
he'd been given by Father, and emerge
transformed into the legendary Che
of grown-up talk.

Strutting around the room,
I'd tell of life in the mountains,
of carnage and rivers of blood,
and of manly feasts with rum and music
to celebrate victories *para la libertad.*

He would listen with a smile
to my tales of battles and brotherhood
until Mother called us to dinner.

She was not amused
by my transformations, sternly forbidding me
from sitting down with them as a man.
She'd order me back to the dark cubicle
that smelled of adventure, to shed
my costume, to braid my hair furiously
with blind hands, and to return invisible,
as myself,
to the real world of her kitchen.

Questions for Journaling and Discussion

1. What is the significance of the cultural reference to Che?
2. Discuss the differences in the reactions of the mother and father to the speaker's behavior.
3. Lyric poetry is spoken in the voice of the poet without the mediation of a narrator. Speculate about whether you would classify this poem as lyric or monologue.

Writing to Explore and Learn

1. Compare and contrast the way that Lorde in "Hanging Fire" and Cofer in "The Changeling" depict crossing the sexual division of the labor characteristic of male-dominated societies.

Open Question for Writing

1. Choose two or three works in this section, and compare and contrast the ways in which the poets and/or writers treat the themes of gender and femininities.

PART II

MASCULINITIES

The changing roles of men and women call into question what it means to be a boy or a girl. In accordance with the idea of gendered biological differences, men have assumed, historically, the role of authority in most cultures. As gender identities are often considered natural, normative masculinity usually encompasses the qualities that are deemed best suited for leadership: a desire for sports and competition, and for wealth, power, and the burying of emotions. Investigations into prescribed gender roles, however, have helped to show that these signifying traits of traditional masculinities may be socially acquired. Since 1980, three areas of research on gender identity have emerged that focus on the meaning of masculinity: masculinity studies; queer theory; and gender, race, ethnic and postcolonial studies.

"Universal masculinity" orders societies in a way that accommodates the interests, needs, and desires of men. Scholar of masculinity R. W. Connell[1] calls this systematic approach "hegemonic masculinity," which she associates with "emphasized femininity," and both of these constructs, she argues, contribute to gender inequality worldwide. This form of masculinity privileges white, middle-class men of European descent over non-European, nonwhite, working class, and/or gay men, all of whom constitute "subordinated masculinities." In non-western settings, men claim privileges as well.

Just as feminism has effected a correlate situational change for men in developed countries, masculinity studies has emerged as a relatively new field of study. Generally a study of the cultural constructions of men and virility, this field recognizes a crisis in masculinity in which men can no longer define themselves against women. Today's understanding of masculinity is in flux.

---

[1] R. W. Connell (1944) is a transgendered woman and notable scholar of masculinities studies. Her groundbreaking text, *Masculinities* (1995), is notable in the field.

Chapter 6

Fatherhood

Because authority is constructed at its very base as male, the father is located at the head of the family, serving as a validating symbol of all the larger forms of rule, law, culture, and religion. Traditionally, the subject position of father is upheld by male economic power. Ongoing negotiations in the balance of power economically, socially, and politically, however, have resulted in a shift in the understanding of the definitions of fatherhood. The following texts explore the lives of fathers in a variety of contexts.

Bharati Mukherjee
(b. 1940)

White America is not the America of the mythological melting pot.

Bharati Mukherjee was born in Calcutta, India. She earned a BA from the University of Calcutta in 1959 and an MA in English and Ancient Indian culture from the University of Baroda in 1961. She came to the United States to attend the Iowa Writers' Workshop and remained to earn an MFA in creative writing in 1963 and a PhD in English and comparative literature in 1969. She is presently a professor of English at the University of California, Berkeley. Her novels and short stories focus on exploration of the North American immigrant identity and the subtleties and complexities added by familial relationships to the construction of the self. She met her husband, Clark Blaise, in Iowa, and, together they researched and wrote a book on terrorist activity related to the Air India tragedy, *The Sorrow and the Terror: The Haunting Legacy of the Air India Tragedy* (1987), as well as a memoir, *Days and Nights in Calcutta* (1977). Important works include the novels *Jasmine* (1989), *Desired Daughters* (2002), and *The Tree Bride* (2004), and the short story collection, *The Middleman and Other Stories* (1988), for which she won the National Book Critics Circle fiction award.

"Fathering" (1988)

In this story, the life of a happy couple is disrupted by the arrival of a child whom the man had fathered in Vietnam. He learns the meaning of fatherhood as he relearns his priorities.

ENG stands just inside our bedroom door, her fidgety fist on the door-knob which Sharon, in a sulk, polished to a gleam yesterday afternoon.

"I'm starved," she says.

I know a sick little girl when I see one. I brought the twins up without much help ten years ago. Eng's got a high fever. Brownish stains stiffen the nap of her terry robe. Sour smells fill the bedroom.

"For God's sake leave us alone," Sharon mutters under the quilt. She turns away from me. We bought the quilt at a garage sale in Rock Springs the Sunday two years ago when she moved in. "Talk to her."

Sharon works on this near-marriage of ours. I'll hand it to her, she really does. I knead her shoulders, and I say, "Easy, easy," though I really hate it when she treats Eng like a deaf-mute. "My girl speaks English, remember?"

Eng can outcuss any freckle-faced kid on the block. Someone in the killing fields must have taught her. Maybe her mama, the honeyest-skinned bar girl with the tiniest feet in Saigon. I was an errand boy with the Combined Military Intelligence. I did the whole war on Dexedrine. Vietnam didn't happen, and I'd put it behind me in marriage and fatherhood and teaching high school. Ten years later came the screw-ups with the marriage, the job, women, the works. Until Eng popped up in my life, I really believed it didn't happen.

"Come here, sweetheart," I beg my daughter. I sidle closer to Sharon, so there'll be room under the quilt for Eng.

"I'm starved," she complains from the doorway. She doesn't budge. The robe and hair are smelling something fierce. She doesn't show any desire to cuddle. She must be sick. She must have thrown up all night. Sharon throws the quilt back. "Then go raid the refrigerator like a normal kid," she snaps.

Once upon a time Sharon used to be a cheerful, accommodating woman. It isn't as if Eng was dumped on us out of the blue. She knew I was tracking my kid. Coming to terms with the past was Sharon's idea. I don't know what happened to *that* Sharon. "For all you know, Jason," she'd said, "the baby died of malaria or something." She said, "Go on, find out and deal with it." She said she could handle being a stepmother—better a fresh chance with some orphan off the streets of Saigon than with my twins from Rochester. My twins are being raised in some organic-farming lesbo commune. Their mother breeds Nubian goats for a living. "Come get in bed with us, baby. Let Dad feel your forehead. You burning up with fever?"

"She isn't hungry, I think she's sick," I tell Sharon, but she's already tugging her sleeping mask back on. "I think she's just letting us know she hurts."

I hold my arms out wide for Eng to run into. If I could, I'd suck the virus right out of her. In the jungle, VC mamas used to do that. Some nights we'd steal right up to a hootch—just a few of us intense sons of bitches on some special mission—and the women would be at their mumbo jumbo. They'd be sticking coins and amulets into napalm burns.

"I'm hungry, Dad." It comes out as a moan. Okay, she doesn't run into my arms, but at least she's come as far in as the foot of our bed. "Dad, let's go down to the kitchen. Just you and me."

I am about to let that pass though I can feel Sharon's body go into weird little jerks and twitches when my baby adds with emphatic viciousness, "Not her, Dad. We don't want her with us in the kitchen."

"She loves you," I protest. Love—not spite—makes Eng so territorial; that's what I want to explain to Sharon. She's a sick, frightened, foreign kid, for Chrissake. "Don't you, Sharon? Sharon's concerned about you."

But Sharon turns over on her stomach. "You know what's wrong with you, Jase? You can't admit you're being manipulated. You can't cut through the 'frightened-foreign-kid' shit."

Eng moves closer. She comes up to the side of my bed, but doesn't touch the hand I'm holding out. She's a fighter.

"I feel fire-hot, Dad. My bones feel pain."

"Sharon?" I want to deserve this woman. "Sharon, I'm so sorry." It isn't anybody's fault. You need uppers to get through peace times, too.

"Dad. Let's go. Chop-chop."

"You're too sick to keep food down, baby. Curl up in here. Just for a bit?"

"I'd throw up, Dad."

"I'll carry you back to your room. I'll read you a story, okay?"

Eng watches me real close as I pull the quilt off. "You got any scars you haven't shown me yet? My mom had a big scar on one leg. Shrapnel. Boom boom. I got scars. See? I got lots of bruises."

I scoop up my poor girl and rush her, terry robe flapping, to her room which Sharon fixed up with white girlish furniture in less complicated days. Waiting for Eng was good. Sharon herself said it was good for our relationship. "Could you bring us some juice and aspirin?" I shout from the hallway.

"Aspirin isn't going to cure Eng," I hear Sharon yell. "I'm going to call Dr. Kearns."

Downstairs I hear Sharon on the phone. She isn't talking flu viruses. She's talking social workers and shrinks. My girl isn't crazy; she's picked up a bug in school as might anyone else.

"The child's arms are covered with bruises," Sharon is saying. "Nothing major. They look like . . . well, they're sort of tiny circles and welts." There's nothing for a while. Then she says, "Christ! no, Jason can't do enough for her! That's not what I'm saying! What's happening to this country? You think we're perverts? What I'm saying is the girl's doing it to herself."

"Who are you talking to?" I ask from the top of the stairs. "What happened to the aspirin?"

I lean as far forward over the railing as I dare so I can see what Sharon's up to. She's getting into her coat and boots. She's having trouble with buttons and snaps. In the bluish light of the foyer's broken chandelier, she looks old, harrowed, depressed. What have I done to her?

"What's going on?" I plead. "You deserting me?"

"Don't be so fucking melodramatic. I'm going to the mall to buy some aspirin."

"How come we don't have any in the house?"

"Why are you always picking on me?"

"Who was that on the phone?"

"So now you want me to account for every call and every trip?" She ties an angry knot into her scarf. But she tells me. "I was talking to Meg Kearns. She says Dr. Kearns has gone hunting for the day."

"Great!"

"She says he has his beeper on him."

I hear the back door stick and Sharon swear. She's having trouble with the latch. "Jiggle it gently," I shout, taking the stairs two at a time. But before I can come down, her Nissan backs out of the parking apron.

Back upstairs I catch Eng in the middle of a dream or delirium. "They got Grandma!" she screams. She goes very rigid in bed. It's a four-poster with canopy and ruffles and stuff that Sharon put on her MasterCard. The twins slept on bunk beds.

With the twins it was different, totally different. Dr. Spock can't be point man for Eng, for us.

"She bring me food," Eng's screaming. "She bring me food from the forest. They shoot Grandma! Bastards!"

"Eng?" I don't dare touch her. I don't know how.

"You shoot my grandmother?" She whacks the air with her bony arms. Now I see the bruises, the small welts all along the insides of her arms. Some have to be weeks old, they're that yellow. The twins' scrapes and cuts never turned that ochre. I can't help wondering if maybe Asian skin bruises differently from ours, even though I want to say skin is skin; especially hers is skin like mine.

"I want to be with Grandma. Grandma loves me. I want to be ghost. I don't want to get better."

I read to her. I read to her because good parents are supposed to read to their kids laid up sick in bed. I want to do it right. I want to be a good father. I read from a sci-fi novel that Sharon must have picked up. She works in a camera store in the mall, right next to a B. Dalton. I read three pages out loud, then I read four chapters to myself because Eng's stopped up her ears. Aliens have taken over small towns all over the country. Idaho, Nebraska: no state is safe from aliens.

Some time after two, the phone rings. Since Sharon doesn't answer it on the second ring, I know she isn't back. She carries a cordless phone everywhere around the house. In the movies, when cops have bad news to deliver, they lean on your doorbell; they don't call. Sharon will come back when she's ready. We'll make up. Things will get back to normal.

"Jason?"

I know Dr. Kearns's voice. He saw the twins through the usual immunizations.

"I have Sharon here. She'll need a ride home. Can you drive over?"

"God! What's happened?"

"Nothing to panic about. Nothing physical. She came for a consultation."

"Give me a half-hour. I have to wrap Eng real warm so I can drag her out in this miserable weather."

"Take your time. This way I can take a look at Eng, too."

"What's wrong with Sharon?"

"She's a little exercised about a situation. I gave her a sedative. See you in a half-hour."

I ease delirious Eng out of the overdecorated four-poster, prop her against my body while I wrap a blanket around her. She's a tiny thing, but she feels stiff and heavy, a sleepwalking mummy. Her eyes are dry-bright, strange.

It's a sunny winter day, and the evergreens in the front yard are glossy with frost. I press Eng against my chest as I negotiate the front steps. Where the gutter leaks, the steps feel spongy. The shrubs and bushes my ex-wife planted clog the front path. I've put twenty years into this house. The steps, the path, the house all have a right to fall apart.

I'm thirty-eight. I've let a lot of people down already.

The inside of the van is deadly cold. Mid-January ice mottles the windshield. I lay the bundled-up child on the long seat behind me and wait for the engine to warm up. It feels good with the radio going and the heat coming on. I don't want the ice on the windshield to melt. Eng and I are safest in the van.

In the rear-view mirror, Eng's wrinkled lips begin to move. "Dad, can I have a quarter?"

"May I, kiddo," I joke.

There's all sorts of junk in the pockets of my parka. Buckshot, dimes and quarters for the vending machine, a Blistex.

"What do you need it for, sweetheart?"

Eng's quick. Like the street kids in Saigon who dove for cigarettes and sticks of gum. She's loosened the blanket folds around her. I watch her tuck the quarter inside her wool mitt. She grins. "Thanks, soldier."

At Dr. Kearns's, Sharon is lying unnaturally slack-bodied on the lone vinyl sofa. Her coat's neatly balled up under her neck, like a bolster. Right now she looks amiable, docile. I don't think she exactly recognizes me, although later she'll say she did. All that stuff about Kearns going hunting must have been a lie. Even the stuff about having to buy aspirins in the mall. She was planning all along to get here.

"What's wrong?"

"It's none of my business, Jason, but you and Sharon might try an honest-to-goodness heart-to-heart." Then he makes a sign to me to lay Eng on the examining table. "We don't look so bad," he says to my daughter. Then he excuses himself and goes into a glass-walled cubicle.

Sharon heaves herself into a sitting position of sorts on the sofa. "Everything was fine until she got here. Send her back, Jase. If you love me, send her back." She's slouched so far forward, her pointed, sweatered breasts nearly touch her corduroy pants. She looks helpless, pathetic. I've brought her to this state. Guilt, not love, is what I feel.

I want to comfort Sharon, but my daughter with the wild, grieving pygmy face won't let go of my hand. "She's bad, Dad. Send *her* back."

Dr. Kearns comes out of the cubicle balancing a sample bottle of pills or caplets on a flattened palm. He has a boxer's tough, squarish hands. "Miraculous stuff, this," he laughs. "But first we'll stick our tongue out and say *ahh*. Come on, open wide."

Eng opens her mouth real wide, then brings her teeth together, hard, on Dr. Kearns's hand. She leaps erect on the examining table, tearing the disposable paper sheet with her toes. Her tiny, funny toes are doing a frantic dance. "Don't let him touch me, Grandma!"

"He's going to make you all better, baby." I can't pull my alien child down, I can't comfort her. The twins had diseases with easy names, diseases we knew what to do with. The thing is, I never felt for them what I feel for her.

"Don't let him touch me, Grandma!" Eng's screaming now. She's hopping on the table and screaming. "Kill him, Grandma! Get me out of here, Grandma!"

"Baby, it's all right."

But she looks through me and the country doctor as though we aren't here, as though we aren't pulling at her to make her lie down.

"Lie back like a good girl," Dr. Kearns commands.

But Eng is listening to other voices. She pulls her mitts off with her teeth, chucks the blanket, the robe, the pajamas to the floor; then, naked, hysterical, she presses the quarter I gave her deep into the soft flesh of her arm. She presses and presses that coin, turning it in nasty half-circles until blood starts to pool under the skin.

"Jason, grab her at the knees. Get her back down on the table."

From the sofa, Sharon moans. "See, I told you the child was crazy. She hates me. She's possessive about Jason."

The doctor comes at us with his syringe. He's sedated Sharon; now he wants to knock out my kid with his cures.

"Get the hell out, you bastard!" Eng yells. *"Vamos!* Bang bang!" She's pointing her arm like a semiautomatic, taking out Sharon, then the doctor. My Rambo. "Old way is good way. Money cure is good cure. When they shoot my grandma, you think pills do her any good? You Yankees, please go home." She looks straight at me. "Scram, Yankee bastard!"

Dr. Kearns has Eng by the wrist now. He has flung the quarter I gave her on the floor. Something incurable is happening to my women.

Then, as in fairy tales, I know what has to be done. "Coming, pardner!" I whisper. "I got no end of coins." I jiggle the change in my pocket. I jerk her away from our enemies. My Saigon kid and me: we're a team. In five minutes we'll be safely away in the cold chariot of our van.

Questions and Ideas for Journaling and Discussion

1. Sharon had made great preparations for Eng's arrival. Describe the kind of child whom she expected and the kind of child Eng actually was.
2. How does Jason come to understand what he must do as a father?
3. Is Eng mad? What do you think might help her?
4. The narrator in this story speaks in the present tense. What is the overall effect of the use of the present tense?

Writing to Explore and Learn

1. Write a letter to Eng explaining the differences between the culture that she left and the culture that she is presently in.

August Strindberg (1849–1912)

I dream, therefore I exist.

August Strindberg was born in Sweden to an upper-class father and servant-class mother. After failed attempts at careers in medicine and acting, he turned to theater. In 1872, he wrote his first important drama, *Master Olaf,* a story about a religious reformer in the sixteenth century. A master of modern drama, Strindberg's output in all genres—plays, fiction, nonfiction, and essays—was astounding. On the personal level, he was dogged by both financial and marital difficulties throughout his life. His primary plays focus on his particular views of the feminine. His major dramatic works include *Miss Julie* (1888), *The Father* (1899), and *Ghost Sonata* (1907).

The Father (1887)

Strindberg's play dramatizes the question of paternity within the context of a fierce battle for supremacy between the sexes. As the play is rooted in the plot of marital conflict, Strindberg depicts how social forces and practices enforce in the family and in the larger culture stringent codes of femininity and masculinity, even in the face of peril and devastation.

ACT One

Early evening. The lamp on the table is lighted. The Captain and the Pastor are sitting on the sofa talking. The Captain is in undress uniform with riding-boots and spurs; the Pastor wears black, with a white cravat in place of his clerical collar, and is smoking a pipe.

The Captain rises and rings a bell. The Orderly enters from the hall.

ORDERLY.   Yes, sir?

CAPTAIN.   Is Nöjd there?

ORDERLY.   Nöjd's in the kitchen, sir, waiting for orders.

CAPTAIN.   In the kitchen again, is he? Send him here at once.

ORDERLY.   Yes, sir.
           Exit.

PASTOR.   Why, what's the trouble?

CAPTAIN.   Oh, the ruffian's been at his tricks again with one of the servant girls! He's a damn nuisance, that fellow!

PASTOR.   Was it Nöjd you said? Didn't he give some trouble back in the spring?

CAPTAIN.   Ah, you remember that, do you? Look here, you give him a bit of a talking to, there's a good chap. That might have some effect. I've sworn at him and thrashed him, without making the least impression.

PASTOR.   So now you want me to preach to him. How much impression do you think God's word is likely to make on a trooper?

CAPTAIN.   Well, my dear brother-in-law, it makes none at all on me, as you know, but . . .

PASTOR.   As I know only too well.

CAPTAIN.   But on him? Worth trying anyhow.
           Enter NÖJD.
           What have you been up to now, Nöjd?

NÖJD.   God bless you, sir, I can't talk about that—not with Pastor here.

PASTOR.   Don't mind me, my lad.

NÖJD.   Well you see, sir, it was like this. We was at a dance at Gabriel's, and then, well then Ludwig said as . . .

CAPTAIN.   What's Ludwig got to do with it? Stick to the point.

NÖJD.   Well then Emma said as we should go in the barn.

CAPTAIN.   I see. I suppose it was Emma who led you astray.

NÖJD.   Well, not far from it. What I mean is if the girl's not game, nothing don't happen.

CAPTAIN.   Once and for all—are you the child's father or are you not?

NÖJD.   How's one to know?

CAPTAIN.   What on earth do you mean? Don't you know?

NÖJD.   No, you see, sir, that's what you never can know.

CAPTAIN.   You mean you weren't the only man?

NÖJD.   That time I was. But you can't tell if you've always been the only one.

CAPTAIN.   Are you trying to put the blame on Ludwig? Is that the idea?

NÖJD.   It's not easy to know who to put the blame on.

CAPTAIN.   But look here, you told Emma you would marry her.

NÖJD.   Oh well, you always have to say that, you know.

CAPTAIN.   *to the* PASTOR. This is atrocious.

PASTOR.   It's the old story. Come now, Nöjd, surely you are man enough to know if you are the father.

NÖJD.   Well, sir, it's true, I did go with her, but you know yourself, Pastor, that don't always lead to nothing.

PASTOR.   Look here, my lad, it's you we are talking about. And you are not going to leave that girl destitute with a child. You can't be forced to marry her, but you must make provision for the child. That you must do.

NÖJD.   So must Ludwig then.

CAPTAIN.   If that's how it is, the case will have to go before the Magistrate: I can't settle it, and it's really nothing to do with me. Dismiss!

PASTOR.   One moment, Nöjd. Ahem. Don't you think it's rather a dirty trick to leave a girl destitute with a child like that? Don't you think so—eh?

NÖJD.   Yes, if I knew I was the father, it would be, but I tell you, Pastor, you never can know that. And it wouldn't be much fun slaving all your life for another chap's brat. You and the Captain must see that for yourselves.

CAPTAIN.   That will do, Nöjd.

NÖJD.   Yes, sir, thank you, sir.

CAPTAIN.   And keep out of the kitchen, you scoundrel!

Exit NÖJD.

Why didn't you haul him over the coals?

PASTOR.   What do you mean? Didn't I?

CAPTAIN.   No, you just sat there muttering to yourself.

PASTOR.   As a matter of fact, I scarcely knew what to say to him. It's hard on the girl, of course, but it's hard on the boy too. Supposing he's not the father? The girl can nurse the baby for four months at the orphanage, and after that it will be taken care of for good. But the boy can't nurse the child, can he? Later on, the girl will get a good place in some respectable family, but if the boy is cashiered, his future may be ruined.

CAPTAIN.   Upon my soul, I'd like to be the magistrate and judge this case! Maybe the boy is responsible—that's what you can't know. But one thing you *can* know—if anybody's guilty, the girl is.

PASTOR.   Well, I never sit in judgment. Now what was it we were talking about when this blessed business' interrupted us? Yes, Bertha and her confirmation, wasn't it?

CAPTAIN.   It's not just a question of confirmation, but of her whole future. The house is full of women, all trying to mould this child of mine. My mother-in-law wants to turn her into a spiritualist; Laura wants her to be an artist; the governess would have her a Methodist, old Margaret a Baptist; and the servant girls a Salvation Army lass. You can't make a character out of patchwork. Meanwhile I . . . I, who have more right than all the rest to guide her, am opposed at every turn. So I must send her away.

PASTOR. You have too many women running your house.

CAPTAIN. You're right there. It's like going into a cage of tigers. They'd soon tear me to pieces, if I didn't hold a red-hot poker under their noses. It's all very well for you to laugh, you blackguard. It wasn't enough that I married your sister; you had to palm off your old stepmother on me too.

PASTOR. Well, good Lord, one can't have stepmothers in one's house!

CAPTAIN. No, you prefer mothers-in-law—in someone else's house, of course.

PASTOR. Well, well, we all have our burdens to bear.

CAPTAIN. I daresay, but I have more than my share. There's my old nurse too, who treats me as if I still wore a bib. She's a good old soul, to be sure, but she shouldn't be here.

PASTOR. You should keep your women-folk in order, Adolf. You give them too much rope.

CAPTAIN. My dear fellow, can you tell me how to keep women in order?

PASTOR. To tell the truth, although she's my sister, Laura was always a bit of a handful.

CAPTAIN. Laura has her faults, of course, but they are not very serious ones.

PASTOR. Oh come now, I know her!

CAPTAIN. She was brought up with romantic ideas and has always found it a little difficult to come to terms with life. But she is my wife and ...

PASTOR. And because she is your wife she must be the best of women. No, brother-in-law, it's she not you who wears the trousers.

CAPTAIN. In any case, the whole household has gone mad. Laura's determined Bertha shan't leave her, and I won't let her stay in this lunatic asylum.

PASTOR. So Laura's determined, is she? Then there's bound to be trouble, I'm afraid. As a child she used to lie down and sham dead until they gave in to her. Then she would calmly hand back whatever she'd set her mind on, explaining it wasn't the thing she wanted, but simply to get her own way.

CAPTAIN. So she was like that even then, was she? Hm. As a matter of fact, she does sometimes get so overwrought I'm frightened for her and think she must be ill.

PASTOR. What is it you want Bertha to do that's such a bone of contention? Can't you come to some agreement?

CAPTAIN.   Don't think I want to turn her into a prodigy—or into some image of myself. But I will not play pander and have my daughter fitted for nothing but the marriage market. For then, if she didn't marry after all, she'd have a wretched time of it. On the other hand, I don't want to start her off in some man's career with a long training that would be entirely wasted if she did marry.

PASTOR.   Well, what do you want then?

CAPTAIN.   I want her to be a teacher. Then, if she doesn't marry she'll be able to support herself, and at least be no worse off than those unfortunate schoolmasters who have to support families on their earnings. And if she does marry, she can educate her own children. Isn't that reasonable?

PASTOR.   Reasonable, yes—but what about her artistic talent? Wouldn't it be against the grain to repress that?

CAPTAIN.   No. I showed her attempts to a well-known painter who told me they were nothing but the usual sort of thing learnt at school. Then, during the summer, some young jackanapes came along who knew better and said she was a genius—whereupon the matter was settled in Laura's favour.

PASTOR.   Was he in love with Bertha?

CAPTAIN.   I take that for granted.

PASTOR.   Well, God help you, old boy, I don't see any solution. But it's a tiresome business, and I suppose Laura has supporters . . . *indicates other rooms* in there.

CAPTAIN.   You may be sure of that. The whole household is in an uproar, and between ourselves the method of attack from that quarter is not exactly chivalrous.

PASTOR,   *rising.* Do you think I haven't been through it?

CAPTAIN.   You too?

PASTOR.   Yes, indeed.

CAPTAIN.   But to me the worst thing about it is that Bertha's future should be decided in there from motives of sheer hate. They do nothing but talk about men being made to see that women can do this and do that. It's man versus woman the whole day long . . . Must you go? Won't you stay to supper? I don't know what there is, but do stay. I'm expecting the new doctor, you know. Have you seen him yet?

PASTOR.   I caught a glimpse of him on my way here. He looks a decent, reliable sort of man.

CAPTAIN.   That's good. Do you think he may be my ally?

PASTOR.   Maybe. It depends how well he knows women.

CAPTAIN.   But won't you stay?

PASTOR.   Thank you, my dear fellow, but I promised to be home this evening, and my wife gets anxious if I'm late.

CAPTAIN.   Anxious! Furious, you mean. Well, as you please. Let me help you on with your coat.

PASTOR.   It's certainly very cold to-night. Thank you. You must look after yourself, Adolf. You seem a bit on edge.

CAPTAIN.   On edge? Do I?

PASTOR.   Yes. You aren't very well, are you?

CAPTAIN.   Did Laura put this into your head? For the last twenty years she's been treating me as if I had one foot in the grave.

PASTOR.   Laura? No, it's just that I'm . . . I'm worried about you. Take my advice and look after yourself. Goodbye, old man. By the way, didn't you want to talk about the confirmation?

CAPTAIN.   By no means. But I give you my word this shall take its own course—and be chalked up to the official conscience. I am neither a witness to the truth, nor a martyr. We have got past that sort of thing. Goodbye. Remember me to your wife.

PASTOR.   Goodbye, Adolf. Give my love to Laura.

Exit PASTOR. *The* CAPTAIN *opens the bureau and settles down to his accounts.*

CAPTAIN.   Thirty-four—nine, forty-three—seven, eight, fifty-six.

LAURA, *entering from the next room.* Will you please . . .

CAPTAIN.   One moment!—Sixty-six, seventy-one, eighty-four, eighty-nine, ninety-two, a hundred. What is it?

LAURA.   Am I disturbing you?

CAPTAIN.   Not in the least. Housekeeping money, I suppose?

LAURA.   Yes, housekeeping money.

CAPTAIN.   If you put the accounts down there, I will go through them.

LAURA.   Accounts?

CAPTAIN.   Yes.

LAURA.   Do you expect me to keep accounts now?

CAPTAIN.   Of course you must keep accounts. Our position's most precarious, and if we go bankrupt, we must have accounts to show. Otherwise we could be accused of negligence.

LAURA.   It's not my fault if we're in debt.

CAPTAIN.   That's what the accounts will show.

LAURA.   It's not my fault the tenant farmer doesn't pay.

CAPTAIN.   Who was it recommended him so strongly? You. Why did you recommend such a—shall we call him a scatterbrain?

LAURA.	Why did you take on such a scatterbrain?
CAPTAIN.	Because I wasn't allowed to eat in peace, sleep in peace or work in peace till you got him here. You wanted him because your brother wanted to get rid of him; my mother-in-law wanted him because I didn't; the governess wanted him because he was a Methodist, and old Margaret because she had known his grandmother as a child. That's why, and if I hadn't taken him I should be in a lunatic asylum by now, or else in the family vault. However, here's the housekeeping allowance and your pin money. You can give me the accounts later. LAURA, *with an ironic bob.* Thank you so much.—By the way, do you keep accounts yourself—of what you spend outside the household?
CAPTAIN.	That's none of your business.
LAURA.	True. As little my business as the future of my own child. Did you gentlemen come to any decision at this evening's conference?
CAPTAIN.	I had already made my decision, so I merely had to communicate it to the only friend I have in the family. Bertha is going to live in town. She will leave in a fortnight's time.
LAURA.	Where, if I may ask, is she going to stay?
CAPTAIN.	At Sävberg's—*the* solicitor's.
LAURA.	That Freethinker!
CAPTAIN.	According to the law as it now stands, children are brought up in their father's faith.
LAURA.	And the mother has no say in the matter?
CAPTAIN.	None whatever. She sells her birthright by legal contract and surrenders all her rights. In return the husband supports her and her children.
LAURA.	So she has no rights over her own child?
CAPTAIN.	None at all. When you have sold something, you don't expect to get it back and keep the money too.
LAURA.	But supposing the father and mother were to decide things together . . . ?
CAPTAIN.	How would that work out? I want her to live in town; you want her to live at home. The mathematical mean would be for her to stop at the railway station, midway between home and town. You see? It's a deadlock.
LAURA.	Then the lock must be forced. . . . What was Nöjd doing here?
CAPTAIN.	That's a professional secret.
LAURA.	Which the whole kitchen knows.
CAPTAIN.	Then doubtless you know it too.

LAURA.   I do.

CAPTAIN. And are ready to sit in judgment?

LAURA.   The law does that.

CAPTAIN. The law doesn't say who the child's father is.

LAURA.   Well, people know that for themselves.

CAPTAIN. Discerning people say that's what one never can know.

LAURA.   How extraordinary! Can't one tell who a child's father is?

CAPTAIN. Apparently not.

LAURA.   How perfectly extraordinary! Then how can the father have those rights over the mother's child?

CAPTAIN. He only has them when he takes on the responsibility—or has it forced on him. But of course in marriage there is no doubt about the paternity.

LAURA.   No doubt?

CAPTAIN. I should hope not.

LAURA.   But supposing the wife has been unfaithful?

CAPTAIN. Well, such a supposition has no bearing on our problem. Is there anything else you want to ask me about?

LAURA.   No, nothing.

CAPTAIN. Then I shall go up to my room. Please let me know when the doctor comes. *Closes the bureau and rises.*

LAURA.   I will.

CAPTAIN, *going out by the wall-papered door.* As soon as he comes, mind. I don't want to be discourteous, you understand.

          Exit.

LAURA.   I understand. *She looks at the bank-notes she is holding.*
          MOTHER-IN-LAW, *off.* Laura!

LAURA.   Yes, Mother?

MOTHER-IN-LAW. Is my tea ready?
          LAURA, *at the door to the next room.* It's coming in a moment.
          The ORDERLY *opens the hall door.*

ORDERLY. Dr. Östermark.
          Enter DOCTOR. *Exit* ORDERLY, *closing the door.*
          LAURA, *shaking hands.* How do you do, Dr. Östermark. Let me welcome you to our home. The Captain is out, but he will be back directly.

DOCTOR.   I must apologize for calling so late, but I have already had to pay some professional visits.

LAURA.   Won't you sit down?

DOCTOR.   Thank you.

LAURA.   Yes, there is a lot of illness about just now, but I hope all the same that you will find this place suits you. It is so important for people in a lonely country district like this to have a doctor who takes a real interest in his patients. I have heard you so warmly spoken of, Dr. Östermark, I hope we shall be on the best of terms.

DOCTOR.   You are too kind, dear lady. I hope, however, for your sake that my visits here will not often be of a professional nature. I take it that the health of your family is, on the whole, good, and that . . .

LAURA.   Yes, we have been fortunate enough not to have any serious illnesses, but all the same things are not quite as they should be.

DOCTOR.   Indeed?

LAURA.   No, I'm afraid not really at all as one would wish.

DOCTOR.   Dear, dear, you quite alarm me!

LAURA.   In a family there are sometimes things which honour and duty compel one to keep hidden from the world.

DOCTOR.   But not from one's doctor.

LAURA.   No. That is why it is my painful duty to tell you the whole truth from the start.

DOCTOR.   May we not postpone this conversation until I have had the honour of meeting the Captain?

LAURA.   No. You must hear what I have to say before you see him.

DOCTOR.   Does it concern him then?

LAURA.   Yes, him. My poor, dear husband.

DOCTOR.   You are making me most uneasy. Whatever your trouble, Madam, you can confide in me.

          LAURA, *taking out her handkerchief.* My husband's mind is affected. Now you know, and later on you will be able to judge for yourself.

DOCTOR.   You astound me. The Captain's learned treatise on mineralogy, for which I have the greatest admiration, shows a clear and powerful intellect.

LAURA.   Does it? I shall be overjoyed if we—his relatives—are mistaken.

DOCTOR.   It is possible, of course, that his mind is disturbed in other ways. Tell me . . .

LAURA.   That is exactly what we fear. You see, at times he has the most peculiar ideas, which wouldn't matter much for a scientist, if they weren't such a burden on his family. For instance, he has an absolute mania for buying things.

DOCTOR. That is significant What kind of things?

LAURA. Books. Whole cases of them, which he never reads.

DOCTOR. Well, that a scholar should buy books isn't so alarming.

LAURA. You don't believe what I am telling you?

DOCTOR. I am convinced, Madam, that you believe what you are telling me.

LAURA. Well, then, is it possible for anyone to see in a microscope what's happening on another planet?

DOCTOR. Does he say he can do that?

LAURA. Yes, that's what he says.

DOCTOR. In a microscope?

LAURA. In a microscope. Yes.

DOCTOR. That is significant, if it is so.

LAURA. If it is so! You don't believe me, Doctor. And here have I let you in to the family secret.

DOCTOR. My dear lady, I am honoured by your confidence, but as a physician I must observe and examine before giving an opinion. Has the Captain shown any symptoms of instability, any lack of will power?

LAURA. Has he, indeed! We have been married twenty years, and he has never yet made a decision without going back on it.

DOCTOR. Is he dogmatic?

LAURA. He certainly lays down the law, but as soon as he gets his own way, he loses interest and leaves everything to me.

DOCTOR. That is significant and requires careful consideration. The will, you see, Madam, is the backbone of the mind. If it is injured, the mind falls to pieces.

LAURA. God knows how I have schooled myself to meet his every wish during these long hard years. Oh, if you knew what I have been through with him, if you only knew!

DOCTOR. I am profoundly distressed to learn of your trouble, Madam, and I promise I will do what I can. You have my deepest sympathy and I beg you to rely on me implicitly. But now you have told me this, I am going to ask one thing of you. Don't allow anything to prey on the patient's mind. In a case of instability, ideas can sometimes take hold and grow into an obsession—or even monomania. Do you follow me?

LAURA. . . . You mean don't let him get ideas into his head.

DOCTOR.   Precisely. For a sick man can be made to believe anything. He is highly susceptible to suggestion.

LAURA.   I see . . . I understand. Yes, indeed. *A bell rings within.* Excuse me. That's my mother ringing. I won't be a moment . . . Oh, here's Adolf!

As LAURA *goes out, the* CAPTAIN *enters by the wallpapered door.*

CAPTAIN.   Ah, so you have arrived, Doctor! You are very welcome.

DOCTOR.   How do you do, Captain. It's a great honour to meet such a distinguished scientist.

CAPTAIN.   Oh please! Unfortunately, my military duties don't give me much time for research . . . All the same, I do believe I am now on the brink of a rather exciting discovery.

DOCTOR.   Really?

CAPTAIN.   You see, I have been subjecting meteoric stones to spectrum analysis, and I have found carbon—an indication of organic life. What do you say to that?

DOCTOR.   Can you see that in a microscope?

CAPTAIN.   No, in a spectroscope, for heaven's sake!

DOCTOR.   Spectroscope! I beg your pardon. Then you will soon be telling us what is happening on Jupiter.

CAPTAIN.   Not what is happening, what *has* happened. If only that blasted Paris bookseller would send my books. I really think the whole book-trade must be in league against me. Think of it, for two months I've not had one single answer to my orders, my letters or my abusive telegrams! It's driving me mad. I can't make out what's happened.

DOCTOR.   Well, what could it be but ordinary carelessness? You shouldn't let it upset you.

CAPTAIN.   Yes, but the devil of it is I shan't be able to get my article finished in time.—I know they're working on the same lines in Berlin . . . However, that's not what we should be talking about now, but about you. If you would care to live here, we can give you a small suite of rooms in that wing. Or would you prefer your predecessor's house?

DOCTOR.   Whichever you please.

CAPTAIN.   No, whichever *you* please. You have only to say.

DOCTOR.   It's for you to decide, Captain.

CAPTAIN.   Nothing of the kind. It's for you to say which you prefer. I don't care one way or the other.

DOCTOR.   But I really can't . . .

CAPTAIN. For Christ's sake, man, say what you want! I haven't any opin-
          ion, any inclination, any choice, any preference at all. Are you
          such a milksop that you don't know what you want? Make up
          your mind, or I shall lose my temper.

DOCTOR.   If I am to choose, I should like to live here.

CAPTAIN. Good!—Thank you. *Rings.* Oh dear me!—I apologise, Doctor,
          but nothing irritates me so much as to hear people say they
          don't care one way or the other.
          The NURSE *enters.*
          Ah, it's you, Margaret. Look here, my dear, do you know if the
          rooms in the wing are ready for the doctor?

NURSE.   Yes, Captain, they're ready.

CAPTAIN. Good. Then I won't detain you, Doctor, for you must be tired.
          Goodnight, and once again—welcome. I look forward to see-
          ing you in the morning.

DOCTOR.   Thank you. Goodnight.

CAPTAIN. By the way, I wonder if my wife told you anything about us—
          if you know at all how the land lies?

DOCTOR.   Your good lady did suggest one or two things it might be as
          well for a newcomer to know. Goodnight, Captain.
          The NURSE *shows the* DOCTOR *out and returns.*

CAPTAIN. What is it, old girl? Anything the matter?

NURSE.   Now listen, Mr. Adolf, dear.

CAPTAIN. Yes, go on, Margaret, talk. You're the only one whose talk
          doesn't get on my nerves.

NURSE.   Then listen, Mr. Adolf. Couldn't you go halfway to meet
          the mistress in all this bother over the child? Think of a
          mother . . .

CAPTAIN. Think of a father, Margaret.

NURSE.   Now, now, now! A father has many things besides his child,
          but a mother has nothing but her child.

CAPTAIN. Quite so, my friend. She has only one burden, while I have three
          and bear hers too. Do you think I'd have been stuck in the army
          all my life if I hadn't had her and her child to support?

NURSE.   I know, but that wasn't what I wanted to talk about.

CAPTAIN. Quite. What you want is to make out I'm in the wrong.

NURSE.   Don't you believe I want what's best for you, Mr. Adolf?

CAPTAIN. I'm sure you do, my dear, but you don't know what is best for
          me. You see, it's not enough to have given the child life. I want
          to give her my very soul.

NURSE.   Oh, that's beyond me, but I do think you two ought to come to terms.

CAPTAIN.   Margaret, you are not my friend.

NURSE.   Not your friend! Ah God, what are you saying, Mr. Adolf? Do you think I ever forget you were my baby when you were little?

CAPTAIN.   Well, my dear, am I likely to forget it? You have been like a mother to me, and stood by me against all the others. But now that things have come to a head, you're deserting—going over to the enemy.

NURSE.   Enemy?

CAPTAIN.   Yes, enemy. You know perfectly well how things are here. You've seen it all from beginning to end.

NURSE.   Aye, I've seen plenty. But, dear God, why must two people torment the lives out of each other? Two people who are so good and kind to everyone else. The mistress never treats me wrong or . . .

CAPTAIN.   Only me. I know. And I tell you, Margaret, if you desert me now, you'll be doing a wicked thing. For a net is closing round me, and that doctor is no friend of mine.

NURSE.   Oh, goodness, Mr. Adolf, you believe the worst of everyone! But that's what comes of not having the true faith. That's your trouble.

CAPTAIN.   While you and the Baptists have found the one true faith, eh? You're lucky.

NURSE.   Aye, luckier than you, Mr. Adolf. Humble your heart and you will see how happy God will make you in your love for your neighbour.

CAPTAIN.   Isn't it strange—as soon as you mention God and love, your voice grows hard and your eyes fill with hate. No, Margaret, I'm sure you haven't found the true faith.

MARGARET.   However proud you are and stuffed with book-learning, that won't get you anywhere when the pinch comes.

CAPTAIN.   How arrogantly thou speakest, O humble heart! I'm well aware that learning means nothing to creatures like you.

NURSE.   Shame on you! Still, old Margaret loves her great big boy best of all. And when the storm breaks, he'll come back to her, sure enough, like the good child he is.

CAPTAIN.   Forgive me, Margaret. You see, you really are the only friend I have here. Help me, for something is going to happen. I don't know what, but I know it's evil, this thing that's on its way. *A scream from within.* What's that? Who's screaming?
BERTHA *runs in.*

BERTHA.	Father, Father! Help me! Save me!
CAPTAIN.	What is it? My darling, tell me.
BERTHA.	Please protect me. I know she'll do something terrible to me.
CAPTAIN.	Who? What do you mean? Tell me at once.
BERTHA.	Grandmother. But it was my fault. I played a trick on her.
CAPTAIN.	Go on.
BERTHA.	Yes, but you mustn't tell anyone. Promise you won't.
CAPTAIN.	Very well, but what happened?

Exit NURSE.

BERTHA.	You see, sometimes in the evening she turns the lamp down and makes me sit at the table holding a pen over a piece of paper. And then she says the spirits write.
CAPTAIN.	Well, I'll be damned! And you never told me.
BERTHA.	I'm sorry, I didn't dare. Grandmother says spirits revenge themselves on people who talk about them. And then the pen writes, but I don't know if it's me doing it or not. Sometimes it goes well, but sometimes it doesn't work at all. And when I get tired nothing happens, but I have to make something happen all the same. This evening I thought I was doing rather well, but then Grandmother said it was all out of Stagnelius* and I had been playing a trick on her. And she was simply furious.
CAPTAIN.	Do you believe there are spirits?
BERTHA.	I don't know.
CAPTAIN.	But I know there are not.
BERTHA.	Grandmother says you don't understand, and that you have worse things that can see into other planets.
CAPTAIN.	She says that, does she? And what else does she say?
BERTHA.	That you can't work miracles.
CAPTAIN.	I never said I could. You know what meteorites are, don't you?—stones that fall from other heavenly bodies. Well, I examine these and see if they contain the same elements as the earth. That's all I do.
BERTHA.	Grandmother says there are things she can see and you can't.
CAPTAIN.	My dear, she is lying.
BERTHA.	Grandmother doesn't lie.
CAPTAIN.	How do you know?
BERTHA.	Then Mother does too.
CAPTAIN.	Hm!

*Erik Johan Stagnelius, Swedish poet and dramatist. (1793–1823.)

BERTHA.	If you say Mother is a liar, I'll never believe a word you say again.
CAPTAIN.	I didn't say that, so now you must believe me. Listen. Your happiness, your whole future depends on your leaving home. Will you do this? Will you go and live in town and learn something useful?
BERTHA.	Oh yes, I'd love to live in town—anywhere away from here! It's always so miserable in there, as gloomy as a winter night. But when you come home, Father, it's like a spring morning when they take the double windows down.
CAPTAIN.	My darling, my beloved child!
BERTHA.	But, Father, listen, you must be kind to Mother. She often cries.
CAPTAIN.	Hm! . . . So you would like to live in town?
BERTHA.	Oh yes!
CAPTAIN.	But supposing your mother doesn't agree?
BERTHA.	She must.
CAPTAIN.	But supposing she doesn't?
BERTHA.	Then I don't know what will happen. But she must, she must!
CAPTAIN.	Will you ask her?
BERTHA.	No, you must ask her—very nicely. She wouldn't pay any attention to me.
CAPTAIN.	Hm! . . . Well now, if you want this and I want it and she doesn't want it, what are we to do then?
BERTHA.	Oh, then the fuss will begin all over again! Why can't you both . . . *Enter* LAURA.
LAURA.	Ah, so you're here, Bertha! Well now, Adolf, as the question of her future is still to be decided, let's hear what she has to say herself.
CAPTAIN.	The child can hardly have anything constructive to say about the development of young girls, but you and I ought to be able to sum up the pros and cons. We've watched a good number grow up.
LAURA.	But as we don't agree, Bertha can give the casting vote.
CAPTAIN.	No. I won't allow anyone to interfere with my rights—neither woman nor child. Bertha, you had better leave us. *Exit* BERTHA.
LAURA.	You were afraid to hear her opinion because you knew she would agree with me.
CAPTAIN.	I know she wants to leave home, but I also know you have the power to make her change her mind.

LAURA.	Oh, have I much power?
CAPTAIN.	Yes, you have a fiendish power of getting your own way, like all people who are unscrupulous about the means they employ. How, for instance, did you get rid of Dr. Norling? And how did you get hold of the new doctor?
LAURA.	Yes, how did I?
CAPTAIN.	You ran the old doctor down until he had to leave, and then you got your brother to canvass for this one.
LAURA.	Well, that was quite simple and perfectly legal. Then is Bertha to leave home?
CAPTAIN.	Yes, in a fortnight's time.
LAURA.	I warn you I shall do my best to prevent it.
CAPTAIN.	You can't.
LAURA.	Can't I? Do you expect me to give up my child to be taught by wicked people that all she has learnt from her mother is nonsense? So that I would be despised by my own daughter for the rest of my life.
CAPTAIN.	Do you expect me to allow ignorant and bumptious women to teach my daughter that her father is a charlatan?
LAURA.	That shouldn't matter so much to you—now.
CAPTAIN.	What on earth do you mean?
LAURA.	Well, the mother's closer to the child, since the discovery that no one can tell who the father is.
CAPTAIN.	What's that got to do with us?
LAURA.	You don't know if you are Bertha's father.
CAPTAIN.	Don't know?
LAURA.	How can you know what nobody knows?
CAPTAIN.	Are you joking?
LAURA.	No, I'm simply applying your own theory. How do you know I haven't been unfaithful to you?
CAPTAIN.	I can believe a good deal of you, but not that. And if it were so, you wouldn't talk about it.
LAURA.	Supposing I were prepared for anything, for being turned out and ostracised, anything to keep my child under my own control. Supposing I am telling the truth now when I say: Bertha is my child but not yours. Supposing . . .
CAPTAIN.	Stop it!
LAURA.	Just supposing . . . then your power would be over.
CAPTAIN.	Not till you had proved I wasn't the father.
LAURA.	That wouldn't be difficult. Do you want me to?

CAPTAIN. Stop.

LAURA. I should only have to give the name of the real father—with particulars of place and time, of course. For that matter—when was Bertha born? In the third year of our marriage . . .

CAPTAIN. Will you stop it now, or . . .

LAURA. Or what? Very well, let's stop. All the same, I should think twice before you decide anything. And, above all, don't make yourself ridiculous.

CAPTAIN. I find the whole thing tragic.

LAURA. Which makes you still more ridiculous.

CAPTAIN. But not you?

LAURA. No, we're in such a strong position.

CAPTAIN. That's why we can't fight you.

LAURA. Why try to fight a superior enemy?

CAPTAIN. Superior?

LAURA. Yes. It's odd, but I have never been able to look at a man without feeling myself his superior.

CAPTAIN. One day you may meet your master—and you'll never forget it.

LAURA. That will be fascinating.
          Enter NURSE.

NURSE. Supper's ready. Come along now, please.

LAURA. Yes, of course. *The* CAPTAIN *lingers and sits down in an armchair near the sofa.* Aren't you coming?

CAPTAIN. No, thank you, I don't want any supper.

LAURA. Why not? Has anything upset you?

CAPTAIN. No, but I'm not hungry.

LAURA. Do come, or they'll start asking questions, and that's not necessary. Do be sensible. You won't? Well, stay where you are then! *Exit.*

NURSE. Mr. Adolf, whatever is it now?

CAPTAIN. I don't know yet. Tell me—why do you women treat a grown man as if he were a child?

NURSE. Well, goodness me, you're all some woman's child, aren't you?—All you men, big or small . . .

CAPTAIN. While no woman is born of man, you mean. True. But I must be Bertha's father. You believe that, Margaret, don't you? Don't you?

NURSE. Lord, what a silly boy you are! Of course you're your own child's father. Come along and eat now. Don't sit here sulking. There now, come along, do.

CAPTAIN, *rising*. Get out, woman! To hell with the hags! *At the hall door.* Svärd! Svärd!

ORDERLY, entering. Yes, sir?

CAPTAIN.   Have the small sleigh got ready at once.
Exit ORDERLY.

NURSE.   Now listen, Captain . . .

CAPTAIN.   Get out, woman! Get out, I say!

NURSE.   God preserve us, whatever's going to happen now?

CAPTAIN, *putting on his cap.* Don't expect me home before midnight.
Exit.

NURSE.   Lord Jesus! What *is* going to happen?

ACT Two

The same as before, late that night. The DOCTOR *and* LAURA *are sitting talking.*

DOCTOR.   My conversation with him has led me to the conclusion that your suspicions are by no means proved. To begin with, you were mistaken in saying that he had made these important astronomical discoveries by using a microscope. Now I have learnt that it was a spectroscope. Not only is there no sign in this of mental derangement—on the contrary, he has rendered a great service to science.

LAURA.   But I never said that.

DOCTOR.   I made a memorandum of our conversation, Madam, and I remember questioning you on this vital point, because I thought I must have misheard. One must be scrupulously accurate when bringing charges which might lead to a man being certified.

LAURA.   Certified?

DOCTOR.   I presume you are aware that if a person is certified insane, he loses both his civil and his family rights.

LAURA.   No, I didn't know that.

DOCTOR.   There is one other point I should like to be clear about. He spoke of not getting any replies from his booksellers. May I ask whether—from the best of intentions, of course—you have been intercepting his correspondence?

LAURA.   Yes, I have. It is my duty to protect the family. I couldn't let him ruin us all and do nothing about it.

DOCTOR.   Excuse me, I do not think you understand the possible consequences of your action. If he realises you have been interfering with his affairs behind his back, his suspicions will be aroused and might even develop into a persecution mania. Particularly, as by thwarting his will, you have already driven him to the end of his tether. Surely you know how enraging it is to have your will opposed and your dearest wishes frustrated.

LAURA.   Do I not!

DOCTOR.   Then think what this means to him.

LAURA, *rising*. It's midnight and he's not back yet. Now we can expect the worst.

DOCTOR.   Tell me what happened this evening after I saw him. I must know everything.

LAURA.   He talked in the wildest way and said the most fantastic things. Can you believe it—he even suggested he wasn't the father of his own child!

DOCTOR.   How extraordinary! What can have put that into his head?

LAURA.   Goodness knows, unless it was an interview he had with one of his men about maintenance for a child. When I took the girl's part, he got very excited and said no one could ever tell who a child's father was. God knows I did everything I could to calm him, but I don't believe anything can help him now. *Weeps.*

DOCTOR.   This can't go on. Something must be done—without rousing his suspicions. Tell me, has he had any such delusions before?

LAURA.   As a matter of fact, he was much the same six years ago, and then he actually admitted—in a letter to his doctor—that he feared for his reason.

DOCTOR.   I see, I see. A deep-seated trouble. But . . . er . . . the sanctity of family life . . . and so forth . . . I mustn't probe too far . . . must keep to the surface. Unfortunately what is done cannot be undone, yet the remedy should have been applied to what is done . . . Where do you think he is now?

LAURA.   I can't imagine. He has such wild notions these days . . .

DOCTOR.   Would you like me to stay until he comes in? I could explain my presence by saying—well, that your mother is ill and I came to see her.

LAURA.   That's a very good idea. Please stand by us, Doctor. If you only knew how worried I am! . . . But wouldn't it be better to tell him straight out what you think of his condition?

DOCTOR.   We never do that with mental patients, unless they bring the subject up themselves, and rarely even then. Everything depends on how the case develops. But we had better not stay here. May I go into some other room, to make it more convincing?

LAURA. Yes, that will be best, and Margaret can come in here. She always waits up for him. *At the door.* Margaret! Margaret! She is the only one who can manage him.
NURSE, *entering.* Did you call, Madam? Is Master back?

LAURA. No, but you are to wait here for him. And when he comes, tell him that my mother is unwell and the doctor is with her.

NURSE. Aye, aye. Leave all that to me.
LAURA, *opening the door.* If you will be so good as to come in here, Doctor . . .

DOCTOR. Thank you.
They go out. The NURSE *sits at the table, puts on her glasses and picks up her hymn-book.*

NURSE. Ah me! Ah me! *Reads softly:*

> *A sorrowful and grievous thing*
> *Is life, so swiftly passing by,*
> *Death shadows with his angel's wing*
> *The whole earth, and this his cry:*
> *'Tis Vanity, all Vanity!*

Ah me! Ah me!

> *All that on earth has life and breath,*
> *Falls low before his awful might,*
> *Sorrow alone is spared by Death,*
> *Upon the yawning grave to write:*
> *'Tis Vanity, all Vanity!*

Ah me! Ah me!
During the last lines, BERTHA *enters, carrying a tray with a coffee-pot and a piece of embroidery.*
BERTHA, *softly.* Margaret, may I sit in here with you? It's so dismal up there.

NURSE. Saints alive! Bertha, are you still up?

BERTHA. Well, you see, I simply must get on with Father's Christmas present. And here's something nice for you.

NURSE. But, sweetheart, this won't do. You have to be up bright and early, and it's past twelve now.

BERTHA. Oh, that doesn't matter! I daren't stay up there all alone. I'm sure there are ghosts.

NURSE. There now! What did I tell you? Mark my words, there's no good fairy in this house. What was it? Did you hear something, Bertha?

BERTHA. Oh Margaret, someone was singing in the attic!

NURSE. In the attic? At this time of night?

BERTHA.   Yes. It was such a sad song; the saddest I ever heard. And it seemed to come from the attic—you know, the one on the left where the cradle is.

NURSE.   Oh dear, dear, dear! And such a fearful night too. I'm sure the chimneys will blow down. "Alas, what is this earthly life? Sorrow, trouble, grief and strife. Even when it seems most fair, Nought but tribulation there."—Ah, dear child, God grant us a happy Christmas!

BERTHA.   Margaret, is it true Father's ill?

NURSE.   Aye, that's true enough.

BERTHA.   Then I don't expect we shall have a Christmas party. But why isn't he in bed if he's ill?

NURSE.   Well, dearie, staying in bed doesn't help his kind of illness. Hush! I hear someone in the porch. Go to bed now—take the tray with you, or the Master will be cross.

BERTHA,   *Going out with the tray.* Goodnight, Margaret.

NURSE.   Goodnight, love. God bless you.
            Enter the CAPTAIN.
            CAPTAIN, *taking off his overcoat.* Are you still up? Go to bed.

NURSE.   Oh, I was only biding till . . .
            The CAPTAIN *lights a candle, opens the bureau, sits down at it and takes letters and newspapers from his pocket.*
            Mr. Adolf . . .

CAPTAIN.   What is it?

NURSE.   The old mistress is ill. Doctor's here.

CAPTAIN.   Anything serious?

NURSE.   No, I don't think so. Just a chill.

            CAPTAIN, *rising.* Who was the father of your child, Margaret?

NURSE.   I've told you often enough, it was that heedless fellow Johansson.

CAPTAIN.   Are you sure it was he?

NURSE.   Don't talk so silly. Of course I'm sure, seeing he was the only one.

CAPTAIN.   Yes, but was he sure he was the only one? No, he couldn't be sure, only you could be. See? That's the difference.

NURSE.   I don't see any difference.

CAPTAIN.   No, you don't see it, but it's there all the same. *Turns the pages of the photograph album on the table.* Do you think Bertha's like me?

NURSE.   You're as like as two peas in a pod.

CAPTAIN.   Did Johansson admit he was the father?

NURSE.	Well, he was forced to.
CAPTAIN.	How dreadfull—Here's the doctor. *Enter* DOCTOR. Good evening, Doctor. How is my mother-in-law?
DOCTOR.	Oh, it's nothing much. Just a slight sprain of the left ankle.
CAPTAIN.	I thought Margaret said it was a chill. There appear to be different diagnoses of the case. Margaret, go to bed. *Exit* NURSE. *Pause.* Won't you sit down, Dr. Östermark?
DOCTOR.	*sitting.* Thank you.
CAPTAIN.	Is it true that if you cross a mare with a zebra you get striped foals? DOCTOR, *astonished.* Perfectly true.
CAPTAIN.	And that if breeding is then continued with a stallion, the foals may still be striped?
DOCTOR.	That is also true.
CAPTAIN.	So, in certain circumstances, a stallion can sire striped foals, and vice versa.
DOCTOR.	That would appear to be the case.
CAPTAIN.	So the offspring's resemblance to the father proves nothing.
DOCTOR.	Oh . . .
CAPTAIN.	You're a widower, aren't you? Any children?
DOCTOR.	Ye-es.
CAPTAIN.	Didn't you sometimes feel rather ridiculous as a father? I myself don't know anything more ludicrous than the sight of a man holding his child's hand in the street, or hearing a father say: "My child." "My wife's child," he ought to say. Didn't you ever see what a false position you were in? Weren't you ever haunted by doubts—I won't say suspicions, as a gentleman I assume your wife was above suspicion?
DOCTOR.	No, I certainly wasn't. There it is, Captain, a man—as I think Goethe says—must take his children on trust.
CAPTAIN.	Trust, where a woman's concerned? A bit of a risk.
DOCTOR.	Ah, but there are many kinds of women!
CAPTAIN.	The latest research shows there is only one kind . . . when I was a young fellow and not, if I may say so, a bad specimen, I had two little experiences which afterwards gave me to think. The first was on a steamer. I was in the saloon with some friends, and the young stewardess told us—with tears running down her cheeks—how her sweetheart had been drowned at sea. We condoled with her and I ordered champagne. After the

second glass I touched her foot after the fourth her knee, and before morning I had consoled her.

DOCTOR. One swallow doesn't make a summer.

CAPTAIN. My second experience was a summer swallow. I was staying at Lysekil and got to know a young married woman who was there with her children—her husband was in town. She was religious and high-minded, kept preaching at me and was—or so I thought—the soul of virtue. I lent her a book or two which, strange to relate, she returned. Three months later, I found her card in one of those books with a pretty outspoken declaration of love. It was innocent—as innocent, that's to say, as such a declaration from a married woman could be—to a stranger who had never made her any advances. Moral: don't believe in anyone too much.

DOCTOR. Don't believe too little either.

CAPTAIN. The happy mean, eh? But you see, Doctor, that woman, was so unaware of her motives she actually told her husband of her infatuation for me. That's where the danger lies, in the fact that women are unconscious of their instinctive wickedness. An extenuating circumstance, perhaps, but that can only mitigate the judgment, not revoke it.

DOCTOR. You have a morbid turn of mind, Captain. You should be on your guard against this.

CAPTAIN. There's nothing morbid about it. Look here. All steam-boilers explode when the pressure-gauge reaches the limit, but the limit isn't the same for all boilers. Got that? After all, you're here to observe me. Now if I were not a man I could sniff and snivel and explain the case to you, with all its past history. But as unfortunately I am a man, like the ancient Roman I must cross my arms upon my breast and hold my breath until I die. Goodnight.

DOCTOR. If you are ill, Captain, there's no reflection on your manhood in telling me about it. Indeed, it is essential for me to hear both sides of the case.

CAPTAIN. I thought you were quite satisfied with one side.

DOCTOR. You're wrong. And I should like you to know, Captain, that when I heard that Mrs. Alving* blackening her late husband's memory, I thought what a damned shame it was that the fellow should be dead.

CAPTAIN. Do you think if he'd been alive he'd have said anything? Do you think if any husband rose from the dead he'd be believed? Goodnight, Doctor. Look how calm I am. It's quite safe for you to go to bed.

---

*Reference to Mrs. Alving in Ibsen's GHOSTS.

DOCTOR. Then I will bid you goodnight. I wash my hands of the whole business.

CAPTAIN. So we're enemies?

DOCTOR. By no means. It's just a pity we can't be friends. Goodnight.
The CAPTAIN *shows the* DOCTOR *out by the hall door, then crosses to the other and slightly opens it.*

CAPTAIN. Come in and let's talk. I knew you were eavesdropping.
Enter LAURA, *embarrassed. The* CAPTAIN *sits at the bureau.*
It's very late, but we'd better have things out now. Sit down. *She sits. Pause.* This evening it was I who went to the post office and fetched the mail, and from my letters it is clear to me that you have been intercepting my correspondence—both in and out. The result of this has been a loss of time which has pretty well shattered the expectations I had for my work.

LAURA. I acted from the best of intentions. You were neglecting your military duties for this other work.

CAPTAIN. Scarcely the best of intentions. You knew very well that one day I should win more distinction in this field than in the Army, but what you wanted was to stop me winning laurels of any kind, because this would stress your own inferiority. Now, for a change, I have intercepted letters addressed to you.

LAURA. How chivalrous!

CAPTAIN. In keeping with the high opinion you have of me. From these letters it appears that for a long time now you've been setting my old friends against me, by spreading rumours about my mental condition. So successful have your efforts been that now scarcely one person from Colonel to kitchen-maid believes I am sane. The actual facts about my condition are these. My reason is, as you know, unaffected, and I am able to discharge my duties both as soldier and father. My emotions are still pretty well under control, but only so long as my will-power remains intact. And you have so gnawed and gnawed at my will that at any moment it may slip its cogs, and then the whole bag of tricks will go to pieces. I won't appeal to your feelings, because you haven't any—that is your strength. I appeal to your own interests.

LAURA. Go on.

CAPTAIN. By behaving in this way you have made me so full of suspicion that my judgment is fogged and my mind is beginning to stray. This means that the insanity you have been waiting for is on its way and may come at any moment. The question you now have to decide is whether it is more to your advantage for me to be well or ill. Consider. If I go to pieces, I shall have to leave the Service, and where will you be then? If I die, you get my life-insurance. But if I take my own life, you get nothing. It is therefore to your advantage that I should live my life out.

LAURA.   Is this a trap?

CAPTAIN.   Certainly. You can avoid it or stick your head in it.

LAURA.   You say you'd kill yourself, but you never would.

CAPTAIN.   Are you so sure? Do you think a man can go on living when he has nothing and nobody to live for?

LAURA.   Then you give in?

CAPTAIN.   No, I offer peace.

LAURA.   On what terms?

CAPTAIN.   That I may keep my reason. Free me from doubt and I will give up the fight.

LAURA.   Doubt about what?

CAPTAIN.   Bertha's parentage.

LAURA.   Are there doubts about that?

CAPTAIN.   Yes, for me there are, and it was you who roused them.

LAURA.   I?

CAPTAIN.   Yes. You dropped them like henbane in my ear, and circumstances encouraged them to grow. Free me from uncertainly. Tell me straight out it is so, and I will forgive you in advance.

LAURA.   I can scarcely admit to guilt that isn't mine.

CAPTAIN.   What can it matter to you, when you know I won't reveal it? Do you think any man would proclaim his shame from the housetops?

LAURA.   If I say it isn't so, you still won't be certain, but if I say it is, you will believe me. You must want it to be true.

CAPTAIN.   Strangely enough I do. Perhaps because the first supposition can't be proved, while the second can.

LAURA.   Have you any grounds for suspicion?

CAPTAIN.   Yes and no.

LAURA.   I believe you want to make out I'm guilty, so you can get rid of me and have absolute control of the child. But you won't catch me in any such trap.

CAPTAIN.   Do you think, if I were convinced of your guilt, I should want to take on another man's child?

LAURA.   No, I'm sure you wouldn't. So evidently you were lying when you said you'd forgive me in advance.

CAPTAIN, *rising.* Laura, save, me and my reason! You can't have understood what I was saying. If the child's not mine, I have no rights over her, nor do I want any. And that's how you'd like it, isn't it? But that's not all. You want complete power over the child, don't you, with me still there to support you both?

LAURA. Power, that's it. What's this whole life and death struggle for if not power?

CAPTAIN. For me, as I don't believe in a life to come, this child was my life after death, my conception of immortality—the only one, perhaps, that's valid. If you take her away, you cut my life short.

LAURA. Why didn't we separate sooner?

CAPTAIN. Because the child bound us together, but the bond became a chain. How was that? I never thought of this before, but now memories return, accusing, perhaps condemning. After two years of marriage we were still childless—you know best why. Then I was ill and almost died. One day, between bouts of fever, I heard voices in the next room. You and the lawyer were discussing the property I still owned then. He was explaining that as there were no children, you could not inherit, and he asked if by any chance you were pregnant. I did not hear your reply. I recovered and we had a child. Who is the father?

LAURA. You are.

CAPTAIN. No, I am not. There's a crime buried here that's beginning to stink. And what a fiendish crime! You women, who were so tender-hearted about freeing black slaves, kept the white ones. I have slaved for you, your child, your mother, your servants. I have sacrificed career and promotion. Tortured, beaten, sleepless—my hair has gone grey through the agony of mind you have inflicted on me. All this I have suffered in order that you might enjoy a care-free life and, when you were old, relive it in your child. This is the lowest form of theft, the cruellest slavery. I have had seventeen years of penal servitude—and I was innocent. How can you make up to me for this?

LAURA. Now you really are mad.

CAPTAIN, *sitting.* So you hope. I have watched you trying to conceal your crime, but because I didn't understand I pitied you. I've soothed your conscience, thinking I was chasing away some nightmare. I've heard you crying out in your sleep without giving your words a second thought. But now . . . now! The other night—Bertha's birthday—comes back to me. I was still up in the early hours, reading, and you suddenly screamed as if someone were trying to strangle you. "Don't! Don't!" you cried. I knocked on the wall—I didn't want to hear any more. For a long time I have had vague suspicions. I did not want them confirmed. This is what I have suffered for you. What will you do for me?

LAURA.   What can I do? Swear before God and all that I hold sacred that you are Bertha's father?

CAPTAIN.   What good would that do? You have already said that a mother can and ought to commit any crime for her child. I implore you by the memory of the past, I implore you as a wounded man begs to be put out of his misery, tell me the truth. Can't you see I'm helpless as a child? Can't you hear me crying to my mother that Fm hurt? Forget I'm a man, a soldier whose word men—and even beasts—obey. I am nothing but a sick creature in need of pity. I renounce every vestige of power and only beg for mercy on my life.

LAURA, *laying her hand on his forehead.* What? You, a man, in tears?

CAPTAIN.   Yes, a man in tears. Has not a man eyes? Has not a man hands, limbs, senses, opinions, passions? Is he not nourished by the same food as a woman, wounded by the same weapons, warmed and chilled by the same winter and summer? If you prick us, do we not bleed? If you tickle us, do we not laugh? If you poison us, do we not die? Why should a man suffer in silence or a soldier hide his tears? Because it's not manly? Why isn't it manly?

LAURA.   Weep, then, my child, and you shall have your mother again. Remember, it was as your second mother that I came into your life. You were big and strong, yet not fully a man. You were a giant child who had come into the world too soon, or perhaps an unwanted child.

CAPTAIN.   That's true. My father and mother had me against their will, and therefore I was born without a will. That is why, when you and I became one, I felt I was completing myself—and that is why you dominated. I—in the army the one to command—became at home the one to obey. I grew up at your side, looked up to you as a superior being and listened to you as if I were your foolish little boy.

LAURA.   Yes, that's how it was, and I loved you as if you were my little boy. But didn't you see how, when your feelings changed and you came to me as a lover, I was ashamed? The joy I felt in your embraces was followed by such a sense of guilt my very blood seemed tainted. The mother became the mistress—horrible!

CAPTAIN.   I saw, but I didn't understand. I thought you despised my lack of virility, so I tried to win you as a woman by proving myself as a man.

LAURA.   That was your mistake. The mother was your friend, you see, but the woman was your enemy. Sexual love is conflict. And don't imagine I gave myself. I didn't give. I only took what I meant to take. Yet you did dominate me . . . I felt it and wanted you to feel it.

CAPTAIN.   You always dominated me. You could hypnotise me when I was wide awake, so that I neither saw nor heard, but simply obeyed. You could give me a raw potato and make me think it was a peach; you could make me take your ridiculous ideas for flashes of genius. You could corrupt me—yes, make me do the shabbiest things. You never had any real intelligence, yet, instead of being guided by me, you would take the reins into your own hands. And when at last I woke to the realisation that I had lost my integrity, I wanted to blot out my humiliation by some heroic action—some feat, some discovery—even by committing *hara-kiri*. I wanted to go to war, but I couldn't. It was then that I gave all my energies to science. And now—now when I should be stretching out my hand to gather the fruit, you chop off my arm. I'm robbed of my laurels; I'm finished. A man cannot live without repute.

LAURA.   Can a woman?

CAPTAIN.   Yes—she has her children, but he has not . . . Yet you and I and everyone else went on living, unconscious as children, full of fancies and ideals and illusions, until we woke up. Right—but we woke topsy-turvy, and what's more, we'd been woken by someone who was talking in his own sleep. When women are old and stop being women, they grow beards on their chins. What do men grow, I wonder, when they are old and stop being men? In this false dawn, the birds that crowed weren't cocks, they were capons, and the hens that answered their call were sexless, too. So when the sun should have risen for us, we found ourselves back among the ruins in the full moonlight, just as in the good old times. Our light morning sleep had only been troubled by fantastic dreams-there had been no awakening.

LAURA.   You should have been a writer, you know.

CAPTAIN.   Perhaps.

LAURA.   But I'm sleepy now, so if you have any more fantasies, keep them till to-morrow.

CAPTAIN.   Just one thing more—a fact. Do you hate me?

LAURA.   Sometimes—as a man.

CAPTAIN.   It's like race-hatred. If it's true we are descended from the ape, it must have been from two different species. There's no likeness between us, is there?

LAURA.   What are you getting at?

CAPTAIN.   In this fight, one of us must go under.

LAURA.   Which?

CAPTAIN.   The weaker naturally.

LAURA.   Then is the stronger in the right?

CAPTAIN.   Bound to be as he has the power.

LAURA.   Then I am in the right.

CAPTAIN.   Why, what power have you?

LAURA.   All I need. And it will be legal power to-morrow when I've put you under restraint.

CAPTAIN.   Under restraint?

LAURA.   Yes. Then I shall decide my child's future myself out of reach of your fantasies.

CAPTAIN.   Who will pay for her if I'm not there?

LAURA.   Your pension.

CAPTAIN, *moving towards her menacingly.* How can you have me put under restraint?

LAURA, *producing a letter.* By means of this letter, an attested copy of which is already in the hands of the authorities.

CAPTAIN.   What letter?

LAURA, *retreating.* Your own. The one in which you told the doctor you were mad. *He stares at her in silence.* Now you have fulfilled the unfortunately necessary functions of father and bread-winner. You are no longer needed, and you must go. You must go, now that you realise my wits are as strong as my will—you won't want to stay and acknowledge my superiority.

The CAPTAIN *goes to the table, picks up the lighted lamp and throws it at* LAURA, *who escapes backward through the door.*

ACT Three

The same. The following evening. A new lamp, lighted, is on the table. The wallpapered door is barricaded with a chair. From the room above comes the sound of pacing footsteps. The NURSE *stands listening, troubled. Enter* LAURA *from within.*

LAURA.   Did he give you the keys?

NURSE.   Give? No, God help us, I took them from the coat Nöjd had out to brush.

LAURA.   Then it's Nöjd who's on duty?

NURSE.   Aye, it's Nöjd.

LAURA.   Give me the keys.

NURSE.   Here you are, but it's no better than stealing. Hark at him up there! To and fro, to and fro.

LAURA.   Are you sure the door's safely bolted?

NURSE.   It's bolted safe enough. *Weeps.*
LAURA, *opening the bureau and sitting down at it*. Pull yourself together, Margaret The only way we can protect ourselves is by keeping calm. A *knock at the hall door*. See who that is.
NURSE, *opening door*. It's Nöjd.

LAURA.   Tell him to come in.
NÖJD, *entering*. Despatch from the Colonel.

LAURA.   Give it to me. *Reads*. I see . . . Nöjd, have you removed the cartridges from all the guns and pouches?

NÖJD.   Yes, Ma'am, just as you said.

LAURA.   Wait outside while I write to the Colonel.
Exit NÖJD. LAURA *writes. Sound of sawing above.*

NURSE.   Listen, Madam. Whatever is he doing now?

LAURA.   Do be quiet. I'm writing.
NURSE, *muttering*. Lord have mercy on us! What will be the end of all this?

LAURA,   *holding out the note*. Here you are. Give it to Nöjd. And, re-member, my mother's to know nothing of all this.
Exit NURSE *with note,* LAURA *opens the bureau drawers and takes out papers. Enter* PASTOR.

PASTOR.   My dear Laura! As you probably gathered, I have been out all day and only just got back. I hear you've been having a terri-ble time.

LAURA.   Yes, brother, I've never been through such a night and day in all my life!

PASTOR.   Well, I see you're looking none the worse for it.

LAURA.   No, thank heaven, I wasn't hurt. But just think what might have happened!

PASTOR.   Tell me all about it. I've only heard rumours. How did it begin?

LAURA.   It began by him raving about not being Bertha's father, and ended by him throwing the lighted lamp in my face.

PASTOR.   But this is appalling. He must be quite out of his mind. What in heaven's name are we to do?

LAURA.   We must try to prevent further violence. The doctor has sent to the hospital for a strait-jacket. I have just written a note to the

Colonel, and now I'm trying to get some idea of the state of our affairs, which Adolf has so shockingly mismanaged. *Opens another drawer.*

PASTOR.   It's a miserable business altogether, but I always feared something of the kind might happen. When fire and water meet, there's bound to be an explosion. *Looks in drawer.* Whatever's all this?

LAURA.   Look! This is where he's kept everything hidden.

PASTOR.   Good heavens! Here's your old doll! And there's your christening cap . . . and Bertha's rattle . . . and your letters . . . and that locket . . . *Wipes his eyes.* He must have loved you very dearly, Laura. I never kept this kind of thing.

LAURA.   I believe he did love me once, but time changes everything.

PASTOR.   What's this imposing document? *Examines it.* The purchase of a gravel Well, better a grave than the asylum! Laura, be frank with me. Aren't you at all to blame?

LAURA.   How can I be to blame because someone goes out of his mind?

PASTOR.   We—elll I will say no more. After all, blood's thicker than water.

LAURA.   Meaning what, if I may ask?

PASTOR, *gazing at her.* Oh come now!

LAURA.   What?

PASTOR.   Come, come! You can scarcely deny that it would suit you down to the ground to have complete control of your daughter.

LAURA.   I don't understand.

PASTOR.   I can't help admiring you.

LAURA.   Really?

PASTOR.   And as for me—I shall be appointed guardian to that Freethinker whom, as you know, I always regarded as a tare among our wheat.

LAURA   *gives a quick laugh which she suppresses.*

LAURA.   You dare say that to me, his wife?

PASTOR.   How strong-willed you are, Laura, how amazingly strong-willed! Like a fox in a trap that would gnaw off its own leg rather than be caught. Like a master-thief working alone, without even a conscience for accomplice. Look in the mirror! You daren't.

LAURA.   I never use a mirror.

PASTOR.   No. You daren't look at yourself. Let me see your hand. Not one tell-tale spot of blood, not a trace of that subtle poison. A little innocent murder that the law cannot touch. An unconscious crime. Unconscious? A stroke of genius that. Listen to him up there! Take care, Laura! If that man gets loose, he will saw you in pieces too.

LAURA.   You must have a bad conscience to talk like that. Pin the guilt on me if you can.

PASTOR.   I can't.

LAURA.   You see? You can't, and so—I am innocent. And now, you look after your charge and I'll take care of mine.
Enter DOCTOR.
Ah, here is the Doctor! *Rises.* I'm so glad to see you, Doctor. I know I can count on you to help me, although I'm afraid not much can be done now. You hear him up there. Are you convinced at last?

DOCTOR.   I am convinced there has been an act of violence. But the question is—should that act of violence be regarded as an outbreak of temper or insanity?

PASTOR.   But apart from this actual outbreak, you must admit that he suffers from fixed ideas.

DOCTOR.   I have a notion, Pastor, that *your* ideas are even more fixed.

PASTOR.   My firmly rooted convictions of spiritual . . .

DOCTOR.   Convictions apart, it rests with you, Madam, to decide if your husband is to be fined or imprisoned or sent to the asylum. How do you regard his conduct?

LAURA.   I can't answer that now.

DOCTOR.   Oh? Have you no—er—firmly rooted convictions of what would be best for the family? And you, Pastor?

PASTOR.   There's bound to be a scandal either way. It's not easy to give an opinion.

LAURA.   But if he were only fined for violence he could be violent again.

DOCTOR.   And if he were sent to prison he would soon be out again. So it seems best for all parties that he should be treated as insane. Where is the nurse?

LAURA.   Why?

DOCTOR.   She must put the strait-jacket on the patient. Not at once, but after I have had a talk with him—and not then until I give the order. I have the—er—garment outside. *Goes out to hall and returns with a large parcel.* Kindly call the nurse.
LAURA *rings. The* DOCTOR *begins to unpack the strait-jacket.*

PASTOR.   Dreadful! Dreadful!
Enter NURSE.

DOCTOR.   Ah, Nurse! Now please pay attention. You see this jacket. When I give you the word I want you to slip it on the Captain from behind. So as to prevent any further violence, you understand. Now it has, you see, unusually long sleeves. That is to restrict his movements. These sleeves must be tied together behind his back. And now here are two straps with buckles, which afterwards you must fasten to the arm of a chair—or to whatever's easiest. Can you do this, do you think?

NURSE.   No, Doctor, I can't. No, not that.

LAURA.   Why not do it yourself, Doctor?

DOCTOR.   Because the patient distrusts me. You, Madam, are the proper person, but I'm afraid he doesn't trust you either, LAURA *grimaces*. Perhaps you, Pastor . . .

PASTOR.   I must beg to decline.
Enter NÖJD.

LAURA.   Did you deliver my note?

NÖJD.   Yes, Madam.

DOCTOR.   Oh, it's you, Nöjd! You know the state of things here, don't you? You know the Captain has had a mental break-down. You must help us look after the patient.

NÖJD.   If there's aught I can do for Captain, he knows I'll do it.

DOCTOR.   You are to put this jacket on him.

NURSE.   He's not to touch him. Nöjd shan't hurt him. I'd rather do it myself, gently, gently. But Nöjd can wait outside and help me if need be—yes, that's what he'd best do.
A pounding on the paper-covered door.

DOCTOR.   Here he is! *To* NURSE. Put the jacket on that chair under your shawl. And now go away, all of you, while the Pastor and I talk to him. That door won't hold long. Hurry!

NURSE, *going* out. Lord Jesus, help us!

LAURA   *shuts the bureau and follows the* NURSE, NÖJD *goes out to the hall. The paper-covered door bursts open, the lock broken and the chair hurled to the floor. The* CAPTAIN *comes out, carrying a pile of books.*

CAPTAIN, *putting the books on the table.* Here it all is. You can read it in every one of these volumes. So I wasn't mad after all. *Picks one up.* Here it is in the Odyssey, Book I, page 6, line 215 in the Uppsala translation. Telemachus speaking to Athene: "My mother says I am Odysseus' son; but for myself I cannot tell. It's a wise child that knows its own father."* And

---

*English translation E. V. Rieu. Penguin Classics.

that's the suspicion Telemachus has about Penelope, the most virtuous of women. Fine state of affairs, eh? *Takes up another book.* And here we have the Prophet Ezekiel: "The fool saith, Lo, here is my father; but who can tell whose loins have engendered him?" That's clear enough. *Picks up another.* And what's this? A history of Russian literature by Merzlyakov. Alexander Pushkin, Russia's greatest poet, was mortally wounded—but more by the rumours of his wife's unfaithfulness than by the bullet he received in his breast at the duel. On his deathbed he swore she was innocent. Jackass! How could he swear any such thing? I *do* read my books, you see! Hullo, Jonas, are you here? And the Doctor, of course. Did I ever tell you what I said to the English lady who was deploring the habit Irishmen have of throwing lighted lamps in their wives' faces? "God, what women!" I said. "Women?" she stammered. "Of course," I replied. "When things get to such a pass that a man who has loved, has worshipped a woman, picks up a lighted lamp and flings it in her face, then you may be sure . . ."

PASTOR.   Sure of what?

CAPTAIN.   Nothing. You can never be sure of anything—you can only believe. That's right, isn't it, Jonas? One believes and so one is saved. Saved, indeed! No. One can be damned through believing. That's what I've learnt.

DOCTOR.   But, Captain . . .

CAPTAIN.   Hold your tongue! I don't want any chat from you. I don't want to hear you relaying all the gossip from in there like a telephone. In there—you know what I mean. Listen to me, Jonas. Do you imagine you're the father of your children? I seem to remember you had a tutor in the house, a pretty boy about whom there was quite a bit of gossip.

PASTOR.   Take care, Adolf!

CAPTAIN.   Feel under your wig and see if you don't find two little nobs. Upon my soul, he's turning pale! Well, well! It was only talk, of course, but my God, how they talked! But we married men are all figures of fun, every man Jack of us. Isn't that right, Doctor? What about your own marriage bed? Didn't you have a certain lieutenant in your house, eh? Wait now, let me guess. He was called . . . *Whispers in the* DOCTOR'S *ear.* By Jove, he's turned pale too! But don't worry. She's dead and buried, so what was done can't be done again. As a matter of fact, I knew him, and he's now—look at me, Doctor—no, straight in the eyes! He is now a major of Dragoons. Good Lord, I believe *he* has horns too!

DOCTOR, *angrily.* Be so good as to change the subject, Captain.

CAPTAIN.   See! As soon as I mention horns he wants to change the subject.

PASTOR.   I suppose you know, brother-in-law, that you're not in your right mind?

CAPTAIN.   Yes, I do know. But if I had the handling of your decorated heads, I should soon have you shut up too. I am mad. But how did I become mad? Doesn't that interest you? No, it doesn't interest anyone. *Takes the photograph album from the table.* Christ Jesus, there is my daughter! Mine? That's what we can never know. Shall I tell you what we should have to do so as to know? First marry, in order to be accepted by society, then immediately divorce; after that become lovers and finally adopt the children. That way one could at least be sure they were one's own adopted children. Eh? But what good's that to me? What good's anything now you have robbed me of my immortality? What can science or philosophy do for me when I have nothing left to live for? How can I live without honour? I grafted my right arm and half my brain and spinal cord on to another stem. I believed they would unite and grow into a single, more perfect tree. Then someone brought a knife and cut below the graft, so now I'm only half a tree. The other part, with my arm and half my brain, goes on growing. But I wither—I am dying, for it was the best part of myself I gave away. Let me die. Do what you like with me. I'm finished.
The DOCTOR *and* PASTOR *whisper, then go out. The* CAPTAIN *sinks into a chair by the table.* BERTHA *enters.*
BERTHA, *going to him.* Are you ill, Father?
CAPTAIN, *looking up stupidly at word "Father."* Me?

BERTHA.   Do you know what you did? You threw a lamp at Mother.

CAPTAIN.   Did I?

BERTHA.   Yes. Supposing she'd been hurt!

CAPTAIN.   Would that have mattered?

BERTHA.   You're not my father if you talk like that.

CAPTAIN.   What d'you say? Not your father? How d'you know? Who told you? Who is your father, then? Who?

BERTHA.   Not you, anyway.

CAPTAIN.   Anyone but me! Who then? Who? You seem well informed. Who told you? That I should live to hear my own child tell me to my face I am not her father! Do you realise you're insulting your mother by saying this? Don't you understand that, if it's true, *she* is disgraced?

BERTHA.   You're not to say anything against Mother, I tell you!

CAPTAIN.   Yes, all in league against me, just as you've always been.

BERTHA. Father!

CAPTAIN. Don't call me that again!

BERTHA. Father, Father!

CAPTAIN, *drawing her to him.* Bertha, my beloved child, yes, you *are* my child. Yes, yes, it must be so—it *is* so. All that was only a sick fancy—it came on the wind like an infection or a fever. Look at me! Let me see my soul in your eyes . . . But I see *her* soul as well. You have two souls. You love me with one and hate me with the other. You must love me and only me. You must have only one soul or you'll have no peace—neither shall I. You must have only one mind, fruit of my mind. You must have only one will-mine!

BERTHA. No, no! I want to be myself.

CAPTAIN. Never! I am a cannibal, you see, and I'm going to eat you. Your mother wanted to eat me, but she didn't succeed. I am Saturn who devoured his children because it was foretold that otherwise they would devour him. To eat or to be eaten—that is the question. If I don't eat you, you will eat me—you've shown your teeth already. *Goes to the rack.* Don't be afraid, my darling child. I shan't hurt you. *Takes down a revolver.*

BERTHA, *dodging away from him.* Help! Mother, help! He wants to kill me!

NURSE, *hurrying in.* What in heaven's name are you doing, Mr. Adolf?

CAPTAIN, *examining the revolver.* Did you remove the cartridges?

NURSE. Well, I did just tidy them away, but sit down here and take it easy and I'll soon fetch them back.

She takes the CAPTAIN *by the arm and leads him to a chair. He slumps down. She picks up the strait-jacket and goes behind the chair.* BERTHA *creeps out.*

Mr. Adolf, do you remember when you were my dear little boy, and I used to tuck you up at night and say your prayers with you? And do you remember how I used to get up in the night to get you a drink when you were thirsty? And how, when you had bad dreams and couldn't go to sleep again, I'd light the candle and tell you pretty stories. Do you remember?

CAPTAIN. Go on talking, Margaret. It soothes my mind. Go on talking.

NURSE. Aye, that I will, but you listen carefully. D'you remember how once you took a great big kitchen knife to carve a boat with, and I came in and had to trick the knife away from you? You were such a silly little lad, one had to trick you, you never would believe what anyone did was for your own good . . . "Give me that snake," I said, "or else he'll bite you." And then, see, you let go of the knife. *Takes the revolver from his hand.* And then, too, when it was time for you to dress yourself, and you wouldn't. I had to coax you, and say you should have a golden coat and be dressed just like a prince. Then I took your little tunic, that was just made of green wool, and held it up in front of you and said: "In with your arms, now, both together." *Gets the jacket on.* And then I said: "Sit nice and still now, while I button it up behind." *Ties the sleeves behind him.* And then I said: "Up with you, and walk across the floor like a good boy, so Nurse can see how it fits." *Leads him to the sofa.* And then I said: "Now you must go to bed."

CAPTAIN. What's that? Go to bed, when I'd just been dressed? My God! What have you done to me? *Tries to get free.* Oh you fiendish woman, what devilish cunning! Who would have thought you had the brains for it? *Lies down on the sofa.* Bound, fleeced, outwitted and unable to die!

NURSE. Forgive me, Mr. Adolf, forgive me! I had to stop you killing the child.

CAPTAIN. Why didn't you let me kill her? If life's hell and death's heaven, and children belong to heaven?

NURSE. What do you know of the hereafter?

CAPTAIN. It's the only thing one does know. Of life one knows nothing. Oh, if one had known from the beginning!

NURSE. Humble your stubborn heart, Mr. Adolf, and cry to God for mercy! Even now it's not too late. It wasn't too late for the thief on the Cross, for Our Saviour said: "To-day shalt thou be with me in paradise."

CAPTAIN. Croaking for a corpse already, old crow? *She takes her hymn-book from her pocket. He calls.* Nöjd! Are you there, Nöjd? *Enter* NÖJD.
Throw this woman out of the house or she'll choke me to death with her hymn-book. Throw her out of the window, stuff her up the chimney, do what you like only get rid of her!
NÖJD, *staring at the* NURSE. God save you, Captain—and that's from the bottom of my heart—but I can't do that, I just can't. If it were six men now, but a woman!

CAPTAIN. What? You can't manage one woman?

NÖJD. I could manage her all right, but there's something stops a man laying hands on a woman.

CAPTAIN. What is this something? Haven't they laid hands on me?

NÖJD. Yes, but I just can't do it, Sir. Same as if you was to tell me to hit Pastor. It's like religion, it's in your bones. I can't do it. *Enter* LAURA. *She signs to* NÖJD, *who goes out.*

CAPTAIN. Omphale! Omphale! Playing with the club while Hercules spins your wool.

LAURA, *approaching the sofa*. Adolf, look at me! Do you believe I'm your enemy?

CAPTAIN. Yes, I do. I believe all you women are my enemies. My mother did not want me to come into the world because my birth would give her pain. She was my enemy. She robbed my embryo of nourishment, so I was born incomplete. My sister was my enemy when she made me knuckle under to her. The first woman I took in my arms was my enemy. She gave me ten years of sickness in return for the love I gave her. When my daughter had to choose between you and me, she became my enemy. And you, you, my wife, have been my mortal enemy, for you have not let go your hold until there is no life left in me.

LAURA. But I didn't mean this to happen. I never really thought it out. I may have had some vague desire to get rid of you—you were in my way—and perhaps, if you see some plan in my actions, there was one, but I was unconscious of it. I have never given a thought to my actions—they simply ran along the rails you laid down. My conscience is clear, and before God I feel innocent, even if I'm not. You weighed me down like a stone, pressing and pressing till my heart tried to shake off its intolerable burden. That's how it's been, and if without meaning to I have brought you to this, I ask your forgiveness.

CAPTAIN. Very plausible, but how does that help me? And whose fault is it? Perhaps our cerebral marriage is to blame. In the old days one married a wife. Now one goes into partnership with a business woman or sets up house with a friend. Then one rapes the partner or violates the friend. What becomes of love, the healthy love of the senses? It dies of neglect. And what happens to the dividends from those love shares, payable to holder, when there's no joint account? Who is the holder when the crash comes? Who is the bodily father of the cerebral child?

LAURA. Your suspicions about our daughter are entirely unfounded.

CAPTAIN. That's the horror of it. If they had some foundation, there would at least be something to catch hold of, to cling to. Now there are only shadows, lurking in the undergrowth, peering out with grinning faces. It's like fighting with air, a mock battle with blank cartridges. Reality, however deadly, puts one on one's mettle, nerves body and soul for action, but as it is . . . my thoughts dissolve in fog, my brain grinds a void till it catches fire . . . Put a pillow under my head. Lay something over me. I'm cold. I'm terribly cold.

LAURA	*takes off her shawl and spreads it over him. Exit* NURSE.
LAURA.	Give me your hand, my dear.
CAPTAIN.	My hand! Which you have bound behind my back. Omphale, Omphale! But I can feel your shawl soft against my mouth. It's warm and gentle like your arms and smells of vanilla like your hair when you were young. When you were young, Laura, and. we used to walk in the birch woods. There were primroses and thrushes—lovely, lovely! Think how beautiful life was then—and what it has become! You did not want it to become like this, neither did I. Yet it has. Who then rules our lives?
LAURA.	God.
CAPTAIN.	The God of strife then—or nowadays the Goddess! *Enter* NURSE *with a pillow.*
	Take away this cat that's lying on me. Take it away! NURSE *removes the shawl and puts the pillow under his head.* Bring my uniform. Put my tunic over me. *The* NURSE *takes the tunic from a peg and spreads it over him. To* LAURA. Ah, my tough lion's-skin that you would take from me! Omphale! Omphale! You cunning woman, lover of peace and contriver of disarmament. Wake, Hercules, before they take away your club! You would trick us out of our armour, calling it tinsel. It was iron, I tell you, before it became tinsel. In the old days the smith forged the soldier's coat, now it is made by the needlewoman. Omphale! Omphale! Rude strength has fallen before treacherous weakness. Shame on you, woman of Satan, and a curse on all your sex! *He raises himself to spit at her, but sinks back again.* What sort of a pillow have you given me, Margaret? How hard and cold it is! So cold! Come and sit beside me on this chair. *She does so.* Yes, like that. Let me put my head on your lap. Ah, that's warmer! Lean over me so I can feel your breast. Oh how sweet it is to sleep upon a woman's breast, be she mother or mistress! But sweetest of all a mother's.
LAURA.	Adolf, tell me, do you want to see your child?
CAPTAIN.	My child? A man has no children. Only women have children. So the future is theirs, while we die childless. O God, who holds all children dear!
NURSE.	Listen! He's praying to God.
CAPTAIN.	No, to you, to put me to sleep. I'm tired, so tired. Goodnight, Margaret. "Blessed art thou among women." *He raises himself, then with a cry falls back on the* NURSES's *knees.*
	LAURA, *at the door, calling.* Doctor!
	Enter DOCTOR *and* PASTOR.

	Help him, Doctor—if it's not too late! Look, he has stopped breathing!
	DOCTOR, *feeling his pulse.* It is a stroke.
PASTOR.	Is he dead?
DOCTOR.	No, he might still wake—but to what, who can say?
PASTOR.	". . . once to die, but after this the judgment."*
DOCTOR.	No judgment—and no recriminations. You who believe that a God rules over human destiny must lay this to his charge.
NURSE.	Ah Pastor, with his last breath he prayed to God!
	PASTOR, *to* LAURA. Is this true?
LAURA.	It is true.
DOCTOR.	If this be so, of which I am as poor a judge as of the cause of his illness, in any case my skill is at an end. Try yours now, Pastor.
LAURA.	Is that all you have to say at this deathbed, Doctor?
DOCTOR.	That is all. I know no more. Let him who knows more, speak.
	BERTHA *comes in and runs to* LAURA.
BERTHA.	Mother! Mother!
LAURA.	My child! My own child!
PASTOR.	Amen.

Questions and Ideas for Journaling and Discussion

1. What is the function of Nojd's story in the first scene of the play?
2. What is the meaning of honor for the captain?
3. Define tragedy. What are the tragic elements in the play?

Writing to Explore and Learn

1. Discuss the issue of paternity in the context of marriage and/or gender relations in the play.
2. In a creative essay, argue with the captain and Laura to try to help them repair their marriage.

Dinty W. Moore
(b. 1955)

What I learned is that pushing form [in an essay] *recasts the existing content and inevitably suggests new content.*

Dinty W. Moore, novelist and essayist, was born and raised in Erie, Pennsylvania. His name was taken from that of a comic strip character of the mid-twentieth century, and, indeed, his work is infused with humor. He earned a BA from the University of Pittsburgh, after which he tried his hand at documentary film, modern dance, zookeeping, and waiting tables in Greenwich Village. Unsuccessful at these endeavors, he earned an MFA in creative writing from Louisiana State University. Moore has won many awards, including a National Endowment for the Arts Fellowship in Fiction. Currently residing in Athens, Ohio, he is a professor of English at Ohio University. *Between Panic and Desire* (University of Nebraska) won the 2009 Grub Street Nonfiction Book Prize; other important books are *The Accidental Buddhist, Toothpick Men,* and *The Emperor's Virtual Clothes*.

"Son of Mr. Green Jeans"; An Essay on Fatherhood, Alphabetically Arranged (2003)

This piece of creative nonfiction presents an alphabetical meditation on fatherhood that references popular culture of the 1950s and examples of fatherhood from the animal world.

Allen, Tim

Best known as the father on ABC's *Home Improvement* (1991–99), the popular comedian was born Timothy Allen Dick on June 13, 1953. When Allen was eleven years old, his father, Gerald Dick, was killed by a drunk driver while driving home from a University of Colorado football game.

Bees

"A man, after impregnating the woman, could drop dead," critic Camille Paglia suggested to Tim Allen in a 1995 *Esquire* interview. "That is how peripheral he is to the whole thing."

"I'm a drone," Allen responded. "Like those bees."

"You are a drone," Paglia agreed. "That's exactly right."

Carp

After the female Japanese carp gives birth to hundreds of tiny babies, the father carp remains nearby. When he senses approaching danger, he sucks the help-less babies into his mouth, and holds them there until the coast is clear.

Divorce

University of Arizona psychologist Sanford Braver tells the story of a woman who felt threatened by her husband's close bond with their young son. The husband had a flexible work schedule but the wife did not, so the boy spent the bulk of his time with the father. The mother became so jealous of the tight father-son relationship that she filed for divorce, and successfully fought for sole custody. The result was that instead of being in the care of his father while the mother worked, the boy was now left in daycare.

Emperor Penguins

Once an emperor penguin male has completed mating, he remains by the fe-male's side for the next month to determine if the act has been successful. When he sees a single greenish-white egg emerge from his mate's egg pouch, he begins to sing. Scientists have characterized his song as "ecstatic."

Father Knows Best

In 1949, Robert Young began *Father Knows Best* as a radio show. Young played Jim Anderson, an average father in an average family. The show later moved to television, where it was a major hit, but Young's successful life was troubled by alcohol and depression.

In January 1991, at age eighty-three, Young attempted suicide by running a hose from his car's exhaust pipe to the interior of the vehicle. The attempt failed because the battery was dead and the car wouldn't start.

Green Genes

In Dublin, Ireland, a team of geneticists is conducting a study to determine the origins of the Irish people. By analyzing segments of DNA from residents across different parts of the Irish countryside, then comparing this DNA with corre-sponding DNA segments from people elsewhere in Europe, the investigators hope to determine the derivation of Ireland's true forefathers.

Hugh Beaumont

The actor who portrayed the benevolent father on the popular TV show *Leave It to Beaver* was a Methodist minister. Tony Dow, who played older brother Wally, reports that Beaumont actually hated kids. "Hugh wanted out of the show after the second season," Dow told the *Toronto Sun*. "He thought he should be doing films and things."

Inheritance

My own Irish forefather was a newspaperman, owned a nightclub, ran for mayor, and smuggled rum in a speedboat during Prohibition. He smoked, drank, ate nothing but red meat, and died of a heart attack in 1938.

His one son, my father, was a teenager when my grandfather died. I never learned more than the barest details about my grandfather from my father, despite my persistent questions. Other relatives tell me that the relationship had been strained.

My father was a skinny, eager-to-please little boy, battered by allergies, and not the tough guy his father had wanted. He lost his mother at age three, and later developed a severe stuttering problem, perhaps as a result of his father's disapproval. My father's adult vocabulary was outstanding, due to his need for alternate words when faltering over hard consonants like *b* or *d*.

The stuttering grew worse over the years, with one notable exception: after downing a few whiskeys, my father could sing like an angel. His Irish tenor became legend in local taverns, and by the time I entered the scene my father was spending every evening visiting the working-class bars. Most nights he would stumble back drunk around midnight; some nights he was so drunk he would stumble through a neighbor's back door, thinking he was home.

As a boy, I coped with the family's embarrassment by staying glued to the television—shows like *Father Knows Best* and *Leave It to Beaver* were my favorites. I desperately wanted someone like Hugh Beaumont to be my father, or maybe Robert Young.

Hugh Brannum, though, would have been my first choice. Brannum played Mr. Green Jeans on *Captain Kangaroo,* and I remember him as being kind, funny, and extremely reliable.

Jaws

My other hobby, besides television, was an aquarium. I loved watching the tropical fish give birth. Unfortunately, guppy fathers, if not moved to a separate tank, will sometimes come along and eat their young.

Kitten

Kitten, the youngest daughter on *Father Knows Best,* was played by Lauren Chapin.

Lauren Chapin

Chapin's father molested her and her mother was a severe alcoholic. After *Father Knows Best* ended in 1960, Chapin's life came apart. At age sixteen, she married an auto mechanic. At age eighteen, she became addicted to heroin and began working as a prostitute.

Male Breadwinners

Wolf fathers spend the daylight hours away from the home—hunting—but return every evening. The wolf cubs, five or six to a litter, rush out of the den when they hear their father approaching and fling themselves at their dad, leaping up to his face. The father backs up a few feet and disgorges food for them, in small, separate piles.

Natural Selection

When my wife Renita confessed to me her ambition, to have children, the very first words out of my mouth were, "You must be crazy." Convinced that she had just proposed the worst imaginable idea, I stood from my chair, looked straight ahead, then marched out of the room.

Ozzie

Oswald Nelson, at thirteen, was the youngest person ever to become an Eagle Scout. Oswald went on to become Ozzie Nelson, the father in *Ozzie and Harriet*. Though the show aired years before the advent of reality television, Harriet was Ozzie's real wife, Ricky and David were his real sons, and eventually Ricky's and David's wives were played by their actual spouses. The current requirements for Eagle Scout make it impossible for anyone to ever beat Ozzie's record.

Penguins, Again

The female emperor penguin "catches the egg with her wings before it touches the ice," Jeffrey Moussaieff Masson writes in his book *The Emperor's Embrace*. She then places it on her feet, to keep it from contact with the frozen ground.

At this point, both penguins will sing in unison, staring at the egg. Eventually, the male penguin will use his beak to lift the egg onto the surface of his own feet, where it remains until hatching.

Not only does the male penguin endure the inconvenience of walking around with an egg balanced on his feet for months, but he also will not eat for the duration.

Quiz

1. What is Camille Paglia's view on the need for fathers?
2. Why did Hugh Beaumont hate kids?

3. Who played Mr. Green Jeans on *Captain Kangaroo?*
4. Who would you rather have as your father: Hugh Beaumont, Hugh Brannum, a wolf, or an emperor penguin?

Religion

In 1979, Lauren Chapin, the troubled actress who played Kitty, had a religious conversion. She credits her belief in Jesus with saving her life. After *his* television career ended, Methodist minister Hugh Beaumont became a Christmas tree farmer.

Sputnik

On October 4, 1957, *Leave It to Beaver* first aired. On that same day, the Soviet Union launched Sputnik I, the world's first artificial satellite. Sputnik I was about the size of a basketball, took roughly ninety-eight minutes to orbit the Earth, and is credited with starting the U.S.-Soviet space race. Later, long after *Leave It to Beaver* ended its network run, a rumor that Jerry Mathers, the actor who played Beaver, had died at the hands of the communists in Vietnam persisted for years. The actress Shelley Winters went so far as to announce it on the *Tonight* show. But the rumor was false.

Toilets

Leave It to Beaver was the first television program to show a toilet.

Use of Drugs

The National Center of Addiction and Substance Abuse at Columbia University claims that the presence of a supportive father is irreplaceable in helping children stay drug-free. Lauren Chapin may be a prime example here, as would Tim Allen, who was arrested for dealing drugs in 1978 and spent two years in prison.

Though I managed to avoid my father's drinking problems, I battled my own drug habit as a young man. Happily, I was never jailed.

Vasectomies

I had a vasectomy in 1994.

Ward's Father

In an episode titled "Beaver's Freckles," the Beaver says that Ward had "a hittin' father," but little else is ever revealed about Ward's fictional family. Despite Wally's constant warning—"Boy, Beav, when Dad finds out, he's gonna clobber ya!"—Ward does not follow his own father's example, and never hits his sons on the show. This is an excellent example of xenogenesis.

Xenogenesis

(zen"*u*-jen'*u*-sis), n. *Biol.* 1. heterogenesis 2. the supposed generation of offspring completely and permanently different from the parent.

Believing in xenogenesis—though at the time I couldn't define it, spell it, *or* pronounce it—I changed my mind about having children about four years after my wife's first suggestion of the idea. Luckily, this was five years before my vasectomy.

Y-Chromosomes

The Y-chromosome of the father determines a child's gender, and is unique, because its genetic code remains relatively unchanged as it passes from father to son. The DNA in other chromosomes, however, is more likely to get mixed between generations, in a process called recombination. What this means, apparently, is that boys have a higher likelihood of inheriting their ancestral traits.

My Y-chromosomes were looking the other way, so my only child is a daughter.

So far Maria has inherited many of what people say are the Moore family's better traits—humor, a facility with words, a stubborn determination. It is yet to be seen what she will do with the negative ones.

Zappa

Similar to the "Beaver died in Vietnam" rumor of the late 1960s, during the late 1990s, Internet discussion lists blasted the news that the actor who played Mr. Green Jeans, Hugh Brannum, was in fact the father of musician Frank Zappa. But Brannum had only one son, and that son was neither Frank Zappa nor this author.

Sometimes, though, I still wonder what it might have been like.

Questions and Ideas for Journaling and Discussion

1. Research Mr. Green Jeans. Why do you think that Moore would have liked to have had him as his own father?
2. An essay is a piece of nonfiction that posits an author's point of view on a topic. What is the relationship between the form of this "essay" and Moore's quote that appears above the essay?
3. This piece of creative nonfiction has a strange-looking format. How would you describe this format and how do you think it adds or detracts from the story. What could Moore have done to structure it differently?

Writing to Explore and Learn

1. In a litany of alphabetically arranged stories, Moore depicts the anxieties inherent in masculinity and fatherhood. What point is he trying to make about these anxieties?

Donald Hall
(b. 1928)

A poem without internal contradiction is not a poem.

Donald Hall was born into a middle-class family in New England and attended private schools and then Harvard and Oxford universities. He wrote poetry as a teenager and began his career by conducting a number of interviews with well-known poets—T.S. Eliot, Ezra Pound, and Marianne Moore. After his first failed marriage, which had produced two children, he met and married Jane Kenyon, a student of his at the University of Michigan. Hall left academia and the two poets lived an idyllic life in his ancestral New Hampshire farmhouse, Eagle Pond farm, until Kenyon's death from leukemia in 1995. Notable works include the poetry collections *Exiles and Marriages* (1955) and *Without* (1999), and the memoir *Unpacking the Boxes* (2006).

"My Son, My Executioner" (1953)

Hall captures the reaction of a young father to the birth of his son. The contrasting metaphors and dark Freudian undertone suggest that parenthood changes a young man's life forever. Hall collapses gender binaries by extending this figurative loss to both parents.

My Son, my executioner,
   I take you in my arms,
Quiet and small and just astir
   And whom my body warms.

Sweet death, small son, our instrument
   Of immortality,
Your cries and hungers document
   Out bodily decay.

We twenty-five and twenty-two,
   Who seemed to live forever,
Observe enduring life in you
   And start to die together.

Questions and Ideas for Journaling and Discussion

1. Freud's Oedipal conflict suggests that in order to be successful in life, a son must, in some way, "kill" his father metaphorically. Discuss the speaker's ambivalence toward the birth of his son in terms of the Oedipal conflict. What is lost? What is gained?
2. In response to the poem, discuss the conflict between parenthood and personal freedom.
3. In English Renaissance poetry, references to the topic of unrelenting change, or the "mutability topos [topic]," was a popular poetic device. In William Shakespeare's *Sonnets*, we learn that the only way to overcome death is to reproduce or write a poem. How do you think Hall is channeling the mutability topos in this poem?

Writing to Explore and Learn

1. Compare and contrast the writer's attitudes toward parenthood in Anne Panning's "The Mother" and Hall's "My Son, My Executioner."

Brett Rutherford
(b. 1947)

Poetry may be the most powerful way to bridge between cultures.

Brett Rutherford, born in Western Pennsylvania, started writing creatively at the age of six. Leaving college to read his poetry in coffee-
houses in San Francisco, he later returned to school before heading to
New York City where he established The Poet's Press in 1971. Active in
the New York City poetry scene of the 1960s and 1970s, Rutherford
eventually left the city for Providence, Rhode Island, when it became
economically impossible for artists to survive in New York City. Currently,
he is editor of the "new" Poet's Press, which publishes more than 175
titles and is available for the world to see on the Internet. Rutherford's
recent publications include *Doctor Jones and Other Terrors* (2009), a
collection of poems that explores the nature of the Gothic.

"All I Know About My Father" (1989)

*Rutherford's poem concerns the father/son relationship as seen through
the eyes of the son. Using this scenario, Rutherford treats the themes
of war, family relations, and responsibility as a way to reveal, in the
yearning for his father, the boy's growing awareness of the stakes of
adult masculinity.*

> When someone asks *Your father?*
> I conjure a blank, a void,
> a vacant place at table, in heart,
> a self-erasing memory.
> Sometimes I envy poets
> who sift from out their childhood days
> a paradigm moment,
> a passing of wisdom,
> a graceless hug,
> eye twinkle of reflected pride.
> I try, and come up empty.
> Once, in the living room,
> he showed me places on a globe;
> I glimpsed

in closely guarded scrapbook
a ruined, barbed-wire Europe
   whose ovens had singed him.
He had a German medal.
Arbeit, it said.
He showed me the tanks,
the marching columns
in which he'd tramped,
GIs like chessmen
   riding and walking
   filling the map
to meet the Red chessmen,
pawns in the *mine* and *yours*
diplomacy of Yalta.
I still recall their farmboy faces,
the broken walls behind their pose.

Once we walked on a slag pile.
He hurled things angrily—
sticks, rocks and bottles—
into a quicksand pool.
I think he meant to tell me something:
The   is a place that draws you to it.
There is a force that sucks you under.
There is a way to walk around it.

Days he kept books at the belching coke ovens,
debits and credits in the sulfurous air;
nights he played jazz at roadside taverns.
One night we even heard him on the radio.

I tried to play his clarinet—just once.
He yanked it away.
Daily and nightly the man was there.
Thirteen years of a father
who wanted a room between himself and sons.
So this is all that I remember:
He was the voice who fought with my mother.
He slept on the couch, then in another house.
Years passed, birthdays and Christmases
unmarked and unremembered.
When I was seventeen he phoned the school,
said he would meet me at the top of the hill.
I walked there, wondering
   what we might have to say,
   what new beginnings—

Sign this, he said.
 What is it?
A policy. Insurance we had
 on you and your brother.
I'd like to cash it in.
I signed. The car sped off.
I never told anyone.

When someone asks *Your father?*
I shrug. He is an empty space,
a vacuum where no bird can fly,
a moon with no planet,
an empty galaxy
 where gravity repels
and dark suns hoard their light.

Questions and Ideas for Journaling and Discussion

1. Characterize the speaker's relationship with his father at the start of the poem. How does their relationship change by the end?
2. How would you explain the father's anger? Is he justified in taking out his anger on his family?
3. Describe the son's expectations when seeing his father after a long absence.
4. Consider Rutherford's description of the "blank void" associated with his recollection of his father and explain what he means by "self-erasing memory."

Writing to Explore and Learn

1. Compare and contrast Hall's and Rutherford's views on the meaning of the relationship between fathers and sons, particularly with respect to the mutability topos.
2. After reading "Veteran's Dance," briefly research Post-Traumatic Stress Disorder (PTSD). PTSD was not fully understood in time to treat World War II veterans. Compare and contrast what might have been done for Rutherford's father and for Lug.

Chapter 7

Boyhood

Perhaps one way of formulating a conceptual understanding of traditional masculinity is to look at boys' behavior in grade school. Recent studies have shown that boys often constitute their masculinities through exhibiting misogyny and homophobia and heterosexual fantasies, often at the expense of girls.[1] That said, performances of masculinity are unstable and vary within specific cultural contexts. The following texts begin to map the structures and restrictions that affect the development of boys and those who play important roles in their lives.

---

[1]See Emma Renold, "If You Don't Kiss Me, You're Dumped: Boys, Boyfriends and Heterosexualised Masculinities in the Primary School," *Educational Review*, Volume 55, Issue 2, June 2003, pp. 179–194; Francis Becky and Christine Skelton, "Men Teachers and the Construction of Heterosexual Masculinity in the Classroom," *Sex Education*, Volume 1, Issue 1, April 2001, pp. 9–21; and Riche Richardson, *Black Masculinity and the U.S. South from Uncle Tom to Gangsta*, Athens: University of Georgia Press, 2007.

Robert Zweig
(b. 1955)

Robert Zweig is a professor of English at the Borough of Manhattan Community College of the City University of New York. He is the author of numerous articles in journals, encyclopedias, and books, and is the author of several textbooks. He has lectured at many universities throughout the United States and abroad, and lives in Westchester, New York, with his wife and two children.

"Bar Mitzvah in Naples" from *Return to Naples: My Italian Bar Mitzvah and Other Discoveries* (2008)

It is in the city of Naples, Italy, that Zweig becomes bar mitzvah, (literally, "son of the commandments"), the Jewish ceremony that brings a male from childhood to adulthood. This defining event intersects with his realization and acceptance of his identity as the child of post-Holocaust European Jews.

I was in the midst of receiving bar mitzvah lessons in the Bronx during the spring of 1968. My six-year-old sister was in the room when the rabbi unexpectedly asked her, "Are you American or Jewish?" At first, she was confused by the question, but after some thought, she answered with satisfaction, "I'm English."

That seemed a reasonable compromise. My father is a German Jew, a survivor of World War II. My mother is an Italian Jew, also a war survivor, who moved with her family from Naples to Florence to Perugia and to Rome in order to evade the advancing Nazis.

I, on the other hand, was many things, and I baffled people by not being as accommodating and self-assertive as my "English" sister. I had to convince others that my mother was not a convert to Judaism but had been born a Jew in Italy, much to the dismay of salesmen who tried to ingratiate themselves to the family by turning on the charm in Yiddish—a language my parents neither understood nor spoke.

The rabbi was hunched over and wore a long black coat and a long white beard. His eyes were older than dust. He had been wandering my Bronx neighborhood looking for business when, one day, he showed up at our house. Before I could complain, I was taking Hebrew lessons instead of shooting my beloved hoops.

The rabbi would leave our house once a week with three dollars in his pocket and a slice of Entenmann's walnut ring under his arm. "You're not listening, Robbie," he would sigh, and I usually wasn't. The three months of lessons were interminable for a boy my age. I had a vague notion that these lessons were important, but the notion did not come from me but rather from the disquieting attitude of others who projected their anxieties onto me.

"If you don't have a bar mitzvah, you are not a real Jew," was the unspoken rebuke by well-meaning relatives. So I accepted the inevitable, buckled down to study, and, with relief, one day found that the lessons were done. Finally we were off to Naples for another summer.

Naples was the home my mother had to flee, but it was also the place she returned to when the war was over; the city therefore tugged at me with special meaning.

In 1968 Naples was exuberant because that was the nature of its people, but it was still largely isolated even from the rest of Italy. As an American, I was always a phenomenon on my grandmother's street, where laundry hung on lines suspended between buildings, and men sat on stoops and wicker chairs in aimless contemplation. I heard of anti-Semitic incidents here and there, but my being Jewish didn't seem to matter to anyone I knew.

This summer of 1968 in Naples, I had more lessons to learn for my bar mitzvah, so every day I walked a narrow, cracked concrete path, which was adorned on both sides by bushes and yellow and red flowers, from my grandmother's house to the lower part of the city. There I would arrive at the only synagogue in the city, which also happened to be the "new" rabbi's house.

The Italian rabbi was a character—he would, without fail, greet me in his underwear. He was in his early thirties, enthusiastic, and when I arrived, he would dart briefly in different directions with the purposeful energy that often accompanies thin people.

Each time, upon seeing me, he would say that he hadn't realized it was so late already. Would I mind waiting? He would have his mother get me a drink while he got dressed. Unfailingly I would agree, and down the hallway he would go, bearded and half-naked, to his room.

Meanwhile, down another hallway, the heavy maroon curtain to the synagogue would be opened a crack, allowing a small, diagonal strip of dancing dust to play in a shaft of light. I would be given a drink, usually a Coke, presented on a silver tray engraved in Hebrew letters, and I would sip it respectfully, given that I was in a house of worship.

The rabbi's mother, a frail woman curved as the letter "C," would wait for me to place the empty glass back on the tray and disappeared into the kitchen, returning only to sit down and stare ahead at her dark and heavy furniture. It felt to me that she had been sitting patiently since the time of Moses.

The synagogue evoked in me a feeling of authentic Jewishness, one I had never known before. It was a feeling that spoke from the old walls of centuries of suffering and oppression. The stones of these walls had seen decades of wars and history. For decades Jews had walked through the dark hallway attached to the rabbi's apartment and laid down their burdens there. I could almost hear the screams of fascists and Nazis.

On the other hand, American synagogues, I thought, had an arbitrary "tinnyness" to them. You would turn into their parking lots off Route 22, walk up a pathway, and look through their too brightly colored "stained glass" windows. The insides usually had the look of a Holiday Inn, with the same bright carpets one might expect at a Las Vegas hotel, paired with the brown plastic and chrome chairs one might see stacked in the corner of the "Embassy Room" at a Sheraton Convention Center. Because of the Holocaust, I had decided, synagogues should not have orange carpets. Orange was too bright a color to suggest the serious historical predicament of Jewish history.

I received my "Italian" Hebrew lessons in a space typical of large Neapolitan apartments—a dining room with high ceilings and white marble floors. When I walked, the sound from the heels of my shoes clicked and echoed throughout the house, adding an appropriate churchlike solemnity.

It is said that God listens to the echoes of voices, not to the voices themselves. The rabbi's feet echoed well too. He wore flip-flops, the kind that hung from strings at kiosks near beaches, where vendors sang for children to buy pails and shovels. In a few weeks the Hebrew symbols, which looked more like little wrought iron sculptures than letters, became coherent, and I knew enough of them to be able to sing my part of the ceremony.

When invitations had to be printed for the big event, a printer was found, a style of card selected, and a simple text in English and Italian written for the printer announcing the occasion. The printer wanted to know what this event was about.

"It's a religious ceremony," I explained briefly.

He was slightly confused but accepted the explanation. A few weeks later the cards were ready to be picked up. Before handing over his beautiful box filled with printed invitations, he announced that he had created something special for us, certain we would be pleased. As this was a unique event, he had embossed a Madonna and child on the cover of each invitation as a bonus—free of charge! I now had 100 bar mitzvah invitations with a Madonna and baby Jesus on each one—a first, I'm certain, for a Jewish boy's entry to manhood.

A new set, Jesus-less, was eventually printed, but I kept the original 100 cards. Occasionally I take them out and look at them, wondering how the guests would have reacted had I sent them as they were.

On the big day, a slow-moving, dignified caravan reminiscent of a funeral cortege drove through the old, cobbled streets of Naples. Pasquale, the wise, folksy caretaker of my Aunt Lietta's building, led the way on his Vespa. He knew this was serious business; this occasion called for a display of the inner gravity that was part of his nature. An appropriately somber expression settled and remained on his face throughout the ceremonies.

Meanwhile "regulars" were already sitting in the synagogue when I arrived. Some were rocking back and forth, human tuning forks to God's music, while others had the familiar "synagogue hunch" and that world-weary stare one can see in any synagogue at any time.

There were an unusual bunch of Jews here, some from Africa, others Neapolitan converts who wanted to follow the "true" religion. They looked out of place with afternoon, Neapolitan beards. It seemed to me that most Neapolitans needed to shave twice a day.

I read my lines robotlike, wishing for time to race past. I heard my voice float from my mouth as if I were outside of my own skin. I wondered if I sounded like other bar mitzvah boys with their too-high voices that did not convey the import of their words.

While I did not understand all that I was reading, that fact did not bother me. Religion, I thought, was not a rational explanation of anything but rather a sentiment, a way of "feeling" the world. The Hebrew words, the old synagogue, the old city of hilly streets outside…I took dominion of these images until they became part of the dance of memories that skims on the surface of conscious thought.

Reading a service in English now seemed like cheating, like sending God a telegram in stunted syntax in order to save money. The true feeling of my Jewishness came from the cultural and historical realities of my parents' lives, made so vivid by being in Naples, the place where they had met. Knowing that they survived the atrocities of war, my living in Europe for long periods of time as a child—at the epicenter of the Holocaust—bore down on me with an immediacy greater than any theological beliefs I could ever envision.

The reception was small, intimate, and bereft of excess. Two waiters set up tables and food at my uncle's house, served, and cleaned up four hours later. The cost: $160.

To some, I was now a man. I didn't feel any closer to God, but because I had some knowledge of what my parents went through during the war, I walked forward with the burden of the past, as if I were walking into a wind.

We left Naples by ship a few weeks later. Once back in the Bronx, I knew I would have more explaining to do about what kind of a Jew I was. This would be my last trip to Italy by sea, and my last long summer visit. Sensing this, I ran to the back of the ship to see the landscape slowly fading, and I listened to the muffled sounds from the port, the city's lungs, expanding and contracting, until Naples took its last breath. That summer, leaving Naples, I had become a different person, having learned of a past that changed my concept of who I really was.

Questions and Ideas for Journaling and Discussion

1. Although initially resistant, Zweig comes to terms with becoming bar mitzvah. What is the relationship between this acceptance and an awareness of his identity?

Writing to Explore and Learn

1. Creative nonfiction is a relatively new genre that uses the techniques and elements of fiction to tell a true story; characterization and the creation of scene are two of these. Discuss the places in which Zweig uses these to enhance the telling of this childhood story.

2. Zweig experienced his new understanding as a burden of the knowledge that he accepted from his parents. Their families were survivors of the Holocaust in Europe, in which six million Jews were murdered. His family had been interned in concentration camps and dislocated from homes, fleeing advancing armies. Speculate how understanding this background might have contributed to his reluctance in accepting this identity.

Seamus Deane
(b. 1940)

A colonized people is without a specific history and even, as in Ireland and other cases, without a specific language.

Born in Derry, Northern Ireland, poet, novelist, and critic Seamus Deane was much affected by the Catholic nationalist movement. He received his education at Queens University in Belfast, his doctorate at Cambridge University, and taught literature at University College, Dublin. At the present time, he is Keough Professor of Irish Studies at the University of Notre Dame in Indiana. His novel, *Reading in the Dark* (1996), won The Irish Times International Fiction Prize and the Irish Literature Prize in 1997. He has written on Irish culture and literature, *Strange Country: Modernity and Nationhood in Irish Writing Since 1790* (Clarendon Lectures in English Literature, 1995), and contributed to a number of anthologies as author and co-editor, recently editing *Irish Times: Temporalities of Modernity*.

"Accident, June 1948" (1996)

Distrust of authority was the customary attitude among the oppressed Catholic majority of Northern Ireland in the 1940s. In this nonfiction account, a boy examines his unquestioning allegiance to this cultural attitude, despite the tragic event that had unfolded before his eyes.

One day I saw a boy from Blucher Street killed by a reversing lorry. He was standing at the rear wheel, ready to jump on the back when the lorry moved off. But the driver reversed suddenly, and the boy went under the wheel as the men at the street corner turned round and began shouting and running. It was too late. He lay there in the darkness under the truck, with his arm spread out and blood creeping out on all sides. The lorry driver collapsed, and the boy's mother appeared and looked and looked and then suddenly sat down as people came to stand in front of her and hide the awful sight.

I was standing on the parapet wall above Meenan's Park, only twenty yards away, and I could see the police car coming up the road from the barracks at the far end. Two policemen got out, and one of them bent down and looked under the lorry. He stood up and pushed his cap back on his head and rubbed his hands on his thighs. I think he felt sick. His distress reached me, airborne, like a smell; in a small vertigo, I sat down on the wall. The lorry seemed to lurch again. The second policeman had a notebook in his hand, and he went round to each of the men who had been standing at the corner when it happened. They all turned their backs on him. Then the ambulance came.

For months, I kept seeing the lorry reversing, and Rory Hannaway's arm going out as he was wound under. Somebody told me that one of the policemen had vomited on the other side of the lorry. I felt the vertigo again on hearing this and, with it, pity for the man. But this seemed wrong; everyone hated the police, told us to stay away from them, that they were a bad lot. So I said nothing, especially as I felt scarcely anything for Rory's mother or the lorry driver, both of whom I knew. No more than a year later, when we were hiding from police in a corn field after they had interrupted us chopping down a tree for the annual bonfire on the fifteenth of August, the Feast of the Assumption, Danny Green told me in detail how young Hannaway had been run over by a police car which had not even stopped. "Bastards," he said, shining the blade of his axe with wet grass. I tightened the hauling rope round my waist and said nothing; somehow this allayed the subtle sense of treachery I had felt from the start. As a result, I began to feel then a real sorrow for Rory's mother and for the driver who had never worked since. The yellow-green corn whistled as the police car slid past on the road below. It was dark before we brought the tree in, combing the back lanes clean with its nervous branches.

Questions and Ideas for Journaling and Discussion

1. Research briefly the political climate in Northern Ireland in the 1940s. Why did the boy speaker of the story keep the details of the accident a secret from the police?
2. What enlightenment did he reach by the end of this piece of creative nonfiction?
3. Images are words that are used to paint pictures in writing. What are some of the images that Deane employs, and what are their effects on readers?

Writing to Explore and Learn

1. Analyze the reasons for the boy's secret. Are there any instances that you can think of where oppressed groups do not cooperate with the police to their own detriment?

Willa Cather
(1873–1947)

Some memories are realities, and are better than anything that can ever happen to one again.

Willa Cather was born into a farming family in Virginia, but it is Red Cloud, Nebraska—a prairie town of pioneers, where her family moved when she was eight—that inspired her greatest novels. She began a career as educator and journalist after graduating from the University of Nebraska. A major writer of American fiction, she produced twelve novels, more than sixty short stories, and several volumes of critical essays. She is best known for her works about immigrants who sought to establish a life on the frontier, including *O Pioneers* (1913), *My Antonia* (1918), and the Pulitzer Prize–winning *One of Ours* (1922).

"Paul's Case" (1906)

This is a story about a working-class high school student who yearns to live the life of an upper-class boy. Paul's escapades and fantasies of escape serve as disguises for exploring how class, as it relates to gender and sexuality, shapes the lives of men in his home town of Pittsburgh, Pennsylvania.

It was paul's afternoon to appear before the faculty of the Pittsburgh High School to account for his various misdemeanours. He had been suspended a week ago, and his father had called the Principal's office and confessed his perplexity about his son. Paul entered the faculty room suave and smiling. His clothes were a trifle outgrown and the tan velvet on the collar of his open overcoat was frayed and worn; but for all that there was something of the dandy about him, and he wore an opal pin in his neatly knotted black four-in-hand, and a red carnation in his button-hole. This latter adornment the faculty somehow felt was not properly significant of the contrite spirit befitting a boy under the ban of suspension.

    Paul was tall for his age and very thin, with high, cramped shoulders and a narrow chest. His eyes were remarkable for a certain hysterical brilliancy and he continually used them in a conscious, theatrical sort of way, peculiarly offensive in a boy. The pupils were abnormally large, as though he were addicted to belladonna, but there was a glassy glitter about them which that drug does not produce.

When questioned by the Principal as to why he was there, Paul stated, politely enough, that he wanted to come back to school. This was a lie, but Paul was quite accustomed to lying; found it, indeed, indispensable for overcoming friction. His teachers were asked to state their respective charges against him, which they did with such a rancour and aggrievedness as evinced that this was not a usual case. Disorder and impertinence were among the offenses named, yet each of his instructors felt that it was scarcely possible to put into words the real cause of the trouble, which lay in a sort of hysterically defiant manner of the boy's; in the contempt which they all knew he felt for them, and which he seemingly made not the least effort to conceal. Once, when he had been making a synopsis of a paragraph at the blackboard, his English teacher had stepped to his side and attempted to guide his hand. Paul had started back with a shudder and thrust his hands violently behind him. The astonished woman could scarcely have been more hurt and embarrassed had he struck at her. The insult was so involuntary and definitely personal as to be unforgettable. In one way and another, he had made all his teachers, men and women alike, conscious of the same feeling of physical aversion. In one class he habitually sat with his hands shading his eyes; in another he always looked out of the window during the recitation; in another he made a running commentary on the lecture, with humorous intention.

His teachers felt this afternoon that his whole attitude was symbolized by his shrug and his flippantly red carnation flower, and they fell upon him without mercy, his English teacher leading the pack. He stood through it smiling, his pale lips parted over his white teeth. (His lips were continually twitching, and he had a habit of raising his eyebrows that was contemptuous and irritating to the last degree.) Older boys than Paul had broken down and shed tears under that baptism of fire, but his set smile did not once desert him, and his only sign of discomfort was the nervous trembling of the fingers that toyed with the buttons of his overcoat, and an occasional jerking of the other hand that held his hat. Paul was always smiling, always glancing about him, seeming to feel that people might be watching him and trying to detect something. This conscious expression, since it was as far as possible from boyish mirthfulness, was usually attributed to insolence or "smartness."

As the inquisition proceeded, one of his instructors repeated an impertinent remark of the boy's, and the Principal asked him whether he thought that a courteous speech to have made a woman. Paul shrugged his shoulders slightly and his eyebrows twitched.

"I don't know," he replied. "I didn't mean to be polite or impolite, either. I guess it's a sort of way I have of saying things regardless."

The Principal, who was a sympathetic man, asked him whether he didn't think that a way it would be well to get rid of. Paul grinned and said he guessed so. When he was told that he could go, he bowed gracefully and went out. His bow was but a repetition of the scandalous red carnation.

His teachers were in despair, and his drawing master voiced the feeling of them all when he declared there was something about the boy which none of them understood. He added: "I don't really believe that smile of his comes altogether from insolence; there's something sort of haunted about it. The boy is not strong, for one thing. I happen to know that he was born in Colorado, only a few months before his mother died out there of a long illness. There is something wrong about the fellow."

The drawing master had come to realize that, in looking at Paul, one saw only his white teeth and the forced animation of his eyes. One warm afternoon the boy had gone to sleep at his drawing-board, and his master had noted with amazement what a white, blue-veined face it was; drawn and wrinkled like an old man's about the eyes, the lips twitching even in his sleep, and stiff with a nervous tension that drew them back from his teeth.

His teachers left the building dissatisfied and unhappy; humiliated to have felt so vindictive toward a mere boy, to have uttered this feeling in cutting terms, and to have set each other on, as it were, in the grewsome game of intemperate reproach. Some of them remembered having seen a miserable street cat set at bay by a ring of tormentors.

As for Paul, he ran down the hill whistling the Soldiers' Chorus from *Faust* looking wildly behind him now and then to see whether some of his teachers were not there to writhe under his light-heartedness. As it was now late in the afternoon and Paul was on duty that evening as usher at Carnegie Hall, he decided that he would not go home to supper. When he reached the concert hall the doors were not yet open and, as it was chilly outside, he decided to go up into the picture gallery—always deserted at this hour—where there were some of Raffalli's gay studies of Paris streets and an airy blue Venetian scene or two that always exhilarated him. He was delighted to find no one in the gallery but the old guard, who sat in one corner, a newspaper on his knee, a black patch over one eye and the other closed. Paul possessed himself of the place and walked confidently up and down, whistling under his breath. After a while he sat down before a blue Rico and lost himself. When he bethought him to look at his watch, it was after seven o'clock, and he rose with a start and ran downstairs, making a face at Augustus, peering out from the cast-room, and an evil gesture at the Venus of Milo as he passed her on the stairway.

When Paul reached the ushers' dressing-room half-a-dozen boys were there already, and he began excitedly to tumble into his uniform. It was one of the few that at all approached fitting, and Paul thought it very becoming—though he knew that the tight, straight coat accentuated his narrow chest, about which he was exceedingly sensitive. He was always considerably excited while he dressed, twanging all over to the tuning of the strings and the preliminary flourishes of the horns in the music-room; but to-night he seemed quite beside himself, and he teased and plagued the boys until, telling him that he was crazy, they put him down on the floor and sat on him.

Somewhat calmed by his suppression, Paul dashed out to the front of the house to seat the early comers. He was a model usher; gracious and smiling he ran up and down the aisles; nothing was too much trouble for him; he carried messages and brought programmes as though it were his greatest pleasure in life, and all the people in his section thought him a charming boy, feeling that he remembered and admired them. As the house filled, he grew more and more vivacious and animated, and the colour came to his cheeks and lips. It was very much as though this were a great reception and Paul were the host. Just as the musicians came out to take their places, his English teacher arrived with checks for the seats which a prominent manufacturer had taken for the season. She betrayed some embarrassment when she handed Paul the tickets, and a *hauteur* which subsequently made her feel very foolish. Paul was startled for a moment, and had the feeling of wanting to put her out; what business had she here among all these fine people and gay colours? He looked her over and decided that she was not appropriately dressed and must be a fool to sit downstairs in such togs. The tickets had probably been sent her out of kindness, he reflected as he put down a seat for her, and she had about as much right to sit there as he had.

When the symphony began Paul sank into one of the rear seats with a long sigh of relief, and lost himself as he had done before the Rico. It was not that symphonies, as such, meant anything in particular to Paul, but the first sigh of the instruments seemed to free some hilarious and potent spirit within him; something that struggled there like the Genius in the bottle found by the Arab fisherman. He felt a sudden zest of life; the lights danced before his eyes and the concert hall blazed into unimaginable splendour. When the soprano soloist came on, Paul forgot even the nastiness of his teacher's being there and gave himself up to the peculiar stimulus such personages always had for him. The soloist chanced to be a German woman, by no means in her first youth, and the mother of many children; but she wore an elaborate gown and a tiara, and above all she had that indefinable air of achievement, the world-shine upon her, which, in Paul's eyes, made her a veritable queen of Romance.

After a concert was over Paul was always irritable and wretched until he got to sleep, and to-night he was even more than usually restless. He had the feeling of not being able to let down, of its being impossible to give up this delicious excitement which was the only thing that could be called living at all. During the last number he withdrew and, after hastily changing his clothes in the dressing-room, slipped out to the side door where the soprano's carriage stood. Here he began pacing rapidly up and down the walk, waiting to see her come out.

Over yonder the Schenley, in its vacant stretch, loomed big and square through the fine rain, the windows of its twelve stories glowing like those of a lighted cardboard house under a Christmas tree. All the actors and singers of the better class stayed there when they were in the city, and a number of the big manufacturers of the place lived there in the winter. Paul had often hung about the hotel, watching the people go in and out, longing to enter and leave schoolmasters and dull care behind him forever.

At last the singer came out, accompanied by the conductor, who helped her into her carriage and closed the door with a cordial *auf wiedersehen* which set Paul to wondering whether she were not an old sweetheart of his. Paul followed the carriage over to the hotel, walking so rapidly as not to be far

from the entrance when the singer alighted and disappeared behind the swinging glass doors that were opened by a negro in a tall hat and a long coat. In the
moment that the door was ajar, it seemed to Paul that he, too, entered. He
seemed to feel himself go after her up the steps, into the warm, lighted building, into an exotic, tropical world of shiny, glistening surfaces and basking ease.
He reflected upon the mysterious dishes that were brought into the dining-
room, the green bottles in buckets of ice, as he had seen them in the supper
party pictures of the *Sunday World* supplement. A quick gust of wind brought
the rain down with sudden vehemence, and Paul was startled to find that he
was still outside in the slush of the gravel driveway; that his boots were letting
in the water and his scanty overcoat was clinging wet about him; that the lights
in front of the concert hall were out, and that the rain was driving in sheets between him and the orange glow of the windows above him. There it was, what
he wanted—tangibly before him, like the fairy world of a Christmas pantomime,
but mocking spirits stood guard at the doors, and, as the rain beat in his face,
Paul wondered whether he were destined always to shiver in the black night
outside, looking up at it.

He turned and walked reluctantly toward the car tracks. The end had to
come sometime; his father in his night-clothes at the top of the stairs, explana-
tions that did not explain, hastily improvised fictions that were forever tripping
him up, his upstairs room and its horrible yellow wall-paper, the creaking bureau with the greasy plush collar-box; and over his painted wooden bed the
pictures of George Washington and John Calvin, and the framed motto, "Feed
my Lambs," which had been worked in red worsted by his mother.

Half an hour later, Paul alighted from his car and went slowly down one
of the side streets off the main thoroughfare. It was a highly respectable street,
where all the houses were exactly alike, and where business men of moderate
means begot and reared large families of children, all of whom went to
Sabbath-school and learned the shorter catechism, and were interested in arithmetic; all of whom were as exactly alike as their homes, and of a piece with the
monotony in which they lived. Paul never went up Cordelia Street without a
shudder of loathing. His home was next the house of the Cumberland minister.
He approached it to-night with the nerveless sense of defeat, the hopeless feeling of sinking back forever into ugliness and commonness that he had always
had when he came home. The moment he turned into Cordelia Street he felt
the waters close above his head. After each of these orgies of living, he experienced all the physical depression which follows a debauch; the loathing of respectable beds, of common food, of a house penetrated by kitchen odours; a
shuddering repulsion for the flavourless, colourless mass of every-day existence; a morbid desire for cool things and soft lights and fresh flowers.

The nearer he approached the house, the more absolutely unequal Paul
felt to the sight of it all; his ugly sleeping chamber; the cold bathroom with the
grimy zinc tub, the cracked mirror, the dripping spigots; his father, at the top of
the stairs, his hairy legs sticking out from his nightshirt, his feet thrust into carpet
slippers. He was so much later than usual that there would certainly be in-
quiries and reproaches. Paul stopped short before the door. He felt that he

could not be accosted by his father to-night; that he could not toss again on that miserable bed. He would not go in. He would tell his father that he had no car fare, and it was raining so hard he had gone home with one of the boys and stayed all night.

Meanwhile, he was wet and cold. He went around to the back of the house and tried one of the basement windows, found it open, raised it cautiously, and scrambled down the cellar wall to the floor. There he stood, holding his breath, terrified by the noise he had made, but the floor above him was silent, and there was no creak on the stairs. He found a soap-box, and carried it over to the soft ring of light that streamed from the furnace door, and sat down. He was horribly afraid of rats, so he did not try to sleep, but sat looking distrustfully at the dark, still terrified lest he might have awakened his father. In such reactions, after one of the experiences which made days and nights out of the dreary blanks of the calendar, when his senses were deadened, Paul's head was always singularly clear. Suppose his father had heard him getting in at the window and had come down and shot him for a burglar? Then, again, suppose his father had come down, pistol in hand, and he had cried out in time to save himself, and his father had been horrified to think how nearly he had killed him? Then, again, suppose a day should come when his father would remember that night, and wish there had been no warning cry to stay his hand? With this last supposition Paul entertained himself until daybreak.

The following Sunday was fine; the sodden November chill was broken by the last flash of autumnal summer. In the morning Paul had to go to church and Sabbath-school, as always. On seasonable Sunday afternoons the burghers of Cordelia Street always sat out on their front "stoops," and talked to their neighbours on the next stoop, or called to those across the street in neighbourly fashion. The men usually sat on gay cushions placed upon the steps that led down to the sidewalk, while the women, in their Sunday "waists," sat in rockers on the cramped porches, pretending to be greatly at their ease. The children played in the streets; there were so many of them that the place resembled the recreation grounds of a kindergarten. The men on the steps—all in their shirt sleeves, their vests unbuttoned—sat with their legs well apart, their stomachs comfortably protruding, and talked of the prices of things, or told anecdotes of the sagacity of their various chiefs and overlords. They occasionally looked over the multitude of squabbling children, listening affectionately to their high-pitched, nasal voices, smiling to see their own proclivities reproduced in their offspring, and interspersed their legends of the iron kings with remarks about their sons' progress at school, their grades in arithmetic, and the amounts they had saved in their toy banks.

On this last Sunday of November, Paul sat all the afternoon on the lowest step of his "stoop," staring into the street, while his sisters, in their rockers, were talking to the minister's daughters next door about how many shirt-waists they had made in the last week, and how many waffles some one had eaten at the last church supper. When the weather was warm, and his father was in a particularly jovial frame of mind, the girls made lemonade, which was always brought out in a red-glass pitcher, ornamented with forget-me-nots in blue enamel. This the girls thought very fine, and the neighbours always joked about the suspicious colour of the pitcher.

To-day Paul's father sat on the top step, talking to a young man who shifted a restless baby from knee to knee. He happened to be the young man who was daily held up to Paul as a model, and after whom it was his father's dearest hope that he would pattern. This young man was of a ruddy complexion, with a compressed, red mouth, and faded, near-sighted eyes, over which he wore thick spectacles, with gold bows that curved about his ears. He was clerk to one of the magnates of a great steel corporation, and was looked upon in Cordelia Street as a young man with a future. There was a story that, some five years ago—he was now barely twenty-six—he had been a trifle dissipated but in order to curb his appetites and save the loss of time and strength that a sowing of wild oats might have entailed, he had taken his chief's advice, oft re-iterated to his employees, and at twenty-one had married the first woman whom he could persuade to share his fortunes. She happened to be an angular school-mistress, much older than he, who also wore thick glasses, and who had now borne him four children, all near-sighted, like herself.

The young man was relating how his chief, now cruising the Mediterranean, kept in touch with all the details of the business, arranging his office hours on his yacht just as though he were at home, and "knocking off work enough to keep two stenographers busy." His father told, in turn, the plan his corporation was considering, of putting in an electric railway plant at Cairo. Paul snapped his teeth; he had an awful apprehension that they might spoil it all before he got there. Yet he rather liked to hear these legends of the iron kings, that were told and retold on Sundays and holidays; these stories of palaces in Venice, yachts on the Mediterranean, and high play at Monte Carlo appealed to his fancy, and he was interested in the triumphs of these cash boys who had become famous, though he had no mind for the cash-boy stage.

After supper was over, and he had helped to dry the dishes, Paul nervously asked his father whether he could go to George's to get some help in his geometry, and still more nervously asked for car fare. This latter request he had to repeat, as his father, on principle, did not like to hear requests for money, whether much or little. He asked Paul whether he could not go to some boy who lived nearer, and told him that he ought not to leave his school work until Sunday; but he gave him the dime. He was not a poor man, but he had a worthy ambition to come up in the world. His only reason for allowing Paul to usher was, that he thought a boy ought to be earning a little.

Paul bounded upstairs, scrubbed the greasy odour of the dish-water from his hands with the ill-smelling soap he hated, and then shook over his fingers a few drops of violet water from the bottle he kept hidden in his drawer. He left the house with his geometry conspicuously under his arm, and the moment he got out of Cordelia Street and boarded a downtown car, he shook off the lethargy of two deadening days, and began to live again.

The leading juvenile of the permanent stock company which played at one of the downtown theatres was an acquaintance of Paul's, and the boy had been invited to drop in at the Sunday-night rehearsals whenever he could. For more than a year Paul had spent every available moment loitering about Charley Edwards's dressing-room. He had won a place among Edwards's following not only because the young actor, who could not afford to employ a dresser, often found him useful, but because he recognized in Paul something akin to what churchmen term "vocation."

It was at the theatre and at Carnegie Hall that Paul really lived; the rest was but a sleep and a forgetting. This was Paul's fairy tale, and it had for him all the allurement of a secret love. The moment he inhaled the gassy, painty, dusty odour behind the scenes, he breathed like a prisoner set free, and felt within him the possibility of doing or saying splendid, brilliant, poetic things. The moment the cracked orchestra beat out the overture from *Martha* or jerked at the serenade from *Rigoletto*, all stupid and ugly things slid from him, and his senses were deliciously, yet delicately fired.

Perhaps it was because, in Paul's world, the natural nearly always wore the guise of ugliness, that a certain element of artificiality seemed to him necessary in beauty. Perhaps it was because his experience of life elsewhere was so full of Sabbath-school picnics, petty economics, wholesome advice as to how to succeed in life, and the unescapable odours of cooking, that he found this existence so alluring, these smartly-clad men and women so attractive, that he was so moved by these starry apple orchards that bloomed perennially under the lime-light.

It would be difficult to put it strongly enough how convincingly the stage entrance of that theatre was for Paul the actual portal of Romance. Certainly none of the company ever suspected it, least of all Charley Edwards. It was very like the old stories that used to float about London of fabulously rich Jews, who had subterranean halls there, with palms, and fountains, and soft lamps and richly apparelled women who never saw the disenchanting light of London day. So, in the midst of that smoke-palled city, enamoured of figures and grimy toil, Paul had his secret temple, his wishing carpet, his bit of blue-and-white Mediterranean shore bathed in perpetual sunshine.

Several of Paul's teachers had a theory that his imagination had been perverted by garish fiction, but the truth was that he scarcely ever read at all. The books at home were not such as would either tempt or corrupt a youthful mind, and as for reading the novels that some of his friends urged upon him—well, he got what he wanted much more quickly from music; any sort of music, from an orchestra to a barrel organ. He needed only the spark, the indescribable thrill that made his imagination master of his senses, and he could make plots and pictures enough of his own. It was equally true that he was not stage struck— not, at any rate, in the usual acceptation of that expression. He had no desire to become an actor, any more than he had to become a musician. He felt no necessity to do any of these things; what he wanted was to see, to be in the atmosphere, float on the wave of it, to be carried out, blue league after blue league, away from everything.

After a night behind the scenes, Paul found the school-room more than ever repulsive; the bare floors and naked walls; the prosy men who never wore frock coats, or violets in their buttonholes; the women with their dull gowns, shrill voices, and pitiful seriousness about prepositions that govern the dative. He could not bear to have the other pupils think, for a moment, that he took these people seriously; he must convey to them that he considered it all trivial, and was there only by way of a jest, anyway. He had autograph pictures of all the members of the stock company which he showed his classmates, telling them the most incredible stories of his familiarity with these people, of his acquaintance with the soloists who came to Carnegie Hall, his suppers with them and the flowers he sent them. When these stories lost their effect, and his audience grew listless, he became desperate and would bid all the boys good-bye, announcing that he was going to travel for awhile; going to Naples, to Venice, to Egypt. Then, next Monday, he would slip back, conscious and nervously smiling; his sister was ill, and he should have to defer his voyage until spring.

Matters went steadily worse with Paul at school. In the itch to let his instructors know how heartily he despised them and their homilies, and how thoroughly he was appreciated elsewhere, he mentioned once or twice that he had no time to fool with theorems; adding—with a twitch of the eyebrows and a touch of that nervous bravado which so perplexed them—that he was helping the people down at the stock company; they were old friends of his.

The upshot of the matter was that the Principal went to Paul's father, and Paul was taken out of school and put to work. The manager at Carnegie Hall was told to get another usher in his stead; the doorkeeper at the theatre was warned not to admit him to the house; and Charley Edwards remorsefully promised the boy's father not to see him again.

The members of the stock company were vastly amused when some of Paul's stories reached them—especially the women. They were hardworking women, most of them supporting indigent husbands or brothers, and they laughed rather bitterly at having stirred the boy to such fervid and florid inventions. They agreed with the faculty and with his father that Paul's was a bad case.

The east-bound train was ploughing through a January snow-storm; the dull dawn was beginning to show grey when the engine whistled a mile out of Newark. Paul started up from the seat where he had lain curled in uneasy slumber, rubbed the breath-misted window glass with his hand, and peered out. The snow was whirling in curling eddies above the white bottom lands, and the drifts lay already deep in the fields and along the fences, while here and there the long dead grass and dried weed stalks protruded black above it. Lights shown from the scattered houses, and a gang of labourers who stood beside the track waved their lanterns.

Paul had slept very little, and he felt grimy and uncomfortable. He had made the all-night journey in a day coach, partly because he was ashamed, dressed as he was, to go into a Pullman, and partly because he was afraid of being seen there by some Pittsburgh business man, who might have noticed him in Denny & Carson's office. When the whistle awoke him, he clutched quickly at his breast pocket, glancing about him with an uncertain smile. But the little, clay-bespattered Italians were still sleeping, the slatternly women across the aisle were in open-mouthed oblivion, and even the crumby, crying babies were for the nonce stilled. Paul settled back to struggle with his impatience as best he could.

When he arrived at the Jersey City station, he hurried through his breakfast, manifestly ill at ease and keeping a sharp eye about him. After he reached the Twenty-third Street station, he consulted a cabman, and had himself driven to a men's furnishing establishment that was just opening for the day. He spent upward of two hours there, buying with endless reconsidering and great care. His new street suit he put on in the fitting-room; the frock coat and dress clothes he had bundled into the cab with his linen. Then he drove to a hatter's and a shoe house. His next errand was at Tiffany's, where he selected his silver and a new scarf-pin. He would not wait to have his silver marked, he said. Lastly, he stopped at a trunk shop on Broadway, and had his purchases packed into various travelling bags.

It was a little after one o'clock when he drove up to the Waldorf, and after settling with the cabman, went into the office. He registered from Washington; said his mother and father had been abroad, and that he had come down to await the arrival of their steamer. He told his story plausibly and had no trouble, since he volunteered to pay for them in advance, in engaging his rooms; a sleeping-room, sitting-room and bath.

Not once, but a hundred times Paul had planned this entry into New York. He had gone over every detail of it with Charley Edwards, and in his scrap book at home there were pages of descriptions about New York hotels, cut from the Sunday papers. When he was shown to his sitting-room on the eighth floor, he saw at a glance that everything was as it should be; there was but one detail in his mental picture that the place did not realize, so he rang for the bell boy and sent him down for flowers. He moved about nervously until the boy returned, putting away his new linen and fingering it delightedly as he did so. When the flowers came, he put them hastily into water, and then tumbled into a hot bath. Presently he came out of his white bath-room, resplendent in his new silk underwear, and playing with the tassels of his red robe. The snow was whirling so fiercely outside his windows that he could scarcely see across the street, but within the air was deliciously soft and fragrant. He put the violets and jonquils on the taboret beside the couch, and threw himself down, with a long sigh, covering himself with a Roman blanket. He was thoroughly tired; he had been in such haste, he had stood up to such a strain, covered so much ground in the last twenty-four hours, that he wanted to think how it had all come about. Lulled by the sound of the wind, the warm air, and the cool fragrance of the flowers, he sank into deep, drowsy retrospection.

It had been wonderfully simple; when they had shut him out of the theatre and concert hall, when they had taken away his bone, the whole thing was virtually determined. The rest was a mere matter of opportunity. The only thing that at all surprised him was his own courage—for he realized well enough that he had always been tormented by fear, a sort of apprehensive dread that, of late years, as the meshes of the lies he had told closed about him, had been pulling the muscles of his body tighter and tighter. Until now, he could not remember the time when he had not been dreading something. Even when he was a little boy, it was always there—behind him, or before, or on either side. There had always been the shadowed corner, the dark place into which he dared not look, but from which something seemed always to be watching him—and Paul had done things that were not pretty to watch, he knew.

But now he had a curious sense of relief, as though he had at last thrown down the gauntlet to the thing in the corner.

Yet it was but a day since he had been sulking in the traces; but yesterday afternoon that he had been sent to the bank with Denny & Carson's deposit, as usual—but this time he was instructed to leave the book to be balanced. There was above two thousand dollars in checks, and nearly a thousand in the bank notes which he had taken from the book and quietly transferred to his pocket. At the bank he had made out a new deposit slip. His nerves had been steady enough to permit of his returning to the office, where he had finished his work and asked for a full day's holiday to-morrow, Saturday, giving a perfectly reasonable pretext. The bank book, he knew, would not be returned before Monday or Tuesday, and his father would be out of town for the next week. From the time he slipped the bank notes into his pocket until he boarded the night train for New York, he had not known a moment's hesitation. It was not the first time Paul had steered through treacherous waters.

How astonishingly easy it had all been; here he was, the thing done; and this time there would be no awakening, no figure at the top of the stairs. He watched the snow flakes whirling by his window until he fell asleep.

When he awoke, it was three o'clock in the afternoon. He bounded up with a start; half of one of his precious days gone already! He spent more than an hour in dressing, watching every stage of his toilet carefully in the mirror. Everything was quite perfect; he was exactly the kind of boy he had always wanted to be.

When he went downstairs, Paul took a carriage and drove up Fifth Avenue toward the Park. The snow had somewhat abated; carriages and tradesmen's wagons were hurrying soundlessly to and fro in the winter twilight; boys in woollen mufflers were shovelling off the doorsteps; the avenue stages made fine spots of colour against the white street. Here and there on the corners were stands, with whole flower gardens blooming under glass cases, against the sides of which the snow flakes stuck and melted; violets, roses, carnations, lilies of the valley—somehow vastly more lovely and alluring that they blossomed thus unnaturally in the snow. The Park itself was a wonderful stage winter-piece.

When he returned, the pause of the twilight had ceased, and the tune of the streets had changed. The snow was falling faster, lights streamed from the hotels that reared their dozen stories fearlessly up into the storm, defying the raging Atlantic winds. A long, black stream of carriages poured down the avenue, intersected here and there by other streams, tending horizontally. There were a score of cabs about the entrance of his hotel, and his driver had to wait. Boys in livery were running in and out of the awning stretched across the sidewalk, up and down the red velvet carpet laid from the door to the street.

Above, about, within it all was the rumble and roar, and hurry and toss of thousands of human beings as hot for pleasure as himself, and on every side of him towered the glaring affirmation of the omnipotence of wealth.

The boy set his teeth and drew his shoulders together in a spasm of realization; the plot of all dramas, the text of all romances, the nerve-stuff of all sensations was whirling about him like the snow flakes. He burnt like a faggot in a tempest.

When Paul went down to dinner, the music of the orchestra came floating up the elevator shaft to greet him. His head whirled as he stepped into the thronged corridor, and he sank back into one of the chairs against the wall to get his breath. The lights, the chatter, the perfumes, the bewildering medley of colour—he had, for a moment, the feeling of not being able to stand it. But only for a moment; these were his own people, he told himself. He went slowly about the corridors, through the writing-rooms, smoking-rooms, reception-rooms, as though he were exploring the chambers of an enchanted palace, built and peopled for him alone.

When he reached the dining-room he sat down at a table near a window. The flowers, the white linen, the many-coloured wine glasses, the gay toilettes of the women, the low popping of corks, the undulating repetitions of the *Blue Danube* from the orchestra, all flooded Paul's dream with bewildering radiance. When the roseate tinge of his champagne was added—that cold, precious, bubbling stuff that creamed and foamed in his glass—Paul wondered that there were honest men in the world at all. This was what all the world was fighting for, he reflected; this was what all the struggle was about. He doubted the reality of his past. Had he ever known a place called Cordelia Street, a place where fagged-looking business men got on the early car; mere rivets in a machine they seemed to Paul,—sickening men with combings of children's hair always hanging to their coats, and the smell of cooking in their clothes. Cordelia Street—Ah! that belonged to another time and country; had he not always been thus, had he not sat here night after night, from as far back as he could remember, looking pensively over just such shimmering textures, and slowly twirling the stem of a glass like this one between his thumb and middle finger? He rather thought he had.

He was not in the least abashed or lonely. He had no especial desire to meet or to know any of these people; all he demanded was the right to look on and conjecture, to watch the pageant. The mere stage properties were all he contended for. Nor was he lonely later in the evening, in his loge at the Metropolitan. He was now entirely rid of his nervous misgivings, of his forced aggressiveness, of the imperative desire to show himself different from his surroundings. He felt now that his surroundings explained him. Nobody questioned the purple; he had only to wear it passively. He had only to glance down at his attire to reassure himself that here it would be impossible for any one to humiliate him.

He found it hard to leave his beautiful sitting-room to go to bed that night, and sat long watching the raging storm from his turret window. When he went to sleep it was with the lights turned on in his bedroom; partly because of his old timidity, and partly so that, if he should wake in the night, there would be no wretched moment of doubt, no horrible suspicion of yellow wall-paper, or of Washington and Calvin above his bed.

Sunday morning the city was practically snowbound. Paul breakfasted late, and in the afternoon he fell in with a wild San Francisco boy, a freshman at Yale, who said he had run down for a "little flyer" over Sunday. The young man offered to show Paul the night side of the town, and the two boys went out together after dinner, not returning to the hotel until seven o'clock the next morning. They had started out in the confiding warmth of a champagne friendship, but their parting in the elevator was singularly cool. The freshman pulled himself together to make his train, and Paul went to bed. He awoke at two o'clock in the afternoon, very thirsty and dizzy, and rang for ice-water, coffee, and the Pittsburgh papers.

On the part of the hotel management, Paul excited no suspicion. There was this to be said for him, that he wore his spoils with dignity and in no way made himself conspicuous. Even under the glow of his wine he was never boisterous, though he found the stuff like a magician's wand for wonder-building. His chief greediness lay in his ears and eyes, and his excesses were not offensive ones. His dearest pleasures were the grey winter twilights in his sitting room; his quiet enjoyment of his flowers, his clothes, his wide divan, his cigarette and his sense of power. He could not remember a time when he had felt so at peace with himself. The mere release from the necessity of petty lying, lying every day and every way, restored his self-respect. He had never lied for pleasure, even at school; but to be noticed and admired, to assert his difference from other Cordelia Street boys; and he felt a good deal more manly, more honest, even now that he had no need for boastful pretensions, now that he could, as his actor friends used to say, "dress the part." It was characteristic that remorse did not occur to him. His golden days went by without a shadow, and he made each as perfect as he could.

On the eighth day after his arrival in New York, he found the whole affair exploited in the Pittsburgh papers, exploited with a wealth of detail which indicated that local news of a sensational nature was at a low ebb. The firm of Denny & Carson announced that the boy's father had refunded the full amount of the theft, and that they had no intention of prosecuting. The Cumberland minister had been interviewed, and expressed his hope of yet reclaiming the motherless lad, and his Sabbath-school teacher declared that she would spare no effort to that end. The rumour had reached Pittsburgh that the boy had been seen in a New York hotel, and his father had gone East to find him and bring him home.

Paul had just come in to dress for dinner; he sank into a chair, weak to the knees, and clasped his head in his hands. It was to be worse than jail, even; the tepid waters of Cordelia Street were to close over him finally and forever. The grey monotony stretched before him in hopeless, unrelieved years; Sabbath-school, Young People's Meeting, the yellow-papered room, the damp dish-towels; it all rushed back upon him with a sickening vividness. He had the old feeling that the orchestra had suddenly stopped, the sinking sensation that the play was over. The sweat broke out on his face, and he sprang to his feet, looked about him with his white, conscious smile, and winked at himself in the mirror. With something of the old childish belief in miracles with which he had so often gone to class, all his lessons unlearned, Paul dressed and dashed whistling down the corridor to the elevator.

He had no sooner entered the dining-room and caught the measure of the music than his remembrance was lightened by his old elastic power of claiming the moment, mounting with it, and finding it all sufficient. The glare and glitter about him, the mere scenic accessories had again, and for the last time, their old potency. He would show himself that he was game, he would finish the thing splendidly. He doubted, more than ever, the existence of Cordelia Street, and for the first time he drank his wine recklessly. Was he not, after all, one of those fortunate beings born to the purple, was he not still himself and in his own place? He drummed a nervous accompaniment to the *Pagliacci* music and looked about him, telling himself over and over that it had paid.

He reflected drowsily, to the swell of the music and the chill sweetness of his wine, that he might have done it more wisely. He might have caught an outbound steamer and been well out of their clutches before now. But the other side of the world had seemed too far away and too uncertain then; he could not have waited for it; his need had been too sharp. If he had to choose over again, he would do the same thing to-morrow. He looked affectionately about the dining-room, now gilded with a soft mist. Ah, it had paid indeed!

Paul was awakened next morning by a painful throbbing in his head and feet. He had thrown himself across the bed without undressing, and had slept with his shoes on. His limbs and hands were lead heavy, and his tongue and throat were parched and burnt. There came upon him one of those fateful attacks of clear-headedness that never occurred except when he was physically exhausted and his nerves hung loose. He lay still and closed his eyes and let the tide of things wash over him.

His father was in New York; "stopping at some joint or other," he told himself. The memory of successive summers on the front stoop fell upon him like a weight of black water. He had not a hundred dollars left; and he knew now, more than ever, that money was everything, the wall that stood between all he loathed and all he wanted. The thing was winding itself up; he had thought of that on his first glorious day in New York, and had even provided a way to snap the thread. It lay on his dressing-table now; he had got it out last night when he came blindly up from dinner, but the shiny metal hurt his eyes, and he disliked the looks of it.

He rose and moved about with a painful effort, succumbing now and again to attacks of nausea. It was the old depression exaggerated; all the world had become Cordelia Street. Yet somehow he was not afraid of anything, was absolutely calm; perhaps because he had looked into the dark corner at last and knew. It was bad enough, what he saw there, but somehow not so bad as his long fear of it had been. He saw everything clearly now. He had a feeling that he had made the best of it, that he had lived the sort of life he was meant to live, and for half an hour he sat staring at the revolver. But he told himself that was not the way, so he went downstairs and took a cab to the ferry.

When Paul arrived at Newark, he got off the train and took another cab, directing the driver to follow the Pennsylvania tracks out of the town. The snow lay heavy on the roadways and had drifted deep in the open fields. Only here and there the dead grass or dried weed stalks projected, singularly black, above it. Once well into the country, Paul dismissed the carriage and walked, floundering along the tracks, his mind a medley of irrelevant things. He seemed to hold in his brain an actual picture of everything he had seen that morning. He remembered every feature of both his drivers, of the toothless old woman from whom he had bought the red flowers in his coat, the agent from whom he had got his ticket, and all of his fellow-passengers on the ferry. His mind, unable to cope with vital matters near at hand, worked feverishly and deftly at sorting and grouping these images. They made for him a part of the ugliness of the world, of the ache in his head, and the bitter burning on his tongue. He stooped and put a handful of snow into his mouth as he walked, but that, too, seemed hot. When he reached a little hillside, where the tracks ran through a cut some twenty feet below him, he stopped and sat down.

The carnations in his coat were drooping with the cold, he noticed; their red glory all over. It occurred to him that all the flowers he had seen in the glass cases that first night must have gone the same way, long before this. It was only one splendid breath they had, in spite of their brave mockery at the winter outside the glass; and it was a losing game in the end, it seemed, this revolt against the homilies by which the world is run. Paul took one of the blossoms carefully from his coat and scooped a little hole in the snow, where he covered it up. Then he dozed a while, from his weak condition, seemingly insensible to the cold.

The sound of an approaching train awoke him, and he started to his feet, remembering only his resolution, and afraid lest he should be too late. He stood watching the approaching locomotive, his teeth chattering, his lips drawn away from them in a frightened smile; once or twice he glanced nervously sidewise, as though he were being watched. When the right moment came, he jumped. As he fell, the folly of his haste occurred to him with merciless clearness, the vastness of what he had left undone. There flashed through his brain, clearer than ever before, the blue of Adriatic water, the yellow of Algerian sands.

He felt something strike his chest, and that his body was being thrown swiftly through the air, on and on, immeasurably far and fast, while his limbs were gently relaxed. Then, because the picture making mechanism was crushed, the disturbing visions flashed into black, and Paul dropped back into the immense design of things.

Questions and Ideas for Journaling and Discussion

1. Compare and contrast Paul's home life with his fantasy life.
2. Describe Paul's attitude toward his family and teachers.
3. What is Paul's predicament toward the end of the story? Do you think that suicide was his only way out?

4. Authors of short stories use the technique of foreshadowing, or presenting hints throughout the story that prepare readers for the ending. What are the clues throughout the story that may indicate the final outcome?

Writing to Explore and Learn

1. Discuss Paul's character in terms of constructions of masculinity and/or gay identity.

Chapter 8

Male Identities

T he phenomenon of challenging established hierarchies of gender has given rise to viewing masculinity, as well as femininity, not as an essential part of an individual, but as a consequence of institutions and social practices. The following texts treat the theme of identity formation in men's lives as identities that are connected to race, class, and ethnicity.

Dexter Jeffries
(b. 1953)

Create yourself.

Dexter Jeffries grew up in New York City and currently resides in Clinton
Hill, Brooklyn. He is proud of his public education, which includes a BA
from Queens College, an MA from City College, and a PhD from the City
University of New York Graduate Center; however, he claims that his ten
years as a New York City cab driver mark his true education in the life of the
city and its people. In between driving a taxi and college, Jeffries served
three years in the United States Army. The time that he spent overseas with
a combat engineer battalion in West Germany instilled in him a "revelatory
perspective on America." Since 1980, he has taught English at various colleges in the City University of New York and the Pratt Institute. In 1996, he
produced and directed a documentary film, *What's Jazz?* Irish bars, graffiti
on the subway, and taking care of an elderly parent are some of the topics
that he has examined in his writing. In 2004, Kensington Press (Dafina
Books) published his autobiographical memoir, *Triple Exposure: Black,
Jewish and Red in the 1950s.* He is currently at work on a second book.

"Source of Comfort" from *Triple Exposure: Black, Jewish and Red in the 1950s* (2004)

As its title implies, the memoir Triple Exposure *treats Jeffries' search for
identity in a world where, he feels, people are not content to let him be himself. He remembers his father, who had served in the Second World War,
"an intelligent black man, Negro, a proud Negro . . . reduced to fodder and
folly," who had, by his life's end, despised his own identity. "Source of
Comfort" points out the difficulty of constructing one's self as masculine in
a complicated milieu made more complex by race, religion, and politics.*

If I had only known that people did not want me to be black or
white, my life would have been a lot simpler. Or, the converse, if I
had known that people wanted me to be black or white, still, my life
would have been a lot simpler. That's what it came down to. And

what they were asking me to do really wasn't so outrageous. I used to brood and cry about the demands put upon me and think they were extraordinarily unfair because the world would not let me be me. Does it ever let anyone be who they are? The only difference in my case is that there were racial connotations intertwined with their demands.

Later in life, after being tortured and self-tortured, I did realize something that was unfair. When you are something that someone does not desire, all you are doing is making them uncomfortable, nothing more, nothing less. But I've come to realize that the word *uncomfortable* possesses a great deal of import. "I really don't feel *comfortable* with that." Yes, that means that you are not going to participate in that person's reality. You are going to avoid, deny, and reject it. Now you're making someone else really feel *uncomfortable*. Do you have a right to do that?

Professor, we've been trying to figure out something all semester.

Professor, we were wondering about something.

Professor, we have a bet about something.

Professor, we had a big discussion about you.

Professor, could you tell us one thing?

Professor, I've been meaning to ask you this since the first day.

Professor, you have to tell us something about yourself.

Professor, we're going crazy trying to figure out something about you.

Yes, most college professors are prepared and enthusiastic about a class that would put so much energy into a series of questions. To see that sort of eagerness in a college classroom is a teacher's dream come true. And I can always tell, now, that it's not going to be a question about literature, James Joyce's life in Dublin, what's the connection between James Baldwin and Richard Wright, or why didn't the Anglo Saxons learn a little Latin during the Roman occupation.

Professor, you see, Doreen and I were wondering if you're Spanish.

That's the question you've been waving your hand about?

Professor Jeffries, aren't you mixed?

A difficult question; I would rather have you ask me about the rhyme scheme of Shakespeare's sonnets than that.

We're positive that you're black but very light.

How can Achilles be a hero if he's down in his tent, crying over losing his girlfriend to Agamemnon; that's a better and more reasonable question.

You're Greek and Puerto Rican, aren't you?

McMurphy, if he's racist, how can he still be the hero of the novel? No problem, I can explain contradictions like that. That's my job.

Professor, it's your hair. That's what threw us off. If it were a little kinkier, we would have positively known that you were . . .

Those are my questions, the ones I can't answer. For the first half of my teaching career or maybe more, I always worried about those questions.

Students, always wondering and thinking about me and not my lectures and investing time and energy. Here I am teaching one of the best Hemingway classes that you'll ever get, and all you can think of is whether I am black, white, Puerto Rican, Greek, Dominican, or *mixed* (I hated that word since it sounded like some sort of breed of dog). I am standing in front of you, presenting you with detailed information about a writer's style and tone, and the only thought occupying your mind is whether I am Russian, Iranian, or from Brazil. And what I didn't realize at the time and only recently have come across this very privileged revelation was that, you're not really asking me about my national origin or race. You're asking me whether I will make you feel *comfortable* by informing you that I am like you. You wanted me to be like you and I was there foolishly trying to look for so many other answers, exploring and sweating as I went through so many different places and all you wanted to hear was that I was like you.

LETTERS

September 1, 1977

Dear Pop,

I just found out that you're dead. Kind of tough to hear it the way I did, a few thousand miles away from home. But I think you could imagine the backdrop because you served during World War II in the Pacific, and you would have no problem envisioning this scene. We were up on the Czechoslovakian border, putting in mine fields. They're all over the place between West Germany, East Germany, and Czechoslovakia. It was a cold morning. Sergeant Walters had told me that Lieutenant Collins wanted to see me.

You know those tents, for the C.O.? We got the same ones you had thirty years ago, shaped like a pentagon with dome for a stovepipe to come out of the top. You open the flap and the light always assaults your eyes. You're blind if you're entering because it's pretty dark, and you're blind if you're leaving because of the light. Funny, you also know *how you're always a little dirty because of the soot that comes out of the space heater? It's just a common condition that exists when you're in an infantry or engineer unit: dirty, unshaven, always a little unkempt.*

LT. COLLINS:	*Jeffries, you better sit down.*
ME:	*Yes sir.*
LT. COLLINS:	*I've got some bad news for you.*
ME:	*Oh, am I in trouble about something?*
LT. COLLINS:	*No, nothing like that. I just got a telegram from the Red Cross. It took a little time to come up here; your father died.*
ME:	*Oh.*
LT. COLLINS:	*I'm sorry. It's a hell of a thing to be way out here in the woods like this . . .*
ME:	*Yeah . . .*
LT. COLLINS:	*Was he ill?*
ME:	*Yeah, he was kinda sick for the last few years; heart.*
LT. COLLINS:	*Oh, I guess it was related to that.*
ME:	*Yeah, he was sick; that's for sure.*
LT. COLLINS:	*According to regulations, you're eligible for an emergency leave. We can put you in a jeep, send you right over to Frankfurt and you'll be back in the world pretty quick.*
ME:	*Nah, that's OK.*
LT. COLLINS:	*Jeffries, wait a second. Take it easy. Maybe you want to think about this.*
ME:	*No, look Lieutenant, I know what I'm doing. I'll stay right here.*

I know that's difficult to hear from your favorite son, but that was what happened. Just like that. I was in the hazy place of being happy that the suffering was over and terribly sad that you wouldn't live to see how things turned out with me. That's what gets to you. I knew you were ill and being handicapped wasn't for you, no, not the rational man who wanted to figure out everything. But for the black side of you, I was happy that the other type of suffering was ended. You would never have to think, feel or dream about it, the thing that made you mad, the thing that tore your soul to shreds. The "color thing" was over. No more battles, past or present. No more thinking, wondering, second-guessing, undermining yourself because you were an intelligent black man, Negro, a proud Negro, who had been reduced to fodder and folly.

You had fought that fight and lost. Not completely. But you lost because you ended up despising Negroes yourself. That was the ultimate proof of that absurd world's power and control over you. You hated them, and I don't know when it started, 1931 or 1946. I suppose it's arbitrary. Maybe "hate" is just not the best way of putting it. White people can't understand. Even I can't understand and I've thought about it long and hard.

Sorry for rambling. Back to the main point. You're dead. That's what I have to deal with. There are some guys in the platoon trying to convince me to go home. I just walked away from the little group sitting on the forest floor in Germany. I've got a lot to think about.

So, my father passed away when I was stationed overseas. He was pretty important to me. Even when he died, he wasn't dead. Not really. I was in for a terrible shock, or reincarnation, or a raising or the dead. About two weeks after my father died, I got the first letter. I thought it was a bad joke played by someone in the U.S. Army Postal Service. But it wasn't. My father was a decent letter writer, and unknowingly he had written me right up until he died. Therefore, I was slated by fate or whatever you might call it, to receive letters from the dead.

You hold a dead man's letter in a far different way from that of the living. It is indeed special. You feel the electricity. It's as though some miracle has been performed on your behalf and as undeserving as you may be, and I was certainly in that category, a waiver has been signed, and the dead are now the living. That first letter was in my hand, and I walked around in a daze.

Because I was so far away, I had to conduct my own funeral oration or memorial service. I didn't cry about specific memories. If anything, I smiled over and over again. AH the things that this Negro, black man, had done. He was a graduate of Brooklyn Technical High School in 1931, with a specialty in drafting. A few years later, in the midst of the Depression, he was an active member of the Communist Party, participating in many rallies, demonstrations, organizing the fledgling labor movement in New York City. When he is stationed overseas during World War II, and is on the island of Tinian, the same little Pacific island that the *Enola Gay* carrying the first atomic bomb took off from, he publishes his own newspaper, *This Small World*. Responsible for the writing, editing, copying, and distribution, the paper, his own version of *Stars and Stripes* with very subtle nuances of left-wing counterpoint. Post-World War II America finds him on the inside cover of *Jet* magazine. He's touted as an up-and-coming Negro businessman with his own automotive dealership and service, catering to a most exclusive clientele because he only accommodates people who own Cords, a fine car built by the Auburn Company. The final segment of my oration was an acknowledgment of his years as a true craftsman, a lithographer whose proudest moment was creating the color plates for the 1960 edition of the *Encyclopedia Britannica*. He was beaming that night when he came home from the lithography plant in lower Manhattan, down near Canal Street, and showed me his copy of Thomas Gainsborough's "Blue Boy." That made me cry. "The Blue Boy" with that tender face, and my old man holding that poster-size print, before my mom put dinner on the table. That got to me.

Other things got to me also. One time I was riding on the C train to Brooklyn, the last local train from Manhattan. I heard someone on the train ranting a bit and shut him out. Then as I listened closer, I noticed that he was mad but there was a pattern to his rambling and put the *Times* down for a second and shut my eyes:

> Ha, ha, ha . . . young black man, yes, you. Stop killing each other. You must stop. You want to fight someone? Fight someone your size. Put on the boxing gloves, man. Yes, you go in right with one who is your weight. You don't fight someone who is not your weight. Ha, ha, ha. . . . you are mad at the white people. Good. But would you kill the black people? Why do you kill black people? I am not sayin' to kill the white people. Oh no. I am a Christian and we are all white when we are in heaven and we are all black when we go to heaven. Yes, ha, ha, ha . . . I have some of you fooled. You thought I was talking about white and black race. No, no, no, ha, ha, ha . . . no, man, I was talking about your spirit. Young black man, stop killing each other. If the man steps on your sneaker, say OK when he says he's sorry. That's all man, that's all man. You don't shoot the man because he stepped on your sneaker. Think about it. The white man got you so mad that you kill a black man. Ha, ha, ha, ha. That's mad.

My father was mad, unfortunately. Unfortunately, he was mad. Either way the country that he had worked for and fought for drove him mad. It was the same country that his family, his grandparents had slaved for. To be made insane by the United States of America happens every day and it's subtle enough that one is not necessarily aware of its insidious power. Race and race consciousness; Kafka himself could not have envisioned a more flawlessly intricate method or scheme for driving a protagonist insane.

What is unique and so special about this landscape? We are race conscious for sure, but it is our guileful manner of using race and its particular parameters that damages so many human beings. It's maddening to the point of producing paranoia, delusions of grandeur, and schizophrenia. Rational men, strong men and women and intelligent people are broken by this disease, by this illness. Khalid Mohammad, Michael Jackson, Lani Guinier, all pushed to breaking points by race, racism, questions that no human beings should ever have to confront. I never realized how maddening and ludicrous it was until I was enlightened that someone with the same last name as I had was ruining my academic career. Man, did I curse the day I changed my name. Irrational things started to happen and there was no way of asserting the truth, any truth. The first time I heard about Dr. Leonard Jeffries I defended him. I had to. A class of students had the mistaken impression that I was him.

It was September 1990, and I had just been hired by Hunter College to teach a course, "The Harlem Renaissance." I was very happy and honored since Hunter College is one of the best schools in the City University of New York. The summer had been an academic one. Preparing, reading, studying, making notes on yellow legal pads, all these activities bring joy to a teacher's heart, and I had boned up for this course just like a prizefighter getting prepared for a major bout in his career. I went to the classroom enthusiastic and buoyant.

I set my books and papers on the desk and looked out at the thirty-five faces, and I was scared and exhilarated. I took the roll and asked if there were any bureaucratic questions that had to be dealt with before commencing the class. About ten students came up to the desk and formed a line on the left. I was baffled, since in the age of computers there are usually only one or two students who have fallen victim to some glitch down in the registrar's office. Ten, something was amiss.

All of the students were requesting to drop out of the class. I was taken aback and was a bit astounded. Without letting the rest of the class discern that a mutiny was occurring within earshot, I whispered to each student. I asked the third student on line why was she dropping the class. There was a sense of ache in my voice as I asked, "Why are you dropping a class before the first lecture?" She said that it did not fit into her schedule. I asked two more students and they replied in the same demurring manner about scheduling conflicts. The sixth student was bold enough to feel sorry for me and said, "They're dropping the class because you're that guy, the racist. The racist from City College."

The reproaches rolled off my tongue with that swift annoyance of a person who has been wrongfully accused of some immoral turpitude of which he knows with conviction he is completely blameless. It was in incredibly awkward situation, with the class delayed now by about five minutes, students whispering at my desk, and a steady murmur and rustling papers and notebooks in the rest of the classroom. I was now standing.

"What guy, who's this guy?" I uttered.

"This guy Jeffries said that the black race is superior to all other races, white, Hispanic, Asian. The black race is first, superior to all others."

With confidence and anger I informed them that no professor of my alma mater would ever pronounce such racist thoughts and if he did, it was within a certain context or possibly he was being incredibly sarcastic and facetious.

My Hunter College students were just as confident. They gave me small details regarding storm trooper guards that surrounded the professor, his habitual lateness to class, and the muffling of academic dialogue. Details such as these made me uncomfortable since they lent credulity to their case. I apologized to the class about the disruption and concluded this little scene with a two-part plea. First, I was not that "guy" even though my last name was Jeffries and second, this Dr. Jeffries had been quoted out of context and was not racist. I reiterated that professors from City College, the place where I earned my MA in English, were not capable of that sort of virulent racism. It was beyond my comprehension.

Later the entire faculty of the City University and I were to learn that Dr. Leonard Jeffries was indeed racist and mad. Something had pushed this scholar over a line of rationality and irrationality, and he was no longer sane. Ice people, anti-Semitism, Sun people, adorned in African regalia, hauptepping his way through class, speaking triumphantly of melanin and other ersatz science. I wrote him a letter informing him of his disservice to the faculty of City University. He never replied. I was to suffer low enrollments due to his notoriety and our similar names. Mad. Madness.

I think my father, had he witnessed this tragi-comic vignette, would have said, "Looks like you should have stayed Puerto Rican." Maybe he was right.

Questions and Ideas for Journaling and Discussion

1. Jeffries talks about occasions when his appearance has made others uncomfortable. Discuss some instances when the way a person looks, or dresses, or speaks makes others uncomfortable. Why does this occur?
2. What do we learn about Jeffries' father? Discuss how his father shaped his attitude about his identity.
3. The tone of a work of literature comes from the attitude of an author toward his or her subject. For more information, research "literary tone." What is Jeffries' attitude toward his subject and what is the tone that results?

Writing to Explore and Learn

1. Imagine that you live in a foreign country where no one looks at all like you. Now imagine that you are that character in a play. Write a monologue in which you explain to the audience how it feels to be so different. Use specific incidents and details.

Jim Northrup (b. 1943)

From harvest to hibernation, sweet spring to summer's wanderings. We know who we are from the seasons.

Jim Northrup was born on the Fond du Lac Indian Reservation in Minnesota where he grew up, the eldest of thirteen. After attending boarding schools and reform school, Northrup became one of the first Native Americans to graduate from high school in the state. Enlisting in the United States Marine Corps, he served combat duty in Vietnam. When he returned to the United States, he found his calling as a writer in a tepee where friends and family would gather to tell stories. Today he is a journalist and creator of fiction and nonfiction who, at the same time, tries to live a traditional Anishinaabeg life. Northrup's works include a nationally syndicated newspaper column, "Fond du Lac Follies," and his highly acclaimed *Walking the Rez Road* (1993), a collection of short stories and poems featuring Luke Warmwater, a Vietnam war veteran.

"Veteran's Dance" (1993)

Northrup tells the tale of a Vietnam War veteran's relationship with his family and community within the context of Native American culture. At the center of the story is a brother/sister relationship in which the process of storytelling helps to heal the soldier, who is suffering from Post-Traumatic Stress Disorder. Reconnecting with his sense of community identity through the ritual of the powwow, the soldier recognizes his new role in the tribe as a means to overcome his challenges in the aftermath of war.

Don't sweat the small shit, Lug thought; it's all small shit unless they're shooting at you.

The tall, skinny Shinnob finished changing the tire on his car. It took longer than usual because he had to improvise with the jack. Summer in Minnesota and Lug was on his way to a powwow.

The powwow was on its second day. The dancers were getting ready for their third grand entry. Singers around the various drums had found their rhythm. Old bones were loosening up. The emcee was entertaining the crowd with jokes. Some of the jokes brought laughs and others brought groans. Kids were weaving through the people that circled the dance arena. The drum-sound knitted the people together.

Lug brushed his long hair away from his face as he looked in the sky for eagles. He had been away from home a long time and was looking forward to seeing his friends and relatives again.

He really enjoyed powwows, although he didn't dance. Lug was content to be with his people again. Ever since the war he had felt disconnected from the things that made people happy.

The first time he walked around the arena he just concentrated on faces. He was looking for family. While walking along he grazed at the food stands. He smelled then sampled the fry bread, moose meat, and wild rice soup.

The Shinnobs walking around the dance arena looked like a river that was going in two directions. Groups of people would stop and talk. Lug smiled at the laughing circles of Shinnobs. He looked at faces and eyes.

That little one there, she looked like his sister Judy did when she was that age. Lug wondered if he would see her here. Judy was a jingle-dress dancer and should be at this powwow. After all, she only lived a mile away from the powwow grounds.

The guy walking in front of him looked like his cousin that went to Vietnam. Nope, couldn't be him. Lug had heard that he died in a single-car accident last fall.

Sitting in a red and white striped powwow chair was an old lady that looked like his grandma. She wore heavy brown stockings that were held up with a big round knot at the knees. She chewed Copenhagen and spit the juice in a coffee can just like his gram. Of course, Lug's grandma had been dead for ten years, but it was still a good feeling to see someone who looked like her.

Lug recognized the woman walking toward him. She was his old used-to-be girlfriend. He hoped she didn't want to talk about what went wrong with them. She didn't, just snapped her eyes and looked away. Lug knew it was his fault he couldn't feel close to anyone. His face was a wooden mask is as they passed each other. He could feel her looking up at him out of the corner of her eyes. Maybe, he thought, just maybe.

He stopped at a food stand called Stand Here. Lug had black coffee and a bag of mini-donuts. The sugar and cinnamon coating stuck to his fingers when he finished. He brushed off his hands and lit a smoke. Lug watched the snaggers 8 to 68 cruising through the river of Shinnobs.

That jingle-dress dancer walking toward him looked like his sister Judy. Yup it was her. The maroon dress made a tinkling, jingling sound as she came closer. She looks healthy, Lug thought. A few more gray hairs, but she moves like she was twenty years younger. They both smiled just hard as their eyes met. Warm brown eyes reached for wary ones.

She noticed the lines on his face were deeper. The lines fanned out from the edges of his eyes. He looked like he had lost some weight since the last time she saw him. His bluejean jacket just hung on him, she thought.

Lug and Judy shook hands and hugged each other. Her black-beaded bag hit him on the back as they embraced. They were together again after a long time apart. Both leaned back to get a better look at each other.

"C'mon over to the house when they break for supper," she said.

"Got any cornbread?" he asked.

"I can whip some up for you," she promised.

"Sounds good," he said.

Eating cornbread was a reminder of when they were young together. Sometimes it was the only thing to eat in the house. Cornbread was the first thing she made him when he came back from Vietnam.

"I have to get in line for the grand entry so I'll see you later. I want to talk to you about something," she said.

"Okay, dance a round for me," Lug said.

"I will, just like I always do."

Lug watched the grand entry. He saw several relatives in their dance outfits. He nodded to friends that were standing around the dance arena. Lug sipped hot coffee as the grand entry song was sung. He saw Judy come dancing by. Lug turned and looked at his car.

He walked to it as the flag song started. He almost moved in time to the beat as he walked. Lug decided to get his tire fixed at the truck stop. He got in and closed the car door as the veterans' song came over the public address system.

Lug left the powwow grounds and slipped a tape in his cassette player. The Animals singing "Sky Pilot" filled the car. Lug sang along with the vintage music.

He drove to the truck stop and read the newspaper while the mechanic fixed his tire. Lug put the tire in his trunk, paid the guy and drove to his sister's house. He listened to the Righteous Brothers do "Soul and Inspiration" on the way.

Judy's car was in the driveway, so he knew she was home. He parked and walked up to the front door. He rang the doorbell and walked in. He smelled combread.

She was in the kitchen making coffee. He sat at the kitchen table as she look the cornbread out of the oven. The steaming yellow bread made his mouth moist. Judy poured him a cup of coffee and sat down at the table.

"How have you been?" she asked.

"Okay, my health is okay."

"Where have you been? I haven't heard from you in quite a while."

"Oh you know, just traveling here and there. I'd work a little bit and then move on. For a while there I was looking for guys I knew in the war."

"Where was that you called from last March?" she asked.

"D.C., I was in Washington D.C. I went to the Wall and after being there I felt like I had to talk to someone I knew."

"You did sound troubled about something."

"I found a friend's name on the Wall. He died after I left Vietnam. I felt like killing myself."

"I'm glad you didn't."

"Me too, we wouldn't be having this conversation if I had gone through with it."

She got up, cut the cornbread and brought it to the table. He buttered a piece and began taking bites from the hot bread. She refilled his cup.

"Remember when we used to have to haul water when we were kids? I was thinking about it the other day, that one time it was thirty below and the cream cans fell off the sled? You somehow convinced me it was my fault. I had to pump the water to fill the cans again. You told me it was so I could stay warm. I guess in your own way you were looking out for me," she said.

"Nahh, I just wanted to see if I could get you to do all the work." Lug smiled at his sister.

"I thought it was good of you to send die folks money from your first military paycheck so we could get our own pump. We didn't have to burn water from die neighbor after that."

"I had to, I didn't want you to break your back lugging those cream cans around."

"Yah, I really hated wash days. Ma had me hauling water all day when she washed clothes."

She got up and got a glass of water from the kitchen faucet. As she came back to the table she said, "I've been talking to a spiritual leader about you. He wants you to come and see him. Don't forget to take him tobacco."

"That sounds like a good idea. I've been wanting to talk to someone," he said.

"What was it like in the war? You never talked much about it."

Lug stared deep into his black medicine water as if expecting an answer to scroll across. He trusted his sister, but it was still difficult talking about the terrible memories.

His eyes retreated into his head as he told her what happened to him what he did in the war. She later learned that this was called the thousand yard stare. His eyes looked like he was trying to see something that was that far away. The laugh lines were erased from his face.

"Sometimes I'd get so scared I couldn't get scared anymore," he said hunched over his coffee cup.

Judy touched his arm. Her face said she was ready to listen to her brother.

"One night they were shooting at us. No one was getting hurt. It got to be a drag ducking every time they fired. The gunfire wasn't very heavy, just a rifle round every couple of minutes. We didn't know if it was the prelude to a big attack or just one guy out there with a case of ammo and a hard on. We laid in our holes, counted the rounds going by and tried to shrink up inside our helmets. The bullets went by for at least a half hour. I counted seventeen of them. The ones that went high made a buzzing noise as they went by. The close ones made a crack sound. First you'd hear the bullet go by then the sound of where it came from."

"I got tired of that shit. I crawled up out of my hole and just stood there. I wanted to see where the bad guy was shooting from. The guys in the next hole told me to get down, but I was in a fuck-it mood. I didn't care what happened, didn't care if I lived or died."

Lug stood up to show his sister what it was like standing in the dark. He was leaning forward trying to see through the night. His hands clutched an imaginary rifle. Lug's head was swiveling back and forth as he looked for the hidden rifleman. He jerked as a rifle bullet came close to him. He turned his head toward the sound.

Judy watched Lug. She could feel her eyes burning and the tears building up. Using only willpower she held the tears back. Judy somehow knew the tears would stop the flood of memories coming out of her brother. She waited.

"I finally saw the muzzle flash. I knew where the bastard was firing from. After he fired the next time we all returned fire. We must have shot 500 rounds at him. The bad guy didn't shoot anymore. We either killed him or scared the shit out of him. After the noise died down I started getting scared. I realized I could have been killed standing up like that."

He paused before speaking again.

"That shows you how dangerous a fuck-it attitude is. I guess I have been living my life with a fuck-it attitude."

Lug sat back down and reached for another piece of cornbread. He ate it silently. When he finished the cornbread he lit a cigarette.

She touched his shoulder as she poured more coffee. Lug accepted this as permission to continue fighting the war. Judy sat down and lit her own cigarette.

"It was really crazy at times. One time we were caught out in this big rice paddy. They started shooting at us. I was close to the front of the formation so I got inside the treeline quick. The bad guys couldn't see me. When I leaned over to catch my breath I heard the snick, snick, bang sound of someone firing a bolt-action rifle. The enemy soldier was firing at the guys still out in the rice paddy. I figured out where the bad guy was from the sound—snick, snick, bang. I fired a three-round burst at the noise. That asshole turned and fired at me. I remember the muzzle flash and the bullet going-by noise happened together. I fired again as I moved closer. Through a little opening in the brush I could see what looked like a pile of rags, bloody rags. I fired another round into his head. We used to do that all the time—one in the head to make sure. The 7.62 bullet knocked his hat off. When the hat came off all this hair came spilling out. It was a woman."

Lug slumped at the kitchen table unable to continue his story. He held his coffee cup as if warming his hands. Judy sat there looking at him. Tears were running down her cheeks and puddling up on the table.

Lug coughed and lit a cigarette. Judy reached for one of her own and Lug lit it for her. Their eyes met. She got up to blow her nose and wipe her eyes. Judy was trembling as she came back and sat at the table. She wanted to cradle her brother but couldn't.

"Her hair looked like grandma's hair used to look. Remember her long, black shiny hair? This woman had hair like that. I knew killing people was wrong somehow but this made it worse when it turned out to be a woman."

Lug was slowly rocking his head back and forth.

When it looked like Lug was not going to talk anymore Judy got up and opened the back door. She poured more coffee and sat there looking at him. He couldn't meet her eyes.

"Tell me how you got wounded. You never did talk about it. All we knew was that you had won a Purple Heart," she probed.

After a long silence, Lug answered. "Ha, won a Purple Heart? We used to call them Idiot Awards. It meant that you fucked up somehow. Standing in the wrong place at the wrong time, something like that."

Lug's shoulders tightened up as he began telling her about his wounds. He reached down for his leg. "I don't know what happened to my leg. It was a long firefight, lots of explosions. After it was over, after the medivac choppers left, we were sitting around talking about what happened.

"I looked down and noticed blood on my leg. I thought it was from the guys we carried in from the listening post. The pain started about then. I rolled up my pants and saw a piece of shrapnel sticking out. Doc came over and pulled it out. He bandaged it up and must have written me up for a Heart. I remember that it took a long time to heal because we were always in the water of the rice paddies."

Lug was absently rubbing his leg as he told his sister about his wound.

He suddenly stood up and changed the subject. He didn't talk about his other wounds. He drained his cup.

"I gotta go, I think I talked too much already. I don't want you to think I am crazy because of what I did in the war. I'll see you at the powwow," said Lug, walking to the door.

As she looked at his back she wished there was something she could do to ease his memories of the war. "Wait a minute," Judy told her brother.

She lit some sage and smudged him with an eagle feather. He stood there with his eyes closed, palms facing out.

He thanked her and walked out the door.

While cleaning up after her brother left, Judy remembered hearing the ads on TV for the Vet's Center. She looked the number up in the book and called. Judy spoke to a counselor who listened. The counselor suggested an Inpatient Post-Traumatic Stress Disorder program.

The closest one was located in southern Minnesota. Judy got die address for her brother.

She went back to the powwow and found Lug standing on the edge of the crowd. "They have a program for treating PTSD," she told Lug.

"Yah, I saw something on TV about PTSD."

"What did you think of it? What do you think of entering a treatment program?"

"It might do some good. I was talking to a guy who went through it. He said it helped him. It might be worth a shot," Lug said.

"I talked to a counselor after you left. She said you can come in anytime."

"How about right now? Do you think they are open right now?"

"Sure, they must keep regular hours."

When she saw him walking to his car she thought it didn't take much to get him started.

Lug left the powwow and drove to the Vet's Center. On the way he listened to Dylan singing "Blowing in the Wind."

At the Vet's Center Lug found out he could enter the program in a couple of days. His stay would be about a month.

Lug talked to the spiritual man before he went in for the program. He remembered to bring him a package of Prince Albert tobacco and a pair of warm socks.

In talking with the man, Lug learned that veterans were respected because of the sacrifices they had made in the war. He told Lug he would pray for him. The spiritual man told Lug to come back and see him when he got out of the Veterans Hospital.

Lug went to see the counselor and she helped him fill out the paperwork. He thanked her and drove to his sister's house. He parked his car and went inside. She showed him where he could leave his car parked while he was gone.

Judy drove Lug to the brick hospital. He took his bag of clothes and walked up the steps. Judy waved from her car. As he turned and looked, he noticed she was parked under an American flag.

He walked into the building. The smell of disinfectant reminded him of other official buildings he had been through.

He was ready for whatever was to come. Don't sweat the small shit, he thought.

Lug quickly learned that he was not the only one having trouble coping with memories of the war. He felt comfortable talking with other vets who had similar experiences.

Living in the Vet's Hospital felt like being in the military again. He slept in a warm bed and ate warm food. He spent most of his time with guys his age who had been to Vietnam. His time was structured for him.

In the group therapy sessions they told war stories at first. After being together a while they began to talk about feelings. Lug became aware that he had been acting normal in what was an abnormal situation. He felt like he was leaving some of his memories at the hospital.

In spite of the camaraderie he felt, Lug was anxious to rejoin his community. He wanted to go home. He knew he would complete the program but didn't expect to spend one extra minute at the hospital.

While he was gone Judy was busy. She was making Lug a pair of moccasins. The toes had the traditional beaded floral design. Around the cuffs she stitched the colors of the Vietnam campaign ribbon. She had called the counselor at the Vet's Center to make sure the colors were right. It was green, then yellow with three red stripes, yellow then green again. The smoke-tanned hide smell came to her as she sewed.

The hardest part was going down in the basement for the trunk her husband had left when he went to Vietnam. The trunk contained the traditional dance outfit he used to wear. It had been packed away because he didn't come back from the war.

Judy drove to the hospital and picked Lug up when he had completed the PTSD program. Looked like he put on some weight she thought when she first saw him.

She drove to the spiritual man's house, and listened to a powwow tape while driving. Lug tapped his hand on his knee in time to the drum. On the way Lug told hospital stories. She could see his laugh lines as he talked about the month with the other vets.

At the house Judy waited outside while the two men talked and smoked. She listened to both sides of the tape twice before Lug came out. He had a smile and walked light on his feet. Lug got in the car.

Judy drove to her house. They listened to the powwow on the way. She could see that Lug was enjoying the music.

"I've got that extra bedroom downstairs. You can stay there until you get your own place," she told him.

"Sounds like a winner. Cornbread every day?"

"Nope, special occasions only."

"I might be eligible for a disability pension, but I'd rather get a job," Lug said.

"Do what you want to do," she said.

"Where are we going now?" Lug asked.

"We're going to a powwow. I got my tent set up already and I want to dance in the first grand entry."

"Okay, it'll feel good to see familiar faces again."

"Did the hospital do anything for you?" she asked.

"I think so, but it felt better talking to the spiritual man," he answered.

When they got to the powwow grounds Judy drove to her tent. Lug perched on the fender when she went inside to change into her jingle dress.

Sure the hospital was nice but it felt better being here with his relatives. Lug thought. He breathed deep in the cool air. He could hear his sister's jingle dress begin to make sounds as she got dressed. He was trying to decide which food stand to start with when his sister came out.

"Tie this up for me, will you?" she asked.

Judy handed him the eagle fluff and medicine wheel. He used rawhide to tie it to her small braid. After she checked to make sure it was the way she wanted it, Judy said, "Go in the tent and get your present."

"Okay," he said, jumping off the fender and unzipping the tent.

Inside the tent he saw a pair of moccasins on top of a traditional dance outfit. The colors of the campaign ribbon on the moccasins caught his eye. He took off his sneakers and put on the moccasins.

"Hey, thanks a lot, I needed some moccasins," said Lug.

"The rest of the outfit belongs to you too," she said.

"Really?" he recognized the dance outfit. He knew who used to own it. He thought of his brother-in-law and the Vietnam war.

"Hurry up and put it on. It is almost time for grand entry," Judy told him.

Lug put on the dance outfit and walked out for the inspection he knew she would give. He did a couple of steps to show her how it fit. She smiled her approval.

They walked to where the people were lining up. He was laughing as he joined the traditional dancers. He saw his cousin Fuzzy who was a Vietnam vet.

"Didja hear? They got a new flavor for Vietnam vets," Lug said.

"Yah, what is it'" asked the guy who had been in Khe San in '68.

"Agent Grape," said Lug.

They both laughed at themselves for laughing.

Lug danced the grand entry song with slow dignity, he felt proud. He moved with the drum during the flag song.

When the veteran's song began Lug moved back to join his sister. Both of them had tears showing as they danced the veteran's honor song together.

Questions and Ideas for Journaling and Discussion

1. Describe Luke Warmwater's life when he returns to Minnesota.
2. Describe Luke's relationship with his sister.
3. Short, simple sentences are often associated with monotony in literature, but they can be used to different effect. The entire third paragraph is a series of short, simple sentences, and much of the story relies on these short sentences as well. What is the result of this rhythm in this short story?

Writing to Explore and Learn

1. Write about the meaning of family, community, and war in "Veteran's Dance."

Mark Simpson
(b. 1965)

British author and journalist Mark Simpson has been called "one of the brightest writers around" by the world press. Famous for "fathering" the metrosexual in 1994, Simpson writes for magazines and newspapers around the globe, including *Playboy* magazine, the *Guardian* newspaper, and *Details* magazine. Notable books include *Male Impersonators: Men Performing Masculinity* (1994) and *Saint Morrissey* (2006).

"Metrosexuals: Male Vanity Steps Out of the Closet" (1994)

Simpson, a cultural critic, examines the ways in which narcissism and homoeroticism play a part in representations of masculinity in contemporary western culture. In deconstructing codes of masculinity and questioning the assumptions of sexual practices, he posits a new male identity, "the metrosexual."

"It's been kept underground for too long," observes one sharply dressed "metrosexual" in his early twenties. He has a perfect complexion and precisely gelled hair, and is inspecting a display of costly aftershaves. "This exhibition shows that male vanity's finally coming out of the closet."

And it's busy filling the extra space in there with expensive clothes and accessories. "It's a Man's World—Britain's first style exhibition for men," organised by *GQ* magazine in London last weekend, proclaims that male narcissism has arrived and we'd better get used to it.

With pavilions representing top men's fashion designers such as Calvin Klein, Ralph Lauren, and Giorgio Armani and all the latest "grooming" products, It's a Man's World is, as Peter Stuart, *GQ* publisher, describes it, "a terrific shopping experience."

Metrosexual man, the single young man with a high disposable income, living or working in the city (because that's where all the best shops are), is perhaps the most promising consumer market of the decade. In the eighties he was only to be found inside fashion magazines such as *GQ*, in television advertisements for Levi's jeans, or in gay bars. In the nineties, he's everywhere, and he's going shopping.

Metrosexual man wears Davidoff "Cool Water" aftershave (the one with the naked bodybuilder on the beach), Paul Smith jackets (Ryan Giggs wears them), corduroy shirts (Elvis wore them), chinos (Steve McQueen wore them), motorcycle boots (Marlon Brando wore them), and Calvin Klein underwear (Marky Mark wore nothing else). Metrosexual man is a commodity fetishist, a collector of fantasies about the male sold to him by advertising.

Even the name of the exhibition reveals how much times have changed. Not so long ago the expression "it's a man's world" conveyed the idea that the world belonged to that half of humanity which shaved; nowadays, it seems to mean that you have to have the right *après-rasage* face cream.

On one of the stands men lie supine while attractive women in white coats rub luxurious moisturisers into their faces; cameras display the beauty treatment in close-up on banks of screens. Behold the metrosexual pampered by women, technology, and capitalism; behold the metrosexual as star.

"It feels nice. Basically you get a free facial out of it," says James, a nineteen-year-old in natty jeans and Italian dad-shirt, face aglow. "This stuff is a bit out of my price range as I'm a student," he confesses. "But if I had the money I might well buy the stuff."

Is all this attention to appearance a good thing? "Yes," says another young man, casually-but-carefully dressed in Caterpillar boots, pristine Levi's, T-shirt, sweatshirt, and bomber jacket. "If women take so much trouble over their appearance it's only fair that men should take a bit more care themselves. My girlfriend would certainly agree!"

But is it really about fairness, or is it about the way you feel when you look in the mirror? "I suppose it's mostly the way you feel," he admits.

A twenty-one-year-old stock manager in Gap jeans agrees: "Men are just as vain as women and it's a good thing that we're able to show it these days."

One of the major interests behind metrosexual pride is, as the impressive list of sponsors of this event shows (Dunhill to Porsche, Timberland to Simpson's of Piccadilly), big business. Metrosexuals are the creation of capitalism's voracious appetite for new markets.

Heterosexual men used to be the world's worst consumers. All they bought was beer, fags, and the occasional Durex; the Wife or Mum bought everything else. In a consumerist world, heterosexual men had no future. So they were replaced by the metrosexual.

The promotion of metrosexuality was left to the men's style press, magazines such as *The Face, GQ, Esquire, Arena,* and *FHM,* the new media which took off in the eighties and is still growing (*GQ* gains 10,000 new readers every month). They filled their magazines with images of narcissistic young men sporting fashionable clothes and accessories. And they persuaded other young men to study them with a mixture of envy and desire.

Some people said unkind things. American *GQ,* for example, was popularly dubbed "Gay Quarterly." Little wonder that all these magazines—with the possible exception of *The Face*—address their readership as if none of them was homosexual or even bisexual. Little wonder that "It's A Man's World" organiser Peter Stuart found it necessary to tell me that "all the men will bring their girlfriends."

The "heterosexual" address of these magazines is a convention, there to reassure the readership and the advertisers that their unmanly passions are in fact manly. Nevertheless, the metrosexual man contradicts the basic premise of traditional heterosexuality—that only women are looked at and only men do the looking. Metrosexual man might prefer women, he might prefer men, but when all's said and done nothing comes between him and his reflection.

Metrosexuality was, of course, test-marketed on gay men—with enormous success. It's a Man's World is billed as the first man's style exhibition—but the Gay Lifestyles Exhibition, which features fashion shows and a whole range of "men's products," is already in its third year. It was in the style-obsessed eighties that the "gay lifestyle"—the single man living in the metropolis and taking himself as his own love object—became a model for nonhomosexuals.

Perhaps this is why *Attitude,* a style magazine launched earlier this year, felt able to break with convention and address itself openly to gay men and what it called "strays" ("gay-acting" straight men).

The New Lad bible, *Loaded,* for all its features on sport, babes, and sport, is metrosexual. Just as its antistyle is a style (last month it carried a supplement for "no-nonsense" clothes, such as jeans and boots), its heterosexuality is so self-conscious, so studied, that it's actually rather camp. New Lads, for all their burping blokeishness, are just as much in love with their own image as any other metrosexual—they just haven't come to terms yet.

Nor is metrosexuality a vice restricted to the poncey Southern middle classes. Working-class boys are, if anything, even more susceptible to it. For example, Newcastle men between the ages of eighteen and thirty-five apparently spend more money per head on clothes than any other men in Europe. If you live with your mother, as do many working-class boys until they marry—and, crucially, you have a job—your disposable income and your metrosexual tendencies are likely to be high.

And metrosexuals have an amazing sense of solidarity. Back at It's a Man's World, Steve and Paul, two fashionably dressed men-about-London in their late twenties, admit to spending "a substantial amount" of their income on male cosmetics and clothes, and think that the exhibition is "great." But they're worried that they might be letting the metrosexual side down.

Says Steve: "It's a shame that you picked us because we're gay and people might think that a show like this is just for gays and wouldn't come. The thing is, straight men are just beginning to discover the joys of shopping and we wouldn't want to scare them off."

Questions and Ideas for Journaling and Discussion

1. Characterize Simpson's conception of "the metrosexual."

Writing to Explore and Learn

1. Consider what Simpson means by "male vanity" and create a profile of your own version of a "man about town."

Vanessa Raymond (b. 1963)

Vanessa Raymond is the editor-in-chief of HowToDoThings.com and general manager of ComoFazerTudo.com.br and Comment-Sur-Tout.fr. Vanessa has written and edited for both print and online publications, including *Glamour*, Sierra Entertainment, Mauny's Kitchen, and *Seattle Weekly*, and has been published internationally in newspapers, including *The Chicago Tribune*, *The Atlanta-Journal Constitution*, and *The Deccan Chronicle*, an Indian regional publication. Vanessa is a graduate of the Radcliffe Publishing Procedures Program and spent the early part of her publishing career at Little, Brown & Company in Boston and New York. Vanessa lives in Seattle with her son.

"How to Know You're a Metrosexual" (2009)

Grounded in humor, this short article points out the sexual oppression faced by men. While women have been universally objectified by society, men have remained in subject positions, defined by their power and not their appearance. What, then, does our culture make of a heterosexual man who steps out of his traditional position of gazer to that of gazed upon and has manicures and pedicures, uses hair products, and has his body hair waxed away?

A metrosexual is a man who spends a certain amount of time and money on his lifestyle, specifically his appearance. Here are a few questions that will help you to ascertain whether or not you are, indeed, a metrosexual.

Do gay men hit on you? If you're a metrosexual, it's already happened. (Who can blame them for trying?) And while you were flattered, you're really a het (and maybe even a "hef") at heart The term, "metrosexual," as originally coined, described heterosexual men who have adopted the dress and appearance of gay men.

Do you carry a purse? A purse gives you an automatic entrée into metrosexualdom. Welcome. And by the way, which designer? See a good-looking manbag at PurseBlog. And find the top ten ultimate metrosexual man bags at Kineda.

How do you feel about your socks? As you read this, do you know what color socks you are wearing? Are they designer socks? Did you put these particular socks on this morning because they were at the top of your drawer or because they go well with your outfit? And finally, do you ever go shopping for socks only? Your consideration of your socks reflects your overall concern with your clothes: Metrosexual men care about socks, along with everything else that adorns their sacred bods.

Do you wear tighty whitties? Sorry about that. A metrosexual would never be caught dead in a pair of tighty whitties. Given the choice, they would rather go without any underwear at all than succumb. And come to think of it, going commando sounds pretty good to a metrosexual (maybe in his new leather pants)!

Do you use more than one product in your hair? Do you refer to your hair products as "product?" Two yeses here make you a met. And you get bonus points if your hair is highlighted.

Have you ever used hair removal services other than shaving? You know—waxing, tweezing, laser, electrolysis? If so, you've entered metro country.

Do you receive spa services? Does a paraffin dip help to calm you? Manicures, pedicures, facials and exfoliation are all part of a metrosexual's routine. Bonus points if you're a regular and/or see your stylist socially.

Do you borrow products from the women in your life? Does your co-worker have a moisturizer that you just can't go without a hit of come mid-afternoon? Does your girlfriend wonder why she seems to be going through her toner so quickly? When she's not looking, do you use her shaving gel instead of yours? And when she is looking, do you use it anyway? Metro alert!

Rumor has it that metrosexuality is on its way out. But I don't believe for a moment that David Beckham will give up his market share (or that Posh will let him) without a fight!

Questions and Ideas for Journaling and Discussion

1. Men have resisted being objects in the same way that women are resisting. According to John Berger in *Ways of Seeing*,[1] the male gaze is the gaze of the subject and it falls upon the object, a woman. Women, as a consequence, and unlike men, always picture themselves walking, talking, or weeping. In what ways does "metrosexuality" subvert that stereotype?

Open Questions for Writing

1. Choose two or three works in this section and compare and contrast each poet's and/or author's representations of gender and masculine identities.

---

[1]New York: Penguin, 1990.

PART III

SEXUALITIES

Sigmund Freud is a rupturing figure—the figure of modernity—who separates the nineteenth century from the twentieth with his institution of psychoanalysis and open questioning of gender and sexuality. French philosopher Michel Foucault, with his groundbreaking text, *The History of Sexuality* (1976), wrote against Freud's psychoanalytic project that posits a separate sexual instinct that is inherent in us, to suggest an "analytics of power," in which he theorizes that sexualities in western civilizations are produced by discourses and deployed into people. Gender and sexualities are not received realities, or essentiality, but are socially constructed by large groups of statements that represent given moments in history, articulated by languages of power, such as medicine, law, and religion. Social identities thus are historically shaped rather than products of "nature."

By denaturalizing dominant understandings of sexual identity, sexualities—homosexuality, bisexuality, and heterosexuality—have come to be understood as cultural categories of difference. Sexual orientations (as well as genders, races, and ethnic identities) have come to be understood as socially constructed rather than essentially, or "naturally," rooted in human beings.

Foucault viewed homosexuality, in particular, as a late nineteenth century formation. Before then, he argues, there were same-sex acts, but no corresponding rank of identification. The implication is that to identify human beings in this way—in terms of sexual acts—is degrading and dehumanizing, opening the door for societal punishment, scapegoating, and group hate.

The constructionist position on sexualities and gender has given rise to a field of study called "Queer Theory," previously known as Lesbian and Gay Studies. Always in a state of flux, "queer," in this context, can be understood as anything that veers away from the norms established by western culture; sexualities and gender identities are fluid and shifting. Generally, this theory takes as its focus any sexual and/or gender identities that fall into or out of deviant or normative categories of difference.

The writers that follow invite readers to consider constructions of sexualities and desire as powerful forces in human relations.

Sappho
(610–580 BCE)

Sappho was considered one of the finest poets of ancient Greece. While the textual history of Sappho's poetry and her private life remain vague, there is no question that throughout the centuries she has been a fascinating figure for poets and writers.[1] Classical scholars believe Sappho to have been actual woman who lived and wrote on the Greek isle of Lesbos in the seventh century BCE; apparently, she ran an academy for women that prepared them for marriage and trained them in deportment, as well as in composition, singing, and performance of poetry. Sappho wrote lyric poetry at a time when Greek poetry was dominated by the epics of Homer; these were mostly lyrics to young women, expressing desire, longing, and love. "Ode to Aphrodite" is one of two complete poems extant among fragments of verses.

"Ode to Aphrodite" (600 BCE)

Sappho, the earliest poet of female desire, invokes the Goddess of Sexuality to intervene on her behalf to effect the transformation of a girl who leaves (most likely Anactoria) to a girl who pursues. A poem of female homoerotic courtship, within an ancient Greek context, Sappho's supplication suggests a discourse on gender that debunks modern categories of sexual difference through the ideas of feminine and masculine.

APHRODITE on your shining throne,
artful daughter of Zeus,
I pray, release me
from sorrow.

Come to me, as you did once before.
You heard my voice from afar,
and listening, left your father's
golden house

---

[1]Throughout western literary history, scholars, writers, and poets produced the "heterosexual" Sappho they wanted, which changed in 1885 with Henry Thorton Wharton's influential translation, which was the first to use the feminine pronoun. See, for example, Joan DeJean's *Fictions of Sappho, 1546–1937*, University of Chicago Press, 1989.

and yoked a chariot with sleek swallows
who quickly brought you from heaven
to dark earth, beating their wings
in midair.

They swiftly left; and you,
goddess, an immortal smile on your face,
ask, "What has happened now? Why do you
call me?

"What does your mad heart crave?
What beauty would you now have me
cause to love you? Who can refuse
you, Sappho?

"No matter if she turns away, she'll soon come around,
and if now she refuses gifts, she'll soon give them,
and if she doesn't love you now, she will soon,
against her will."

Come, I pray, now, and relieve me
of this unrelenting heartache. All
that my heart longs for, may you achieve,
and be my accomplice.

Questions and Ideas for Journaling and Discussion

1. Do we read the speaker's supplication to the goddess as an acceptable expression of human emotion? Or is it an exaggeration and why might this be so?

Writing to Explore and Learn

1. Sappho has been called "the original poet of female desire." How does "Ode to Aphrodite" demonstrate this quality?

Christina Rossetti
(1830–1894)

My heart is like a singing bird.

Christina Rossetti was a Victorian poet whose compact, mysterious lyrics and experimental narrative poems examine the religious, social, and sexual issues of her time in an unconventional way. Born in London to Italian émigré parents, she was the youngest member of a family of poets, artists, and critics. She was a devout evangelical Anglican who refused two marriage proposals and led a retiring life. Living vicariously through other people, her inner circle included her brother Dante' Gabriel's friends—Algernon Charles Swinburne, James McNeill Whistler, and Lewis Carroll of the Pre-Raphaelite arts movement. Her most well known collection of poetry is *Goblin Market and Other Poems* (1862); she wrote two volumes of short stories, six volumes of unorthodox religious prose, and, among others, the collection *The Princess Progress and Other Poems* (1866).

Goblin Market (1859)

Rossetti's long poem is an unsettling fairy tale about two sisters, Laura and Lizzie, whose life of virginal domesticity is upset when they venture away from home into the world of the marketplace of goblin men. In this poem of proto-feminist politics, Rossetti combines the Victorian erotic and spiritual to treat themes of sexuality, temptation, and redemption.

    Morning and evening
    Maids heard the goblins cry:
    "Come buy our orchard fruits.
    Come buy, come buy:
5   Apples and quinces,
    Lemons and oranges,
    Plump unpecked cherries,
    Melons and raspberries,
    Bloom-down-cheeked peaches,
10   Swart-beaded mulberries,
    Wild free-born cranberries,
    Crab-apples, dewberries,

Pine-apples, blackberries,
Apricots, strawberries;—
All ripe together   15
In summer weather,—
Morns that pass by,
Fair eves that fly;
Come buy, come buy:
Our grapes fresh from the vine,   20
Pomegranates full and fine,
Dates and sharp bullaces,
Rare pears and greengages,
Damsons and bilberries,
Taste them and try: 25
Currants and gooseberries,
Bright-fire-like barberries,
Figs to fill your mouth,
Citrons from the South,
Sweet to tongue and sound to eye: 30
Come buy, come buy."

Evening by evening
Among the brookside rushes,
Laura bowed her head to hear,
Lizzie veiled her blushes: 35
Crouching close together
In the cooling weather,
With clasping arms and cautioning lips,
With tingling cheeks and finger tips.
"Lie close," Laura said,   40
Pricking up her golden head:
"We must not look at goblin men,
We must not buy their fruits:
Who knows upon what soil they fed
Their hungry thirsty roots:"   45
"Come buy," call the goblins
Hobbling down the glen.
"Oh," cried Lizzie. "Laura, Laura,
You should not peep at goblin men."
Lizzie covered up her eyes,   50
Covered close lest they should look:
Laura reared her glossy head,
And whispered like the restless brook:
"Look, Lizzie, look, Lizzie,
Down the glen tramp little men.   55
One hauls a basket,
One bears a plate,

One lugs a golden dish
Of many pounds weight.
60   How fair the vine must grow
Whose grapes are so luscious;
How warm the wind must blow
Thro' those fruit bushes."
"No," said Lizzie: "No, no, no,
65   Their offers should not charm us,
Their evil gifts would harm us."
She thrust a dimpled finger
In each ear, shut eyes and ran:
Curious Laura chose to linger
70   Wondering at each merchant man.
One had a cat's face,
One whisked a tail,
One tramped at a rat's pace,
One crawled like a snail,
75   One like a wombat prowled obtuse and furry,
One like a ratel tumbled hurry skurry.
She heard a voice like voice of doves
Cooing all together:
They sounded kind and full of loves
80   In the pleasant weather.

Laura stretched her gleaming neck
Like a rush-imbedded swan,
Like a lily from the beck,
Like a moonlit poplar branch,
85   Like a vessel at the launch
When its last restraint is gone.

Backwards up the mossy glen
Turned and trooped the goblin men,
With their shrill repeated cry,
90   "Come buy, come buy."
When they reached where Laura was
They stood stock still upon the moss.
Leering at each other,
Brother with queer brother;
95   Signalling each other,
Brother with sly brother.
One set his basket down,
One reared his plate;
One began to weave a crown
100   Of tendrils, leaves and rough nuts brown
(Men sell not such in any town);
One heaved the golden weight

Of dish and fruit to offer her:
"Come buy, come buy," was still their cry.
Laura stared but did not stir,   105
Longed but had no money;
The whisk-tailed merchant bade her taste
In tones as smooth as honey,
The cat-faced purr'd,
The rat-paced spoke a word   110
Of welcome, and the snail-paced even was heard;
One parrot-voiced and jolly
Cried "Pretty Goblin" still for "Pretty Polly:"—
One whistled like a bird.

But sweet-tooth Laura spoke in haste: 115
"Good folk, I have no coin;
To take were to purloin:
I have no copper in my purse,
I have no silver either,
And all my gold is on the furze   120
That shakes in windy weather
Above the rusty heather."
"You have much gold upon your head,"
They answered all together:
"Buy from us with a golden curl."   125
She clipped a precious golden lock,
She dropped a tear more rare than pearl,
Then sucked their fruit globes fair or red:
Sweeter than honey from the rock.
Stronger than man-rejoicing wine,   130
Clearer than water flowed that juice;
She never tasted such before,
How should it cloy with length of use?
She sucked and sucked and sucked the more
Fruits which that unknown orchard bore;   135
She sucked until her lips were sore;
Then flung the emptied rinds away
But gathered up one kernel-stone,
And knew not was it night or day
As she turned home alone.   140

Lizzie met her at the gate
Full of wise upbraidings:
"Dear, you should not stay so late,
Twilight is not good for maidens:
Should not loiter in the glen   145
In the haunts of goblin men.
Do you not remember Jeanie,

How she met them in the moonlight,
Took their gifts both choice and many,
150   Ate their fruits and wore their flowers
Plucked from bowers
Where summer ripens at all hours?
But ever in the noonlight
She pined and pined away:
155   Sought them by night and day,
Found them no more but dwindled and grew grey;
Then fell with the first snow,
While to this day no grass will grow
Where she lies low:
160   I planted daisies there a year ago
That never blow.
You should not loiter so."
"Nay, hush," said Laura:
"Nay, hush, my sister:
165   I ate and ate my fill,
Yet my mouth waters still:
Tomorrow night I will
Buy more:" and kissed her:
"Have done with sorrow;
170   I'll bring you plums tomorrow
Fresh on their mother twigs,
Cherries worth getting;
You cannot think what figs
My teeth have met in,
175   What melons icy-cold
Piled on a dish of gold
Too huge for me to hold,
What peaches with a velvet nap,
Pellucid grapes without one seed:
180   Odorous indeed must be the mead
Whereon they grow, and pure the wave they drink
With lilies at the brink,
And sugar-sweet their sap."

Golden head by golden head,
185   Like two pigeons in one nest
Folded in each other's wings,
They lay down in their curtained bed:
Like two blossoms on one stem,
Like two flakes of new-fall'n snow,
190   Like two wands of ivory
Tipped with gold for awful kings,
Moon and stars gazed in at them,

Wind sang to them lullaby,
Lumbering owls forbore to fly,
Not a bat flapped to and fro   195
Round their rest:
Cheek to cheek and breast to breast
Locked together in one nest.

Early in the morning
When the first cock crowed his warning,   200
Neat like bees, as sweet and busy,
Laura rose with Lizzie:
Fetched in honey, milked the cows,
Aired and set to rights the house,
Kneaded cakes of whitest wheat,   205
Cakes for dainty mouths to eat,
Next churned butter, whipped up cream,
Fed their poultry, sat and sewed;
Talked as modest maidens should:
Lizzie with an open heart,   210
Laura in an absent dream,
One content, one sick in part;
One warbling for the mere bright day's delight,
One longing for the night.

At length slow evening came: 215
They went with pitchers to the reedy brook;
Lizzie most placid in her look,
Laura most like a leaping flame.
They drew the gurgling water from its deep;
Lizzie plucked purple and rich golden flags,   220
Then turning homewards said: "The sunset flushes
Those furthest loftiest crags;
Come, Laura, not another maiden lags,
No wilful squirrel wags,
The beasts and birds are fast asleep,"   225
But Laura loitered still among the rushes
And said the bank was steep.

And said the hour was early still,
The dew not fall'n, the wind not chill:
Listening ever, but not catching   230
The customary cry,
"Come buy, come buy,"
With its iterated jingle
Of sugar-baited words:
Not for all her watching   235
Once discerning even one goblin

Racing, whisking, tumbling, hobbling;
Let alone the herds
That used to tramp along the glen,
240   In groups or single,
Of brisk fruit-merchant men,
Till Lizzie urged, "O Laura, come;
I hear the fruit-call but I dare not look:
You should not loiter longer at this brook:
245   Come with me home.
The stars rise, the moon bends her arc,
Each glowworm winks her spark,
Let us get home before the night grows dark:
For clouds may gather
250   Tho' this is summer weather,
Put out the lights and drench us thro';
Then if we lost our way what should we do?"

Laura turned cold as stone
To find her sister heard that cry alone,
255   That goblin cry,
"Come buy our fruits, come buy."
Must she then buy no more such dainty fruit?
Must she no more such succous pasture find,
Gone deaf and blind?
260   Her tree of life drooped from the root:
She said not one word in her heart's sore ache;
But peering thro' the dimness, nought discerning,
Trudged home, her pitcher dripping all the way;
So crept to bed, and lay
265   Silent till Lizzie slept;
Then sat up in a passionate yearning,
And gnashed her teeth for baulked desire, and wept
As if her heart would break.

Day after day, night after night,
270   Laura kept watch in vain
In sullen silence of exceeding pain.
She never caught again the goblin cry:
"Come buy, come buy:"—
She never spied the goblin men
275   Hawking their fruits along the glen;
But when the noon waved bright
Her hair grew thin and gray;
She dwindled, as the fair full moon doth turn
To swift decay and burn
280   Her fire away.

One day remembering her kernel-stone
She set it by a wall that faced the south:
Dewed it with tears, hoped for a root,
Watched for a waxing shoot,
But there came none;   285
It never saw the sun,
It never felt the trickling moisture run:
While with sunk eyes and faded mouth
She dreamed of melons, as a traveller sees
False waves in desert drouth   290
With shade of leaf-crowned trees,
And burns the thirstier in the sandful breeze.

She no more swept the house,
Tended the fowls or cows,
Fetched honey, kneaded cakes of wheat,   295
Brought water from the brook:
But sat down listless in the chimney-nook
And would not eat.

Tender Lizzie could not bear
To watch her sister's cankerous care   300
Yet not to share.
She night and morning
Caught the goblins' cry:
"Come buy our orchard fruits,
Come buy, come buy:"—   305
Beside the brook, along the glen,
She heard the tramp of goblin men,
The voice and stir
Poor Laura could not hear;
Longed to buy fruit to comfort her,   310
But feared to pay too dear.
She thought of Jeanie in her grave,
Who should have been a bride;
But who for joys brides hope to have
Fell sick and died   315
In her gay prime,
In earliest Winter time,
With the first glazing rime,
With the first snow-fall of crisp Winter time.

Till Laura dwindling   320
Seemed knocking at Death's door:
Then Lizzie weighed no more
Better and worse;
But put a silver penny in her purse,

325   Kissed Laura, crossed the heath with clumps of furze
　　　At twilight, halted by the brook:
　　　And for the first time in her life
　　　Began to listen and look.

　　　Laughed every goblin
330　When they spied her peeping:
　　　Came towards her hobbling,
　　　Flying, running, leaping,
　　　Puffing and blowing,
　　　Chuckling, clapping, crowing,
335　Clucking and gobbling,
　　　Mopping and mowing,
　　　Full of airs and graces,
　　　Pulling wry faces,
　　　Demure grimaces,
340　Cat-like and rat-like,
　　　Ratel- and wombat-like,
　　　Snail-paced in a hurry,
　　　Parrot-voiced and whistler,
　　　Helter skelter, hurry skurry,
345　Chattering like magpies,
　　　Fluttering like pigeons,
　　　Gliding like fishes,—
　　　Hugged her and kissed her,
　　　Squeezed and caressed her:
350　Stretched up their dishes,
　　　Panniers, and plates:
　　　"Look at our apples
　　　　Russet and dun,
　　　Bob at our cherries,
355　Bite at our peaches,
　　　Citrons and dates,
　　　Grapes for the asking,
　　　Pears red with basking
　　　Out in the sun,
360　Plums on their twigs;
　　　Pluck them and suck them,
　　　Pomegranates, figs,"—

　　　"Good folk," said Lizzie,
　　　Mindful of Jeanie:
365　"Give me much and many:"—
　　　Held out her apron,
　　　Tossed them her penny.
　　　"Nay, take a seat with us,
　　　Honour and eat with us,"

They answered grinning: 370
"Our feast is but beginning.
Night yet is early,
Warm and dew-pearly,
Wakeful and starry:
Such fruits as these   375
No man can carry;
Half their bloom would fly,
Half their dew would dry,
Half their flavour would pass by.
Sit down and feast with us,   380
Be welcome guest with us,
Cheer you and rest with us,"—
"Thank you," said Lizzie: "But one waits
At home alone for me:
So without further parleying,   385
If you will not sell me any
Of your fruits tho' much and many,
Give me back my silver penny
I tossed you for a fee."—
They began to scratch their pates.   390
No longer wagging, purring,
But visibly demurring.
Grunting and snarling.
One called her proud,
Cross-grained, uncivil;   395
Their tones waved loud,
Their looks were evil.
Lashing their tails
They trod and hustled her,
Elbowed and jostled her,   400
Clawed with their nails,
Barking, mewing, hissing, mocking,
Tore her gown and soiled her stocking,
Twitched her hair out by the roots,
Stamped upon her tender feet,   405
Held her hands and squeezed their fruits
Against her mouth to make her eat.

White and golden Lizzie stood,
Like a lily in a flood,—
Like a rock of blue-veined stone   410
Lashed by tides obstreperously,—
Like a beacon left alone
In a hoary roaring sea,
Sending up a golden fire,—

415   Like a fruit-crowned orange-tree
              White with blossoms honey-sweet
              Sore beset by wasp and bee,—
              Like a royal virgin town
              Topped with gilded dome and spire
420   Close beleaguerred by a fleet
              Mad to tug her standard down.

              One may lead a horse to water,
              Twenty cannot make him drink.
              Tho' the goblins cuffed and caught her,
425   Coaxed and fought her,
              Bullied and besought her,
              Scratched her, pinched her black as ink,
              Kicked and knocked her,
              Mauled and mocked her,
430   Lizzie uttered not a word;
              Would not open lip from lip
              Lest they should cram a mouthful in:
              But laughed in heart to feel the drip
              Of juice that syruped all her face,
435   And lodged in dimples of her chin.
              And streaked her neck which quaked like curd.
              At last the evil people
              Worn out by her resistance
              Flung back her penny, kicked their fruit
440   Along whichever road they took,
              Not leaving root or stone or shoot;
              Some writhed into the ground,
              Some dived into the brook
              With ring and ripple,
445   Some scudded on the gale without a sound,
              Some vanished in the distance.
              In a smart, ache, tingle,
              Lizzie went her way;
              Knew not was it night or day;
450   Sprang up the bank, tore thro' the furze,
              Threaded copse and dingle,
              And heard her penny jingle
              Bouncing in her purse,
              Its bounce was music to her ear.
455   She ran and ran
              As if she feared some goblin man
              Dogged her with gibe or curse
              Or something worse:
              But not one goblin skurried after,

Nor was she pricked by fear; 460
The kind heart made her windy-paced
That urged her home quite out of breath with haste
And inward laughter.

She cried "Laura," up the garden,
"Did you miss me? 465
Come and kiss me.
Never mind my bruises,
Hug me, kiss me, suck my juices
Squeezed from goblin fruits for you,
Goblin pulp and goblin dew. 470
Eat me, drink me, love me;
Laura, make much of me:
For your sake I have braved the glen
And had to do with goblin merchant men."

Laura started from her chair, 475
Flung her arms up in the air,
Clutched her hair:
"Lizzie, Lizzie, have you tasted
For my sake the fruit forbidden?
Must your light like mine be hidden, 480
Your young life like mine be wasted,
Undone in mine undoing
And ruined in my ruin,
Thirsty, cankered, goblin-ridden?"—
She clung about her sister, 485
Kissed and kissed and kissed her:
Tears once again
Refreshed her shrunken eyes,
Dropping like rain
After long sultry drouth; 490
Shaking with aguish fear, and pain,
She kissed and kissed her with a hungry mouth.
Her lips began to scorch,
That juice was wormwood to her tongue,
She loathed the feast: 495
Writhing as one possessed she leaped and sung,
Rent all her robe, and wrung
Her hands in lamentable haste,
And beat her breast,
Her locks streamed like the torch 500
Borne by a racer at full speed,
Or like the mane of horses in their flight,
Or like an eagle when she stems the light

Straight toward the sun,
505   Or like a caged thing freed,
Or like a flying flag when armies run.

Swift fire spread thro' her veins, knocked at her heart,
Met the fire smouldering there
And overbore its lesser flame;
510   She gorged on bitterness without a name:
Ah! fool, to choose such part
Of soul-consuming care!
Sense failed in the mortal strife:
Like the watch-tower of a town
515   Which an earthquake shatters down,
Like a lightning-stricken mast.
Like a wind-uprooted tree
Spun about,
Like a foam-topped waterspout
520   Cast down headlong in the sea,
She fell at last:
Pleasure past and anguish past,
Is it death or is it life?

Life out of death.
525   That night long Lizzie watched by her,
Counted her pulse's flagging stir,
Felt for her breath,
Held water to her lips, and cooled her face
With tears and fanning leaves:
530   But when the first birds chirped about their eaves,
And early reapers plodded to the place
Of golden sheaves,
And dew-wet grass
Bowed in the morning winds so brisk to pass.
535   And new buds with new day
Opened of cup-like lilies on the stream,
Laura awoke as from a dream,
Laughed in the innocent old way,
Hugged Lizzie but not twice or thrice;
540   Her gleaming locks showed not one thread of grey,
Her breath was sweet as May
And light danced in her eyes.

Days, weeks, months, years
Afterwards, when both were wives
545   With children of their own;
Their mother-hearts beset with fears,
Their lives bound up in tender lives;

Laura would call the little ones
And tell them of her early prime,
Those pleasant days long gone   550
Of not-returning time:
Would talk about the haunted glen,
The wicked, quaint fruit-merchant men,
Their fruits like honey to the throat
But poison in the blood;   555
(Men sell not such in any town:)
Would tell them how her sister stood
In deadly peril to do her good,
And win the fiery antidote:
Then joining hands to little hands   560
Would bid them cling together,
"For there is no friend like a sister
In calm or stormy weather;
To cheer one on the tedious way,
To fetch one if one goes astray,   565
To lift one if one totters down,
To strengthen whilst one stands."

Questions and Ideas for Journaling and Discussion

1. Characterize Lizzie and Laura. How are they alike? How are they different?
2. Who is the redeemer figure? Why?
3. What do the images of the fruits represent?
4. How does the poem depict a clash of gender?
5. A poetic foot is a unit within a line of poetry; it contains stressed and unstressed syllables in varying positions. (For further information, research "poetic meter" on the Internet.) Note the number of poetic feet in each line of the poem and explain what effect is produced. How does the meter influence our overall understanding of the poem?

Writing to Explore and Learn

1. How do you think the theme of sexual desire is expressed in "Goblin Market"?

Luisa Coelho
(b. 1954)

Portuguese in nationality, but born in Angola, Luisa Coelho holds a PhD in Portuguese literature from the University of Utrecht, Netherlands, and has taught at European universities. In addition, she has degrees in German philology and theories of political science. She has mastered eight European languages and has published a number of academic articles. Her works of fiction include *The Love Song of the Whales*, *Riding a Beam of Light*, and *The Spaces of Desire: Erotic Tales*, and she has edited *Intimacies: An Anthology of Portuguese and Brazilian Women's Erotic Tales*. She has taught at the University of Brasilia and at the University of Agostinho Neto in Luanda, Angola.

from *Monique* Trans. Dolores DeLuise and Maria do Carmo de Vasconcelos (2007)

In 1929, French author Marguerite Yourcenar published Alexis, *a novella in the form of a letter from a husband to the wife he had abandoned, explaining his actions. Yourcenar never wrote the answering letter/novella, but expressed a desire that it be written. Coelho took up the challenge and produced* Monique. *A brilliant musician—and homosexual—Alexis felt trapped in a marriage to a woman whom he considered to be good and beautiful but lacking in passion; he knew nothing of her immense creativity and lesbian sexuality that had taught her to long for a passionate sexual relationship.* Monique *allows a rereading of* Alexis *that makes clear his lack of knowledge of his wife of three years. This selection describes the childhood awakening of her sexuality.*

Concerning my body: I only knew about its childhood. Its freedom. The pleasure of feeling the touch of my father's lips on my baby cheeks, and the unending kisses all over my hair that made me so happy. His hands on mine, the sugary smell of his tobacco, the arms that picked me up, and, above all, the gaze that pacified me. The pleasure of caressing the feathers of my talkative birds and pelicans' pouch, that membranous pouch under his beak where he hid his fish. I was the only one who shared his secret. Feeling his closeness on my neck.

My birds were so sweet and their contact gave me so much pleasure. Yes, I knew my body well when I was a child. It wasn't forbidden to me. I could explore it and show it off. The fine long legs that weren't united because of the "*montanha pelada*." The short silky hair that adorned the entrance, so good to touch. The hair that got goose bumps and laughed. Small pleasures that would make you catch your breath while exploring the sacred fire hidden in the tunnel that existed there inside. That's where life was: discovering the immense possibilities of the body.

Let me tell you about my first time. My first sexual pleasure. Like every other thing that I didn't share with my father, I found it by myself. It was completely unexpected; I didn't know there was a physical pleasure that could come all by itself from inside my body. I was flying, suspended in the air. I had already learned the pleasures of watching the sea, of finding birds in their nests, eating salty grains of sand, passing my hand over my skin, and caressing the beard and the wrinkles on the corner of my father's lips as soon as he fell asleep on his chaise lounge in the late afternoon. Those pleasures existed by themselves—they were things, or representations of things, I was able to describe—but that day the pleasure happened all by itself. It came about without any intervention and it existed inside me only. What power! It was an experience that took me over.

There was a tree in my garden, more friendly than the others, who allowed me to ride her, galloping. It was a chestnut tree, *sloanea,* whose thick branches, cascading down to the ground, made it easy to climb, and where my father had hung two ropes that made up a swing. When it rained hard, I liked listening to it as I sat on the branches surrounded by the leaves. The rain's conversation became clear and understandable, more organic. By nightfall on that day, I hadn't yet returned home. Suspended on the swing by the legs with my head down, I propelled my body back and forth and saw the garden upside down. The shadows projected a universe into that space. With the movements that I made by swinging my body, I approached the ground and immediately glided away from it again. Then, after that exhilarating and sensuous dance, when I wanted to get up so I could sit over the seat, the effort of pulling my body slowly erect made me feel a sudden enormous pleasure. It began inside the labia, covered by small hair, animating a tunnel that I was able to imagine but didn't yet know very well. My heart was in that spot. I pulsated from pleasure. It invited me to become abandoned, to feel it and be closer to my body. Unexpected wildness invaded first the lower part of my abdomen and then spread throughout my body. It affected my head the most, hanging down as though it weren't attached to the rest of me. For a while I was able to balance comfort and surprise. Pleasure. I tried once again and still again, but it never happened a second time. It was a revelation and a revolution. Something had looked inside me and understood sensations I didn't know I had and couldn't control. This discovery distracted my attention from my own body and focused it onto the bodies of others. I wanted to talk to my father about my discovery, but I didn't know the Latin words that could describe it *verbo adverbum*. So I kept everything to myself because the words I knew couldn't describe such an amplitude of intensity. It wasn't modesty, no, it was that I didn't want to spoil the importance of this memory with inappropriate description. Describing too much disturbs the described. Later on, when I did learn the Latin words that could describe what happened, my father wasn't available to me.

I was able to understand all this much better when I read *The School of Women,* a work that revealed the secrets of forbidden emotions, said to have been written by a woman in the seventeenth century in Castilian and then translated into Latin. This was probably the only experience I didn't share with my father throughout my entire childhood because immediately afterwards I became an adolescent, and we became separated by all the taboos of the adult world, which kept us from remaining close. In our conversations.

After I moved to France, I had to hide my body. And my emotions as well, but all I could do was disguise them. My grandparents had no bodies. They were only shadows. Undemonstrative and uncommunicative. They never touched me and avoided looking directly into my eyes. Everything took place in an oblique way. It was as if the denizens of that house existed only to contemplate the past, immobile, like the oil portrait hanging over the fireplace in one of the badly lit and shadowy rooms: A young blond man in military uniform looked straight ahead, gazing directly at the painter and the world of the living that wanted to view him. He had no secrets. The secret was that he disappeared. He had stepped out of himself, overflowing the picture frame, filling up the house, leaving no empty spaces that could contain my presence. So I had to pretend, to act as if I weren't there. To hide my repugnance for the food too acidic, sheets too harsh, water too cold, furniture too austere, glances too critical, tea too much perfumed, clothing without age. To hide my pleasure in well ripened fruit, truly profound books, tranquilizing dreams of heavy rains, letters from my father, family portraits, walks along the sea, touching the horses' manes, and the awakening of my senses.

On a calm fall day, I left for boarding school. My grandparents were sitting in the back seat of the car and I sat next to the driver. My grandmother had told me, quite early that day at breakfast, that I needed to earn the right to receive knowledge. The desire to know, *libido sciendi,* had been born along with me, and I didn't have to cultivate it. My grandmother didn't mean knowledge of the world as a way to attain knowledge of oneself, but she meant knowledge of the world as a way to accept suffering. To learn the life of Jesus and the Saints and the History of Humanity filled with wars, debts, and barbarity. The geography of lost feelings and the mathematical calculations that subtracted days until the moment of the Last Judgment. To learn to live in the future where we would have the status of *animarum post mortem,* when we would already have been judged by God and resting in peace.

The Catholic boarding school didn't make me accept suffering for the simple reason that I had not yet truly found it. I had accepted my mother's death well, and leaving my island had become my ritual of initiation. It was the search for the Firebird that was to mark my passage from adolescence to adulthood. Boarding school made me discover the indifference that was able to dampen my passion, my internal agitation. I never forgot my island, but it remained forever in my childhood. I became another person and began to understand how rare precious things were.

We had to get up early at school. Very early. The sun was still asleep when we awakened tired. We met the new day when a light was suddenly switched on and a prayer—resembling a psalm of the suffering—was mechanically recited aloud by the nun who slept near us. We wore dark uniforms that hid all our femininity. Our bodies needed to be protected from the serpent, they admonished us. He copulated with young virgin women, the cause of the fall from paradise. And in the mornings, above all, there was the mass. Half asleep, we used to go to the small, dark, silent chapel where the candles also seemed sleepy as they flickered reflections of the living dead on the images of the saints.

We listened to the chaplain's prayers and responded automatically, charmed by the music, its cadence, the sonority of the words, and the aroma of sugar and cinnamon. Above all the scent. I remember the gentle warmth filling the air that never left the sacred places during the summer. I can also remember the perfume of the grass, "hunting-devil," the *millepertuis,* that exhales a sugary fragrance of incense that still haunts my memory today. The image of the Virgin with her Son devoured us with their eyes. It was imperative that we not deceive her. We all went through the same motions and we all had the same fears—that we wouldn't deserve their love. On our knees, mouths open, eyes closed, we accepted invasion by the pleasures of the senses. The sensation of a body on our mouths. Our salvation. *Hoc est enim corpus meum.*

Mass was brief; erotic religious ecstasy was long. After the service, we had to receive the chaplain's blessing. He approached us and we kissed his hand. Then he asked us about the state of our souls, and with his man's hand touched our hearts in the place where he could feel our small breasts perfectly. That began to want to grow. Later, we laughed nervously about that intimacy, already waiting impatiently for the end of the next mass. He was our only contact with the world of men. He was the one who chose us, but we stood in line to receive his blessing and unchaste caresses, making us accomplices in a pleasure that we ardently desired to know.

The act of confession was another privileged moment when each of us had the man to herself for that brief space of time. We couldn't make him out very well and he couldn't see us clearly either. All these dark, dense environments helped bring us closer to sin and salvation. We were almost there, but still, there we were not. The soft, sibilant whisper, the lasciviousness of shared sinful intimacy. We could make out his body, especially those hands that we knew so well, his breath, and the noise of his breathing that spoke to our hearts and emotions, and we took great pleasure from the act of telling him what he wanted to hear. He was the one who guided our confessions: what we had done, fantasized, or simply invented at that moment—imaginary things. In that chapel there was no anonymity, unlike confession in any other church. Our chaplain, who should have personified chastity, took part in our game as we imagined ourselves as the Marquesa of Merteuil:

"The good priest caused me such deep suffering that I came to the conclusion that pleasure, too, ought to be extreme; and with the desire to learn about pleasure, then came the desire to taste it." You know, Alexis, young women are only mysterious to boys their own age; mature men, they understand women very well. On the other hand, women of your age are incomprehensible to men, as you may well testify.

After attending mass and all its ritual sensuality, we had to return to the dormitory to make our beds and organize our clothing. The newborn day found us a bit ecstatic. Each of us took care of her own space, which was also the communal space. It was difficult for a young only child to share the intimacy of her sleeping quarters with others that she didn't know from Adam. It was during those moments that I think I understood my grandparents' reason for always wanting me to put things in their rightful order—so that I would understand that there was no place for me in France. My space remained in Sainte-Pierre. I had to conquer this new space by suffering, as usual. My life, like religion, was founded on sacrifice and suffering. We left the dorm and went to the refectory, always in silence. Breakfast was brief. We ate, silently, standing, frugally, to the sound of religious music.

We had to get to our classes quickly and begin our studies. We learned a little bit of everything that could be useful to a young woman destined for marriage, children, and becoming the owner and manager of a house. We learned to be docile and obedient, suffer in silence, and love God with all our strength. The kingdom of heaven was a future reality, but we had to earn it here on earth. To the nuns, the present time was already the end of time although its terminus was yet to occur. Hypocrisy and contradiction screamed at us from all sides, but we weren't able to discuss it.

At noon we ate, and after lunch we were busy with classes until five o'clock. Classics—language and literature—was the discipline that I liked the best. I imagined Diderot's nun singing litanies, rope around her neck, in the middle of the chapel, at night. In my mind, Susanne was a race in chiaroscuro that followed me; and that, along with my grandmother's blessing, was what I had to remind myself about the dangers of loneliness. Her body was always falling into apparent death. Pleasure and pain revealed themselves as inseparable.

After classes, we had a break. Before we said the rosary, we were allowed to stay together for a while, and we talked about our lives. What brought us together was what time would unearth about the mysteries of the body. We liked to solve the riddle of our future by comparing it to the act of peeling an apple, which, we thought, could reveal how close we were to marriage. The wedding was our future, and the apple, we already knew from Paradise in the Bible. It reminded us that we would always face the need to choose. To choose not between freedom and dependency, but between the quality and the level of our spiritual submission. Freedom only existed within us, we had to keep it hidden. The only way we would be able to discover our bodies was through the signals it sent us. At my grandparents' home all body language was censored. Blood, menstruation, pregnancy. Swollen breasts, pimples on the skin, hair. Although maternity was seldom discussed, the suffering of childbirth was inscribed in our memories. Fear spread without words. My classmates' mothers never spoke of it, and neither of my grandmothers did either. Engraved on women's nature was the understanding that we mustn't complain. We could tell from the expressions of acceptance on their faces that it was not a joyous act. The representations of women we were able to see were bodiless—fully dressed, shrouded by veils. They were mothers and sisters. They were the faces of acceptance and renunciation. Thus: Woman.

The nun who slept nearby us was always dressed. Even in the middle of the night, when one of us who wasn't feeling well called to her, she would suddenly appear all dressed up like a wandering ghost. We referred to our bodies as though they didn't belong to us; they weren't part of who we were. We did-not look at them because there wasn't enough privacy. Even the mirrors were so small that we could only see our faces in them; our bodies weren't surfaces that could be reflected. And my body had grown and changed so much that I could not recognize my childhood body in the shape I perceived under my clothing. I was living in a body that wasn't mine.

The bodies of others—men—existed in images. In art etchings and religious books. The images in the chapel: Christ was always naked on the cross. And there was, above all, Saint Sebastian, his body so beautiful, naked, ripped up by arrows, his clothing spread out on the floor, and his expression so lost, with his sex covered only by a loincloth, a very fine white cloth, that hid everything we wanted so much to see. What was there underneath the cloth that we weren't able to see? Each of us had our own ideas and fantasized individually about the hidden parts in those images of masculine bodies. This forbidden act caused us some fear, and I think it was more than anything else the fear of disillusion. But fear was only a guide that served to accentuate our refusal to submit. What they kept hidden from us actually awakened our desire.

I'm going to try to describe to you, Alexis, what existed in the imaginary of my fifteen-year-old mind, under the veil that covered Saint Sebastian. During the night I dreamed of his body. On my bed, I saw an image step out of Van Dyck's painting. It was the young Roman officer, Saint Sebastian, tied to a tree. His body was full of holes made by arrows, and he suffered. The suffering of a man touches a young woman's own fragility. It throws the world out of balance. I approached him and suffered along with his injured modesty. I liberated him from his martyrdom, removing the arrows and caressing his wounds. I raised the cloth that hid his difference and discovered another arrow—much bigger and more pointed. I woke up frightened.

After dinner we still had to go to the chapel for a little while to say our last prayers before we went to bed. During the day, we had been together but were very isolated in our own tasks and thoughts. A complicit glance, a partly hidden smile, a clandestine message written on a scrap of paper was our way of staying in touch, of not losing our sense of reality, of weaving the bonds of friendship. Getting back to the dormitory at the end of the day, we took off very few clothes because we needed to keep the rest of them on underneath our nightgowns.

I can confess now, Alexis, that it was because of this former promiscuity that our mutual nighttime loneliness was unbearable to me. This was the reason I asked you to turn out the lights; I was afraid you would see my desire. But you were a sensitive man, my dear friend, and therefore truly good, and always gave in to my whims.

But, as I was saying, the nun watched over us, and as soon as we got into bed, she turned off the light and began to prepare her own body for the night. Her bed was separated from ours by a paneled screen that gave her a little privacy. We heard the cold water run. She made her ablutions, purifying herself so she could give her body to the god of her dreams. We imagined that she allowed her hands to touch her neck, taking pleasure in it. We would have liked to have seen her hair scattered over her shoulders and the color of the skin between her breasts, in that very place that no look had yet touched. And we tried to make our eyes become used to the dark, so that we could make out her shadows and contours. We guessed more than we could really see. We exchanged silent and suggestive glances that betrayed our desire. That desire that had to be invented, constructed, because we couldn't attribute a real shape to it.

Later, during the night, when the great majority of girls slept, there were always a few who sought each other out. Who explored the nooks and crannies of bodies they could only see with their hands, their mouths, and their breathing. Identical bodies but not the same. Bodies that could have pleasure without a man's intercession. Petal-like skin appeared from between the sheets and aroused the workings of desire. A moan or a nightmare. The fear and the loneliness. The absence of the maternal kiss. Of a true caress. A complicity that we never spoke about the next day because pleasure had no place in our discourse. When dawn arrived, our bodies became transformed once more into objects of morality.

However, at school there were rumors that contained the truths that we needed to believe in. The rumors spoke about the nocturnal love between a nun and a student. Because of the magnitude of the scandal, this rumor allowed them the privilege of distance and respect. They didn't sleep in my dormitory, but I knew them well; they were both names and faces to me. The young woman was pointed out while people talked about the most daring details of the lost paradise of her body, but I never heard a single word from her own mouth. It was better that way because it conferred more mystery to my desire, which was based on absence. She was the only one of us who had something real between her legs, because she had dared to challenge her body's absent identity by transgressing. When I mentioned this rumor during confession, the chaplain, who assuredly knew about it first hand, referred me to the teaching of Father Morel, the priest in *The Nun*: "What is it about the caresses of a woman that could represent danger to another woman?" I thought about it and decided that if there were something forbidden about it, it was not because the body of one woman desired the body of another woman, but because one of those women was the wife of Christ. Was this adultery, I asked myself from within my internal chaos. The chaplain then instructed me that a young woman must reserve her love, first, for God and, next, for her husband. He didn't talk to me about bodies. The nun took the place of God in his absence. The ninth commandment had not been transgressed.

During summer vacations, I returned to my grandparents' home to spend three months relaxing. Sometimes my father was there also, and we were able to come together only on the realities of the past because everything in our present kept us apart. We took very long walks. We observed nature, acknowledged its changes, its beauty, and listened to the industrious movement of the bees. We focused our attention on the beehives. We could only see them from afar and that distance invested their communal existence with another meaning. They were a real family and we envied them. When I felt that my father was nearby and available, I asked him to tell me a story as if I were still a child. He very much liked to tell stories, wondrous tales, because the words of those timeless stories gave him comfort and security, he who had so much need of internal tranquility from *perpetuum mobili,* erratic and without rest. Simultaneously, because time's transformations on me hurt him, this return to my childhood helped him continue on his way. He didn't recognize me in my adolescent body, and he couldn't bear to touch me or approach my face with his beard to kiss me. He pretended to caress me then turned away immediately. My new body had become an obstacle that placed itself between our affections, and I felt his nostalgia for our former spontaneity. It hurt both of us to think that those moments of plenitude would never return.

Questions and Ideas for Journaling and Discussion

1. Define poetry and prose. Prose may become "poetic" when heightened emotion is the topic of discourse. Identify places in the text where it seems more like poetry than prose.
2. Freud first identified childhood sexuality and pointed out that it is often associated with games children play with others. Monique is a child who has no playmates; why is the swing an appropriate image?
3. Do you believe that such sexual experiences exist for children in real life?
4. What is the narrator's attitude toward lesbian sexuality?

Angela Costa*

"Gauguin's Stars" (for Laura Nyro Who Loved Gauguin) (1996)

Costa's poem evokes the artistry of Paul Gauguin,[2] tenets of eastern belief, and images of natural landscapes to explore the significance and relatedness of sexuality, creativity, and spirituality. A mystical celebration of pleasure, imagination, and the body, Costa's sensual vision offers a way in which to think through and beyond the dominant discourses on sex, sexuality, and gender.

these are not regular stars
these are Gauguin's stars
corresponding to the seven
interior stars and we

feel kundalini rise until
the dragon's fire is in our eyes
and we feel love as the hot thing
the penetrating warmth

the great eastern sun inside.

we are full of moon tide and
cradle rock in the realm of rivers
and wetness we sail oceans and expanse
we speak through gesture and objects left

in the hidden language of watermarks.

we climb upper deck realm
of mountains realm
of peaks where we love and lay
on straw mats

to contemplate the after midnight sky.

the blue of our flame splits

---

[2]Paul Gauguin (1848–1903) was a prominent French post-Impressionist painter whose career was distinguished by his exotic paintings of the inhabitants of Tahiti.

*See page 49 for author biography.

the shadow and the darkness opens up
no longer a scary black but lush
sexual, erotic

like hands over velvet.

voices whisper from unseen lips
this is it   this is it
higher   higher
to the place where great imaginations reach
higher.

to where the bird wings brush
against your face

this is the place of dreams
the manifestation of love song

and lullaby.

free from thoughts of yesterday and tomorrow's
expectation inside
the perpetual now
of a Gauguin star

lost in the light of kisses that
amplify all dimensions of
time and you
feel like forever

to me.

Questions and Ideas for Journaling and Discussion

1. Strong figurative language (similes, metaphors, symbols, and images) is usually concrete, brief, and interesting. Think about the sources from which the images are drawn, and the types of metaphors and similes. What are the patterns in this figurative language?
2. Where are the images located and what are the connections among the related images?

Writing to Explore and Learn

1. How does the poem communicate the speaker's state of mind? Consider the function of the artist Gauguin, the eastern elements, and the natural landscapes.
2. Research the life and music of Laura Nyro. Why do you think that the poet dedicated the poem to her?
3. Discuss the ways in which Costa represents sexual union as a mystical, inspirational, as well as physical act.
4. Compare and contrast representations of sexual desire in Costa's "Gauguin's Stars" with those in Rossetti's "Goblin Market."

Angela Carter
(1940–1992)

"It's not very pleasant for women to find out about how they are represented in the world," said Angela Carter in response to a question about her controversial work, *The Sadeian Woman and the Ideology of Pornography* (1978). One of the most original writers of our time, Carter was born in Eastbourne, England, to a Scottish father and British mother and grew up in south London. Both an essayist and a fiction writer, Carter wrote mysterious, magical realist and subversive fiction and essays of feminist and socialist persuasions. Seeing femininity as "male impersonation," Carter challenged traditional female icons and narratives with a bold "demythologizing" style. Notable works include *The Magic Toyshop* (1967) and *The Bloody Chamber* (1979), both of which have been made into films.

"The Company of Wolves" (1976)

In this short story, Carter reimagines the fairy tale "Little Red Riding Hood" as a feminist and Gothic story of seduction, danger, and desire. In a daring twist on the original tale, Carter, in this sexually charged retelling, draws out an eroticism of violence and beauty in gender and sexual formations as the young girl owns her newfound sexual power by destabilizing the predatory advances of the wolf.

One beast and only one howls in the woods by night.

The wolf is carnivore incarnate and he's as cunning as he is ferocious; once he's had a taste of flesh then nothing else will do.

At night, the eyes of wolves shine like candle flames, yellowish, reddish, but that is because the pupils of their eyes fatten on darkness and catch the light from your lantern to flash it back to you—red for danger; if a wolf's eyes reflect only moonlight, then they gleam a cold and unnatural green, a mineral, a piercing colour. If the benighted traveller spies those luminous, terrible sequins stitched suddenly on the black thickets, then he knows he must run, if fear has not struck him stock-still.

But those eyes are all you will be able to glimpse of the forest assassins as they cluster invisibly round your smell of meat as you go through the wood unwisely late. They will be like shadows, they will be like wraiths, grey members of a congregation of nightmare; hark! his long, wavering howl . . . an aria of fear made audible.

The wolfsong is the sound of the rending you will suffer, in itself a murdering.

It is winter and cold weather. In this region of mountain and forest, there is now nothing for the wolves to eat. Goats and sheep are locked up in the byre, the deer departed for the remaining pasturage on the southern slopes—wolves grow lean and famished. There is so little flesh on them that you could count the starveling ribs through their pelts, if they gave you time before they pounced. Those slavering jaws; the lolling tongue; the rime of saliva on the grizzled chops—of all the teeming perils of the night and the forest, ghosts, hobgoblins, ogres that grill babies upon gridirons, witches that fatten their captives in cages for cannibal tables, the wolf is worst for he cannot listen to reason.

You are always in danger in the forest, where no people are. Step between the portals of the great pines where the shaggy branches tangle about you, trapping the unwary traveller in nets as if the vegetation itself were in a plot with the wolves who live there, as though the wicked trees go fishing on behalf of their friends—step between the gateposts of the forest with the greatest trepidation and infinite precautions, for if you stray from the path for one instant, the wolves will eat you. They are grey as famine, they are as unkind as plague.

The grave-eyed children of the sparse villages always carry knives with them when they go out to tend the little flocks of goats that provide the homesteads with acrid milk and rank, maggoty cheeses. Their knives are half as big as they are, the blades are sharpened daily.

But the wolves have ways of arriving at your own hearthside. We try and try but sometimes we cannot keep them out. There is no winter's night the cottager does not fear to see a lean, grey, famished snout questing under the door, and there was a woman once bitten in her own kitchen as she was straining the macaroni.

Fear and flee the wolf; for, worst of all, the wolf may be more than he seems.

There was a hunter once, near here, that trapped a wolf in a pit. This wolf had massacred the sheep and goats; eaten up a mad old man who used to live by himself in a hut halfway up the mountain and sing to Jesus all day; pounced on a girl looking after the sheep, but she made such a commotion that men came with rifles and scared him away and tried to track him into the forest but he was cunning and easily gave them the slip. So this hunter dug a pit and put a duck in it, for bait, all alive-oh; and he covered the pit with straw smeared with wolf dung. Quack, quack! went the duck and a wolf came slinking out of the forest, a big one, a heavy one, he weighed as much as a grown man and the straw gave way beneath him—into the pit he tumbled. The hunter jumped down after him, slit his throat, cut off all his paws for a trophy.

And then no wolf at all lay in front of the hunter but the bloody trunk of a man, headless, footless, dying, dead.

A witch from up the valley once turned an entire wedding party into wolves because the groom had settled on another girl. She used to order them to visit her, at night, from spite, and they would sit and howl around her cottage for her, serenading her with their misery.

Not so very long ago, a young woman in our village married a man who vanished clean away on her wedding night. The bed was made with new sheets and the bride lay down in it; the groom said he was going out to relieve himself, insisted on it, for the sake of decency, and she drew the coverlet up to her chin and she lay there. And she waited and she waited and then she waited again—surely he's been gone a long time? Until she jumps up in bed and shrieks to hear a howling, coming on the wind from the forest.

That long-drawn, wavering howl has, for all its fearful resonance, some inherent sadness in it, as if the beasts would love to be less beastly if only they knew how and never cease to mourn their own condition. There is a vast melancholy in the canticles of the wolves, melancholy infinite as the forest, endless as these long nights of winter and yet that ghastly sadness, that mourning for their own irremediable appetites, can never move the heart for not one phrase in it hints at the possibility of redemption; grace could not come to the wolf from its own despair, only through some external mediator, so that, sometimes, the beast will look as if he half welcomes the knife that despatches him.

The young woman's brothers searched the outhouses and the haystacks but never found any remains so the sensible girl dried her eyes and found herself another husband not too shy to piss into a pot who spent the nights indoors. She gave him a pair of bonny babies and all went right as a trivet until, one freezing night, the night of the solstice, the hinge of the year when things do not fit together as well as they should, the longest night, her first good man came home again.

A great thump on the door announced him as she was stirring the soup for the father of her children and she knew him the moment she lifted the latch to him although it was years since she'd worn black for him and now he was in rags and his hair hung down his back and never saw a comb, alive with lice.

'Here I am again, missus,' he said.' Get me my bowl of cabbage and be quick about it.'

Then her second husband came in with wood for the fire and when the first one saw she'd slept with another man and, worse, clapped his red eyes on her little children who'd crept into the kitchen to see what all the din was about, he shouted: 'I wish I were a wolf again, to teach this whore a lesson!' So a wolf he instantly became and tore off the eldest boy's left foot before he was chopped up with the hatchet they used for chopping logs. But when the wolf lay bleeding and gasping its last, the pelt peeled off again and he was just as he had been, years ago, when he ran away from his marriage bed, so that she wept and her second husband beat her.

They say there's an ointment the Devil gives you that turns you into a wolf the minute you rub it on. Or, that he was born feet first and had a wolf for his father and his torso is a man's but his legs and genitals are a wolf's. And he has a wolf's heart.

Seven years is a werewolf's natural span but if you burn his human clothing you condemn him to wolfishness for the rest of his life, so old wives hereabouts think it some protection to throw a hat or an apron at the werewolf, as if clothes made the man. Yet by the eyes, those phosphorescent eyes, you know him in all his shapes; the eyes alone unchanged by metamorphosis.

Before he can become a wolf, the lycanthrope strips stark naked. If you spy a naked man among the pines, you must run as if the Devil were after you.

It is midwinter and the robin, the friend of man, sits on the handle of the gardener's spade and sings. It is the worst time in all the year for wolves but this strong-minded child insists she will go off through the wood. She is quite sure the wild beasts cannot harm her although, well-warned, she lays a carving knife in the basket her mother has packed with cheeses. There is a bottle of harsh liquor distilled from brambles; a batch of flat oatcakes baked on the hearth-stone; a pot or two of jam. The flaxen-haired girl will take these delicious gifts to a reclusive grandmother so old the burden of her years is crushing her to death. Granny lives two hours' trudge through the winter woods; the child wraps herself up in her thick shawl, draws it over her head. She steps into her stout wooden shoes; she is dressed and ready and it is Christmas Eve. The ma-lign door of the solstice still swings upon its hinges but she has been too much loved ever to feel scared.

Children do not stay young for long in this savage country. There are no toys for them to play with so they work hard and grow wise but this one, so pretty and the youngest of her family, a little late-comer, had been indulged by her mother and the grandmother who'd knitted her the red shawl that, today, has the ominous if brilliant look of blood on snow. Her breasts have just begun to swell; her hair is like lint, so fair it hardly makes a shadow on her pale fore-head; her cheeks are an emblematic scarlet and white and she has just started her woman's bleeding, the clock inside her that will strike, henceforward, once a month.

She stands and moves within the invisible pentacle of her own virginity. She is an unbroken egg; she is a sealed vessel; she has inside her a magic space the entrance to which is shut tight with a plug of membrane; she is a closed sys-tem; she does not know how to shiver. She has her knife and she is afraid of nothing.

Her father might forbid her, if he were home, but he is away in the forest, gathering wood, and her mother cannot deny her.

The forest closed upon her like a pair of jaws.

There is always something to look at in the forest, even in the middle of winter—the huddled mounds of birds, succumbed to the lethargy of the season, heaped on the creaking boughs and too forlorn to sing; the bright frills of the winter fungi on the blotched trunks of the trees; the cuneiform slots of rabbits and deer, the herringbone tracks of the birds, a hare as lean as a rasher of bacon streaking across the path where the thin sunlight dapples the russet brakes of last year's bracken.

When she heard the freezing howl of a distant wolf, her practised hand sprang to the handle of her knife, but she saw no sign of a wolf at all, nor of a naked man, neither, but then she heard a clattering among the brushwood and there sprang on to the path a fully clothed one, a very handsome young one, in the green coat and wideawake hat of a hunter, laden with carcasses of game birds. She had her hand on her knife at the first rustle of twigs but he laughed with a flash of white teeth when he saw her and made her a comic yet flattering little bow; she'd never seen such a fine fellow before, not among the rustic clowns of her native vil-lage. So on they went together, through the thickening light of the afternoon.

Soon they were laughing and joking like old friends. When he offered to carry her basket, she gave it to him although her knife was in it because he told her his rifle would protect them. As the day darkened, it began to snow again; she felt the first flakes settle on her eyelashes but now there was only half a mile to go and there would be a fire, and hot tea, and a welcome, a warm one, surely, for the dashing huntsman as well as for herself.

This young man had a remarkable object in his pocket. It was a compass. She looked at the little round glass face in the palm of his hand and watched the wavering needle with a vague wonder. He assured her this compass had taken him safely through the wood on his hunting trip because the needle always told him with perfect accuracy where the north was. She did not believe it; she knew she should never leave the path on the way through the wood or else she would be lost instantly. He laughed at her again; gleaming trails of spittle clung to his teeth. He said, if he plunged off the path into the forest that surrounded them, he could guarantee to arrive at her grandmother's house a good quarter of an hour before she did, plotting his way through the undergrowth with his compass, while she trudged the long way, along the winding path.

I don't believe you. Besides, aren't you afraid of the wolves?

He only tapped the gleaming butt of his rifle and grinned.

Is it a bet? he asked her. Shall we make a game of it? What will you give me if I get to your grandmother's house before you?

What would you like? she asked disingenuously.

A kiss.

Commonplaces of a rustic seduction; she lowered her eyes and blushed.

He went through the undergrowth and took her basket with him but she forgot to be afraid of the beasts, although now the moon was rising, for she wanted to dawdle on her way to make sure the handsome gentleman would win his wager.

Grandmother's house stood by itself a little way out of the village. The freshly falling snow blew in eddies about the kitchen garden and the young man stepped delicately up the snowy path to the door as if he were reluctant to get his feet wet, swinging his bundle of game and the girl's basket and humming a little tune to himself.

There is a faint trace blood on his chin; he has been snacking on his catch.

He rapped upon the panels with his knuckles.

Aged and frail, granny is three-quarters succumbed to the mortality the ache in her bones promises her and almost ready to give in entirely. A boy came out from the village to build up her hearth for the night an hour ago and the kitchen crackles with busy firelight. She has her Bible for company, she is a pious old woman. She is propped up on several pillows in the bed set into the wall peasant-fashion, wrapped up in the patchwork quilt she made before she was married, more years ago than she cares to remember. Two china spaniels with liver-coloured blotches on their coats and black noses sit on either side of the fireplace. There is a bright rug of woven rags on the pantiles. The grandfather clock ticks away her eroding time.

We keep the wolves outside by living well.

He rapped upon the panels with his hairy knuckles.

It is your granddaughter, he mimicked in a high soprano.

Lift up the latch and walk in, my darling.

You can tell them by their eyes, eyes of a beast of prey, nocturnal, devastating eyes as red as a wound; you can hurl your Bible at him and your apron after, granny, you thought that was a sure prophylactic against these infernal vermin . . . now call on Christ and his mother and all the angels in heaven to protect you but it won't do you any good.

His feral muzzle is sharp as a knife; he drops his golden burden of gnawed pheasant on the table and puts down your dear girl's basket, too. Oh, my God, what have you done with her?

Off with his disguise, that coat of forest-coloured cloth, the hat with the feather tucked into the ribbon; his matted hair streams down his white shirt and she can see the lice moving in it. The sticks in the hearth shift and hiss; night and the forest has come into the kitchen with darkness tangled in its hair.

He strips off his shirt. His skin is the colour and texture of vellum. A crisp stripe of hair runs down his belly, his nipples are ripe and dark as poison fruit but he's so thin you could count the ribs under his skin if only he gave you the time. He strips off his trousers and she can see how hairy his legs are. His genitals, huge. Ah! huge.

The last thing the old lady saw in all this world was a young man, eyes like cinders, naked as a stone, approaching her bed.

The wolf is carnivore incarnate.

When he had finished with her, he licked his chops and quickly dressed himself again, until he was just as he had been when he came through her door. He burned the inedible hair in the fireplace and wrapped the bones up in a napkin that he hid away under the bed in the wooden chest in which he found a clean pair of sheets. These he carefully put on the bed instead of the tell-tale stained ones he stowed away in the laundry basket. He plumped up the pillows and shook out the patchwork quilt, he picked up the Bible from the floor, closed it and laid it on the table. All was as it had been before except that grandmother was gone. The sticks twitched in the grate, the clock ticked and the young man sat patiently, deceitfully beside the bed in granny's nightcap.

Rat-a-tap-tap.

Who's there, he quavers in granny's antique falsetto.

Only your granddaughter.

So she came in, bringing with her a flurry of snow that melted in tears on the tiles, and perhaps she was a little disappointed to see only her grandmother sitting beside the fire. But then he flung off the blanket and sprang to the door, pressing his back against it so that she could not get out again.

The girl looked round the room and saw there was not even the indentation of a head on the smooth cheek of the pillow and how, for the first time she'd seen it so, the Bible lay closed on the table. The tick of the clock cracked like a whip. She wanted her knife from her basket but she did not dare reach for it because his eyes were fixed upon her—huge eyes that now seemed to shine with a unique, interior light, eyes the size of saucers, saucers full of Greek fire, diabolic phosphorescence.

What big eyes you have.

All the better to see you with.

No trace at all of the old woman except for a tuft of white hair that had caught in the bark of an unburned log. When the girl saw that, she knew she was in danger of death.

Where is my grandmother?

There's nobody here but we two, my darling.

Now a great howling rose up all around them, near, very near, as close as the kitchen garden, the howling of a multitude of wolves; she knew the worst wolves are hairy on the inside and she shivered, in spite of the scarlet shawl she pulled more closely round herself as if it could protect her although it was as red as the blood she must spill.

Who has come to sing us carols, she said.

Those are the voices of my brothers, darling; I love the company of wolves. Look out of the window and you'll see them.

Snow half-caked the lattice and she opened it to look into the garden. It was a white night of moon and snow; the blizzard whirled round the gaunt, grey beasts who squatted on their haunches among the rows of winter cabbage, pointing their sharp snouts to the moon and howling as if their hearts would break. Ten wolves; twenty wolves—so many wolves she could not count them, howling in concert as if demented or deranged. Their eyes reflected the light from the kitchen and shone like a hundred candles.

It is very cold, poor things, she said; no wonder they howl so.

She closed the window on the wolves' threnody and took off her scarlet shawl, the colour of poppies, the colour of sacrifices, the colour of her menses, and, since her fear did her no good, she ceased to be afraid.

What shall I do with my shawl?

Throw it on the fire, dear one. You won't need it again.

She bundled up her shawl and threw it on the blaze, which instantly consumed it. Then she drew her blouse over her head; her small breasts gleamed as if the snow had invaded the room.

What shall I do with my blouse?

Into the fire with it, too, my pet.

The thin muslin went flaring up the chimney like a magic bird and now off came her skirt, her woollen stockings, her shoes, and on to the fire they went, too, and were gone for good. The firelight shone through the edges of her skin; now she was clothed only in her untouched integument of flesh. Thus dazzling, naked she combed out her hair with her fingers; her hair looked white as the snow outside. Then went directly to the man with red eyes in whose unkempt mane the lice moved; she stood up on tiptoe and unbuttoned the collar of his shirt.

What big arms you have.

All the better to hug you with.

Every wolf in the world now howled a prothalamion outside the window as she freely gave the kiss she owed him.

What big teeth you have!

She saw how his jaw began to slaver and the room was full of the clamour of the forest's Liebestod but the wise child never flinched, even when he answered:

All the better to eat you with.

The girl burst out laughing; she knew she was nobody's meat. She laughed at him full in the face, she ripped off his shirt for him and flung it into the fire, in the fiery wake of her own discarded clothing. The flames danced like dead souls on Walpurgisnacht and the old bones under the bed set up a terrible clattering but she did not pay them any heed.

Carnivore incarnate, only immaculate flesh appeases him.

She will lay his fearful head on her lap and she will pick out the lice from his pelt and perhaps she will put the lice into her mouth and eat them, as he will bid her, as she would do in a savage marriage ceremony.

The blizzard will die down.

The blizzard died down, leaving the mountains as randomly covered with snow as if a blind woman had thrown a sheet over them, the upper branches of the forest pines limed, creaking, swollen with the fall.

Snowlight, moonlight, a confusion of paw-prints.

All silent, all still.

Midnight; and the clock strikes. It is Christmas Day, the werewolves' birthday, the door of the solstice stands wide open; let them all sink through.

See! sweet and sound she sleeps in granny's bed, between the paws of the tender wolf.

Questions and Ideas for Journaling and Discussion

1. Discuss the representation of male sexual desire in the story.
2. Characterize the sexual act in terms of the theme of deception and gender expectations.
3. There are several mentions of blood in the story, and through this use of foreshadowing, Carter has readers understand that the story will end violently. How does she overturn our expectations at the end of the story?
4. One topos (topic) in Renaissance literature was the notion that an orgasm was a kind of death. Write about the use of this device in "The Company of Wolves."

Writing to Explore and Learn

1. Read the original fairy tale, "Little Red Riding Hood." Write about how Carter reinterprets the tale in "The Company of Wolves."

Paul Lisicky
(b. 1959)

Maybe everything I write wants to live somewhere on the borders.

Paul Lisicky, novelist, poet, and memoirist, grew up in Cherry Hill, New Jersey, and earned a BA and an MA from Rutgers University and an MFA in creative writing from the University of Iowa Writers' Workshop. He currently lives in Manhattan. Lisicky is the author of *Lawnboy* (2006) and *Famous Builder* (2002), both published by Graywolf Press. His work has appeared in *Story Quarterly*, *Mississippi Review*, *The Seattle Review*, and *Prairie Schooner*, among others. He won a National Endowment for the Arts Fellowship and awards from the James Michener/Copernicus Society, the Henfield Foundation, and others. He has taught in the writing programs at Cornell University; Rutgers University, Newark; Sarah Lawrence College; and Antioch University, Los Angeles. He currently teaches at New York University and in the low-residency MFA program at Fairfield University. A new novel, *The Burning House*, is forthcoming from Etruscan Press in summer 2011.

"Afternoon with Canals" (2002)

In this short piece of creative nonfiction, we learn of a tender love between the author and his partner that occurs in a setting that we would not have imagined possible: a bathhouse in Amsterdam that contains a high-end nightclub with restaurant, pool, and bar. The love story and the beautiful description of the canals undercut the stigma attached to bathhouses.

It's the hour when the heels are inevitably blistered, when we've strolled past as many canals, funky houseboats, and tall, glamorous windows as we can for one day. Even the obsessive pleasure we've taken in trying to perfect our pronunciations of *Prinsengracht* or *Leidesgracht*—the burr of those "g's" scratching the backs of our throats—is no longer of interest. All those rainy pavements, those brooding clouds blown in from the North Sea: we're sodden, saturated, and we can't help but wish to be warmed, to feel the heat of a candle's flame drying us out from inside.

"So now what should we do?" I say.

My boyfriend leans against a stone wall in his leather jacket. He shifts his weight from leg to leg. He holds me entirely in his gaze, brows raised, a hint of mischief in his grin. We know it's too early to head back to the guest house. We shrug at exactly the same moment, tensing our shoulders, then laugh, nervous but relieved we've been thinking alike.

Of course, it shouldn't come as any shock that we're strolling past these burnished cherry red boxes (I think of elegant Japanese furniture) inside of which handsome men, in varying degrees of light, lie back with their hands latched behind their heads or on their stomachs. Now that we've calmed down—the fingers fill with blood; the pulse slows—we're tempted to walk downstairs till I'm reminded of my tattooist's instructions: no steam room, no hot tub. I press my hand to the freshly pierced flesh, bewildered that the crown-capped heart will be on my arm for the rest of my life.

Then my boyfriend's arm is around my waist.

Just across the hall, inside one of the boxes, sits a man with an amazingly hard chest. A honeyed light shadows the planes of his rough, bearded face. What does he want? Is it just me, or am I simply in the way? Are we, together, two large Americans with our shaven heads, just the ticket for a dreary, lowlit afternoon? We try our best to read him, the flares of interest, the averted eyes, as he shifts inside the frame of the box, soulful and startling: a Vermeer in the flesh.

Only hours ago we stood before a still life in the Rijks-museum. Tulip, dragonfly, conch shell, lemon peel, all of it entered me, soaking through my skin and bones, like dye. If only for a moment, I stood before the easel, missing paints. Poppy seed oil, lead, red upon blue—twilight falls, while just outside the window, on the other side of the wall, horseshoes clomp on cobblestone, bakers pound their dough. Time hurries away from me as I try my best to still it, to anchor it within its frame.

We walk around the system of boxes. It takes us but two minutes to find out that our dear Vermeer is gone, his space empty. We look at each other and shrug, smile. No matter. Maybe this is what we'd wanted anyway. Without saying a word, I draw my arm over his shoulder and lead him inside the box. It doesn't take long. The warmth beneath my fingers, the density and heft of his muscles—he feels like gold in my hands as I touch my lips to his neck. His palms press against my skull. Then what: a kick against the wall? We laugh. So many footsteps down these halls, so much longing and release, little cries, and breaths pulled in, while far from the range of our hearing, the car horns beep, the motorboats chug in the canals, cell phones ring, forks chime against the dinner plates of Amsterdam. "*Prinsengracht,*" he rasps. "*Leidesgracht.*"

We walk down the street again, arm in arm this time. In two days we'll be back on the plane, rushing off to meetings, appointments. My feet hurt inside my shoes. But we've framed time at least: we'll travel back inside it, again and again, and beyond.

Questions and Ideas for Journaling and Discussion

1. The canals of Amsterdam are readily viewable on the Internet; they are extraordinarily beautiful and aesthetically pleasing. What ideas might they represent in this story?

Writing to Explore and Learn

1. Discuss the tension between the physical and the spiritual in the story.
2. The story contains many sensory details. How do readers get a sense of place, that is, Amsterdam, through these details?

Dorothy Allison
(b. 1949)

"A lot of women are storytellers . . . but mostly we believe our stories aren't worth anything, that our stories aren't important, and that if they are important, they're dangerous, and therefore too dangerous to tell anyone," said Dorothy Allison when asked about her transition from storyteller to writer, which she attributes to the influence of the women's movement. Born in Greenville, South Carolina, to a poor fifteen-year-old girl who dropped out of high school to become a waitress, Allison grew up in South Carolina and Florida. Deeply rooted in feminist and lesbian-feminist politics, her work can be found on the edge of Southern and working-class literature. Since the 1970s, she has written for feminist, gay, and lesbian publications, but it was the publication of her first novel, *Bastard Out of Carolina* (1992), that catapulted her into the national spotlight. A prolific writer of fiction, poetry, and nonfiction and winner of various literary awards, Allison currently resides with her partner, son, and dogs in northern California.

"The Women Who Hate Me" (1983)

Allison employs a subversive humanist strategy to contest dominant gender and sexual ideologies as they intersect with the social force of class. In this poem of social protest, the lesbian speaker rails against conformist women who serve as agents of a male-dominated society as a way to condemn, torture, and degrade other women who upset the status quo. In seeking justice for the outsider, Allison deconstructs the historical working-class female narrative, hoping to find in her rage the power to create a feminist utopia.

1

The women who do not know me.

The women who, not knowing me, hate me
mark my life, rise in my dreams and shake their loose hair
throw out their thin wrists, narrow their already sharp eyes
say "Who do you think you are?"

"Lazy, useless, cuntsucking, scared, stupid
What you scared of anyway?"

Their eyes, their hands, their voices
Terrifying.

The women who hate me cut me
as men can't. Men don't count.
I can handle men. Never expected better
of any man anyway.
But the women,
shallow-cheeked young girls the world was made for
safe little girls who think nothing of bravado
who never got over by playing it tough.

What do they know of my fear?

What do they know of the women in my body?
My weakening hips, sharp good teeth
angry nightmares, scarred cheeks,
fat thighs, fat everything.

"Don't smile too wide. You look like a fool."
"Don't want too much. You an't gonna get it."
An't gonna get it.
Goddamn.

Say Goddamn and kick somebody's ass
that I am not even half what I should be,
full of terrified angry bravado
      BRAVADO.

The women who hate me
don't know
can't imagine
life-saving, precious bravado.

       2

God on their right shoulder
righteousness on their left,
the women who hate me never use words
like hate, speak instead of nature
of the spirit not housed in the flesh
as if my body, a temple of sin,
didn't mirror their own.

Their measured careful words echo
earlier coarser stuff, say

"What do you think you're doing?"
"Who do you think you are?"

"Whitetrash
no-count
bastard
mean-eyed
garbage-mouth
cuntsucker
cuntsucker
no good to anybody, never did diddlyshit anyway."

"You figured out yet who you an't gonna be?"

The women who hate me hate
their insistent desires, their fat lusts
swallowed and hidden, disciplined to nothing
narrowed to bone and dry hot dreams.
The women who hate me deny
hunger and appetite,
the cream delight
of a scream
that arches the thighs and fills
the mouth with singing.

3

Something hides here
a secret thing shameful and complicated.
Something hides in a tight mouth
a life too easily rendered
a childhood of inappropriate longing
girl's desire to grow into a man
a boyish desire to stretch and sweat

Every three years I discover again
that No I knew nothing before.
Everything must be dragged out,
looked over again. The unexamined life
is the lie, but still
must I every time deny
everything I knew before?

4

My older sister tells me flatly
she don't care who I take to my bed
what I do there. Tells me finally
she sees no difference between
her husbands, my lovers. Behind it all
we are too much the same to deny.

My little sister thinks my older crazy
thinks me sick
more shameful to be queer than crazy
as if her years hustling ass,
her pitiful junky whiteboy
saved through methadone and marriage, all that
asslicking interspersed with asskicking
all those pragmatic family skills we share mean nothing
measured against the little difference
of who and what I am.

My little sister too
is one of the women who hate me.

5

I measure it differently, what's shared,
what's denied, what no one wants recognized.
My first lover's skill at mystery,
how one day she was there, the next gone;
the woman with whom I lived for eight years
but slept with less than one;
the lover who tied me to the foot of her bed
when I didn't really want that
but didn't really know
what else I could get.

What else can I get?
Must I rewrite my life
edit it down to a parable where everything
turns out for the best?
But then what would I do with the lovers
too powerful to disappear, the women
too hard to melt to soft stuff?
Now that I know that soft stuff
was never where I wanted to put my hand.

6

The women who hate me
hate too my older sister
with her many children, her weakness for
good whiskey, country music, bad men.
She says the thing "women's lib" has given her
is a sense she don't have to stay too long
though she does
still she does
much too long.

7

I am not so sure anymore of the difference.
I do not believe anymore in the natural superiority
of the lesbian, the difference between my sisters and me.

Fact is, for all I tell my sisters
I turned out terrific at it myself:
sucking cunt, stroking ego, provoking
manipulating, comforting and keeping.
Plotting my life around mothering
other women's desperation
the way my sisters
build their lives
around their men.
Til I found myself sitting at the kitchen table
shattered glass, blood in my lap and her
the good one with her stern insistence
just standing there wanting me
to explain it to her, save her from being
alone with herself.

Or that other one
another baby-butch wounded girl
How can any of us forget how wounded
any of us have to be to get that hard?
Never to forget that working class says nothing
does not say who she was how she was
fucking me helpless. Her hand on my arm
raising lust to my throat, that lust
everyone says does not happen
though it goes on happening
all the time.

How can I speak of her, us together?
Her touch drawing heat from my crotch to my face
her face, terrifying, wonderful.
Me saying, *"Yeah, goddamn it, yeah,*
put it to me, ease me, fuck me, anything . . ."
til the one thing I refused
then back up against a wall
her rage ugly in the muscles of her neck
her fist swinging up to make a wind,
a wind blowing back to my mama's cheek
past my stepfather's arm

I ask myself over and over how I
came to be standing in such a wind?
How I came to be held up like my mama

with my jeans, my shoes locked in a drawer
and the woman I loved breathing on me
  "You bitch. You damned fool."

  "You want to try it?"
  "You want to walk to Brooklyn
    barefooted?"
  "You want to try it
    mothernaked?"

Which meant, of course, I had to decide
how naked I was willing to go where.

Do I forget all that?
Deny all that?
Pretend I am not
my mama's daughter
my sisters' mirror.
Pretend I have not
at least as much lust
in my life as pain?

Where then will I find the country
where women never wrong women
where we will sit knee to knee
finally listening
to the whole
naked truth
of our lives?

Questions and Ideas for Journaling and Discussion

1. Who are the women who hate the speaker? Why do they hate her? How is this hatred a comment on relationships among women?
2. What does the speaker conclude about her relationships and those of her mother and sisters?

Writing to Explore and Learn

1. Research "woman on woman" abuse and write a short essay about how it is referenced by Allison in the poem.
2. This is a "lyric" poem, but it is not "lyrical" in the common usage of the term. Research these two terms and write a short essay explaining why this is so.

Xiaolu Guo
(b. 1973)

I think that [capitalism] *is the most horrible monster which affects the way you think, the way you write and the creative.*

Chinese novelist, screenwriter, and filmmaker Xiaolu Guo is considered by her generation to be the voice of modern China. Her work explores the themes of alienation and personal journeys. She graduated from the Beijing Film Academy and has won numerous awards for both her visual and written work. Her third novel, *A Concise Chinese–English Dictionary for Lovers* (2007), is the first work that she has written in English.

"Reunion" (2008)

Guo exposes the harsh realities of the life of a young prostitute who is caught between the past and the present in a seedy karaoke bar in Beijing. Central to the story is a meeting between old classmates, which serves as a subterfuge for how gender shapes the roles of women and men in matters of sex, money, and power.

Men's faces always appear old to me. Most of the ones who visit the karaoke parlor are aging, with wives and children at home. They were born in the '50s, dedicated the prime of their lives to the socialist cause. They say to me:

"Bastard, life is so unfair to us, girl, I tell you, I was looking after stinky chicken farms for thirty years, now I'm fifty and got some spare money to spend on you. How will you satisfy me tonight for my thirty years of misery?"

Or even worse: "This is my plan: I'm going to divorce my old wife and have different girls every week. Why not? I have got money now and you have to respect me tonight, understand?"

It's their revenge, perhaps.

Monday night, not much going on. Contracts still to be negotiated, deals being discussed in white office buildings. Bored, I start to watch a soap on TV with two other girls. It's called "I fell in love with a police officer's wife." It's not bad. A man walks in. I can't be bothered to raise my eyes, but he picks me out. I stand up and lead him into the karaoke room he's hired, handing him a menu on the way.

He orders some Bordeaux. Instead of talking, he starts to study my face. He is surprisingly young, about thirty, and doesn't seem too confident about having his hands on my lap.

Then he says, "You know what? I think that . . . you look like a classmate of mine."

I give him a smile. "Sure. Was she cute?"

"Yes she was. But really, you look like her."

"Come on, there are millions of girls in this city with my kind of looks."

He carries on studying me as he takes the wineglass from my hand. I'm getting nervous: there's something familiar about his face, as if it comes from an old dream. But no one should know who I am. Nobody is allowed to know.

"You definitely look like someone I've known," he insists.

I turn away towards the TV and change the channel at random.

"Where are you from?" he goes on.

Where am I from? That accent is so familiar. I start to panic. I glance at him—I must have known this man in my former life, back home. My mind starts to reel, searching for ways to escape his questions, to make up a story. I'll say I'm from some tiny unknown town in Shan Dong or in Hu Nan province, something like that.

But he doesn't wait for my answer. He says the dreaded words: "Are you Zhang Yan?"

I am lost. I pretend I have never heard that name before. Impatient, he carries on:

"Your hometown is Jiu Long, in Fu Jian Province, right?"

He knows my past. Definitely. I can't escape. Or can I? Trying to sound cool and casual, I reply, "You must be mistaking me for someone else, mister. You are too drunk."

"I am totally sober!" He protests angrily. "You are Zhang Yan from Jiu Long primary school and I am your former classmate Ma Yue San."

My eyes leave the TV screen and look at his face, trying to recall my old classmates. Yes, this man really looks like Ma Yue San from Jiu Long primary school. I remember he was good with numbers and always got top grades on our math tests.

"I don't know what you're talking about, mister. I am from Si Chuan province, so I can't be your schoolmate."

"So you have a twin sister then?"

I turn the TV on louder, a Hong Kong song covers his voice.

"Sorry, mister, I don't care about your classmate. The only thing I care about is making you feel good. Shall we have another drink? Do you have enough money for this?"

"I haven't made my millions yet. But I am not poor, we design anti-virus software that sells all over the country."

"Anti-virus software huh?" I repeat, trying to think of something to say.

"Yes. We just bought a building on the Fourth Ring Road." He pauses, scrutinizing my face again. He sighs and continues.

"You don't want to admit who you are. But I have a good memory."

He's got a good memory, but I have a thick skin, and I don't let the world upset me, particularly when it comes to men. But this schoolmate's rambling unsettles me. If the people in Jiu Long know how I make my living, I won't be able to return home anymore. Zhang Yan works in a state-run factory in the capital, that's what my parents know. And she has a good boyfriend who is her colleague. I can feel a tingle of anxiety creeping down my spine. I must make this Ma Yue San shut up. I'll drown his brain in liquor and make sure that when he crawls out of bed tomorrow morning, he'll have no memory of any Zhang Yan schoolmate working in a karaoke parlor. Besides, nobody here knows my name. Here, I am Ai Lian, Lotus Lover, a name men like to spend a night with. There has never been a Zhang Yan here, never.

And so after a few songs by Faye Wong, the Bordeaux is finished. I persuade him to order some whisky, the most expensive thing here, the boss always tells us we should get the men to order it.

We drink scotch until Ma Yue San is soaked in it. Twice already I've gone to the bathroom, my throat is raw. I learned the trick from the other girls: when you drink a lot, you stick your fingers down your throat and vomit it up again. It's the only way you can last the night. After my third trip to the toilet, I taste a trickle of blood dripping down my throat. But that doesn't matter right now. My mission is to persuade Ma Yue San to drink even more and to sing karaoke with me.

My classmate has passed out on the sofa, he is as dead as a drunken shrimp. I don't think I need to worry any more. I get back to the counter, write down the list of what he's drunk, and tell the waiter that he'll pay in the morning. Then I get back to the reception room and drink some tea while waiting for my next customer.

Four in the morning. Sitting alone under a neon light in a windowless room, I reach for the remote control and mute the TV. Laughing and singing is coming from every corner. I'm tired. My only other customer tonight was an overweight businessman from Hu Nan with a coarse drawl that reminded me of old videos of Chairman Mao. The weight of his enormous body made me choke, and as I lay under what seemed like a ton of stale sweat and beer, the tang of sour vomit seeped back into my mouth.

I drink a cup of green tea, then another one, and then a third. I start to feel better. Ma Yue San's words are ringing in my ears. I'm hungry. I miss the South. I miss a bowl of congee and the smell of boiled rice. An image of rice fields spreads out in front of my eyes, covering the vast horizon of Beijing. The wind is warm and fermented, I can smell the grain, the soil, the grass, the sweetness of those fields, the fields where I grew up with my hometown kids. I look at the dim carpet, the red neon illuminating my skin. The high heels are hurting my feet.

Questions and Ideas for Journaling and Discussion

1. Examine the narrator's double life. Why does she deny her identity when she meets her former classmate?
2. Discuss the significance of sex, money, and power in the story.
3. The narrator lived and worked in a place where no one knew her. What was the result of her not being recognized?

Writing to Explore and Learn

1. Write your own story in which a character leads a double life.

Carol Ann Duffy
(b. 1955)

I look on it as recognition of the great women poets we now have writing.

The "it" to which Carol Ann Duffy refers is the poet laureateship of Great Britain to which she was appointed in 2009, becoming the first woman in Britain to hold the job in 341 years. Born in 1955 in Glasgow, Scotland, to a working-class family, Duffy, the eldest of five, began writing poetry in grade school after the family moved to England when she was five years old. She earned a degree in philosophy from Liverpool University and published her first pamphlet of poems in 1973. Duffy, a highly esteemed poet and playwright, is the author of award-winning poetry collections, poetry for children, and plays and adaptations of fairy tales. She is a professor of writing at Manchester Metropolitan University and lives in Manchester with her partner and daughter, defining herself as "a poet and a mother—that's all."

"Mrs Rip Van Winkle" (1999)

All Duffy's dramatic monologues give voice to members of the culture who are not usually heard; in this case, the wife of Washington Irving's fictional character Rip Van Winkle. Discovering self-fulfillment and enjoying freedom from sexual duties during her husband's long sleep, she is glad to be on her own, but her husband wakes up wanting to resume sexual activities. In retelling the folktale, Duffy explores the significance of gender politics, destabilizing it, as a means to resist the ways in which both women and men have been socialized into a gendered society.

> I sank like a stone
> into the still, deep waters of late middle age,
> aching from head to foot.
>
> I took up food
> and gave up exercise.
> It did me good.

And while he slept
I found some hobbies for myself.
Painting. Seeing the sights I'd always dreamed about:
The Leaning Tower.
The Pyramids. The Taj Mahal.
I made a little watercolour of them all.

But what was best,
what hands-down beat the rest,
was saying a none-too-fond farewell to sex.

Until the day
I came home with this pastel of Niagara
and he was sitting up in bed rattling Viagra.

Questions and Ideas for Journaling and Discussion

1. Describe the predicament of the middle-class housewife. What might her attitudes be toward her life and marriage?

Writing to Explore and Learn

1. Read Washington Irving's short story "Rip Van Winkle." Analyze how Duffy retells the tale.
2. Write an essay in which you compare the themes in Chopin's "The Story of an Hour" with those in "Mrs Rip Van Winkle."

Ree Dragonette
(1918–1979)

Born, we are promised sleep.

Ree Dragonette was born into an Italian American family in Philadelphia. She migrated to New York to become an artist, and she and her third husband, John Corsiglia, with whom she bore three children, lived in Greenwich Village. Dragonette believed that, as a Scorpio, she had a potent "sting." Fascinated with the relationship of science to poetry, Dragonette soon became a vital figure on the New York poetry scene, culminating in a performance with jazz saxophonist Eric Dolphy at Town Hall. Dragonette, a jazz poet of the 1950s and 1960s, sought to rescue poetry from the sterility of academia and to engage the working classes. She is known for her Calliope Poetry Theater, open poetry readings that she organized in her apartment at Westbeth. Notable works include *This Is the Way We Wash Our Hands* (1977) and *Remember Zion: A Woman's Existential, Tragic Love Poem* (1970).

"Say It in Sanskrit" (1971)

This poem meditates on the effect of language in gender relations, as it relates to the female body and sexuality. Dragonette, through a witty wordplay on male constructs of the female body, shows the ways in which women in the dominant culture have been reduced to the sum of their body parts.

Signor, my horned <u>bambino</u>,
speak not to me of lays
but of libido.

<u>Caronome</u>, sonny, dirty old fellow,
when you come courting
tell me that mating call in chimes,
in <u>serenata</u>
or ballade of jasmine-roses.

In case you care, dad,
girls are persons;

and grandma poets can feel feminine
and outraged.

My many parts are human
without brass or chrome.
I am an older female,
not a Waring blender
or a worn meat-grinder.
No spark plugs occupy my chambers;
no recriprocating piston engines.

Sorry, my body-soul are not the
freeways of Long Island
or race course at Le Mans or Aqueduct.
My energies are solar, more direct
than those collected In
Standard Oil refineries, or caged by
General Motors.

You, sir, and I are living matter
beyond our sifted metals;
are much more than coal stacks,
grids or levers.
We cannot truly know each other
through flippant data "read-out," by
smudged ink dots, lines and dashes.

I thank you not to call me a
cold or hot potato,
a piece of overripe tomato; or a
chip of processed silicon or steel.

Among your cronies at the club,
in cafes where you sit to rap; do not
refer to me as being made of only
skin, bones, hanks of hair: or
brick by brick, a kind of shit house.

Old bags are what you hide your
infant lust in;
witches and hags are transfers of
your frightened dreams.
To reach me
do not talk of ploughing, digging,
Save those terms for
a field of wheat; an archeology of
graves and ditches.

Soon enough, dear buddy,
sadistic engineers
with brains from Saturn, or Moguls
from Uranus
will have their will with us
to twist our genes.
Crazed technocrats will
violate our organs, will blend them
with scissored alloys and disasters.

But not yet, man!
If you would have me bended, prone;
surrendered between your arms
and thighs, to make love from our
loins together: if self-to-self, you
want us interfaced, by radiant
exchange combined and lifted—
call me by some other
sweet endearments
than doll, chick; or
your weird old lady.

My parents signed my life with
Christian saint, Egyptian goddess,
Hebrew mother.
And all three women that I am
have no desire to be turned on
or ripped off like a tag, a button;
a water tap or faucet.

I hold no slick, aluminum, cold socket
into which you can jump and dive
to ball me.

FUCK; CUNT
are chauvinistic and pretensious.
We cannot ever make it or
make each other.
Our genetic codes did that
some time ago.
If you cannot resist to mention
my vagina or my breasts, do so
without your stealthy, puerile slang.

Get smart, Jack. Mira. mira. learn
or hit the road!

A cock is what I check at dinner
on the stove
to save my children's stew
from burning.
And boobs are rural simpletons to me.

Listen, my fragile lover boy,
I have to tell you that you
coveted your mother's body
when you were just a sapling-baby.
I do not fear your longing for
her several sphincters; but I
despise your puritan concealments.

Right on, pal! If you yen
for my allurements, woo me
in something more eclectic,
fresh and clean.

Tit, in my dictionary, is a bird,
a mouse; is sly repayment for a hurt
belonging, properly, to tat. It has
nothing to do with
plain, good mammary glands.

Don't be so patronizing and so British!
You say you're with it;
if you really are
and we should get together: if black
is beautiful and hard-hat, right wing
Protestant, middle, middle pig is sick
and overthrowable—
so are you Charley!
You come on like a plastic bigot.

So gather up your bangs,
your screws and nuts; and your
feeble gonads and depart.
You sound more like a plumber, welder
or garage mechanic to this woman, than
you do a hot, erotic lady killer.

Seduce me in Sanskrit, for a change;
or wax melodious in Spanish.
Tell me you want me, if you do,
in Aramaic;
In Arawakan or in Grecian-Yiddish.

Questions and Ideas for Journaling and Discussion

1. Discuss the significance of the title, "Say It in Sanskrit", in terms of the larger context of the poem.
2. What does the language of the poem tell us about the poet's views on gender relations?

Writing to Explore and Learn

1. Write about the way in which the poem raises awareness about the significance of words in reflecting the western obsession with the sexualization of women and women's bodies.
2. The Beat poetry movement is best known as a male-dominated American undertaking, spearheaded by Allen Ginsberg. The Beats, generally, challenged literary conventions and rejected social conformity. Research Beat literature and then discuss how "Say It in Sanskrit" might represent a female interpretation of the genre.

Leslie Marmon Silko
(b. 1948)

We know we are part of the trees, and the earth, and water.

Leslie Marmon Silko was born into a prominent family in Albuquerque, New Mexico, and grew up in Laguna Pueblo. She is of mixed ancestry— Laguna Pueblo, Mexican, and white; she identifies, however, primarily with Laguna culture. In 1969, she earned a bachelor's degree from the University of New Mexico, and taught oral tradition and creative writing there. As a child, Silko became familiar with the cultural folklore of the Laguna and Keres peoples through stories passed down to her by her grandmother and aunt, and these had a profound effect on her. Her first book of poetry is titled *Laguna Woman* (1974), and her debut novel, *Ceremony* (1977), was published to high critical acclaim.

"Yellow Woman" (1974)

Silko carries on the Native American tradition of storytelling by detailing, in this short story, the journey of a woman who leaves home to find adventure and sex with a handsome stranger. Set in the terrain of the Southwest, the story combines the ordinary and the mythic to show the intersections among gender, sexuality, and the category of difference in race.

I

My thigh clung to his with dampness, and I watched the sun rising up through the tamaracks and willows. The small brown water birds came to the river and hopped across the mud, leaving brown scratches in the alkali-white crust. They bathed in the river silently. I could hear the water, almost at our feet where the narrow fast channel bubbled and washed green ragged moss and fern leaves. I looked at him beside me, rolled in the red blanket on the white river sand. I cleaned the sand out of the cracks between my toes, squinting because the sun was above the willow trees. I looked at him for the last time, sleeping on the white river sand.

I felt hungry and followed the river south the way we had come the afternoon before, following our footprints that were already blurred by lizard tracks and bug trails. The horses were still lying down, and the black one whinnied when he saw me but he did not get up—maybe it was because the corral was made out of thick cedar branches and the horses had not yet felt the sun like I had. I tried to look beyond the pale red mesas to the pueblo. I knew it was there, even if I could not see it, on the sand rock hill above the river, the same river that moved past me now and had reflected the moon last night.

The horse felt warm underneath me. He shook his head and pawed the sand. The bay whinnied and leaned against the gate trying to follow, and I remembered him asleep in the red blanket beside the river. I slid off the horse and tied him close to the other horse. I walked north with the river again, and the white sand broke loose in footprints over footprints.

"Wake up."

He moved in the blanket and turned his face to me with his eyes still closed. I knelt down to touch him.

"I'm leaving."

He smiled now, eyes still closed. "You are coming with me, remember?" He sat up now with his bare dark chest and belly in the sun.

"Where?"

"To my place."

"And will I come back?"

He pulled his pants on. I walked away from him, feeling him behind me and smelling the willows.

"Yellow Woman," he said.

I turned to face him. "Who are you?" I asked.

He laughed and knelt on the low, sandy bank, washing his face in the river. "Last night you guessed my name, and you knew why I had come."

I stared past him at the shallow moving water and tried to remember the night, but I could only see the moon in the water and remember his warmth around me.

"But I only said that you were him and that I was Yellow Woman—I'm not really her—I have my own name and I come from the pueblo on the other side of the mesa. Your name is Silva and you are a stranger I met by the river yesterday afternoon."

He laughed softly. "What happened yesterday has nothing to do with what you will do today, Yellow Woman."

"I know—that's what I'm saying—the old stories about the ka'tsina spirit and Yellow Woman can't mean us."

My old grandpa liked to tell those stories best. There is one about Badger and Coyote who went hunting and were gone all day, and when the sun was going down they found a house. There was a girl living there alone, and she had light hair and eyes and she told them that they could sleep with her. Coyote wanted to be with her all night so he sent Badger into a prairie-dog hole, telling him he thought he saw something in it. As soon as Badger crawled in, Coyote blocked up the entrance with rocks and hurried back to Yellow Woman.

"Come here," he said gently.

He touched my neck and I moved close to him to feel his breathing and to hear his heart. I was wondering if Yellow Woman had known who she was—if she knew that she would become part of the stories. Maybe she'd had another name that her husband and relatives called her so that only the ka'tsina from the north and the storytellers would know her as Yellow Woman. But I didn't go on; I felt him all around me, pushing me down into the white river sand.

Yellow Woman went away with the spirit from the north and lived with him and his relatives. She was gone for a long time, but then one day she came back and she brought twin boys.

"Do you know the story?"

"What story?" He smiled and pulled me close to him as he said this. I was afraid lying there on the red blanket. All I could know was the way he felt, warm, damp, his body beside me. This is the way it happens in the stories, I was thinking, with no thought beyond the moment she meets the ka'tsina spirit and they go.

"I don't have to go. What they tell in stories was real only then, back in time immemorial, like they say."

He stood up and pointed at my clothes tangled in the blanket. "Let's go," he said.

I walked beside him, breathing hard because he walked fast, his hand around my wrist. I had stopped trying to pull away from him, because his hand felt cool and the sun was high, drying the river bed into alkali. I will see someone, eventually. I will see someone, and then I will be certain that he is only a man—some man from nearby—and I will be sure that I am not Yellow Woman. Because she is from out of time past and I live now and I've been to school and there are highways and pickup trucks that Yellow Woman never saw.

It was an easy ride north on horseback. I watched the change from the cottonwood trees along the river to the junipers that brushed past us in the foothills, and finally there were only piñons, and when I looked up at the rim of the mountain plateau I could see pine trees growing on the edge. Once I stopped to look down, but the pale sandstone had disappeared and the river was gone and the dark lava hills were all around. He touched my hand, not speaking, but always singing softly a mountain song and looking into my eyes.

I felt hungry and wondered what they were doing at home now—my mother, my grandmother, my husband, and the baby. Cooking breakfast, saying, "Where did she go?—maybe kidnapped," and Al going to the tribal police with the details: "She went walking along the river."

The house was made with black lava rock and red mud. It was high above the spreading miles of arroyos and long mesas. I smelled a mountain smell of pitch and buck brush. I stood there beside the black horse, looking down on the small, dim country we had passed, and I shivered.

"Yellow Woman, come inside where it's warm."

II

He lit a fire in the stove. It was an old stove with a round belly and an enamel coffeepot on top. There was only the stove, some faded Navajo blankets, and a bedroll and cardboard box. The floor was made of smooth adobe plaster, and there was one small window facing east. He pointed at the box.

"There's some potatoes and the frying pan." He sat on the floor with his arms around his knees pulling them close to his chest and he watched me fry the potatoes. I didn't mind him watching me because he was always watching me—he had been watching me since I came upon him sitting on the river bank trimming leaves from a willow twig with his knife. We ate from the pan and he wiped the grease from his fingers on his Levis.

"Have you brought women here before?" He smiled and kept chewing, so I said, "Do you always use the same tricks?"

"What tricks?" He looked at me like he didn't understand.

"The story about being a ka'tsina from the mountains. The story about Yellow Woman."

Silva was silent; his face was calm.

"I don't believe it. Those stories couldn't happen now," I said.

He shook his head and said softly, "But someday they will talk about us, and they will say, 'Those two lived long ago when things like that happened.'"

He stood up and went out. I ate the rest of the potatoes and thought about things—about the noise the stove was making and the sound of the mountain wind outside. I remembered yesterday and the day before, and then I went outside.

I walked past the corral to the edge where the narrow trail cut through the black rim rock. I was standing in the sky with nothing around me but the wind that came down from the blue mountain peak behind me. I could see faint mountain images in the distance miles across the vast spread of mesas and valleys and plains. I wondered who was over there to feel the mountain wind on those sheer blue edges—who walks on the pine needles in those blue mountains.

"Can you see the pueblo?" Silva was standing behind me.

I shook my head. "We're too far away."

"From here I can see the world." He stepped out on the edge. "The Navajo reservation begins over there." He pointed to the east. "The Pueblo boundaries are over here." He looked below us to the south, where the narrow trail seemed to come from. "The Texans have their ranches over there, starting with that valley, the Concho Valley. The Mexicans run some cattle over there too."

"Do you ever work for them?"

"I steal from them," Silva answered. The sun was dropping behind us and shadows were filling the land below. I turned away from the edge that dropped forever into the valleys below.

"I'm cold," I said; "I'm going inside." I started wondering about this man who could speak the Pueblo language so well but who lived on a mountain and rustled cattle. I decided that this man Silva must be Navajo, because Pueblo men didn't do things like that.

"You must be a Navajo."

Silva shook his head gently. "Little Yellow Woman," he said, "you never give up, do you? I have told you who I am. The Navajo people know me, too."

He knelt down and unrolled the bedroll and spread the extra blankets out on a piece of canvas. The sun was down, and the only light in the house came from outside—the dim orange light from sundown.

I stood there and waited for him to crawl under the blankets.

"What are you waiting for?" he said, and I lay down beside him. He undressed me slowly like the night before beside the river—kissing my face gently and running his hands up and down my belly and legs. He took off my pants and then he laughed.

"Why are you laughing?"

"You are breathing so hard."

I pulled away from him and turned my back to him.

He pulled me around and pinned me down with his arms and chest. "You don't understand, do you, little Yellow Woman? You will do what I want."

And again he was all around me with his skin slippery against mine, and I was afraid because I understood that his strength could hurt me. I lay underneath him and I knew that he could destroy me. But later, while he slept beside me, I touched his face and I had a feeling—the kind of feeling for him that overcame me that morning along the river. I kissed him on the forehead and he reached out for me.

When I woke up in the morning he was gone. It gave me a strange feeling because for a long time I sat there on the blankets and looked around the little house for some object of his—some proof that he had been there or maybe that he was coming back. Only the blankets and the cardboard box remained. The .30-30 that had been leaning in the corner was gone, and so was the knife I had used the night before. He was gone, and I had my chance to go now. But first I had to eat, because I knew it would be a long walk home.

I found some dried apricots in the cardboard box, and I sat down on a rock at the edge of the plateau rim. There was no wind and the sun warmed me. I was surrounded by silence. I drowsed with apricots in my mouth, and I didn't believe that there were highways or railroads or cattle to steal.

When I woke up, I stared down at my feet in the black mountain dirt. Little black ants were swarming over the pine needles around my foot. They must have smelled the apricots. I thought about my family far below me. They would be wondering about me, because this had never happened to me before. The tribal police would file a report. But if old Grandpa weren't dead he would tell them what happened—he would laugh and say, "Stolen by a ka'tsina, a mountain spirit. She'll come home—they usually do." There are enough of them to handle things. My mother and grandmother will raise the baby like they raised me. Al will find someone else, and they will go on like before, except that there will be a story about the day I disappeared while I was walking along the river. Silva had come for me; he said he had. I did not decide to go. I just went. Moonflowers blossom in the sand hills before dawn, just as I followed him. That's what I was thinking as I wandered along the trail through the pine trees.

It was noon when I got back. When I saw the stone house I remembered that I had meant to go home. But that didn't seem important any more, maybe because there were little blue flowers growing in the meadow behind the stone house and the gray squirrels were playing in the pines next to the house. The horses were standing in the corral, and there was a beef carcass hanging on the shady side of a big pine in front of the house. Flies buzzed around the clotted blood that hung from the carcass. Silva was washing his hands in a bucket full of water. He must have heard me coming because he spoke to me without turning to face me.

"I've been waiting for you."

"I went walking in the big pine trees."

I looked into the bucket full of bloody water with brown-and-white animal hairs floating in it. Silva stood there letting his hand drip, examining me intently.

"Are you coming with me?"

"Where?" I asked him.

"To sell the meat in Marquez."

"If you're sure it's O.K."

"I wouldn't ask you if it wasn't," he answered.

He sloshed the water around in the bucket before he dumped it out and set the bucket upside down near the door. I followed him to the corral and watched him saddle the horses. Even beside the horses he looked tall, and I asked him again if he wasn't Navajo. He didn't say anything; he just shook his head and kept cinching up the saddle.

"But Navajos are tall."

"Get on the horse," he said "and let's go."

The last thing he did before we started down the steep trail was to grab the .30-30 from the corner. He slid the rifle into the scabbard that hung from his saddle.

"Do they ever try to catch you?" I asked.

"They don't know who I am."

"Then why did you bring the rifle?"

"Because we are going to Marquez where the Mexicans live."

III

The trail leveled out on a narrow ridge that was steep on both sides like an animal spine. On one side I could see where the trail went around the rocky gray hills and disappeared into the southeast where the pale sandrock mesas stood in the distance near my home. On the other side was a trail that went west, and as I looked far into the distance I thought I saw the little town. But Silva said no, that I was looking in the wrong place, that I just thought I saw houses. After that I quit looking off into the distance; it was hot and the wildflowers were closing up their deep-yellow petals. Only the waxy cactus flowers bloomed in the bright sun, and I saw every color that a cactus blossom can be; the white ones and the red ones were still buds, but the purple and the yellow were blossoms, open full and the most beautiful of all.

Silva saw him before I did. The white man was riding a big gray horse, coming up the trail toward us. He was traveling fast and the gray horse's feet sent rocks rolling off the trail into the dry tumbleweeds. Silva motioned for me to stop and we watched the white man. He didn't see us right away, but finally his horse whinnied at our horses and he stopped. He looked at us briefly before he loped the gray horse across the three hundred yards that separated us. He stopped his horse in front of Silva, and his young fat face was shadowed by the brim of his hat. He didn't look mad, but his small, pale eyes moved from the blood-soaked gunny sacks hanging from my saddle to Silva's face and then back to my face.

"Where did you get the fresh meat?" the white man asked.

"I've been hunting," Silva said, and when he shifted his weight in the saddle the leather creaked.

"The hell you have, Indian. You've been rustling cattle. We've been looking for the thief for a long time."

The rancher was fat, and sweat began to soak through his white cowboy shirt and the wet cloth stuck to the thick rolls of belly fat. He almost seemed to be panting from the exertion of talking, and he smelled rancid, maybe because Silva scared him.

Silva turned to me and smiled. "Go back up the mountain, Yellow Woman."

The white man got angry when he heard Silva speak in a language he couldn't understand. "Don't try anything, Indian. Just keep riding to Marquez. We'll call the state police from there."

The rancher must have been unarmed because he was very frightened and if he had a gun he would have pulled it out then. I turned my horse around and the rancher yelled, "Stop!" I looked at Silva for an instant and there was something ancient and dark—something I could feel in my stomach—in his eyes, and when I glanced at his hand I saw his finger on the trigger of the .30-30 that was still in the saddle scabbard. I slapped my horse across the flank and the sacks of raw meat swung against my knees as the horse leaped up the trail. It was hard to keep my balance, and once I thought I felt the saddle slipping backward; it was because of this that I could not look back.

I didn't stop until I reached the ridge where the trail forked. The horse was breathing deep gasps and there was a dark film of sweat on its neck. I looked down in the direction I had come from, but I couldn't see the place. I waited. The wind came up and pushed warm air past me. I looked up at the sky, pale blue and full of thin clouds and fading vapor trails left by jets.

I think four shots were fired—I remember hearing four hollow explosions that reminded me of deer hunting. There could have been more shots after that, but I couldn't have heard them because my horse was running again and the loose rocks were making too much noise as they scattered around his feet.

Horses have a hard time running downhill, but I went that way instead of uphill to the mountain because I thought it was safer. I felt better with the horse running southeast past the round gray hills that were covered with cedar trees and black lava rock. When I got to the plain in the distance I could see the dark green patches of tamaracks that grew along the river; and beyond the river I could see the beginning of the pale sandrock mesas. I stopped the horse and looked back to see if anyone was coming; then I got off the horse and turned the horse around, wondering if it would go back to its corral under the pines on the mountain. It looked back at me for a moment and then plucked a mouthful of green tumbleweeds before it trotted back up the trail with its ears pointed forward, carrying its head daintily to one side to avoid stepping on the dragging reins. When the horse disappeared over the last hill, the gunny sacks full of meat were still swinging and bouncing.

IV

I walked toward the river on a wood-hauler's road that I knew would eventually lead to the paved road. I was thinking about waiting beside the road for someone to drive by, but by the time I got to the pavement I had decided it wasn't very far to walk if I followed the river back the way Silva and I had come.

The river water tasted good, and I sat in the shade under a cluster of silvery willows. I thought about Silva, and I felt sad at leaving him; still, there was something strange about him, and I tried to figure it out all the way back home.

I came back to the place on the river bank where he had been sitting the first time I saw him. The green willow leaves that he had trimmed from the branch were still lying there, wilted in the sand. I saw the leaves and I wanted to go back to him—to kiss him and to touch him—but the mountains were too far away now. And I told myself, because I believe it, he will come back sometime and be waiting again by the river.

I followed the path up from the river into the village. The sun was getting low, and I could smell supper cooking when I got to the screen door of my house. I could hear their voices inside—my mother was telling my grandmother how to fix the Jell-o and my husband, Al, was playing with the baby. I decided to tell them that some Navajo had kidnapped me, but I was sorry that old Grandpa wasn't alive to hear my story because it was the Yellow Woman stories he liked to tell best.

Questions and Ideas for Journaling and Discussion

1. Examine the story as a narrative of the female quest.

Writing to Explore and Learn

1. Discuss the function of the figure of Yellow Woman in the story.
2. How does your opinion of the narrator change when you learn that she has a husband and a child?
3. Do you think that the narrator would have remained if the incident with the rancher had not occurred?

Open Question for Writing

1. Compare and contrast the ways in which two or more of the poets and/or writers treat the theme of gender and sexualities.

PART IV

ETHNICITIES AND IDENTITIES

Ethnicity is a relatively new concept when viewed through the lens of American immigration. During the Great Depression, the term was used to describe the large immigrant populations that came from the heterogeneous lands of Europe. The idea of ethnicity for European immigrants—those of Italian, Irish, and Jewish descent, for example—was connected to race because members of these groups knew that the way to achievement and advancement in their new country was to remain attached to the status conferred by being white. While these immigrant groups held onto some cultural markers, such as food, language, and religion, they intended that their children let go of those markers, especially language, so that they could "be American."

Today, the national conversation about race and diversity has changed. People of different races and ethnicities generally are encouraged both to maintain their individual cultural identities and to acculturate into American society. Definitions of race and ethnicity are wide and varied and can include identities such as African American, Afro-Caribbean, Native American, Latin American, Middle Eastern, and Asian. Diversity connotes not only people of various cultures and races, but various sexualities and genders as well. Indeed, the issues of race and ethnicity overlap the issues of class, sexuality, and gender.

To explain the dynamics of race, ethnicity, and diversity is too large a task to perform here, and would most likely raise more questions than provide answers. The texts that follow invite the reader to consider, although not exclusively, these questions: "What does it mean to be an American?" "What are the models of cultural difference?" "What does it mean to live on the border between cultures?"

Walt Whitman (1819–1892)

If anything is sacred, the human body is sacred.

Largely self-taught, Walt Whitman fell in love with the written word as a child. He was born to working-class parents in Long Island, New York, and was the second son of nine children. The family moved to Brooklyn where he attended public schools, but it was his boyhood reminiscences of the Long Island countryside and sea shore that inspired him to become a poet. Printer, teacher, and journalist, he founded a weekly newspaper, *Long Islander*, and, following a trip to New Orleans, he founded the "free soil" newspaper, *Brooklyn Freeman*, in response to the cruelties of slavery. Whitman began writing poetry in 1855 towards a lifelong project, which was to become his major collection, *Leaves of Grass* (1891). He lived in Washington, DC, after the Civil War, working in hospitals in order to help the wounded; he took a job as a clerk at the U.S. Department of the Interior. He was fired when it was discovered that he was the author of *Leaves of Grass*. Settling in Camden, New Jersey, in the 1870s after years of financial struggle, he was able to live on the revenue produced by the 1882 edition of *Leaves of Grass*. Whitman was buried in a self-designed tomb. Notable works include "Crossing Brooklyn Ferry" (1856) and *Good-Bye, My Fancy* (1891).

"I Hear America Singing" (1867)

In this poem, Whitman celebrates the ordinary working people of America.

> I hear America singing, the varied carols I hear,
> Those of mechanics each one singing his as it should be
>   blithe and strong,
> The carpenter singing his as he measures his plank or beam,
> The mason singing his as he makes ready for work, or leaves
>   off work,
5
> The boatman singing what belongs to him in his boat the
> deckhand singing on the steamboat deck,

The shoemaker singing as he sits on his bench, the hatter
    singing as he stands,
The wood-cutter's song, the ploughboy's on his way in the morning,
    or at noon intermissions, or at sundown,
The delicious singing of the mother, or of the young wife at work, or
    of the girl sewing or washing,
Each singing what belongs to him or her and to none else,
The day what belongs to the day—at night the party of young fellows,
    robust, friendly,
Singing with open mouths their strong melodious songs.   10

Questions and Ideas for Journaling and Discussion

1. Describe the sexual division of labor in the poem.
2. What is the tone of the poem? What does the tone tell us about Whitman's attitude
toward the people of America?
3. How does Whitman construct American identity?
4. Discuss the rhythm produced by the lack of sentence divisions.
5. What is the effect of the repetitions of words?

Langston Hughes
(1902–1967)

I have discovered in life that there are ways of getting almost anywhere you want to go, if you really want to go.

Langston Hughes began writing creatively in high school where his talent was recognized early by teachers and classmates. Born into a prominent African American family in Joplin, Missouri, he was raised by his grandmother in Lawrence, Kansas, after his parents divorced. He graduated from high school in Cleveland, Ohio, where he lived with his mother, later spending time in Mexico with his father and a year at Columbia University before graduating from Lincoln University in Pennsylvania. A poet, fiction writer, and playwright, Hughes came into his own when he discovered the burgeoning African American arts scene in Harlem and became one of the key players in what we now call the Harlem Renaissance. He was influenced by the jazz and blues music of his era, and his work portrays black life in America from the 1920s through the 1960s. His major works include "The Negro Speaks of Rivers" (1921), "Montage of a Dream Deferred" (1951), and a critically acclaimed autobiography, *The Big Sea* (1940).

"I, Too" (1925)

Hughes addresses Whitman's assumption that the "ordinary" people in America are white.

I, too, sing America.

I am the darker brother.
They send me to eat in the kitchen
When company comes,
But I laugh,
And eat well,
And grow strong.

Tomorrow,
I'll sit at the table
When company comes.

Nobody'll dare
Say to me,
"Eat in the kitchen,"
Then.

Besides,   15
They'll see how beautiful I am
And be ashamed—

I, too, am America.

Questions and Ideas for Journaling and Discussion

1. Discuss the realities and possibilities for African American experience and identity addressed in the poem.
2. What is the effect of the short poetic line and conversational tone of the poem?

Writing to Explore and Learn

1. Compare and contrast Whitman's vision of "I Hear America Singing" with Hughes's vision in the poem "I, Too."

Elizabeth Primamore*
(b. 1956)

Just Fine (2008)

This solo play tells the tale of a college professor who finds herself in an unlikely place, a Manhattan police station, after suffering the tragic loss of her life partner. The play simultaneously explores the darker side of humanity and the nature of reality and contests, among other concerns, the core categories of sexual identification, in the setting of a police investigation.

(SUSAN PONTI, *a middle-age professional woman, sits in an open waiting area of a police station.*)

SUSAN: I did nothing wrong. If I did, wouldn't I be handcuffed? I'm not drunk. Forget smoking pot. You get arrested for that. In my day, you could toke in the street—8th Street—and the cops would walk right past you—Back home in New Jersey we'd ride in the car and smoke—driving round and round aimlessly. Even high it was boring! (*Beat*) That cop is eyeballing me. I am so sick and tired of people looking at me. Everywhere I go. Even in this filthy shit hole.

(*She looks up.*)

Diana, get me out of here! (*Beat*) She was doing just fine. (*Beat*) I know this is about that white coat who called himself a doctor—

(*She holds her back as if in pain.*)

I am not answering any questions without my attorney. I may not know much about what happens in places like this. But I do watch *Law and Order*. Never say a word without a lawyer. Even if you're innocent. Look what happened to Martha Stewart! Our mouths hung open when we heard the jury's verdict! Diana said, "America hates women!"

(*She looks up*)

You should've seen what happened to Hillary.

---

*See page xii for author's biography.

I don't look at anyone anymore. When I see people I know coming my way, I try as hard as I can to avoid them. Before Diana died—we'd walk in our neighborhood, and I say "hi" to everybody. Diana would say to me, "Who the hell are you, the mayor?" Things were so different then.

I'm too young to be a widow. That's what I am.

Even babies in baby carriages stare at me. All over Tribeca! Here we are, two artists alien in our own neighborhood. Isn't that what places like New York are for? Misfits? Queers? Outcasts? Now we got battalions of fucking baby carriages. Just like the suburbs we escaped! I'm not talking one or two here. That would be cute. I'm talking zillions! Looking at me! (Beat) Like the way those nurses in the hospital looked at us. No one wants to be pitied. Not even the dying.

(*She looks around her.*)

Where is my bag? A woman needs to know where her pocketbook is. (Beat) I'm going on and on here. Where is he? Where is my lawyer! (*Beat*) Where are you, bitch!

I know what people say to their significant others—There she is, poor thing! (*Beat*) Did I say significant others? That doesn't sound right anymore. What is it? Oh Lord, my memory—Partner.

In England, partner is straight and gay. How can a human being squeeze her life into a three letter word. Gay. We were so much bigger that that! To define your life by a sexuality is dehumanizing! So fucking American! Labeling everything! Sound it out. Lezzzzzzzzz. I always get stuck there. On the "Z". Lezzzzzz. (*Beat*) Who cares about this shit. Lesbian, lesbian. I said it—

This had to be the day my lawyer is tied up in court . . . .

(*Pause*) Lesbian. We always thought it sounded like a disease! I have lesbian today. I'm staying home from work. You've got what? Lesbian. Don't come near me!

You were doing just fine. I'm in a fog without you.

If it were up to me, I'd never see anyone again. Ever. Not my mother, my father, my brother, the kids, friends—students—Too many people care about me. What a burden. People caring about you. That's how she must have felt. Burdened.

Burdened by me.

We were so happy. Still in the prime of our destinies. Together for twenty-seven years. With support from no one! We didn't give a shit. (*Beat*) She was doing just fine. (*Beat*) Waiting is excruciating! (*Beat*) I'd rather be at work!

College teaching is my line.

I was sitting at my desk eating an apple and my phone rings. This is Detective So-and-So. I almost choked. Who? What? Precinct? As in police? Something about a doctor. They think I saw something . . .

(*She holds her lower back.*)

He said if I don't come in for questioning that they would come and get me. I left the half-eaten apple on my desk! All covered in saliva!

This doctor they want me to tell them about? He was in his seventies-and (*Beat*) I'm so thirsty—Officer, excuse me, officer? Can I please get—

I can't have anything I fucking want! Not even a glass of water! (*Beat*) Everything's killing us! (*Beat*) Doctors are killing us, too. I'm not saying they're all terrible. But some of them? Look out! (*Beat*) I know because you told me, Diana—

She was doing just fine. Nobody could tell she had cancer. She looked like a regular person. This big shot oncologist—everybody's praising to the high heavens, cajoled her—like Satan tempted Eve with the apple in the Garden of Eden. She begged him to fractionate the chemotherapy, but he said no.

(*She looks up*)

Why the fuck didn't you insist, Diana?

It was downhill from there. The patient knows more than one thinks— We were lying in bed and she looked at me with those rich blue eyes and said, "I hope that Dr. So-and-So dies so he'll know what he did to me." I was stunned. I didn't know what she meant then, but I do now. (*Beat*) I hate that place! Lethal memories. I had no choice the other night. The library I need is near there. That's why I went—

(*She lowers her voice.*)

I did see something . . . He was murdered. The doctor. That doctor. HER doctor. Someone . . . I don't know who . . . walked up real close to him as he was leaving the cancer center. Then he was lying on the ground, bleeding. His smug expression dissipating into thin air. I saw this big man running—The doctor's credit cards were strewn all over the sidewalk . . . I ran the other way. The stones on my vintage bag—(*She holds up the bag.*) These gems refracted the streetlight into some guy's video— Somehow, through lots of questioning, photos and computers, they found me. It must have been the receptionist who gave them the tip because she—the pretty Hispanic girl—knows where I teach. She has the diamond cheek piercing.

(*She points to her cheek.*)

They call it the Marilyn Monroe. When Diana and I would go for her treatments, that cute, little receptionist always commented on my Vintage bag. (*Beat*) He was killed. So what! Why should this bastard walk around and enjoy his children and grandchildren—The bastard wouldn't LISTEN. (*Looks up*) Diana, all I wanted was you! Help me, Diana!!

(*She whispers.*)

It wasn't the gems on my bag here that reflected the light. It was a big, shiny knife that I carried inside my bag. I took the knife and drove it into his back real hard—then I twisted and twisted it. When I saw blood spurt-ing, I tossed it into the sewer. He stumbled, his wallet fell out of his pocket. I kicked it with my high heels. A big guy was walking by and when he heard the doctor scream, he ran. I wanted to level the playing field.

Could I really do something like that? I'm a professor, not a murderer. I always wanted to be an actor. Diana thought I'd be great.

I have to go now. My attorney. (*Beat*) I'm hungry. I wish I had an apple . . .

(*She leaves. End of play.*)

Questions and Ideas for Journaling and Discussion

1. Conflict (or tension) is at the core of drama. What does Susan want and what are the obstacles in her way?
2. Are you sympathetic toward her plight?
3. Is Susan a reliable narrator?
4. Describe Susan's rage. Is she justified in her rage?
5. What are Susan's criticisms of the medical profession?
6. Briefly, tragedy involves the downfall of a heroic character with a fatal flaw. Research tragedy further on the Internet. What are the tragic elements of the play? How does Susan fit the description of a heroic character?

Writing to Explore and Learn

1. Analyze the way that Primamore constructs lesbian and gay identities in the play.
2. Write your own story in which the main character finds herself or himself on the wrong side of the law.

E. Pauline Johnson
(1861–1914)

Emily Pauline Johnson was born into a middle-class family in Canada. Her father was a Mohawk chief, George Henry Martin Johnson, and her mother was Emily Susann Howells, the British-born cousin of William Dean Howells. She was schooled mostly at home by her mother, who instilled in her a love of English literature. Her enjoyment of performing in plays and pageants led to the writing of poetry. After the death of her father in 1864, Johnson began writing more seriously and, before long, was touring Ontario and the East Coast of the United States, performing her work to enthusiastic audiences. Billed as the "Mohawk Princess," she performed one half of her show dressed in buckskin and the other half in an evening gown. Johnson is regarded primarily as a Native American writer who took as her subjects the plight of those with "mixed blood," searching for an identity and issues affecting Native American women. Notable works include *The White Wampum* (1895), the poem "The Song My Paddle Sings" (1892), and *Flint and Feather* (1913).

"As It Was in the Beginning" (1913)

In this first-person narrative, Johnson tells a story about a young mixed-blood Native American girl whose father sends her to a Christian mission school against her mother's wishes. In a tale of social injustice combined with domestic romance, the author addresses the themes of betrayal and white Protestant religious hypocrisy to show the ways in which gender is inextricably tied to the issues of race, class, and ethnicity.

They account for it by the fact that I am a Redskin, but I am something else, too—I am a woman.

I remember the first time I saw him. He came up the trail with some Hudson's Bay trappers, and they stopped at the door of my father's tepee. He seemed even then, fourteen years ago, an old man; his hair seemed just as thin and white, his hands just as trembling and fleshless as they were a month since, when I saw him for what I pray his God is the last time.

My father sat in the tepee, polishing buffalo horns and smoking; my mother, wrapped in her blanket, crouched over her quill-work, on the buffalo-skin at his side; I was lounging at the doorway, idling, watching, as I always watched, the thin, distant line of sky and prairie; wondering, as I always wondered, what lay beyond it. Then he came, this gentle old man with his white hair and thin, pale face. He wore a long black coat, which I now know was the sign of his office, and he carried a black leather-covered book, which, in all the years I have known him, I have never seen him without.

The trappers explained to my father who he was, the Great Teacher, the heart's Medicine Man, the "Blackcoat" we had heard of, who brought peace where there was war, and the magic of whose black book brought greater things than all the Happy Hunting Grounds of our ancestors.

He told us many things that day, for he could speak the Cree tongue, and my father listened, and listened, and when at last they left us, my father said for him to come and sit within the tepee again.

He came, all the time he came, and my father welcomed him, but my mother always sat in silence at work with the quills; my mother never liked the Great "Blackcoat."

His stories fascinated me. I used to listen intently to the tale of the strange new place he called "heaven," of the gold crown, of the white dress, of the great music; and then he would tell of that other strange place—hell. My father and I hated it; we feared it, we dreamt of it, we trembled at it. Oh, if the "Blackcoat" would only cease to talk of it! Now I know he saw its effect upon us, and he used it as a whip to lash us into his new religion, but even then my mother must have known, for each time he left the tepee she would watch him going slowly away across the prairie; then when he was disappearing into the far horizon she would laugh scornfully, and say:

"If the white man made this Blackcoat's hell, let him go to it. It is for the man who found it first. No hell for Indians, just Happy Hunting Grounds. Blackcoat can't scare me."

And then, after weeks had passed, one day as he stood at the tepee door he laid his white, old hand on my head and said to my father: "Give me this little girl' chief. Let me take her to the mission schools, let me keep her, and teach her of the great God and His eternal heaven. She will grow to be a noble woman, and return perhaps to bring her people to the Christ."

My mother's eyes snapped. "No," she said. It was the first word she ever spoke to the "Blackcoat." My father sat and smoked. At the end of a half-hour he said:

"I am an old man, Blackcoat. I shall not leave the God of my fathers. I like not your strange God's ways—all of them. I like not His two new places for me when I am dead. Take the child, Blackcoat, and save her from hell."

The first grief of my life was when we reached the mission. They took my buckskin dress off, saying I was now a little Christian girl and must dress like all the white people at the mission. Oh, how I hated that stiff new calico dress and those leather shoes! But, little as I was, I said nothing, only thought of the time when I should be grown, and do as my mother did, and wear the buckskins and the blanket.

My next serious grief was when I began to speak the English, that they forbade me to use any Cree words whatever. The rule of the school was that any child heard using its native tongue must get a slight punishment. I never understood it, I cannot understand it now, why the use of my dear Cree tongue could be a matter for correction or an action deserving punishment.

She was strict, the matron of the school, but only justly so, for she had a heart and a face like her brother's, the "Blackcoat." I had long since ceased to call him that. The trappers at the post called him "St. Paul," because, they told me of his self-sacrificing life, his kindly deeds, his rarely beautiful old face; so I, too, called him "St. Paul," though oftener "Father Paul," though he never liked the latter title, for he was a Protestant. But as I was his pet, his darling of the whole school, he let me speak of him as I would, knowing it was but my heart speaking in love. His sister was a widow, and mother to a laughing yellow-haired little boy of about my own age, who was my constant playmate and who taught me much of English in his own childish way. I used to be fond of this child, just as I was fond of his mother and of his uncle, my "Father Paul," but as my girlhood passed away, as womanhood came upon me, I got strangely wearied of them all; I longed, oh, God, how I longed for the old wild life! It came with my womanhood, with my years.

What mattered it to me now that they had taught me all their ways?—their tricks of dress, their reading, their writing, their books. What mattered it that "Father Paul" loved me, that the traders at the post called me pretty, that I was a pet of all, from the factor to the poorest trapper in the service? I wanted my own people, my own old life, my blood called out for it, but they always said I must not return to my father's tepee. I heard them talk amongst themselves of keeping me away from pagan influences; they told each other that if I returned to the prairies, the tepees, I would degenerate, slip back to paganism, as other girls had done; marry, perhaps, with a ********—and all their years of labor and teaching would be lost.

I said nothing, but I waited. And then one night the feeling overcame me. I was in the Hudson's Bay store when an Indian came in from the north with a large pack of buckskin. As they unrolled it a dash of its insinuating odor filled the store. I went over and leaned above the skins a second, then buried my face in them, swallowing, drinking the fragrance of them, that went to my head like wine. Oh, the wild wonder of that wood-smoked tan, the subtilty [*sic*] of it, the untamed smell of it! I drank it into my lungs, my innermost being was saturated with it, till my mind reeled and my heart seemed twisted with a physical agony. My childhood recollections rushed upon me, devoured me. I left the store in a strange, calm frenzy, and going rapidly to the mission house I confronted my Father Paul and demanded to be allowed to go "home," if only for a day. He received the request with the same refusal and the same gentle sigh that I had so often been greeted with, but *this* time the desire, the smoke-tan, the heart-ache, never lessened.

Night after night I would steal away by myself and go to the border of the village to watch the sun set in the foothills, to gaze at the far line of sky and prairie, to long and long for my father's lodge. And Laurence—always Laurence—my fair-haired, laughing, child playmate, would come calling and calling for me: "Esther, where are you? We miss you; come in, Esther, come in with me." And if I did not turn at once to him and follow, he would come and place his strong hands on my shoulders and laugh into my eyes and say, "Truant, truant, Esther; can't *we* make you happy?"

My old child playmate had vanished years ago. He was a tall, slender young man now, handsome as a young chief, but with laughing blue eyes, and always those yellow curls about his temples. He was my solace in my half-exile, my comrade, my brother, until one night it was, "Esther, Esther, can't *I* make you happy?"

I did not answer him; only looked out across the plains and thought of the tepees. He came close, close. He locked his arms about me, and with my face pressed up to his throat he stood silent. I felt the blood from my heart sweep to my very finger-tips. I loved him. O God, how I loved him! In a wild, blind instant it all came, just because he held me so and was whispering brokenly, "Don't leave me, don't leave me, Esther; *my* Esther, my child-love, my playmate, my girl-comrade, my little Cree sweetheart, will you go away to your people, or stay, stay for me, for my arms, as I have you now?"

No more, no more the tepees; no more the wild stretch of prairie, the intoxicating fragrance of the smoke-tanned buckskin; no more the bed of buffalo hide, the soft, silent moccasin; no more the dark faces of my people, the dulcet cadence of the sweet Cree tongue—only this man, this fair, proud, tender man who held me in his arms, in his heart. My soul prayed his great white God, in that moment, that He let me have only this. It was twilight when we re-entered the mission gate. We were both excited, feverish. Father Paul was reading evening prayers in the large room beyond the hallway his saint-like voice stole beyond the doors like a ********* upon us. I went noiselessly upstairs to my own room and sat there undisturbed for hours.

The clock downstairs struck one, startling me from my dreams of happiness, and at the same moment a flash of light attracted me. My room was in an angle of the building, and my window looked almost directly down into those of Father Paul's study, into which at that instant he was entering, carrying a lamp. "Why, Laurence," I heard him exclaim, "what are you doing here? I thought, my boy, you were in bed hours ago."

"No, uncle, not in bed, but in dreamland," replied Laurence, arising from the window, where evidently he, too, had spent the night hours as I had done.

Father Paul fumbled about a moment, found his large black book, which for once he seemed to have got separated from, and was turning to leave, when the curious circumstance of Laurence being there at so unusual an hour seemed to strike him anew. "Better go to sleep, my son," he said simply, then added curiously, "Has anything occurred to keep you up?"

Then Laurence spoke: "No, uncle, only—only, I'm happy, that's all."

Father Paul stood irresolute. Then: "It is—?"

"Esther," said Laurence quietly, but he was at the old man's side, his hand was on the bent old shoulder, his eyes proud and appealing.

Father Paul set the lamp on the table, but, as usual, one hand held that black book, the great text of his life. His face was paler than I had ever seen it—graver.

"Tell me of it," he requested.

I leaned far out of my window and watched them both. I listened with my very heart, for Laurence was telling him of me, of his love, of the newfound joy of that night.

"You have said nothing of marriage to her?" asked Father Paul.

"Well—no; but she surely understands that—"

"Did you speak of *marriage?*" repeated Father Paul, with a harsh ring in his voice that was new to me.

"No, uncle, but—"

"Very well, then; very well."

There was a brief silence. Laurence stood staring at the old man as though he were a stranger; he watched him push a large chair up to the table, slowly seat himself; then mechanically following his movements, he dropped on to a lounge. The old man's head bent low, but his eyes were bright and strangely fascinating. He began:

"Laurence, my boy, your future is the dearest thing to me of all earthly interests. Why, you *can't* marry this girl—no, no, sit, sit until I have finished," he added, with raised voice, as Laurence sprang up, remonstrating. "I have long since decided that you marry well; for instance, the Hudson's Bay factor's daughter."

Laurence broke into a fresh, rollicking laugh. "What, uncle," he said, "little Ida McIntosh? Marry that little yellow-haired fluff ball, that kitten, that pretty little dolly?"

"Stop," said Father Paul. Then, with a low, soft persuasiveness, "She is *white,* Laurence."

My lover started. "Why, uncle, what do you mean?" he faltered.

"Only this, my son: poor Esther comes of uncertain blood; would it do for you—the missionary's nephew, and adopted son, you might say—to marry the daughter of a pagan Indian? Her mother is hopelessly uncivilized; her father has a dash of French somewhere—half-breed, you know, my boy, half-breed." Then, with still lower tone and half-shut, crafty eyes, he added: "The blood is a bad, bad mixture, *you* know that; you know, too, that I am very fond of the girl, poor dear Esther. I have tried to separate her from evil pagan influences; she is the daughter of the Church; I want her to have no other parent; but you never can tell what lurks in *a caged animal that has once been wild.* My whole heart is with the Indian people, my son; my whole heart, my whole life, has been devoted to bringing them to Christ, *but it is a different thing to marry with one of them.*"

His small old eyes were riveted on Laurence like a hawk's on a rat. My heart lay like ice in my bosom.

Laurence, speechless and white, stared at him breathlessly.

"Go away somewhere," the old man was urging; "to Winnipeg, Toronto, Montreal; forget her, then come back to Ida McIntosh. A union of the Church and the Hudson's Bay will mean great things, and may ultimately result in my life's ambition, the civilization of this entire tribe, that we have worked so long to bring to God."

I listened, sitting like one frozen. Could those words have been uttered by my venerable teacher, by him whom I revered as I would one of the saints in his own black book? Ah, there was no mistaking it. My white father, my life-long friend who pretended to love me, to care for my happiness, was urging the man I worshipped to forget me, to marry with the factor's daughter—because of what? Of my red skin; my good, old, honest pagan mother; my confiding French-Indian father. In a second all the care, the hollow love he had given me since my childhood, were as things that never existed. I hated that old mission priest as I hated his white man's hell. I hated his long, white hair; I hated his thin, white hands; I hated his body, his soul, his voice, his black book—oh, how I hated the very atmosphere of him!

Laurence sat motionless, his face buried in his hands, but the old man continued, "No, no; not the child of that pagan mother; you can't trust her, my son. What would you do with a wife who might any day break from you to return to her prairies and her buckskins? *You can't trust her.*" His eyes grew smaller, more glittering, more fascinating then, and leaning with an odd, secret sort of movement towards Laurence, he almost whispered, "Think of her silent ways, her noiseless step; the girl glides about like an apparition; her quick fingers, her wild longings—I don't know why, but with all my fondness for her, she reminds me sometimes of a strange—*snake.*"

Laurence shuddered, lifted his face, and said hoarsely: "You're right, uncle; perhaps I'd better not; I'll go away, I'll forget her, and then—well, then— yes, you are right, it *is* a different thing to marry one of them." The old man arose. His feeble fingers still clasped his black book; his soft white hair clung about his forehead like that of an Apostle; his eyes lost their peering, crafty expression; his bent shoulders resumed the dignity of a minister of the living God; he was the picture of what the traders called him—"St. Paul."

"Good-night, son," he said.

"Good-night, uncle, and thank you for bringing me to myself."

They were the last words I ever heard uttered by either that old archfiend or his weak, miserable kinsman. Father Paul turned and left the room. I watched his withered hand—the hand I had so often felt resting on my head in holy benedictions—clasp the door-knob, turn it slowly, then, with bowed head and his pale face wrapped in thought, he left the room—left it with the mad venom of my hate pursuing him like the very Evil One he taught me of.

What were his years of kindness and care now? What did I care for his God, his heaven, his hell? He had robbed me of my native faith, of my parents, of my people, of this last, this life of love that would have made a great, good woman of me. God! how I hated him!

I crept to the closet in my dark little room. I felt for a bundle I had not looked at for years—yes, it was there, the buckskin dress I had worn as a little child when they brought me to the mission. I tucked it under my arm and descended the stairs noiselessly. I would look into the study and speak good-bye to Laurence; then I would—

I pushed open the door. He was lying on the couch where a short time previously he had sat, white and speechless, listening to Father Paul, I moved towards him softly. God in heaven, he was already asleep. As I bent over him the fullness of his perfect beauty impressed me for the first time; his slender form, his curving mouth that almost laughed even in sleep, his fair, tossed hair, his smooth, strong-pulsing throat. God! how I loved him!

Then there arose the picture of the factor's daughter. I hated her. I hated her baby face, her yellow hair, her whitish skin. "She shall not marry him," my soul said. "I will kill him first—kill his beautiful body, his lying, false heart." Something in my heart seemed to speak; it said over and over again, "Kill him, kill him; she will never have him then. Kill him. It will break Father Paul's heart and blight his life. He has killed the best of you, of your womanhood; kill *his* best, his pride, his hope—his sister's son, his nephew Laurence." But how? how?

What had that terrible old man said I was like? A *strange snake*. A snake? The idea wound itself about me like the very coils of a serpent. What was this in the beaded bag of my buckskin dress? this little thing rolled in tan that my mother had given me at parting with the words, "Don't touch much, but some time maybe you want it!" Oh! I knew well enough what it was—a small flint arrow-head dipped in the venom of some *strange snake*.

I knelt beside him and laid my hot lips on his hand. I worshipped him, oh, how, how I worshipped him! Then again the vision of *her* baby face, *her* yellow hair—I scratched his wrist twice with the arrow-tip. A single drop of red blood oozed up; he stirred. I turned the lamp down and slipped out of the room—out of the house.

I dream nightly of the horrors of the white man's hell. Why did they teach me of it, only to fling me into it?

Last night as I crouched beside my mother on the buffalo-hide, Dan Henderson, the trapper, came in to smoke with my father. He said old Father Paul was bowed with grief, that with my disappearance I was suspected, but that there was no proof. Was it not merely a snake bite?

They account for it by the fact that I am a Redskin.

They seem to have forgotten I am a woman.

Writing to Explore and Learn

1. Describe what you think Esther, the narrator, means by identifying herself as both a "Redskin" and a "woman."
2. How is Esther is caught between two cultures?
3. In fiction, authors tell their stories through first-person or third-person narrators. In the first case, the narrator, who often is a character as well, tells the story as he or she experienced it, and in the second case, the narrator relates the events of the story as it happened to others. Johnson chose a first-person narrator for this story; what is the effect of this decision?

Writing to Explore and Learn

1. Write about themes of hypocrisy and romance and how these shape Esther's life.

Patricia Smith
(b. 1955)

Writer, poet, and playwright Patricia Smith was born in Chicago and educated at Southern Illinois and Northwestern Universities. She began her writing career as a columnist for the *Boston Globe* and has gained national recognition as a performance poet in poetry slam competitions and is a four-time champion in the National Poetry Slam. Smith is a winner of many literary awards, including the Carl Sandburg Literary Award (1998), the Paterson Poetry Prize (2007), and the Pushcart Prize (2006); a *Publishers Weekly* critic called her "that rarest of creatures, a charismatic slam and performance poet whose artistry truly survives on the printed page." Her major works include *Close to Death* (1993), *Teahouse of the Almighty* (2006), and *Blood Dazzler* (2008).

"Undertaker" (1993)

The eponymous undertaker attempts to recreate the facial features of a young boy from a photo provided by his mother. A powerful, dark, and disturbing work, the poem grieves the senseless loss of life as a means to question the codes of masculinity that are deeply connected to issues of race.

When a bullet enters the brain, the head explodes.
    I can think of no softer warning for the mothers
        who sit doubled before my desk,
        knotting their smooth brown hands,
        and begging, fix my boy, fix my boy.
    Here's his high school picture.
And the smirking, mildly mustachioed player
        in the crinkled snapshot
        looks nothing like the plastic bag of boy
        stored and dated in the cold room downstairs.
    In the picture, he is cocky and chiseled,
        clutching the world by the balls. I know the look.
    Now he is flaps of cheek,
        slivers of jawbone, a surprised eye,
        assorted teeth, bloody tufts of napped hair.

The building blocks of my business.

So I swallow hard, turn the photo face down
    and talk numbers instead. The high price
    of miracles startles the still-young woman,
    but she is prepared. I know that she has sold
    everything she owns, that cousins and uncles
    have emptied their empty bank accounts,
    that she dreams of her baby
    in tuxedoed satin, flawless in an open casket,
    a cross or blood red rose tacked to his fingers,
    his halo set at a cocky angle.
I write a figure on a piece of paper
    and push it across to her
    while her chest heaves with hoping.
She stares at the number, pulls in
    a slow weepy breath: "*Jesus.*"

But Jesus isn't on this payroll. I work alone
    until the dim insistence of morning,
    bent over my grisly puzzle pieces, gluing,
    stitching, creating a chin with a brushstroke.
I plop glass eyes into rigid sockets,
    then carve eyelids from a forearm, an inner thigh.
I plump shattered skulls, and paint the skin
    to suggest warmth, an impending breath.
I reach into collapsed cavities to rescue
    a tongue, an ear. Lips are never easy to recreate.

And I try not to remember the stories,
    the tales the mothers must bring me
    to ease their own hearts. *Oh,* they cry,
    my Ronnie, my Willie, my Michael, my Chico.
It was self-defense. He was on his way home,
    a dark car slowed down, they must have thought
    he was someone else. He stepped between
    two warring gang members at a party.
Really, he was trying to get off the streets,
    trying to pull away from the crowd.
He was just trying to help a friend.
He was in the wrong place at the wrong time.
Fix my boy; he was a good boy. Make him the way he was.

But I have explored the jagged gaps
    in the boy's body, smoothed the angry edges
    of bulletholes. I have touched him in places
    no mother knows, and I have birthed

his new face. I know he believed himself
invincible, that he most likely hissed
"Fuck you, man" before the bullets lifted him
    off his feet. I try not to imagine
    his swagger, his lizard-lidded gaze,
    his young mother screaming into the phone.
She says she will find the money, and I know
    this is the truth that fuels her, forces her
    to place one foot in front of the other.
Suddenly, I want to take her down
    to the chilly room, open the bag
    and shake its terrible bounty onto the
    gleaming steel table. I want her to see him,
    to touch him, to press her lips to the flap of cheek.
The woman needs to wither, finally, and move on.

We both jump as the phone rattles in its hook.
I pray it's my wife, a bill collector, a wrong number.
But the wide, questioning silence on the other end
    is too familiar. Another mother needing a miracle.
Another homeboy coming home.

Questions and Ideas for Journaling and Discussion

1. What is the attitude of the undertaker toward the mother of the dead boy?
2. Study stanza three. Why do you think that Smith describes the undertaker's task to reconstruct the dead bodies of the boys in such vivid detail?
3. Discuss the significance of the last line, "Another homeboy coming home."
4. What do we learn about the speaker of this modern version of a dramatic monologue?

Writing to Explore and Learn

1. Explain the undertaker's concept of codes of masculinity and African American male identity.

George Guida
(b. 1967)

Born in Brooklyn and raised on Long Island, New York, George Guida began writing poems on the consciousness of ethnicity in 1992 while studying multicultural American literature at the City University of New York and performing his work at the Nuyorican Poets Cafe with other members of the Italian American Writers Association, of which he is an incorporating officer. He has published two collections of poems: *New York and Other Lovers* (Smalls Books, 2008) and *Low Italian* (Bordighera Press, 2006). His poem "Left Behind" won a 2009 North Sea Poetry Scene Prize, and his 2009 Pushcart Prize-nominated story, "Rome," appeared in *J Journal* in 2008. Guida received a 2009 Puffin Grant for "The Pope Play," which was given a 2009 workshop production in New York City. His chapbook of comic fiction, *The Pope Stories* (Sutton Press), appeared in 2005; his critical works include *The Peasant and the Pen: Men, Enterprise and the Recovery of Culture in Italian American Narrative* (Peter Lang, 2003) and various essays on Italian-American literature and popular culture, which appear widely.

"Fear of Crossing Over" (2006)

The speaker of this poem explains all of the stereotypical aspects of Italian American culture that he "fears," such as speaking, eating, and fighting "Italian," ending with what he fears most of all. He is ambivalent about his ethnicity while wary of his attraction to it. Guida pinpoints the dilemma of the ethnically drawn masculine identity.

> I too much fear speaking Italian,
> > that while trilling an r
> > my tongue will get stuck
> > and stay that way.
> I too much fear eating Italian,
> > that I'll continue to like it too much.
> I too much fear fighting Italian,
> > that I'll either give up and go home
> > or pull out a baseball bat and go to jail.
> I too much fear loving Italian,
> > the damage I'll do when I love and lose.

I too much fear carousing Italian,
   that the wine will run out,
   that the sex will turn out to be merely human.
I too much fear pledging Italian,
   that I'll have to cheer soccer teams
   and vote in every election
   or never vote at all
   and damn other dark races.
But most of all I fear
   denying Italian,
   unlearning it,
   and leaving it to ghosts
   who whistle tarantellas in my ear.

Questions and Ideas for Journaling and Discussion

1. What does Guida mean by "crossing over"?
2. Research Yusuf Hawkins on the Internet and then explain the third stanza.
3. Discuss the uses and effects of repetition in the poem.

Writing to Explore and Learn

1. "Ambivalent" means having equal emotions of love and hatred toward a person or thing. Explain the expressions of ambivalence in Guida's poem.

Roger Sedarat
(b. 1971)

As an Iranian-American, I'm privy . . . to . . . a 'Third Space,' a formative place between two fixed positions.

Roger Sedarat was born in Normal, Illinois, to an Iranian father and an American mother. He earned a BA in sociology from the University of Texas, Austin; an MA in English and creative writing from Queens College/City University of New York; and a PhD in English from Tufts University. Currently, he is chair of the MFA Poetry and Translation program at Queens College/City University of New York, where he also teaches. His background is reflected in his poetry as he negotiates languages as a translator of Persian literature, as well as in his writings in English, where he crosses formal traditions. His collection, *Dear Regime: Letters to the Islamic Republic,* won Ohio University Press's Hollis Summers Prize (David Lehman, judge). He has authored the chapbook *From Tehran to Texas,* and his poems and translations have appeared in such journals as *New England Review*, *Atlanta Review*, *Zoland Poetry*, *Green Mountains Review*, and *Drunken Boat*.

"Sonnet *Ghazal*" for Janette (2009)

A "ghazal" is an ancient Persian poetic form; Sedarat's contemporary interpretation of the ghazal honors both the Persian form and the four-teen-line love sonnet of the western tradition; note particularly the use of the author's name in the last stanza. The feminine inspiration in this poem, much like Dante's Beatrice, is an idealized woman beyond his attainment.

> Hafez, the baker, could see what I mean;
> If she were a spice, she'd be cinnamon.
>
> It's both terrifying and exciting,
> The idea that she'd see other men.
>
> Oh God, I'd sell my soul to watch her walk;
> Hear my prayer, and grant me this sin. Amen.
>
> I heard the great poets of Shiraz sing
> Through olive vein-lines of her Persian skin.

I know; this ghazal objectifies her,
Ignoring feminist criticism.

Reversing the Cinderella story,
She turns all princes into cindermen.

"Your next patient, doctor. It's Roger S."
"The one love sick for his wife? Send him in."

Questions and Ideas for Journaling and Discussion

1. Research "sonnet" and "ghazal." How does Sedarat combine these disparate forms?
2. Discuss how Sedarat inverts the traditional role of women—muse, object of the gaze—in this love poem.

Writing to Explore and Learn

1. Compare the male speaker in this poem with the hero in "Sleeping Beauty."

Sojourner Truth
(1797–1883)

I suppose I am about the only colored woman that goes about to speak for the rights of the colored woman.

Sojourner Truth was born Isabella Baumfree on a farm in New York; her owners were Dutch. In 1827, at the age of thirty, she gained her freedom after a law was passed in New York that freed slaves born before 1799. Truth was an evangelist, abolitionist, and women's rights activist and made history when she sued and won her son's freedom from an Alabama slave owner; subsequently, she used the courts many times to win rights for African Americans. Around 1835, Truth had a life-changing spiritual experience after which she engaged in a new life of traveling in order to spread the Gospel, hence renaming herself "Sojourner Truth." She gained national prominence with the publication of her 1850 autobiography, *Narrative of Sojourner Truth*.

"Ain't I a Woman" (1851)

Truth exemplifies the rhetorical tradition of speechmaking to represent a reality about the nature of the African American female experience during slavery. The text takes aim at cultural beliefs about the inferiority of women and brings up, for the first time, the role of race in the construction of gender.

Delivered 1851, Women's Convention, Akron, Ohio

Well, children, where there is so much racket there must be something out of kilter. I think that 'twixt the negroes of the South and the women at the North, all talking about rights, the white men will be in a fix pretty soon. But what's all this here talking about?

That man over there says that women need to be helped into carriages, and lifted over ditches, and to have the best place everywhere. Nobody ever helps me into carriages, or over mud-puddles, or gives me any best place! And ain't I a woman? Look at me! Look at my arm! I have ploughed and planted, and gathered into barns, and no man could head me! And ain't I a woman? I could work as much and eat as much as a man—when I could get it—and bear the lash as well! And ain't I a woman? I have borne thirteen children, and seen most all sold off to slavery, and when I cried out with my mother's grief, none but Jesus heard me! And ain't I a woman?

Then they talk about this thing in the head; what's this they call it? [member of audience whispers, "intellect"] That's it, honey. What's that got to do with women's rights or negroes' rights? If my cup won't hold but a pint, and yours holds a quart, wouldn't you be mean not to let me have my little half measure full?

Then that little man in black there, he says women can't have as much rights as men, 'cause Christ wasn't a woman! Where did your Christ come from? Where did your Christ come from? From God and a woman! Man had nothing to do with Him.

If the first woman God ever made was strong enough to turn the world upside down all alone, these women together ought to be able to turn it back, and get it right side up again! And now they is asking to do it, the men better let them.

Obliged to you for hearing me, and now old Sojourner ain't got nothing more to say.

Writing to Explore and Learn

1. Why do you think Truth repeats the question "Ain't I a Woman?" How does this repetition help us to understand her predicament?
2. Discuss the significance of gender in the religious references.
3. Explain the ways in which Truth points out the discrepancy between the perception of white women and the perception of African American women in western culture.

Joyce Zonana
(b. 1949)

Because I have never learned the language of my homeland, there has been a strange lacuna in my identity, a wound I have been unable to heal.

Joyce Zonana was born in Cairo, Egypt. Following the independence of the State of Israel, anti-Semitic street riots and shouts of "Down with the Jews!" motivated her father to move the family to New York when she was eighteen months old, where she discovered, while growing up, that her ethnicity—Egyptian and Sephardic Jew—did not match others' expectations of Brooklyn Jewishness. A graduate of Brooklyn College, she earned a PhD from the University of Pennsylvania and has taught in Oklahoma, Louisiana, and New Jersey. She is Professor of English at Borough of Manhattan Community College/City University of New York. Her scholarly articles and personal essays have appeared in *Tulsa Studies in Women's Literature*, *Signs*, *Meridians*, and *The Hudson Review*, and she is the recipient of the Florence Howe Award for feminist scholarship. *Dream Homes: From Cairo to Katrina, an Exile's Journey,* is a memoir in which she explores her identity through recollection and remembrance. Zonana has recently undertaken the study of Arabic.

"Heirloom" from *Dream Homes: From Cairo to Katrina, An Exile's Journey* (2008)

In this first chapter of her memoir, Zonana tells about the reasons for her family's immigration from Cairo, Egypt, to Brooklyn, New York. She explores the meaning of "heirloom" and its relationship to ethnicity and identity formation.

My own grandmothers were left behind in Cairo in 1951 when my parents, Egyptian Jews, brought me, eighteen months old, on a boat to the United States. They didn't carry much—a little money, clothes, linens, some silver trays and prayer rugs—nothing that couldn't be squeezed into a few worn suitcases. Although they had waited five years for the visa granting them entrance to the United States, they didn't want the officials in Cairo to suspect them of planning to emigrate. They were slipping away quietly, taking with them only what they could carry, trying to make it look as if they were simply taking a short vacation in Italy. Silver trays? Prayer rugs? Gold jewelry? For a brief vacation? Apparently the customs officer let these pass. Left behind, though, were the bed and dresser crafted for them when they married, the dining table and chairs my father had known since infancy. Because they reasoned that no one would think to examine an eighteen-month-old child, I served as the bearer of the family legacy: Dressed in several layers of clothing, I was decked with the additional jewels my parents thought the customs officer might balk at. I wore rings, necklaces, bracelets, pins—anything they could manage to secure on me. They were of gold and silver, embellished with turquoise, rubies, and tiny seed pearls; among them were a filigreed gold *khamsa* to ward off the evil eye; an eighteen-carat gold mesh bracelet in the form of a snake; silver mezuzahs; enameled brooches; and a pale gold locket, heart shaped, etched with flowers.

I know this not because I remember but because I have been told, because I have listened avidly to the few words my parents have let drop about this voyage. Much as I would like to, I remember nothing of the boat, nothing of my infant days in Cairo, not much even of the first years in New York. And my parents—Felix was thirty-six, Nelly thirty, when they left their home—have been reluctant to talk about it. They appear to suffer from a kind of amnesia, an involuntary—or is it willed?—failure to recollect. Obsessively, I ask questions, but I obtain only fragments, bits and pieces I painstakingly arrange and rearrange in my effort to grasp the whole. "What was it like?" I plead. "How did it feel?" "What did you think?" The answers I receive are fixed, rigid, laconic: a few details, ritually repeated, like verses of an ancient prayer; rough, unsanded boards—nothing like even the most rudimentary chair or table where I might sit, dream, feed my imagination.

The year was 1951, the boat the *Fiorello La Guardia,* our destination New York City. The trip lasted twenty-one days.

"Tu étais très malade," my mother tells me. "You were very sick. You had a high fever, and they told us we had to stay in our room."

"We were quarantined?" The idea is exotic, simultaneously romantic and frightening, evoking scenes of turn-of-the-century immigration, the long lines and cold examination rooms at Ellis Island. Where were we? On the boat? In New York Harbor? My mother's focus drifts.

"Yes, quarantined," she repeats. "That's the word. *On était si bête.* We were so stupid. I stayed with you in the hotel for three days while Felix went out. No one ever checked."

"We were in a hotel? You mean the boat was docked?" I ask, struggling for precision. "Where were we?"

"Yes," my mother replies, returning from her reverie. "The boat was docked in Naples." By then, the pretense of the short Italian vacation had been abandoned. We were on our way to New York. "I wanted to see the city," my mother continues, "but they said I had to stay in the room. We were so stupid. We didn't know anything. On the boat they brought me tea in little bags, and I had never seen anything like that before. I opened the bags and put the tea leaves in the cup. *J' étais si bête.* I was so stupid. They must have been laughing at me."

Part of the reason she can't remember, I suddenly realize, must be because she is embarrassed, ashamed of her ignorance. It is a trait we share. Living in what still often feels to me like an alien land, I retain her fear of saying or doing the wrong thing, letting slip a word or a gesture that will betray me, revealing my foreignness. Like her, I call myself "stupid"—*bête*—worry, stay silent.

"Not stupid," I try to reassure her, "you just didn't know."

My mother tells me she was seasick for the entire voyage, remaining below deck, vomiting, drinking black tea littered with leaves.

"Don't you remember anything else?" I persist. "What was the ocean like?"

"I went out only once," she eventually concedes, "at Gibraltar. I remember the sky, the stars. There were—how do you say it?—*falaises,* like in England—big cliffs—on both sides. It was very beautiful."

I picture a young woman, traveling with her husband and child, leaving behind parents, siblings, cousins, friends. She is alone and frightened, barely able to stand. Perhaps her husband tells her they are about to pass the Straits of Gibraltar. She has studied geography at the lycée in Cairo, knows where this is. She climbs up to the deck, holds her husband's arm, breathes deeply of the night air, takes her last look at the Mediterranean. The *Fiorello La Guardia* steams out into the Atlantic, as my mother succumbs once more to vertigo.

Five, six, seven years later, in our meticulously kept kitchen in Brooklyn, my mother sings, encouraging me to eat:

> *"Il était un petit navire,*
> *Il était un petit navire,*
> *Qui n'avait ja-ja-jamais navigué*
> *Qui n'avait ja-ja-jamais navigué*
> *O-wais-o-wais-o-wais. . . ."*

The song describes the adventures of a young sailor on his first ocean voyage, a trip across the Mediterranean:

> *"Sur la mer-mer-mer Méditerranée*
> *Sur la mer-mer-mer Méditerranée*
> *Sur la mer-mer-mer Méditerranée*
> *O-wais-o wais-o wais. . . ."*

After several weeks at sea, the ship is becalmed, and food supplies are exhausted. The starving sailors draw lots to determine who will be eaten. The *petit navire,* the song's young hero, is chosen. Moments before he is to be sacrificed, a landward wind arises and the ship sails safely to port.

I loved this macabre little song, with its cheerfully matter-of-fact threat of cannibalism, and I would often deliberately not eat, just to hear it again. While my mother sang, I dreamed of the *Méditerranée,* that mysterious blue sea she evoked with such love—the sea where innocent sailors might be eaten without remorse, the sea that glittered in her memory, forever shining on the other side of Gibraltar.

"What was it like," I ask, "to leave everybody behind in Cairo? Did *Nonna* and *Nonno* come to the dock to see you off?" My mother cannot answer, turns away, tells me that *Tante* Suze and *Oncle* Joe—my Aunt Suze and Uncle Joe—met us in New York. "But what was it like in Cairo?" I ask again, "Who came to the dock?" My mother remains silent, doesn't even tell me that the ship left from Alexandria, not Cairo.

I recall a moment several years back at one of the large train stations in Prague. Kay and I had spent a weekend in the city, and now she was leaving to return to Austria, while I was to remain in the Czech Republic for another week. Her train left early, and I accompanied her to the crowded station before dawn. Together we walked along the echoing platform to her carriage, located her compartment and her seat, put up her luggage. I said good-bye, then stood outside, watching the long train pull away. We waved, blew kisses, laughed as I pretended to cry.

But as the train receded into the brown countryside, I was surprised by the real tears that suddenly burned my face. Within moments I was sobbing, my shoulders convulsed. Embarrassed, I tried to stop myself. These tears made no sense. Kay and I would be separated for less than a week; we would be seeing one another before long. Yet I was inconsolable. Alone on that empty platform in a city where I could not speak the language, I sank into the pain of my first departure, the pain that awaits me at every good-bye. It is the memory I do not have, the experience that shapes all memory. The boat sails; the train pulls away. I hear the echoing blast of the steamship, the receding cry of the train. And I do not know if I am the one left behind or if I am the one leaving, if I am the one on the dock or on the ship, the platform or the train. What I know are the tears, the loss, the terrified certainty that I will never again see the loved face.

I decide to stop badgering my mother.

My mother's parents—*Nonna* and *Nonno,* Allegra and Selim Chalom—came to New York in 1956, five years after we had left Cairo. My father and *Oncle* Joe had tried for many years to obtain entry visas for them, but U.S. immigration quotas admitted only one hundred Egyptians a year. In Egypt most Jews were not regarded as citizens. Some had passports from European nations, and many were simply stateless, *apatride.* Yet from the point of view of U.S. immigration, they were Egyptians. During the Suez Crisis—when Britain, France, and Israel attacked Egypt after Nasser nationalized the Suez Canal—more than twenty thousand Jews either fled or were expelled from the country. Although the United States did not classify them as political refugees, some managed to enter the States; most emigrated to Israel or to Latin America. Along with *Tante* Diane, and my *Oncles* Albert, Lucien, and Eli, my maternal grandparents were moving to Brazil, where they would settle in São Paulo.

My mother, my two-year-old brother, Victor, and I drove to Idlewild Airport in the used Mercury my parents had just bought. At the age of seven, I already knew the airport well. We would go whenever a relative came to visit, and relatives were always visiting, strange men and elaborately made-up women who slept on the living room couch and talked loudly in French and Arabic, greeting me with astonished comments about how much I had grown, how closely I resembled my mother and grandmother. In time, my parents discovered that a trip to the airport could be as entertaining as a picnic at the

Cloisters or a stroll through the Brooklyn Botanical Gardens. We would park the car in a large outdoor lot, then walk to the observation tower, where we spent happy hours watching planes taking off and landing.

But this trip to the airport was not an excursion. My mother was on edge, anxious. Her parents were arriving, and though I had no conscious memory of them, I had been told that they loved me, that they would be happy to see me again. From photographs I knew that my grandfather wore a soft Fedora and that my grandmother's white hair fell in thin strands from a loose bun; they were both stooped, with rounded shoulders and bent necks. We were to meet them at the International Arrivals Building, after they passed through customs, *"la douane." La douane.* The words were ominous, frightening, uttered always with a kind of hushed respect. I sensed that they referred to a mystery one could not fathom, a force one could not control. What would the officials do? What would they find? Could they turn one back? I worried for my unknown grandparents who would have to go through *la douane.*

In the mid-1950s the customs area at Idlewild was in a huge rectangular room at the center of the International Arrivals Building. People awaiting family or visitors from abroad could look down from a glassed-in gallery high above the bare white room. When we learned that my grandparents' plane had landed, my mother and brother and I made our way to that gallery, watching the hundreds of people slowly moving through *la douane.*

"How will we recognize them?" I asked my mother. "How will we know who they are? Will they know we're here?"

The crowd seemed huge, a dull mass of solemn adults in heavy coats and hats. My mother was eager, holding my hand tightly, ceaselessly scanning the room below.

Then suddenly she pointed. *"Là. Ils sont là. Là. Regarde!"*

And she started banging against the glass, waving, jumping. *"Maman! Papa! Maman!"* She hurried us down the corridor so that we would be standing directly in front of the line where my grandparents waited, holding their passports, not even knowing to look up.

"Maman! Papa!" she continued to cry, banging the glass. I was self-conscious, not wanting her to call attention to our family. But of course that's exactly what my mother was intending to do. Call attention to us, get her mother and father to see us all. In those days, I hated to be out with my mother in public. There she would be, obviously attached to me, speaking in her awkward, accented English, asking questions that embarrassed me, acting so unmistakably foreign, while I ached to be like everyone else. But here everyone else was also banging on the glass, waving, trying to attract the attention of disoriented relatives stumbling across this last hurdle before the embrace of arrival.

Eventually, *Nonna* and *Nonno* looked up; they must have noticed others doing it, glimpsed the broad smiles illuminating otherwise bewildered faces. It was *Nonno* who saw us first, and he bent gently toward his wife, taking her hand, pointing upwards, showing her Nelly, Nelly and the children. Allegra smiled, burst into tears. My mother waved with both hands, her body pressed against the glass. She held my young brother up so they could see him, pulled me in front of her proudly.

And then we waited, waited and watched and worried as we saw the customs man order them to open their bags, to undo carefully wrapped packages, to answer questions. I could see the man my mother called Papa, whom I was to call *Nonno*. He was shaking his head, spreading his hands in a gesture that seemed to say, "I'm sorry, this is the best I can do."

"Do they speak any English?" I asked my mother.

"*Non,*" she replied, "*Ils ne* speak *pas* English."

"Shouldn't we help them?" I wondered. I wanted to run down to these old people trapped behind that glass wall, unable to speak the language, lost. I wanted to take their hands, to talk to the customs officer in my perfect, unaccented English, to lead them proudly from the chaos of the airport to the order of our small apartment in the Shore Haven housing complex. I still see them there, *Nonna* and *Nonno,* bewildered in that huge room at Idlewild, speechless and alone; I still want to go to them, to take them home with me, introduce them to the United States, our home. Of their visit itself—did my grandmother hold me? did my grandfather smile?—I, like my mother, have no memory. I only know that, after a month, *Nonna* and *Nonno* left us, moving to Brazil with my *Tante* Diane and *Oncles* Albert, Lucien, and Eli.

On the *Fiorello La Guardia,* because my mother was sick in the second-class cabin, I was out every day with my father, as he paced the deck. I like to think that sometimes he held me, lifting me in his arms so that I might look over the rails.

"What was it like?" I begged him to tell me in the years before his death. "What did we do all day? How did you feel?"

My mother would answer for him. "He was nervous. Your father had never spent any time with you before, and he was nervous. He didn't know what to do with you."

And I would turn again to my father, "What was it like? How did you feel?"

"I was scared," he would finally say, emerging with difficulty from the rigidity of advanced Parkinson's disease. "I was very nervous. We didn't know what we were going to find. I didn't know what I was going to do. I was scared."

In Cairo, my father—who had earned a French law degree—held a job as an interpreter of French and Arabic in the Mixed Courts. The courts, established in 1875, had jurisdiction over civil disputes between foreigners—among whom many Jews were counted—and Egyptians. Most Jewish men in Cairo worked in business and the professions, often as textile merchants or bankers, but my father cherished the security and prestige of his civil service appointment, as well as his status as an Egyptian citizen. Working for the Egyptian government, he would have a pension, the guarantee of a lifetime job. It was not something he could have given up easily.

"So why did you decide to leave?" I continued to probe.

"*J'ai vu l'écriture sur le mur,*" he whispered, pointing a trembling finger and opening his eyes wide, as if to show me the crumbling wall he could still see, inscribed with anti-Semitic comments. "I saw the writing on the wall I could see what was coming." He was pleased with himself, proud of his prophetic acumen, yet annoyed with my question. I shouldn't have to ask.

During and after World War II, in addition to working in the Mixed Courts, my father served as social secretary for Haim Nahum Effendi, the Chief Rabbi of Cairo. An esteemed scholar and astute diplomat, the Chief Rabbi worked to defuse the developing tensions between Jews and Arabs, refusing to identify himself—and the larger Sephardic Jewish community he represented—with either extreme Zionism or radical Egyptian nationalism. I imagine the rabbi talking with my father about the mounting signs that Jews might no longer be welcome in Egypt; I wonder if he didn't encourage my father to make his plans to leave.

"He was a great man," my father said of the Chief Rabbi. "He always worked for peace."

My mother interjects: "We have a card from him; he gave us a card," and she rummages through a box of old papers and photos until she finds it, the engraved calling card signed with flourishes by Cairo's Chief Rabbi, wishing *"chères Félix et Nelly bonne chance"* in the United States.

My father made his decision to emigrate early in 1946, a year after he married my mother and a few months after the terrible Cairo riots that erupted on November 2 and 3, 1945, the anniversary of the 1917 Balfour Declaration promising the establishment of a Jewish homeland in Palestine. Members of Young Egypt and the Muslim Brotherhood transformed what was to have been a peaceful anti-Zionist demonstration into an anti-Jewish riot. The Ashkenazi synagogue on al-Noubi Street was pillaged and set ablaze, Jewish-owned department stores in the elegant downtown were looted, and shouts of "Down with the Jews, down with colonization," echoed through the streets of the city. On the second day of the riots, Jewish shops on my grandparents' street were stoned.

My father's older brother applied for a visa a month after my father did; although our chance to emigrate came in 1951, my uncle's visa was not granted until late in 1956. In the month between the two brothers' applications, hundreds, perhaps thousands, of Jews must have been making the difficult decision to leave the nation where they had prospered for more than half a century.

Even during World War II—with the exception of the days when Rommel's troops threatened Alexandria—the more than eighty thousand Jews of Egypt had lived well. "We didn't care about a thing," a relative once told me. "We had our heads in the sand. Life was good." But in 1945 and 1946, emerging Egyptian nationalism, coupled with sympathy for Palestinian Arabs who were about to lose *their* homeland, triggered attacks against Jews, who were suspected of Zionism and of identifying with the British occupiers of Egypt. In the years after 1946, attacks against Jews increased, culminating in seizures of property, arrests, and, finally, expulsions.

I consider how, until his death, my father worried about our family's safety and security. "Explain to me," he often asked, "tell me what tenure means. Does it mean you can't lose your job?"

"Yes," I would assure him, "I can keep this job as long as I want." I was an associate professor in the English Department of the University of New Orleans, the city's major public university. After a long probation, I had acquired what few people in the United States have—a permanent, full-time, relatively well paying, and, best of all, extremely fulfilling job.

"Good," my father would say, comforted. "But don't do anything to make them upset with you."

My father was convinced that one cannot be too careful. Haunted by a keen sense of the fragility of social life, he knew that one could be jettisoned at a moment's notice, one's livelihood gone, one's standing lost. With alarming regularity, he asked me how much I made, if I was saving for retirement, if I got along with my neighbors and colleagues. When I moved to Oklahoma for my first teaching job, he had worried. "Do they know about Jews there? Will you be safe?"

My father's fears may have been a legacy from childhood. His own father died suddenly when he was four, and his mother, alone with three boys, was forced to turn to her widowed mother and mother-in-law for help. In that financially strained house-hold with no adult men, my father, the sensitive middle son, would have imbibed the women's anxious determination to act *comme il faut*—as one must—in order to maintain their hold on middle-class respectability. He grew to be a cautious man troubled by a concern for order, propriety, the opinions of others. Yet sometimes I think his anxieties should be attributed to the collective traumas of World War II and its aftermath rather than to individual family psychology. He never forgot those days before Al-Alamein, when Rommel's forces were poised to overtake Alexandria, and Jews throughout Egypt feared the worst; he always remembered how, daring the 1948 war with Israel, while my mother was pregnant with me, he was arrested, imprisoned, and interrogated by Egyptian soldiers who suspected him of having constructed a bomb in the family's apartment kitchen.

I struggle to picture this timid, delicate man—at the end nearly paralyzed with Parkinson's disease—pacing the decks of the *Fiorello La Guardia,* holding my small hand, seeking answers to what I'm sure even then were my incessant, though barely articulate, questions. "Where are we going?" "Why?" "When will we get there?" He had no job, no prospects. A man reliant on his ability to follow rules precisely, he was entering a country where he did not know the rules, where he would be forced to find his way without coordinates. When, in elementary school, I was introduced to graph paper, I would spend hours carefully drawing objects to scale. Later, I became fascinated with the use of the x and y axes to chart points. On a road trip, no matter who is driving, I appoint myself navigator. I pore over maps, plan routes, check constantly to see if we have reached the markers indicated in the guidebooks. I am my father's daughter. I need always to know where I am Like him, I fear the horrible free fall of being lost, at sea.

I have inherited neither antique furniture nor an ancestral home. I do not have a grandmother's house. What I have instead are fragments of stories and tiny pieces of moveable property—what Wemmick, in *Great Expectations,* advises Pip to get his hands on—that made the journey with my parents from Cairo. Jewelry, embroidery, books, silver: These are my heirlooms, my relics of the past. On my wall is a delicate needlepoint canvas depicting sailboats—feluccas—at sunset on the Nile; in my cupboard are engraved silver trays that once adorned my grandmother's table; and although it is much battered, I still have one of the beautifully woven prayer rugs my mother received at her wedding. Jewish peoples, I remind myself, rarely owned land; they invested whatever wealth they could amass in precious objects that moved quietly from hand to hand. Small things, nearly invisible—certainly unnoticeable to those who do not know what to look for. A migratory people, my ancestors learned to love what they could carry, and to carry what they loved.

I remember a gold locket that belonged to my maternal grandmother: eighteen karat, heart shaped, with delicate roses etched on its face. One summer evening in New York I sat with a friend at dusk on a bench in Central Park, talking after a pleasant dinner, prolonging our time together. The locket was on my neck, cool against my sun-warmed skin. A man approached us, asking for a match. When I said I didn't have one, he stepped back, then lunged suddenly toward me, with a knife I thought, directed at my throat. What he wanted, I realized too late, was the locket, glinting in the fading light. His hand grasped it, twisted the chain, and wrenched it from me as he jumped away, into the bushes across from us and out into the street. Stunned, I clutched my throat, and began to cry with grief and rage. He could not have known what it meant to me, this tiny piece of worked gold. What would it bring in a pawn shop? Surely not its worth. My grandmother's locket. What stories does it hold?

Questions and Ideas for Journaling and Discussion

1. Why do you think Nellie said that she could not remember what it had been like in Cairo?
2. Why is the setting of this story important? What do we learn from it about the realities of Egyptian-Jewish immigration as experienced by the Zonana family?
3. Talk about the theme of this piece of creative nonfiction.

Writing to Explore and Learn

1. Define "heirloom." Write a short essay in which you analyze the differences between Kay's heirlooms and Zonana's heirlooms.

Open Question for Writing

1. Choose two or three works in this section and compare and contrast each poet's and/or writer's representations of gender and ethnicity and/or identity.

PART V

THE CHANGING ROLES OF WOMEN AND MEN IN SOCIETY

Individual societies, including subcultures, have a great influence on gender roles and identities. In the west, the loosening of social expectations for women and men has affected our conception of gender differences. Since human desires and abilities often exceed, or resist, the narrow confines of our traditional social roles, a continuing change in attitude toward gender norms is necessary for the further evolution of society.

Both the civil rights and feminist movements of the 1960s and 1970s have effected political, economic, and social gains for minorities and women. Women of all races have gained access to birth control and abortion rights. With the increasing rise of minorities and women entering medicine, law, business, and the trades, the gender-based division of labor has shifted. Taking into consideration cultural and class variants, women are no longer confined to the domestic sphere of home and hearth, and men have increasingly assumed nontraditional roles in the home. In middle-class life, dual-earner marriages are not uncommon, and men are more likely to play a more involved role in the functioning of the family than they have done in the past. A progressive model of marriage consists of both woman and man working outside the home, sharing domestic chores and child-rearing responsibilities.

The gay rights movement has fought for equal rights, including marriage equality, for lesbians and gays. The aim is to continue to move toward a paradigm shift in which the idea of family and legitimacy in relationships will take on new social significance.

These fundamental transformations in the lives of women and men afford them more choices in lifestyle, work, and family arrangements, and indicate that there is no "one size fits all" formula when it comes to issues of gender, gender relations, and sexuality. As society moves forward, there is more work to be done to achieve full sexual egalitarianism and independence.

We raise these issues of contemporary representations of the changing roles of women and men in society for further discussion. The sections below will explore the dimensions of these evolving gender norms.

Kate Chopin
(1850–1904)

To succeed, the artist must possess the courageous soul . . . the brave
soul. The soul that dares and defies.

Kate Chopin's earliest writings are diary entries; she did not write seriously until becoming a widow at the age of thirty-two, with six children
to raise. Born in St. Louis, Missouri, to a Creole mother and father of
Irish descent, she grew up speaking both French and English. She moved
to New Orleans upon her marriage to Oscar Chopin—"the right man."
A fiction writer of short stories, children's stories, and novels, she was
well known in her lifetime. Most of her work, set in Louisiana, is known
for her depiction of sensitive, intelligent, and recalcitrant women.
Chopin's major works include *Bayou Folk* (1894) and *The Awakening*
(1899), which was widely condemned for its radical narrative of a dis-
contented wife and mother.

"The Story of an Hour" (1894)

Chopin tells the story of Mrs. Mallard, who believes that her husband
was killed in a train wreck as a way to question the significance of mar-
riage at a time when women and men lived by strict codes of femininity
and masculinity.

Knowing that Mrs. Mallard was afflicted with a heart trouble,
great care was taken to break to her as gently as possible the news of
her husband's death.

It was her sister Josephine who told her, in broken sentences:
veiled hints that revealed in half concealing. Her husband's friend
Richards was there, too, near her. It was he who had been in the newspaper office when intelligence of the railroad disaster was received,
with Brently Mallard's name leading the list of "killed." He had only
taken the time to assure himself of its truth by a second telegram, and
had hastened to forestall any less careful, less tender friend in bearing
the sad message.

She did not hear the story as many women have heard the same,
with a paralyzed inability to accept its significance. She wept at once,
with sudden, wild abandonment, in her sister's arms. When the storm

of grief had spent itself she went away to her room alone. She would have no one follow her.

There stood, facing the open window, a comfortable, roomy armchair. Into this she sank, pressed down by a physical exhaustion that haunted her body and seemed to reach into her soul.

She could see in the open square before her house the tops of trees that were all aquiver with the new spring life. The delicious breath of rain was in the air. In the street below a peddler was crying his wares. The notes of a distant song which some one was singing reached her faintly, and countless sparrows were twittering in the eaves.

There were patches of blue sky showing here and there through the clouds that had met and piled one above the other in the west facing her window.

She sat with her head thrown back upon the cushion of the chair, quite motionless, except when a sob came up into her throat and shook her, as a child who has cried itself to sleep continues to sob in its dreams.

She was young, with a fair, calm face, whose lines bespoke repression and even a certain strength. But now there was a dull stare in her eyes, whose gaze was fixed away off yonder on one of those patches of blue sky. It was not a glance of reflection, but rather indicated a suspension of intelligent thought.

There was something coming to her and she was waiting for it, fearfully. What was it? She did not know; it was too subtle and elusive to name. But she felt it, creeping out of the sky, reaching toward her through the sounds, the scents, the color that filled the air.

Now her bosom rose and fell tumultuously. She was beginning to recognize this thing that was approaching to possess her, and she was striving to beat it back with her will—as powerless as her two white slender hands would have been.

When she abandoned herself a little whispered word escaped her slightly parted lips. She said it over and over under her breath: "free, free, free!" The vacant stare and the look of terror that had followed it went from her eyes. They stayed keen and bright. Her pulses beat fast, and the coursing blood warmed and relaxed every inch of her body.

She did not stop to ask if it were or were not a monstrous joy that held her. A clear and exalted perception enabled her to dismiss the suggestion as trivial.

She knew that she would weep again when she saw the kind, tender hands folded in death; the face that had never looked save with love upon her, fixed and gray and dead. But she saw beyond that bitter moment a long procession of years to come that would belong to her absolutely. And she opened and spread her arms out to them in welcome.

There would be no one to live for during those coming years; she would live for herself. There would be no powerful will bending hers in that blind persistence with which men and women believe they have a right to impose a private will upon a fellow-creature. A kind intention or a cruel intention made the act seem no less a crime as she looked upon it in that brief moment of illumination.

15   And yet she had loved him—sometimes. Often she had not. What did it matter! What could love, the unsolved mystery, count for in face of this possession of self-assertion which she suddenly recognized as the strongest impulse of her being!

"Free! Body and soul free!" she kept whispering.

Josephine was kneeling before the closed door with her lips to the keyhole, imploring for admission. "Louise, open the door! I beg; open the door—you will make yourself ill. What are you doing, Louise? For heaven's sake open the door."

"Go away. I am not making myself ill." No; she was drinking in a very elixir of life through that open window.

Her fancy was running riot along those days ahead of her. Spring days, and summer days, and all sorts of days that would be her own. She breathed a quick prayer that life might be long. It was only yesterday she had thought with a shudder that life might be long.

20   She arose at length and opened the door to her sister's importunities. There was a feverish triumph in her eyes, and she carried herself unwittingly like a goddess of Victory. She clasped her sister's waist, and together they descended the stairs. Richards stood waiting for them at the bottom.

Some one was opening the front door with a latchkey. It was Brently Mallard who entered, a little travel-stained, composedly carrying his grip-sack and umbrella. He had been far from the scene of the accident, and did not even know there had been one. He stood amazed at Josephine's piercing cry: at Richards' quick motion to screen him from the view of his wife.

But Richards was too late.

When the doctors came they said she had died of heart disease—of joy that kills.

Questions and Ideas for Journaling and Discussion

1. What is Mrs. Mallard's reaction to the news of her husband's death?
2. How do we understand that Mrs. Mallard suppressed her true feelings about her husband?
3. What is the central irony of the story?
4. Discuss the doctor's conclusions about the cause of Mrs. Mallard's death.

Writing to Explore and Learn

1. Write about Chopin's view of the state of marriage in Victorian America.

Gwendolyn Brooks
(1917–2000)

Art hurts. Art urges voyages—and it is easier to stay home.

Gwendolyn Brooks began writing as a child and became the first African American to receive the Pulitzer Prize in 1950. Born in Kansas, she grew up on the impoverished South Side of Chicago, which was the inspiration for her writing. She graduated from Wilson Junior College in 1936, married, and had two children. She was a university professor, publicity director, and founder of a publishing house, and she won the American Academy of Arts and Letters Award, Guggenheim Fellowships, and honorary doctorates. Brooks is best known for her depiction of the struggles and hardships of ordinary African American life, as well as bringing poetry to the people. Her major works include *A Street in Bronzeville* (1945), *The Bean Eaters* (1960), "We Real Cool" (1966), and *Primer for Blacks* (1981).

"The Mother" (1963)

Brooks imagines a mother addressing her unborn children, those she had aborted. The poet's bold perspective on women and abortion problematizes and complicates standard notions of motherhood.

> Abortions will not let you forget.
> You remember the children you got that you did not get,
> The damp small pulps with a little or with no hair,
> The singers and workers that never handled the air.
> You will never neglect or beat
> Them, or silence or buy with a sweet.
> You will never wind up the sucking-thumb
> Or scuttle off ghosts that come.
> You will never leave them, controlling your luscious sigh,
> Return for a snack of them, with gobbling mother-eye.
>
> I have heard in the voices of the wind the voices of my dim
>   killed children.
> I have contracted. I have eased
> My dim dears at the breasts they could never suck.
> I have said, Sweets, if I sinned, if I seized

Your luck
And your lives from your unfinished reach,
If I stole your births and your names,
Your straight baby tears and your games,
Your stilted or lovely loves, your tumults, your marriages, aches, and
     your deaths,
If I poisoned the beginnings of your breaths,
Believe that even in my deliberateness I was not deliberate.
Though why should I whine,
Whine that the crime was other than mine?—
Since anyhow you are dead.
Or rather, or instead,
You were never made.
But that too, I am afraid,
Is faulty: oh, what shall I say, how is the truth to be said?
You were born, you had body, you died.
It is just that you never giggled or planned or cried.
Believe me, I loved you all.
Believe me, I knew you, though faintly, and I loved, I loved you All.

Questions and Ideas for Journaling and Discussion

1. Think about the kind of mother whom Brooks describes in the poem. Is it possible
   for a woman who has had abortions to consider herself a mother?
2. Do you believe Brooks when she tells her unborn children that she loves them? How
   can this be possible?
3. Diction is the result of a writer's use of word choice, phrasing, vocabulary, and sentence structure. What is the effect of the rhymes on the conversational diction of this
   poem?

Anne Panning
(b. 1966)

I feel the best writing is peppered with things and objects that speak about life or the narrator in a way straight narrative cannot.

Originally from Minnesota, Anne Panning has lived in the Philippines, Vietnam, Hawaii, northern Idaho, and Ohio; she now lives in upstate New York with her husband and two children and teaches creative writing at the State University of New York, Brockport. Panning writes fiction and creative nonfiction and is the winner of the 2006 Flannery O'Connor Award for Short Fiction for the collection *Super America: Stories* (2006). Her newest completed work, *Viet*Mom: An American Mother of Two Moves to the Mekong*, is a memoir. Both her fiction and nonfiction deal with American family issues, often infused with dark humor.

"The Mother" (2005)

The universally held cultural belief that women possess an essential feminine nature is subverted in Panning's short personal essay.

After I give birth to my son, I reach for my eyeglasses so I can see him. There's a photograph of me crying immediately post-birth, and I'm wearing nothing but a blue and white hospital gown and my tiny brown glasses that people—total strangers—used to always compliment me on back when they were still in style.

But life with baby wears on me. Nursing in the middle of the night in the near-dark, glasses off, all is a blur. In fact, day and night bleed into one cloudy gray. I lose the baby weight but also lose all energy or insight. I simply want to eat potato chips and watch reruns of *Providence* and cry.

When the baby is almost a year-old, I fly to California for a friend's wedding. I'm so unused to a lack of responsibility for others that I'm giddy just to ride solo on the airplane. I fall asleep before we're even out of my time zone. When I wake up, mountains and buttery sunshine fill the window. In the taxi, I sit back and imagine staying here forever. I will live in a bungalow, wear linen pants, and eat salad every day.

I stay in a hotel with fresh cedar shingles that's located next to a mall. This is Marin Country, which I've heard about and have associations:

wealth, convertibles with their tops down, women wearing white, fancy sunglasses, health food stores. I am not incorrect. But it is also sunny and warm and invigorating. Somehow living in the grim gray cold of New York State seems to be the reason for much of my exhaustion. I have been missing simple sunshine.

The day before the ceremony, I walk over to the mall and pass a vitamin shop. What catches my eye is the display case of eyeglass frames advertised for twenty-five dollars. "Latest styles from Italy," a sign says, and I am perplexed. Thinking they must be drugstore magnifying lenses, I almost pass, but hesitate. The frames are so stylish, so rich in color, so differently shaped that I want to own a pair and start over and not look like a "mom."

Inside, the clerk explains that the owner takes a yearly vacation to Italy and brings back last year's models at deep discounts. There's no catch, she says. It's just something he does. I pore over the black velvet tray of frames, finally deciding on an elongated rectangular pair in a color much like toffee with a tiny tiny hint of orange blended in. When I try them on, even without my prescription lenses, I think I look European.

On the plane ride home, I keep the red velvet glasses' case in my carry-on. I am torn: a deep, almost primal urge to get back to my child, smell him, hold him, feel his small soft hands, and another competing urge to live in California in a light and airy house with eucalyptus trees and an open porch and childless friends who mix sangrias on Saturday afternoons and eat tapas.

Back home, my husband and I both teach and tag-team with our child. When the winter gets particularly unbearable, I take my son to the community toddler gym to let him blow off steam. Before we are allowed entrance into the stark, padded room, we must pose for photo ID cards. When mine is handed back to me, I'm flummoxed, out of focus, and feel I'm looking at a stranger. I've got my "pimp" coat on, a black Persian lamb's wool with shiny buttons, which is really an old-lady Presbyterian church sale coat I got for three dollars. My bangs are cut very short and my California eyeglasses look almost bright orange, too European, too West Coast, too something. Holding a toddler in flannel shirt and overalls in my arms, I am completely mismatched with my life—an impostor, a stand-in, a woman I barely recognize.

Questions and Ideas for Journaling and Discussion

1. What is the effect of motherhood on the author's sense of self? How does she experience herself before the baby was born and afterwards?
2. In literature, a symbol is one thing that stands for another. What possible symbolic meaning do the eyeglasses have in the story?

Audre Lorde*

"Black Mother Woman" (1973)

This poem celebrates blackness in the context of the mother/daughter relationship. Lorde explores the role of a mother who affects the development of her daughter's identity as a means to instill a sense of pride in African American women. The personal tone of the poem reveals the speaker's awareness of her coming of age as being deeply connected to the issue of race.

I cannot recall you gentle
yet through your heavy love
I have become
an image of your once delicate flesh
split with deceitful longings.

When strangers come and compliment me
your aged spirit takes a bow
jingling with pride
bat once you hid that secret
in the center of furies
hanging me
with deep breasts and wiry hair
with your own split flesh
and long suffering eyes
buried in myths of little worth.

But I have peeled away your anger
down to the core of love
and look mother
I Am
a dark temple where your true spirit rises
beautiful
and tough as chestnut
stanchion against your nightmare of weakness
and if my eyes conceal
a squadron of conflicting rebellions

*See page 68 for author's biography.

I learned from you
to define myself
through your denials.

Questions and Ideas for Journaling and Discussion

1. Describe the daughter's attitude toward her mother in the poem.
2. Discuss Lorde's construction of female African American identity.

Writing to Explore and Learn

1. Analyze the last phrase, "I learned from you to define myself through your denials," in terms of your understanding of the mother/daughter relationship.
2. An oxymoron is a figure of speech that contrasts contradictory terms. What does Lorde mean by the oxymoron "heavy love"? Write a poem about "heavy love."

Barbara A. Holland
(1925–1988)

Poetry was my personal rebellion against the second-handedness of the scholarly criticism which comprises doctoral work in literature and the file-clerky business of it.

Barbara A. Holland was born into an intellectual family in Maine—both parents were college professors. She attended private schools and then earned both a BA and an MA in English literature from the University of Pennsylvania. In the 1960s, after working at a series of jobs, she moved to Greenwich Village in New York to write full time, living on scant income from freelance work. An iconoclast and feminist, Holland's poems are both funny and terrifying. She was also known for her captivating dramatic readings. Notable works include the collection *Crises of Rejuvenation* (1986) and the poem "Not Now, Wanderer," an audience favorite.

"The Consultation" (1983)

In a discussion with her doctor, the speaker unapologetically insists on ending an unwanted pregnancy regardless of the father's desire to keep the baby. In this poem of personal protest, the poet resists gender ideologies as a means to assert female autonomy, the state in which women are in full control of their bodies.

Doctor, I must not have this child,
for it will have no bones to support it.
A poor little thing that can neither
stand nor sit or use its hands, with a sponge
for a skull throughout a lifetime.
Can you imagine such a being as an adult?

None of this would come about
were I to drink of its father's blood,
but I am allergic to blood
or influenced by conditioning.

Its clotting, its curdling,
its fibrinous texture estranges
my stomach; my pyloric sphincter rebels.

And is there any guarantee
that death will in any way alter
or adjust my digestive system?
Doctor, I refuse to vomit the blood
of anyone all over the landscape
and perhaps forever.

                                  No,
I must cling to my beliefs
in the powers of garlic,
trust every weekend to its down home
savor and daily keep my windows
curtained against .that mournful face
which entreats me nightly and politely
from the fire escape and try not
to hear his fingernails squealing
in frustration against the glass.

Doctor, this child to be
has got to go.

Questions and Ideas for Journaling and Discussion

1. Why does Holland tell us that the child "will have no bones to support it"?
2. Discuss how the poem supports abortion rights for women.
3. What do you notice about the diction employed in this poem?

Writing to Explore and Learn

1. Explore Holland's use of the vampire myth as a way to represent her vision of gender relations.
2. Society has constructed an idealized version of mothers. Write an essay in which you first explain what has been traditionally believed about motherhood and then describe alternate versions of motherhood taken from Brooks' "The Mother," Holland's "The Consultation," and Panning's "The Mother."

Matthew Arnold
(1822–1888)

Culture is to know the best that has been said and thought in the world.

Matthew Arnold, poet and critic, won prizes for his poetry at an early age, going on to win the prestigious Newdigate Prize for "Cromwell, A Prize Poem," when a student at Oxford University. He was born into an educated family at Laleham on Thames, England. After a stint as a teacher of classics, Arnold married in 1851 and began work as a government school inspector, a position that he held for thirty-five years. His life in education benefitted both his critical works and his poetry. After the publication of *Empedocles on Etna* (1852) and *Poems* (1853) established him as a poet, he was offered a position as professor of poetry at Oxford. Arnold's criticism is core to the tradition, influencing almost every important English critic since that time. After suffering the tragic deaths of three of his sons, Arnold embarked on extended lecture tours in the United States. His major works include *The Function of Criticism at the Present Time* (1864, 1865), the poem "Dover Beach" (1867), and *Culture and Anarchy* (1869).

"The Forsaken Merman" (1853)

In this poem, simply written as though it were a children's story, Arnold sharply criticizes the hypocrisy of organized religion and calls into question the relevance of the afterlife.

Come, dear children, let us away;
Down and away below!
Now my brothers call from the bay,
Now the great winds shoreward blow,
5   Now the salt tides seaward flow;
Now the wild white horses play,
Champ and chafe and toss in the spray.
Children dear, let us away!
This way, this way!

10   Call her once before you go—
Call once yet!

In a voice that she will know:
"Margaret! Margaret!"
Children's voices should be dear
15   (Call once more) to a mother's ear;

Children's voices, wild with pain—
Surely she will come again!
Call her once and come away;
This way, this way!
20   "Mother dear, we cannot stay!
The wild white horses foam and fret."
Margaret! Margaret!

Come, dear children, come away down;
Call no more!
25   One last look at the white-wall'd town
And the little grey church on the windy shore,
Then come down!
She will not come though you call all day;
Come away, come away!

30   Children dear, was it yesterday
We heard the sweet bells over the bay?
In the caverns where we lay,
Through the surf and through the swell,
The far-off sound of a silver bell?
35   Sand-strewn caverns, cool and deep,
Where the winds are all asleep;
Where the spent lights quiver and gleam,
Where the salt weed sways in the stream,
Where the sea-beasts, ranged all round,
40   Feed in the ooze (if their pasture-ground;
Where the sea-snakes coil and twine,
Dry their mail and bask in the brine;
Where great whales come sailing by,
Sail and sail, with unshut eye,
45   Round the world for ever and aye?
When did music come this way?
Children dear, was it yesterday?

Children dear, was it yesterday
(Call yet once) that she went away?
50   Once she sate with you and me,
On a red gold throne in the heart of the sea,
And the youngest sate on her knee.
She comb'd its bright hair, and she tended it well,

When down swung the sound of a far-off bell.
She sigh'd, she look'd up through the clear green sea;   55
She said: "I must go, to my kinsfolk pray
In the little grey church on the shore today.
T will be Easter-time in the world—ah me!
And I lose my poor soul, Merman! here with thee."
I said: "Go up, dear heart, through the waves;   60
Say thy prayer, and come back to the kind sea-caves!"
She smiled, she went up through the surf in the bay.
Children dear, was it yesterday?

Children dear, were we long alone?
"The sea grows stormy, the little ones moan;   65
Long prayers," I said, "in the world they say;
Come!" I said; and we rose through the surf in the bay.
We went up the beach, by the sandy down
Where the sea-stocks bloom, to the white-wall'd town;
Through the narrow paved streets, where all was still,   70
To the little grey church on the windy hill.
From the church came a murmur of folk at their prayers,
But we stood without in the cold blowing airs.
We climb'd on the graves, on the stones worn with rains,
And we gazed up the aisle through the small leaded panes.   75
She sate by the pillar; we saw her clear:
"Margaret, hist! come quick, we are here!
Dear heart," I said, "we are long alone;
The sea grows stormy, the little ones moan."
But, ah, she gave me never a look,   80
For her eyes were seal'd to the holy book!
Loud prays the priest; shut stands the door.
Come away, children, call no more!
Come away, come down, call no more!

Down, down, down!   85
Down to the depths of the sea!
She sits at her wheel in the humming town,
Singing most joyfully.
Hark what she sings: "O joy, O joy,
For the humming street, and the child with its toy!   90
For the priest, and the bell, and the holy well;
For the wheel where I spun,
And the blessed light of the sun!"
And so she sings her fill,
Singing most joyfully,   95
Till the spindle drops from her hand,
And the whizzing wheel stands still.

She steals to the window, and looks at the sand,
And over the sand at the sea;
100 And her eyes are set in a stare;
And anon there breaks a sigh,
And anon there drops a tear,
From a sorrow-clouded eye,
And a heart sorrow-laden,
105 A long, long sigh;
For the cold strange eyes of a little Mermaiden
And the gleam of her golden hair.

Come away, away children
Come children, come down!
110 The hoarse wind blows coldly;
Lights shine in the town.
She will start from her slumber
When gusts shake the door;
She will hear the winds howling,
115 Will hear the waves roar.
We shall see, while above us
The waves roar and whirl,
A ceiling of amber,
A pavement of pearl.
120 Singing: "Here came a mortal,
But faithless was she!
And alone dwell for ever
The kings of the sea."

But, children, at midnight,
125 When soft the winds blow,
When clear falls the moonlight,
When spring-tides are low;
When sweet airs come seaward
From heaths starr'd with broom,
130 And high rocks throw mildly
On die blanch'd sands a gloom;
Up the still, glistening beaches,
Up die creeks we will hie,
Over banks of bright seaweed
135 The ebb-tide leaves dry.
We will gaze, from the sand-hills,
At the white, sleeping town;
At the church on the hill-side—
And then come back down.
140 Singing: "There dwells a loved one,
But cruel is she!

She left lonely for ever
The kings of the sea."

Questions and Ideas for Journaling and Discussion

1. Identify the images in the poem.
2. Through the images, how would you describe the town?
3. Because Margaret was brought up in the town, what kinds of values might she have?
4. What are the images that describe what it's like under the sea?
5. Because the Merman came from beneath the sea, what might his values be?

Writing to Explore and Learn

1. Think about the relationship between Margaret and the Merman. In real life, what kind of relationship might this be?
2. Was it a greater moral wrong for Margaret to abandon her religion and condemn her soul to hell in the next life or to abandon her children in this life?

Adrienne Rich*

"Living in Sin" (1955)

Rich asks us to imagine a woman living during a time when cohabitating unmarried women were harshly criticized and, in some cases, ostracized by a society wherein only marriage conferred respectability on a relationship. Despite exhibiting sexually transgressive behavior, the speaker cannot escape the prescribed gender roles, which prove to be unfulfilling and limiting for her.

She had thought the studio would keep itself;
no dust upon the furniture of love.
Half heresy, to wish the taps less vocal,
the panes relieved of grime. A plate of pears,
5   a piano with a Persian shawl, a cat
stalking the picturesque amusing mouse
had risen at his urging.
Not that at five each separate stair would writhe
under the milkman's tramp; that morning light
10 so coldly would delineate the scraps
of last night's cheese and three sepulchral bottles;
that on the kitchen shelf among the saucers
a pair of beetle-eyes would fix her own—
envoy from some village in the moldings . . .
15 Meanwhile, he, with a yawn,
sounded a dozen notes upon the keyboard,
declared it out of tune, shrugged at the mirror,
rubbed at his beard, went out for cigarettes;
while she, jeered by the minor demons,
20 pulled back the sheets and made the bed and found
a towel to dust the table-top,
and let the coffee-pot boil over on the stove.
By evening she was back in love again,
though not so wholly but throughout the night
25 she woke sometimes to feel the daylight coming
like a relentless milkman up the stairs.

*See page 21 for author biography.

Questions and Ideas for Journaling and Discussion

1. Discuss the significance of the title, "Living in Sin."
2. Compare and contrast the speaker's expectations of her love affair with the realities of her situation.
3. What are the images that help readers learn the speaker's state of mind?

Merle Feld
(b. 1947)

The story of poetry and me is a lot like the story of Judaism and me.

Born in Brooklyn, New York, poet, playwright, activist, and educator Merle Feld is the wife of a rabbi and a mother of two. She has pioneered the teaching of writing as a spiritual practice and is the founding director of the Rabbinic Writing Institute. She has traveled extensively, working with Jewish women's groups in Russia, Ukraine, and Belarus, organizing dialogue groups for Israeli and Palestinian women on the West Bank, teaching educators and community leaders from the Middle East and South Asia through the auspices of Seeds of Peace, and leading writing workshops for rabbis, rabbinical students, and lay leaders. Her book, *A Spiritual Life: Exploring the Heart and Jewish Tradition* (2007), combines poetry and memoir, and provides prompts for journaling and discussion.

"We All Stood Together" for Rachel Adler (2007)

Feld's poem takes place on Mount Sinai at the time that God gave the Torah, the Hebrew Bible, to the Jewish people. Until recently, only men have participated in synagogue readings of the Torah, where only consonants appear in the text. In this work, Feld suggests an unwritten feminine interpretation of the Torah, in which the vowels were heard and passed down by women.

My brother and I were at Sinai.
He kept a journal
of what he saw,
of what he heard,
of what it all meant to him.

I wish I had such a record
of what happened to me there.

It seems like every time I want to write
I can't—
I'm always holding a baby,
one of my own,

or one for a friend,
always holding a baby,
so my hands are never free
to write things down.

And then
as time passes,
the particulars,
the hard data,
the who what when where why,
slip away from me,
and all I'm left with is
the feeling.

But feelings are just sounds
the vowel barking of a mute.

My brother is so sure of what he heard—
after all he's got a record of it—
consonant after consonant after consonant.

If we remembered it together
we could recreate holy time
sparks flying.

Questions and Ideas for Journaling and Discussion

1. What might have been the role of women at the time that the Israelites wandered in the desert for forty years?
2. Explore what Feld means when she says that sparks will fly if "we remembered it together."
3. Discuss the differences in women's roles in society in ancient times and in the present. Why do you think that it might be possible for Judaism to include women in ritual activities today?

Writing to Explore and Learn

1. Write a short story about what the giving of the Torah might have been like if a female God had written the commandments.

Angela Costa*

And They Call It Puppy Love (A Trans-Species Farce) (2006)

Costa's original, radical take on the themes of motherhood, family relations, and friendship in this play unpacks the myth of motherhood that defines and sustains western social and sexual unions. A farcical twist on the mother/daughter relationship plot with a dog at its center, the play stages in provocative ways the conflicts and struggles between a narcissistic, baby-boomer parent and her conservative daughter as a means to challenge the rules and conventions of cultural contexts in which we find ourselves today.

(*Baby boomer,* ALYSON ST. PIERRE, *sits on a park bench smoking a joint. She's surrounded by a pup tent, doggie bowl, and boom box. Chronic pot-smoking, wine drinking, codependent best friend,* JEAN MELLING, *approaches carrying two bottles of wine. Crickets chirp.*)

(ALYSON *inhales a joint and holds her breath.*)

ALYSON   Will somebody shut those fuckin things up!

JEAN   ALYSON. WHERE ARE YOU? ALYSON. I'M LOST!

ALYSON   I'M RIGHT HERE, JEAN. FOR GOD'S SAKE! I'M RIGHT HERE!

(JEAN *sits, lights up.*)

JEAN   Why . . . why are we here?

ALYSON   I don't have time for the BIG questions, today, Jean. I just don't!

JEAN   What happened?

ALYSON   The kid's home from school. The box. Don't ask.

(JEAN *inhales joint. Holds her breath.*)

JEAN   So what—what happened?

ALYSON   She was rummaging around upstairs. And I forgot that I forgot to put the box away.

*See page 49 for author biography.

JEAN   NO! What'd she do? Flush it all?

ALYSON   Not that box, Jean! The other box.

JEAN   Oh, with the—the um, um, thee, um, um, uh, uh, the, um, uh—

ALYSON   Squeeky toys, Jean. The squeeky toys.

JEAN   I love those things.

ALYSON   Well, she was digging in that box like an obsessed little crab and I'm like, "Honey, what are you doing?" And she's like, "MOM, what are YOU doing!" And I say, "Being fabulous. Being me."

JEAN   Damn right!

ALYSON   And then, in that condescending little voice of hers, she says, "despicable." And, I'm like, "who is, honey?" And she's like, "YOU are mom and so are these—these squeeky toys, this leash, these handcuffs, this b-b-bone." And THEN she finds the magazines and starts waving them in the air, screaming, "HOT DIGGITY DOG? DOGGIE STYLE? What the HELL is going on, MOM?"

JEAN   She's so anal—

ALYSON   Accusatory—

JEAN   Tedious—

ALYSON   Like her father, without the salary—

JEAN   For sure.

ALYSON   Believe me, she was his idea. I thought, oh, a baby, that could be fun. Frankly, I would of rather had pups. Anyway, the condom broke and the rest is histrionics. What can you do?

JEAN   ABORT!

ALYSON   Could of, would of, should of. Anyway—

JEAN   Yeah—

ALYSON   Pepper hears the commotion—

JEAN   He was there!?

ALYSON   Yep.

JEAN   She doesn't know yet, right?

ALYSON   No. But I need to tell her.

JEAN   You've got NOTHING to hide!

ALYSON   So, Pepper starts barking, panting, scratching the door. And Sarah's like, "WHO'S in the closet? WHO'S in the closet?"

JEAN   And—

ALYSON   And I'm like, honey . . . this is MOMMY'S house and in MOMMY'S house, no one's in the closet. Your choices are your choices and mine are not yours, and—

JEAN   (*sings*)

Give peace a chance—

ALYSON and if by chance, there go I and . . . blah, blah, blah. And I don't even know what I m saying anymore.

JEAN and ALYSON
(*both wasted, sing and sway*)
All we are saying / is give peace a chance.

ALYSON Then Pepper comes—

JEAN Where?

ALYSON JUMPING out of the closet and knocks her right the fuck over.

JEAN GOOD!

ALYSON So, in answer to your question, Jean . . . that's why we're here . . . in the park, so Pepper can be comfortable with who he is, and I can get a little, needed peace of mind for a change. I do exist too now, don't I?

JEAN You're a visionary! An exception to every rule. An incredible mother!

ALYSON EVERYONE ADORES me, except my daughter.

JEAN What's SHE want?

ALYSON More love—

JEAN More wine—

ALYSON I'll call her—

JEAN Must you.

(ALYSON *phones* SARAH *on her cell phone.*)

ALYSON Hi honey. It's mommy. Yes. Wanna come hang out in the park a little bit? Just a little bit, then go, okay. Mommy loves you, you know that. Of course, you do.

JEAN Don't encourage her.

ALYSON Yes honey . . . we'll have a pajama party . . . the night's young, and me too (*Beat*). . . NO! NOT just the two of us, of course NOT . . . (*Beat*) Jean is here and there's someone else I want you to meet. Oh, and could you do mommy a tiny, little favor, pleeeaaase . . . fetch, I mean get, mommy that case of wine from the basement and bring it to the park. It's not heavy, honey. It's white! White wine. The red is heavy, not the white.

JEAN Just drop it off!

ALYSON Yes, honey . . . We're by the bench, near the road. I love you too. (*Beat*) NO! What do I have to do to convince you that I've given it up . . .

(*Lights change.*)

(*Boom box plays a slow blues while* ALYSON *dances alone and Jean smokes weed. A stern, conservatively dressed* SARAH ST. PIERRE *approaches, wearing practical pumps and struggling with a case of wine.*)

SARAH   Mom. Mom!

ALYSON   Hi honey. Just leave it there. See ya.

SARAH   Mom! I came here to BE with you.

ALYSON   Oh, I have something I need to—

SARAH   Give me?

ALYSON   Tell you.

SARAH   (*sees* PEPPER)

God!

ALYSON   What?

SARAH   What's that?!

ALYSON   What?

SARAH   That—that drunken animal!

ALYSON   You remember Jean.

SARAH   Not her.

ALYSON   Who?

SARAH   Him.

ALYSON   Pepper?

SARAH   That's—that DOG in the closet—

JEAN   And this is MOMMY'S house and in MOMMY'S house—

ALYSON   I don't know what you're trying to say, honey . . . but . . . yes, Pepper's a DOG, but he's NOT in the closet—

SARAH   He—he's drinking, mom!

ALYSON   Party, honey! PAARTAY!

SARAH   He's DRUNK, mom!

ALYSON   Mommy is an animal lover. You know that, don't you?

SARAH   Well .

ALYSON   Don't you?

SARAH   I guess. But . . . my hamster . . . I always felt you might have killed my—

ALYSON   That wasn't me! (*Beat*) Tell me again, you know mommy is an animal lover, right? Say yes.

SARAH   Yes.

ALYSON   Well, now . . . guess what?

SARAH   What?

ALYSON   Mommy's lover . . . IS an animal.

SARAH   What?!

ALYSON   Great, huh?

SARAH   No.

ALYSON   Why?

SARAH   Another defenseless creature for you to exploit. You're—you're SELFISH!

JEAN   Shhhellfish? Where's the shhhellfish?

ALYSON   It's Trans, honey. The word is Trans. And they call it Puppy Love. You're just not up on things, that's all.

SARAH   Trans?

ALYSON   Trans-species. Big in the U.K. . . . Exploding in Berlin.

SARAH   NO, no, ma.

ALYSON   Don't fight me? Be nice. Make friends.

(PEPPER *rubs up against* SARAH, *tries to lick her.*)

ALYSON   Sarah, this is Pepper. Pepper, Sarah. Pepper's my partner. Significant Animal-Other. Lover. Or whatever we're calling it now. We're having, FUN. Aren't we?

SARAH   Fun?

JEAN   Fun. That's beautiful, man. I love it. I do.

(ALYSON *pours some wine into Pepper's doggie bowl. He wags his tail.*)

SARAH   Pepper's a dog and you should treat him like a dog, instead of using him like you use everything you come in contact with. He's a defenseless animal and you're a treacherous BITCH. I want you to STOP!

ALYSON   Gee. Your more interesting when you're angry. (Beat) Come on, honey, tell me, aren't some of your best friends, you know, dogs?

SARAH   It's not the same, mom.

ALYSON   I get it. It's fine to have a dog as a pet, a best friend, but when your mother's sleeping with—

SARAH   Sleeping with—

ALYSON   With—

SARAH   Where?

JEAN   In the pup pup pup PUP tent! Pup, pup, pup, PUP, tent . . .

(PEPPER *paws* ALYSON.)

ALYSON   Yeah Pepper. Yeah baby. You're my top dog. Kiss me. Lick me—

SARAH   Everything and anything for your own amusement!

ALYSON   What!

SARAH   He's an animal!

JEAN   You're a pig!

SARAH   You're a stupid ass!

ALYSON   I'M ONLY HUMAN!

SARAH   He's a MUTT! A MUTT!

ALYSON   What?

JEAN   What?

(PEPPER *barks, cries, runs off.*)

ALYSON   How dare you use the "M" word in front of him. You racist, little
animal, phobe—

JEAN   Selma, Alabama 19— . . .

ALYSON   Shut up Jean! Where's Pepper?

(*Sound of screeching tires.*)

ALYSON   Oh my God. Pepper! PEPPER!

(*Yelping sounds from* PEPPER.)

JEAN   You killed him! You little murderer! You're going to jail. FOR LIFE!
(*Beat*) I could of been a contender.

(*Lights change.* ALYSON, PEPPER, JEAN and SARAH *walk together in the
park. Pepper's head and leg are bandaged.* ALYSON *carries a picnic basket.* JEAN *smokes a joint and* SARAH *lugs a case of wine.* ALYSON *spreads
a red-checkered table cloth on the grass. Birds chirp.*)

ALYSON   Will somebody shut those fuckin' things up!

SARAH   I like Pepper, ma. I do. At first, I didn't understand—

ALYSON-   It's over.

SARAH   Over?

ALYSON   He won't let me shave his back and that doesn't work for me,
honey. I need something a little more . . . Metrosexual, now.

SARAH   But, mom, he's—

ALYSON   He's history and you're giving me a headache.

SARAH   But for the first time in my life, I—I feel happy.

ALYSON   I can't be responsible for that now! I've got myself to think about
. . . and—and Jean—

JEAN   (*almost passed out*)

Pup pup pup PUP tent—

SARAH   But mom, I really need—I just need—

ALYSON   I can't talk about your needs, honey. I just can't.

(*Blackout*)

Questions and Ideas for Journaling and Discussion

1. A farce is a play (or television show or film) designed to encourage laughter by presenting broadly humorous situations and playing down the importance of character and plot. A comedy is a play centered on humor and an expectation of a happy ending. Identify the farcical elements of the play. Identify the comedic elements. Do you think that the play is a farce, a comedy, or both?
2. Characterize Alyson and her daughter Sarah. How are they different? How are they alike?
3. Describe the conflict between Sarah and her mother's best friend, Jean.
4. How is Pepper presented? How are we supposed to react to his character?

Writing to Explore and Learn

1. Research the counterculture of the 1960s. Analyze the play in terms of some of the beliefs and attitudes inherent in that culture.
2. Write your own story or play in which the protagonist is involved in a "nontraditional" relationship, which could be one of mixed race, mixed ethnicity, and/or same sex.
3. Discuss the metaphor of the nonhuman lovers in Costa's *And They Call It Puppy Love* and Arnold's "The Forsaken Merman."
4. In the play *And They Call It Puppy Love*, the piece of creative nonfiction "The Mother," and the poem "The Mother," by Costa, Panning, and Brooks, respectively, address the challenges and meanings of motherhood in different ways. Drawing on the three works, discuss this issue. Is there any such thing as a "perfect" mother?

Galway Kinnell
(b. 1927)

Self-knowledge is always helpful to our well-being.

Born and raised in Rhode Island, Galway Kinnell began to write poetry as a teenager. He was attracted at a young age to the poetry of Edgar Allan Poe and Emily Dickinson. He graduated from Princeton University in 1948, and earned an MA from the University of Rochester in 1949. After teaching in Europe and the Middle East, he realized that he could be more productive outside an academic environment. He worked odd jobs and became involved in the civil rights and anti-Vietnam War movements of the 1960s. His poetry addresses a wide range of themes, including animals, children, social issues, relations of the self to violence, love of nature, the transience of life, and the significance of life through daily human existence. His first publication, *Selected Poems* (1980), won the Pulitzer Prize and National Book Award. His major works include *Body Rags* (1968), *The Book of Nightmares* (1971), and *Strong Is Your Hold: Poems* (2008).

"After Making Love We Hear Footsteps" (1980)

In this decidedly personal poem, Kinnell uses irony and humor to write about his son, Fergus, to show both marital love and parental love in ways that reflect the quotidian and transcendent.

> For I can snore like a bullhorn
> or play loud music
> or sit up talking with any reasonably sober Irishman
> and Fergus will only sink deeper
> into his dreamless sleep, which goes by all in one flash,
> but let there be that heavy breathing
> or a stifled come-cry anywhere in the house
> and he will wrench himself awake
> and make for it on the run—as now, we lie together,
> after making love, quiet, touching along the length of our
>   bodies,
> familiar touch of the long-married,
> and he appears—in his baseball pajamas, it happens,

the neck opening so small he has to screw them on—
and flops down between us and hugs us and snuggles himself to
    sleep,
his face gleaming with satisfaction at being this very child.

In the half darkness we look at each other
and smile
and touch arms across this little, startlingly muscled body—
his one whom habit of memory propels to the ground of his making,
sleeper only the mortal sounds can sing awake,
this blessing love gives again into our arms.

Questions and Ideas for Journaling and Discussion

1. Describe the uses of humor in the poem.
2. Irony is a literary device that may produce a sarcastic disproportion. Where does Kinnell use irony in the poem?
3. What does the poem suggest about the role of the child in the couple's life?

Writing to Explore and Learn

1. Discuss the ways in which the poem represents the everyday and the transcendent in family life.

Chitra Banerjee Divakaruni (b. 1957)

The art of dissolving boundaries is what living is all about.

Chitra Banerjee Divakaruni, fiction writer and poet, was born in India, immigrating to the United States in 1976 at the age of nineteen. She earned an MA in English from Wright State University in Dayton, Ohio, and a PhD from the University of California, Berkeley. She currently lives in Sunnydale, California, with her husband and two children and teaches creative writing at Foothill College in Los Altos Hills, California. Since 1991, she has been the president of Maitri, a helpline for South Asian women that particularly assists victims of domestic violence and other abusive situations. Divakaruni's work is widely anthologized, including pieces in *Best American Short Stories*, *The O'Henry Prize Stories*, and *The Pushcart Prize Anthology*. Her book of short stories, *Arranged Marriage*, won critical acclaim and the 1996 American Book Award, the Bay Area Book Reviewers Award, and the PEN Josephine Miles Award for Fiction. *The Mistress of Spices* was on several "Best Books" lists, including the *San Francisco Chronicle*'s 100 Best Books of the 20th Century.

"Clothes" (1995)

The traditional dress of Indian women is the sari, whose colors symbolize their position in life, for example, marriage, the hope of auspicious fortune, and widowhood. This short story tells how a young woman's clothing and her acceptance and ultimate rejection of traditional clothing and color reflect her rejection of the role of a woman in a society that restricts women's autonomy.

The water of the women's lake laps against my breasts, cool, calming. I can feel it beginning to wash the hot nervousness away from my body. The little waves tickle my armpits, make my sari float up around me, wet and yellow, like a sunflower after rain. I close my eyes and smell the sweet brown odor of the *ritha* pulp my friends Deepali and Radha are working into my hair so it will glisten with little lights this evening. They scrub with more vigor than usual and wash it out more carefully, because today is a special day. It is the day of my bride-viewing.

"Ei, Sumita! Mita! Are you deaf?" Radha says. "This is the third time I've asked you the same question."

"Look at her, already dreaming about her husband, and she hasn't even seen him yet!" Deepali jokes. Then she adds, the envy in her voice only half hidden, "Who cares about friends from a little Indian village when you're about to go live in America?"

I want to deny it, to say that I will always love them and all the things we did together through my growing-up years—visiting the *charak* fair where we always ate too many sweets, raiding the neighbor's guava tree summer afternoons while the grown-ups slept, telling fairy tales while we braided each other's hair in elaborate patterns we'd invented. *And she married the handsome prince who took her to his kingdom beyond the seven seas.* But already the activities of our girlhood seem to be far in my past, the colors leached out of them, like old sepia photographs.

His name is Somesh Sen, the man who is coming to our house with his parents today and who will be my husband "if I'm lucky enough to be chosen," as my aunt says. He is coming all the way from California. Father showed it to me yesterday, on the metal globe that sits on his desk, a chunky pink wedge on the side of a multicolored slab marked *Untd. Sts. of America*. I touched it and felt the excitement leap all the way up my arm like an electric shock. Then it died away, leaving only a beaten-metal coldness against my fingertips.

For the first time it occurred to me that if things worked out the way everyone was hoping, I'd be going halfway around the world to live with a man I hadn't even met. Would I ever see my parents again? *Don't send me so far away,* I wanted to cry, but of course I didn't. It would be ungrateful. Father had worked so hard to find this match for me. Besides, wasn't it every woman's destiny, as Mother was always telling me, to leave the known for the unknown? She had done it, and her mother before her. A *married woman belongs to her husband, her in-laws.* Hot seeds of tears pricked my eyelids at the unfairness of it.

"Mita Moni, little jewel," Father said, calling me by my childhood name. He put out his hand as though he wanted to touch my face, then let it fall to his side. "He's a good man. Comes from a fine family. He will be kind to you." He was silent for a while. Finally he said, "Come, let me show you the special sari I bought in Calcutta for you to wear at the bride-viewing."

"Are you nervous?" Radha asks as she wraps my hair in a soft cotton towel. Her parents are also trying to arrange a marriage for her. So far three families have come to see her, but no one has chosen her because her skin-color is considered too dark. "Isn't it terrible, not knowing what's going to happen?"

I nod because I don't want to disagree, don't want to make her feel bad by saying that sometimes it's worse when you know what's coming, like I do. I knew it as soon as Father unlocked his mahogany *almirah* and took out the sari.

It was the most expensive sari I had ever seen, and surely the most beautiful. Its body was a pale pink, like the dawn sky over the women's lake. The color of transition. Embroidered all over it were tiny stars made out of real gold *zari* thread.

"Here, hold it," said Father.

The sari was unexpectedly heavy in my hands, silk-slippery, a sari to walk carefully in. A sari that could change one's life. I stood there holding it, wanting to weep. I knew that when I wore it, it would hang in perfect pleats to my feet and shimmer in the light of the evening lamps. It would dazzle Somesh and his parents and they would choose me to be his bride.

When the plane takes off, I try to stay calm, to take deep, slow breaths like Father does when he practices yoga. But my hands clench themselves on to the folds of my sari and when I force them open, after the *fasten seat belt* and *no smoking* signs have blinked off, I see they have left damp blotches on the delicate crushed fabric.

We had some arguments about this sari. I wanted a blue one for the journey, because blue is the color of possibility, the color of the sky through which I would be traveling. But Mother said there must be red in it because red is the color of luck for married women. Finally, Father found one to satisfy us both: midnight-blue with a thin red border the same color as the marriage mark I'm wearing on my forehead.

It is hard for me to think of myself as a married woman. I whisper my new name to myself, Mrs. Sumita Sen, but the syllables rustle uneasily in my mouth like a stiff satin that's never been worn.

Somesh had to leave for America just a week after the wedding. He had to get back to the store, he explained to me. He had promised his partner. The store. It seems more real to me than Somesh—perhaps because I know more about it. It was what we had mostly talked about the night after the wedding, the first night we were together alone. It stayed open twenty-four hours, yes, all night, every night, not like the Indian stores which closed at dinnertime and sometimes in the hottest part of the afternoon. That's why his partner needed him back.

The store was called *7-Eleven*. I thought it a strange name, exotic, risky. All the stores I knew were piously named after gods and goddesses—*Ganesh Sweet House, Lakshmi Vastralaya for Fine Saris*—to bring the owners luck.

The store sold all kinds of amazing things—apple juice in cardboard cartons that never leaked; American bread that came in cellophane packages, already cut up; canisters of potato chips, each large grainy flake curved exactly like the next. The large refrigerator with see-through glass doors held beer and wine, which Somesh said were the most popular items.

"That's where the money comes from, especially in the neighborhood where our store is," said Somesh, smiling at the shocked look on my face. (The only places I knew of that sold alcohol were the village toddy shops, "dark, stinking dens of vice," Father called them.) "A lot of Americans drink, you know. It's a part of their culture, not considered immoral, like it is here. And really, there's nothing wrong with it." He touched my lips lightly with his finger. "When you come to California, I'll get you some sweet white wine and you'll see how good it makes you feel. . . ." Now his fingers were stroking my cheeks, my throat, moving downward. I closed my eyes and tried not to jerk away because after all it was my wifely duty.

"It helps if you can think about something else," my friend Madhavi had said when she warned me about what most husbands demanded on the very first night. Two years married, she already had one child and was pregnant with a second one.

I tried to think of the women's lake, the dark cloudy green of the *shapla* leaves that float on the water, but his lips were hot against my skin, his fingers fumbling with buttons, pulling at the cotton night-sari I wore. I couldn't breathe.

"Bite hard on your tongue," Madhavi had advised. "The pain will keep your mind off what's going on down there."

But when I bit down, it hurt so much that I cried out. I couldn't help it although I was ashamed. Somesh lifted his head. I don't know what he saw on my face, but he stopped right away. "Shhh," he said, although I had made myself silent already. "It's OK, we'll wait until you feel like it." I tried to apologize but he smiled it away and started telling me some more about the store.

And that's how it was the rest of the week until he left. We would lie side by side on the big white bridal pillow I had embroidered with a pair of doves for married harmony, and Somesh would describe how the store's front windows were decorated with a flashing neon Dewar's sign and a lighted Budweiser waterfall *this big*. I would watch his hands moving excitedly through the dim air of the bedroom and think that Father had been right, he was a good man, my husband, a kind, patient man. And so handsome, too, I would add, stealing a quick look at the strong curve of his jaw, feeling luckier than I had any right to be.

The night before he left, Somesh confessed that the store wasn't making much money yet. "I'm not worried, I'm sure it soon will," he added, his fingers pleating the edge of my sari. "But I just don't want to give you the wrong impression, don't want you to be disappointed."

In the half dark I could see he had turned toward me. His face, with two vertical lines between the brows, looked young, apprehensive, in need of protection. I'd never seen that on a man's face before. Something rose in me like a wave.

"It's all right," I said, as though to a child, and pulled his head down to my breast. His hair smelled faintly of the American cigarettes he smoked. "I won't be disappointed. I'll help you." And a sudden happiness filled me.

That night I dreamed I was at the store. Soft American music floated in the background as I moved between shelves stocked high with brightly colored cans and elegant-necked bottles, turning their labels carefully to the front, polishing them until they shone.

Now, sitting inside this metal shell that is hurtling through emptiness, I try to remember other things about my husband: how gentle his hands had been, and his lips, surprisingly soft, like a woman's. How I've longed for them through those drawn-out nights while I waited for my visa to arrive. He will be standing at the customs gate, and when I reach him, he will lower his face to mine. We will kiss in front of everyone, not caring, like Americans, then pull back, look each other in the eye, and smile.

But suddenly, as I am thinking this, I realize I cannot recall Somesh's face. I try and try until my head hurts, but I can only visualize the black air swirling outside the plane, too thin for breathing. My own breath grows ragged with panic as I think of it and my mouth fills with sour fluid the way it does just before I throw up.

I grope for something to hold on to, something beautiful and talismanic from my old life. And then I remember. Somewhere down under me, low in the belly of the plane, inside my new brown case which is stacked in the dark with a hundred others, are my saris. Thick Kanjeepuram silks in solid purples and golden yellows, the thin hand-woven cottons of the Bengal countryside, green as a young banana plant, gray as the women's lake on a monsoon morning. Already I can feel my shoulders loosening up, my breath steadying. My wedding Benarasi, flame-orange, with a wide *pelloo* of gold-embroidered dancing peacocks. Fold upon fold of Dhakais so fine they can be pulled through a ring. Into each fold my mother has tucked a small sachet of sandalwood powder to protect the saris from the unknown insects of America. Little silk sachets, made from *her* old saris—I can smell their calm fragrance as I watch the American air hostess wheeling the dinner cart toward my seat. It is the smell of my mother's hands.

I know then that everything will be all right. And when the air hostess bends her curly golden head to ask me what I would like to eat, I understand every word in spite of her strange accent and answer her without stumbling even once over the unfamiliar English phrases.

Late at night I stand in front of our bedroom mirror trying on the clothes Somesh has bought for me and smuggled in past his parents. I model each one for him, walking back and forth, clasping my hands behind my head, lips pouted, left hip thrust out just like the models on TV, while he whispers applause. I'm breathless with suppressed laughter (Father and Mother Sen must not hear us) and my cheeks are hot with the delicious excitement of conspiracy. We've stuffed a towel at the bottom of the door so no light will shine through.

I'm wearing a pair of jeans now, marveling at the curves of my hips and thighs, which have always been hidden under the flowing lines of my saris. I love the color, the same pale blue as the *nayantara* flowers that grow in my parents' garden. The solid comforting weight. The jeans come with a close-fitting T-shirt which outlines my breasts.

I scold Somesh to hide my embarrassed pleasure. He shouldn't have been so extravagant. We can't afford it. He just smiles.

The T-shirt is sunrise-orange—the color, I decide, of joy, of my new American life. Across its middle, in large black letters, is written *Great America.* I was sure the letters referred to the country, but Somesh told me it is the name of an amusement park, a place where people go to have fun. I think it a wonderful concept, novel. Above the letters is the picture of a train. Only it's not a train, Somesh tells me, it's a roller coaster. He tries to explain how it moves, the insane speed, the dizzy ground falling away, then gives up. "I'll take you there, Mita sweetheart," he says, "as soon as we move into our own place."

That's our dream (mine more than his, I suspect)—moving out of this two-room apartment where it seems to me if we all breathed in at once, there would be no air left. Where I must cover my head with the edge of my Japan nylon sari (my expensive Indian ones are to be saved for special occasions—trips to the temple, Bengali New Year) and serve tea to the old women that come to visit Mother Sen, where like a good

Indian wife I must never address my husband by his name. Where even in our bed we kiss guiltily, uneasily, listening for the giveaway creak of springs. Sometimes I laugh to myself, thinking how ironic it is that after all my fears about America, my life has turned out to be no different from Deepali's or Radha's. But at other times I feel caught in a world where everything is frozen in place, like a scene inside a glass paperweight. It is a world so small that if I were to stretch out my arms, I would touch its cold unyielding edges. I stand inside this glass world, watching helplessly as America rushes by, wanting to scream. Then I'm ashamed. Mita, I tell myself, you're growing westernized. Back home you'd never have felt this way.

We must be patient. I know that. Tactful, loving children. That is the Indian way. "I'm their life," Somesh tells me as we lie beside each other, lazy from lovemaking. He's not boasting, merely stating a fact. "They've always been there when I needed them. I could never abandon them at some old people's home." For a moment I feel rage. You're constantly thinking of them, I want to scream. But what about me? Then I remember my own parents, Mother's hands cool on my sweat-drenched body through nights of fever, Father teaching me to read, his finger moving along the crisp black angles of the alphabet, transforming them magically into things I knew, water, dog, mango tree. I beat back my unreasonable desire and nod agreement.

Somesh has bought me a cream blouse with a long brown skirt. They match beautifully, like the inside and outside of an almond. "For when you begin working," he says. But first he wants me to start college. Get a degree, perhaps in teaching. I picture myself in front of a classroom of girls with blond pigtails and blue uniforms, like a scene out of an English movie I saw long ago in Calcutta. They raise their hands respectfully when I ask a question. "Do you really think I can?" I ask. "Of course," he replies.

I am gratified he has such confidence in me. But I have another plan, a secret that I will divulge to him once we move. What I really want is to work in the store. I want to stand behind the counter in the cream-and-brown skirt set (color of earth, color of seeds) and ring up purchases. The register drawer will glide open. Confident, I will count out green dollars and silver quarters. Gleaming copper pennies. I will dust the jars of gilt-wrapped chocolates on the counter. Will straighten, on the far wall, posters of smiling young men raising their beer mugs to toast scantily clad redheads with huge spiky eyelashes. (I have never visited the store—my in-laws don't consider it proper for a wife—but of course I know exactly what it looks like.) I will charm the customers with my smile, so that they will return again and again just to hear me telling them to have a nice day.

Meanwhile, I will the store to make money for us. Quickly. Because when we move, we'll be paying for two households. But so far it hasn't worked.

They're running at a loss, Somesh tells me. They had to let the hired help go. This means most nights Somesh has to take the graveyard shift (that horrible word, like a cold hand up my spine) because his partner refuses to.

"The bastard!" Somesh spat out once. "Just because he put in more money he thinks he can order me around. I'll show him!" I was frightened by the vicious twist of his mouth. Somehow I'd never imagined that he could be angry.

Often Somesh leaves as soon as he has dinner and doesn't get back till after I've made morning tea for Father and Mother Sen. I lie mostly awake those nights, picturing masked intruders crouching in the shadowed back of the store, like I've seen on the police shows that Father Sen sometimes watches. But Somesh insists there's nothing to worry about, they have bars on the windows and a burglar alarm. "And remember," he says, "the extra cash will help us move out that much quicker."

I'm wearing a nightie now, my very first one. It's black and lacy, with a bit of a shine to it, and it glides over my hips to stop outrageously at mid-thigh. My mouth is an O of surprise in the mirror, my legs long and pale and sleek from the hair remover I asked Somesh to buy me last week. The legs of a movie star. Somesh laughs at the look on my face, then says, "You're beautiful." His voice starts a flutter low in my belly. "Do you really think so," I ask, mostly because I want to hear him say it again. No one has called me beautiful before. My father would have thought it inappropriate, my mother that it would make me vain.

Somesh draws me close. "Very beautiful," he whispers. "The most beautiful woman in the whole world." His eyes are not joking as they usually are. I want to turn off the light, but "Please," he says, "I want to keep seeing your face." His fingers are taking the pins from my hair, undoing my braids. The escaped strands fall on his face like dark rain. We have already decided where we will hide my new American clothes—the jeans and T-shirt camouflaged on a hanger among Somesh's pants, the skirt set and nightie at the bottom of my suitcase, a sandalwood sachet tucked between them, waiting.

I stand in the middle of our empty bedroom, my hair still wet from the purification bath, my back to the stripped bed I can't bear to look at. I hold in my hands the plain white sari I'm supposed to wear. I must hurry. Any minute now there'll be a knock at the door. They are afraid to leave me alone too long, afraid I might do something to myself.

The sari, a thick voile that will bunch around the waist when worn, is borrowed. White, Widow's color, color of endings. I try to tuck it into the top of the petticoat, but my fingers are numb, disobedient. It spills through them and there are waves and waves of white around my feet. I kick out in sudden rage, but the sari is too soft, it gives too easily. I grab up an edge, clamp down with my teeth and pull, feeling a fierce, bitter satisfaction when I hear it rip.

There's a cut, still stinging, on the side of my right arm, halfway to the elbow. It is from the bangle-breaking ceremony. Old Mrs. Ghosh performed the ritual, since she's a widow, too. She took my hands in hers and brought them down hard on the bedpost, so that the glass bangles I was wearing shattered and multicolored shards flew out in every direction. Some landed on the body that was on the bed, covered with a sheet. I can't call it Somesh. He was gone already. She took an edge of the sheet and rubbed the red marriage mark off my forehead. She was crying. All the women in the room were crying except me. I watched them as though from the far end of a tunnel. Their flared nostrils, their red-veined eyes, the runnels of tears, salt-corrosive, down their cheeks.

It happened last night. He was at the store. "It isn't too bad," he would tell me on the days when he was in a good mood. "Not too many customers. I can put up my feet and watch MTV all night. I can sing along with Michael Jackson as loud as I want." He had a good voice, Somesh. Sometimes he would sing softly at night, lying in bed, holding me. Hindi songs of love, *Mere Sapnon Ki Rani,* queen of my dreams. (He would not sing American songs at home out of respect for his parents, who thought they were decadent.) I would feel his warm breath on my hair as I fell asleep.

Someone came into the store last night. He took all the money, even the little rolls of pennies I had helped Somesh make up. Before he left he emptied the bullets from his gun into my husband's chest.

"Only thing is," Somesh would say about the night shifts, "I really miss you. I sit there and think of you asleep in bed. Do you know that when you sleep you make your hands into fists, like a baby? When we move out, will you come along some nights to keep me company?"

My in-laws are good people, kind. They made sure the body was covered before they let me into the room. When someone asked if my hair should be cut off, as they sometimes do with widows back home, they said no. They said I could stay at the apartment with Mrs. Ghosh if I didn't want to go to the crematorium. They asked Dr. Das to give me something to calm me down when I couldn't stop shivering. They didn't say, even once, as people would surely have in the village, that it was my bad luck that brought death to their son so soon after his marriage.

They will probably go back to India now. There's nothing here for them anymore. They will want me to go with them. You're like our daughter, they will say. Your home is with us, for as long as you want. For the rest of your life. *The rest of my life.* I can't think about that yet. It makes me dizzy. Fragments are flying about my head, multicolored and piercing sharp like bits of bangle glass.

I want you to go to college. Choose a career. I stand in front of a classroom of smiling children who love me in my cream-and-brown American dress. A faceless parade straggles across my eyelids: all those customers at the store that I will never meet. The lace nightie, fragrant with sandalwood, waiting in its blackness inside my suitcase. The savings book where we have $3605.33. *Four thousand and we can move out, maybe next month.* The name of the panty hose I'd asked him to buy me for my birthday: sheer golden-beige. His lips, unexpectedly soft, woman-smooth. Elegant-necked wine bottles swept off shelves, shattering on the floor.

I know Somesh would not have tried to stop the gunman. I can picture his silhouette against the lighted Dewar's sign, hands raised. He is trying to find the right expression to put on his face, calm, reassuring, reasonable. *OK, take the money. No, I won't call the police.* His hands tremble just a little. His eyes darken with disbelief as his fingers touch his chest and come away wet.

I yanked away the cover. I had to see. *Great America, a place where people go to have fun.* My breath roller-coasting through my body, my unlived life gathering itself into a scream. I'd expected blood, a lot of blood, the deep red-black of it crusting his chest. But they must have cleaned him up at the hospital. He was dressed in his silk wedding *kurta*. Against its warm ivory his face appeared remote, stern. The musky aroma of his aftershave lotion that someone must have sprinkled on the body. It didn't quite hide that other smell, thin, sour, metallic. The smell of death. The floor shifted under me, tilting like a wave.

I'm lying on the floor now, on the spilled white sari. I feel sleepy. Or perhaps it is some other feeling I don't have a word for. The sari is seductive-soft, drawing me into its folds.

Sometimes, bathing at the lake, I would move away from my friends, their endless chatter. I'd swim toward the middle of the water with a lazy backstroke, gazing at the sky, its enormous blueness drawing me up until I felt weightless and dizzy. Once in a while there would be a plane, a small silver needle drawn through the clouds, in and out, until it disappeared. Sometimes the thought came to me, as I floated in the middle of the lake with the sun beating down on my closed eyelids, that it would be so easy to let go, to drop into the dim brown world of mud, of water weeds fine as hair.

Once I almost did it. I curled my body inward, tight as a fist, and felt it start to sink. The sun grew pale and shapeless; the water, suddenly cold, licked at the insides of my ears in welcome. But in the end I couldn't.

They are knocking on the door now, calling my name. I push myself off the floor, my body almost too heavy to lift up, as when one climbs out after a long swim. I'm surprised at how vividly it comes to me, this memory I haven't called up in years: the desperate flailing of arms and legs as I fought my way upward; the press of the water on me, heavy as terror; the wild animal trapped inside my chest, clawing at my lungs. The day returning to me as searing air, the way I drew it in, in, in, as though I would never have enough of it.

That's when I know I cannot go back. I don't know yet how I'll manage, here in this new, dangerous land. I only know I must. Because all over India, at this very moment, widows in white saris are bowing their veiled heads, serving tea to in-laws. Doves with cut-off wings.

I am standing in front of the mirror now, gathering up the sari. I tuck in the ripped end so it lies next to my skin, my secret. I make myself think of the store, although it hurts. Inside the refrigerated unit, blue milk cartons neatly lined up by Somesh's hands. The exotic smell of Hills Brothers coffee brewed black and strong, the glisten of sugar-glazed donuts nestled in tissue. The neon Budweiser emblem winking on and off like a risky invitation.

I straighten my shoulders and stand taller, take a deep breath. Air fills me—the same air that traveled through Somesh's lungs a little while ago. The thought is like an unexpected, intimate gift. I tilt my chin, readying myself for the arguments of the coming weeks, the remonstrations. In the mirror a woman holds my gaze, her eyes apprehensive yet steady. She wears a blouse and skirt the color of almonds.

Questions and Ideas for Journaling and Discussion

1. This story describes an arranged marriage. What do you think the pros and cons of such a marriage would be?
2. Why did Sumita have to hide her American clothes?
3. What do we learn about the traditional attitudes and roles of Indian women in this story?

Writing to Explore and Learn

1. Track the colors of the clothes that Sumita wore, and discuss the relationship between the colors and their meanings. Why do you think white might symbolize widowhood?

Susan Glaspell
(1876–1948)

The biggest stories are written about the things which draw human beings closer together.

Susan Glaspell began writing and publishing short stories in magazines such as *Harper's Monthly* and *American Magazine* while a college student at Drake University. She was born into a middle-class family in Davenport, Iowa, where she grew up. After a stint as a reporter for the *Des Moines News*, she gave up her job to write full time. Having published two works of fiction, Glaspell moved to New York and turned to playwriting, and she and her husband, the bohemian George Cram Cook, became pioneers in New York's little theater movement. Together they presented works of new American drama, including writers such as Djuna Barnes, Edna St. Vincent Millay, and Eugene O'Neil. Writing from a feminist perspective, Glaspell was well known in her lifetime as "the playwright of woman's selfhood." She won the Pulitzer Prize for her play *Alison's House* (1931), which is loosely based on the life of Emily Dickinson. In her later years, she left New York to live in Providence, Rhode Island, and to write novels. Her major works include *Lifted Masks* (1912), *Trifles* (1916), and "A Jury of Her Peers" (1917).

Trifles (1916)

Weaving a daring tale of law, justice, and female revenge, Glaspell dramatizes the police investigation of a murder by exploring the stabilizing yet destructive effects of subscribing to strict gender codes. A year later, Glaspell refashioned the play as an equally powerful short story called "A Jury of Her Peers."

A Play in One Act

SCENE: *The kitchen in the now abandoned farmhouse of* JOHN WRIGHT, *a gloomy kitchen, and left without having been put in order—unwashed pans under the sink, a loaf of bread outside the bread-box, a dish-towel on the table—other signs of incompleted work. At the rear the outer door opens and the* SHERIFF *comes in followed by the* COUNTY   ATTORNEY *and* HALE. *The* SHERIFF *and* HALE *are men in middle life, the* COUNTY ATTORNEY *is a young man; all are much bundled up and go at once to the stove. They are followed by two women—the* SHERIFF'S *wife first; she is a slight wiry woman, a thin nervous face.* MRS. HALE *is larger and would ordinarily be called more comfortable looking, but she is disturbed now and looks fearfully about as she enters. The women have come in slowly, and stand close together near the door.*

COUNTY ATTORNEY: [*Rubbing his hands.*] This feels good. Come up to the fire, ladies.

MRS. PETERS: [*After taking a step forward.*] I'm not—cold.

SHERIFF: [*Unbuttoning his overcoat and stepping away from the stove as if to mark the beginning of official business.*] Now, Mr. Hale, before we move things about, you explain to Mr. Henderson just what you saw when you came here yesterday morning.

COUNTY ATTORNEY: By the way, has anything been moved? Are things just as you left them yesterday?

SHERIFF: [*Looking about.*] It's just the same. When it dropped below zero last night I thought I'd better send Frank out this morning to make a fire for us—no use getting pneumonia with a big case on, but I told him not to touch anything except the stove—and you know Frank.

COUNTY ATTORNEY: Somebody should have been left here yesterday.

SHERIFF: Oh—yesterday. When I had to send Frank to Morris Center for that man who went crazy—I want you to know I had my hands full yesterday. I knew you could get back from Omaha by today and as long as I went over everything here myself—

COUNTY ATTORNEY: Well, Mr. Hale, tell just what happened when you came here yesterday morning.

HALE: Harry and I had started to town with a load of potatoes. We came along the road from my place and as I got here I said, "I'm going to see if I can't get John Wright to go in with me on a party telephone." I spoke to Wright about it once before and he put me off, saying folks talked too much anyway, and all he asked was peace and quiet—I guess you know about how much he talked himself; but I thought maybe if I went to the house and talked about it before his wife, though I said to Harry that I didn't know as what his wife wanted made much difference to John—

COUNTY ATTORNEY: Let's talk about that later, Mr. Hale. I do want to talk about that, but tell now just what happened when you got to the house.

HALE: I didn't hear or see anything; I knocked at the door, and still it was all quiet inside. I knew they must be up, it was past eight o'clock. So I knocked again, and I thought I heard somebody say, "Come in." I wasn't sure, I'm not sure yet, but I opened the door—this door [*indicating the door by which the two women are still standing*] and there in that rocker—[*pointing to it*] sat Mrs. Wright.

They all look at the rocker.

COUNTY ATTORNEY: What—was she doing?

HALE: She was rockin' back and forth. She had her apron in her hand and was kind of—pleating it.

COUNTY ATTORNEY: And how did she—look?

HALE: Well, she looked queer.

COUNTY ATTORNEY: How do you mean—queer?

HALE: Well, as if she didn't know what she was going to do next. And kind of done up.

COUNTY ATTORNEY: How did she seem to feel about your coming?

HALE: Why, I don't think she minded—one way or other. She didn't pay much attention. I said, "How do, Mrs. Wright, it's cold, ain't it?" And she said, "Is it?"—and went on kind of pleating at her apron. Well, I was surprised; she didn't ask me to come up to the stove, or to set down, but just sat there, not even looking at me, so I said, "I want to see John." And then she—laughed. I guess you would call it a laugh. I thought of Harry and the team outside, so I said a little sharp: "Can't I see John?" "No," she says, kind o' dull like. "Ain't he home?" says I. "Yes," says she, "he's home." "Then why can't I see him?" I asked her, out of patience. "'Cause he's dead," says she. "*Dead?*" says I. She just nodded her head, not getting a bit excited, but rockin' back and forth. "Why—where is he?" says I, not knowing what to say. She just pointed upstairs—like that [*himself pointing to the room above*]. I got up, with the idea of going up there. I walked from there to here—then I says, "Why, what did he die of?" "He died of a rope round his neck," says she, and just went on pleatin' at her apron. Well, I went out and called Harry. I thought I might—need help. We went upstairs and there he was lyin'—

COUNTY ATTORNEY: I think I'd rather have you go into that upstairs, where you can point it all out. Just go on now with the rest of the story.

HALE: Well, my first thought was to get that rope off. It looked . . . [*Stops, his face twitches*] . . . but Harry, he went up to him, and he said, "No, he's dead all right, and we'd better not touch anything." So we went back down stairs. She was still sitting that same way. "Has anybody been notified?" I asked. "No," says she, unconcerned. "Who did this, Mrs. Wright?" said Harry. He said it business-like—and she stopped pleatin' of her apron. "I don't know," she says. "You don't *know?*" says Harry. "No," says she. "Weren't you sleepin' in the bed with him?" says Harry. "Yes," says she, "but I was on the inside." "Somebody slipped a rope round his neck and strangled him and you didn't wake up?" says Harry. "I didn't wake up," she said after him. We must 'a looked as if we didn't see how that could be, for after a minute she said, "I sleep sound." Harry was going to ask her more questions but I said maybe we ought to let her tell her story first to the coroner, or the sheriff, so Harry went fast as he could to Rivers' place, where there's a telephone.

COUNTY ATTORNEY: And what did Mrs. Wright do when she knew that you had gone for the coroner?

HALE: She moved from that chair to this one over here [*Pointing to a small chair in the corner*] and just sat there with her hands held together and looking down. I got a feeling that I ought to make some conversation, so I said I had come in to see if John wanted to put in a telephone, and at that she started to laugh, and then she stopped and looked at me—scared. [*The* COUNTY ATTORNEY, *who has had his notebook out, makes a note.*] I dunno, maybe it wasn't scared. I wouldn't like to say it was. Soon Harry got back, and then Dr. Lloyd came, and you, Mr. Peters, and so I guess that's all I know that you don't.

COUNTY ATTORNEY: [*Looking around.*] I guess we'll go upstairs first—and then out to the barn and around there. [*To the* SHERIFF] You're convinced that there was nothing important here—nothing that would point to any motive.

SHERIFF: Nothing here but kitchen things.

The COUNTY ATTORNEY, *after again looking around the kitchen, opens the door of a cupboard closet. He gets up on a chair and looks on a shelf. Pulls his hand away, sticky.*

COUNTY ATTORNEY: Here's a nice mess.

The women draw nearer.

MRS. PETERS: [*To the other woman.*] Oh, her fruit; it did freeze. (*To the* LAWYER.) She worried about that when it turned so cold. She said the fire'd go out and her jars would break.

SHERIFF: Well, can you beat the women! Held for murder and worryin' about her preserves.

COUNTY ATTORNEY: I guess before we're through she may have something more serious than preserves to worry about.

HALE: Well, women are used to worrying over trifles.

The two women move a little closer together.

COUNTY ATTORNEY: [*With the gallantry of a young politician.*] And yet, for all their worries, what would we do without the ladies? [*The women do not unbend. He goes to the sink, takes a dipperful of water from the pail and pouring it into a basin, washes his hands. Starts to wipe them on the roller towel, turns it for a cleaner place.*] Dirty towels! [*Kicks his foot against the pans under the sink.*] Not much of a housekeeper, would you say, ladies?

MRS. HALE: [*Stiffly.*] There's a great deal of work to be done on a farm.

COUNTY ATTORNEY: To be sure. And yet [*With a little bow to her*] I know there are some Dickson county farmhouses which do not have such roller towels.

He gives it a pull to expose its full length again.

MRS. HALE: Those towels get dirty awful quick. Men's hands aren't always as clean as they might be.

COUNTY ATTORNEY: Ah, loyal to your sex, I see. But you and Mrs. Wright were neighbors. I suppose you were friends, too.

MRS. HALE: [*Shaking her head.*] I've not seen much of her of late years. I've not been in this house—it's more than a year.

COUNTY ATTORNEY: And why was that? You didn't like her?

MRS. HALE: I liked her all well enough. Farmers' wives have their hands full, Mr. Henderson. And then—

COUNTY ATTORNEY: Yes—?

MRS. HALE: [*Looking about.*] It never seemed a very cheerful place.

COUNTY ATTORNEY: No—it's not cheerful. I shouldn't say she had the homemaking instinct.

MRS. HALE: Well, I don't know as Wright had, either.

COUNTY ATTORNEY: You mean that they didn't get on very well?

MRS. HALE: No, I don't mean anything. But I don't think a place'd be any cheerfuller for John Wright's being in it.

COUNTY ATTORNEY: I'd like to talk more of that a little later. I want to get the lay of things upstairs now.

He goes to the left, where three steps lead to a stair door.

SHERIFF: I suppose anything Mrs. Peters does'll be all right. She was to take in some clothes for her, you know, and a few little things. We left in such a hurry yesterday.

COUNTY ATTORNEY: Yes, but I would like to see what you take, Mrs. Peters, and keep an eye out for anything that might be of use to us.

MRS. PETERS: Yes, Mr. Henderson.

The women listen to the men's steps on the stairs, then look about the kitchen.

MRS. HALE: I'd hate to have men coming into my kitchen, snooping around and criticizing.

She arranges the pans under sink which the LAWYER *had shoved out of place.*

MRS. PETERS: Of course it's no more than their duty.

MRS. HALE: Duty's all right, but I guess that deputy sheriff that came out to make the fire might have got a little of this on. [*Gives the roller towel a pull.*] Wish I'd thought of that sooner. Seems mean to talk about her for not having things slicked up when she had to come away in such a hurry.

MRS. PETERS: [*Who has gone to a small table in the left rear corner of the room, and lifted one end of a towel that covers a pan.*] She had bread set.

Stands still.

MRS. HALE: [*Eyes fixed on a loaf of bread beside the bread-box, which is on a low shelf at the other side of the room. Moves slowly toward it.*] She was going to put this in there. [*Picks up loaf, then abruptly drops it. In a manner of returning to familiar things.*] It's a shame about her fruit. I wonder if it's all gone. [*Gets up on the chair and looks.*] I think there's some here that's all right, Mrs. Peters. Yes—here; [*Holding it toward the window*] this is cherries, too. [*Looking again.*] I declare I believe that's the only one. [*Gets down, bottle in her hand. Goes to the sink and wipes it off on the outside.*] She'll feel awful bad after all her hard work in the hot weather. I remember the afternoon I put up my cherries last summer.

She puts the bottle on the big kitchen table, center of the room. With a sigh, is about to sit down in the rocking-chair. Before she is seated realizes what chair it is; with a slow look at it, steps back. The chair which she has touched rocks back and forth.

MRS. PETERS: Well, I must get those things from the front room closet. [*She goes to the door at the right, but after looking into the other room, steps back.*] You coming with me, Mrs. Hale? You could help me carry them.

They go in the other room; reappear, MRS. PETERS *carrying a dress and skirt,* MRS. HALE *following with a pair of shoes.*

MRS. PETERS: My, it's cold in there.

She puts the clothes on the big table, and hurries to the stove.

MRS. HALE: [*Examining the skirt.*] Wright was close. I think maybe that's why she kept so much to herself. She didn't even belong to the Ladies Aid. I suppose she felt she couldn't do her part, and then you don't enjoy things when you feel shabby. She used to wear pretty clothes and be lively, when she was Minnie Foster, one of the town girls singing in the choir. But that—oh, that was thirty years ago. This all you was to take in?

MRS. PETERS: She said she wanted an apron. Funny thing to want, for there isn't much to get you dirty in jail, goodness knows. But I suppose just to make her feel more natural. She said they was in the top drawer in this cupboard. Yes, here. And then her little shawl that always hung behind the door. [*Opens stair door and looks.*] Yes, here it is.

Quickly shuts door leading upstairs.

MRS. HALE: [*Abruptly moving toward her.*] Mrs. Peters?

MRS. PETERS: Yes, Mrs. Hale?

MRS. HALE: Do you think she did it?

MRS. PETERS: [*In a frightened voice.*] Oh, I don't know.

MRS. HALE: Well, I don't think she did. Asking for an apron and her little shawl. Worrying about her fruit.

MRS. PETERS: [*Starts to speak, glances up, where footsteps are heard in the room above. In a low voice.*] Mr. Peters says it looks bad for her. Mr. Henderson is awful sarcastic in a speech and he'll make fun of her sayin' she didn't wake up.

MRS. HALE: Well, I guess John Wright didn't wake when they was slipping that rope under his neck.

MRS. PETERS: No, it's strange. It must have been done awful crafty and still. They say it was such a—funny way to kill a man, rigging it all up like that.

MRS. HALE: That's just what Mr. Hale said. There was a gun in the house. He says that's what he can't understand.

MRS. PETERS: Mr. Henderson said coming out that what was needed for the case was a motive; something to show anger, or— sudden feeling.

MRS. HALE: [*Who is standing by the table.*] Well, I don't see any signs of anger around here. [*She puts her hand on the dish towel which lies on the table, stands looking down at table, one half of which is clean, the other half messy.*] It's wiped to here. [*Makes a move as if to finish work, then turns and looks at loaf of bread outside the breadbox. Drops towel. In that voice of coming back to familiar things.*] Wonder how they are finding things upstairs. I hope she had it a little more red-up up there. You know, it seems kind of *sneaking*. Locking her up in town and then coming out here and trying to get her own house to turn against her!

MRS. PETERS: But Mrs. Hale, the law is the law.

MRS. HALE: I s'pose 'tis. [*Unbuttoning her coat.*] Better loosen up your things, Mrs. Peters. You won't feel them when you go out.

MRS. PETERS *takes off her fur tippet, goes to hang it on hook at back of room, stands looking at the under part of the small corner table.*

MRS. PETERS: She was piecing a quilt.

She brings the large sewing basket and they look at the bright pieces.

MRS. HALE: It's a log cabin pattern. Pretty, isn't it? I wonder if she was goin' to quilt it or just knot it?

Footsteps have been heard coming down the stairs. The Sheriff enters followed by HALE *and the* COUNTY ATTORNEY.

SHERIFF: They wonder if she was going to quilt it or just knot it!

The men laugh, the women look abashed.

COUNTY ATTORNEY: [*Rubbing his hands over the stove.*] Frank's fire didn't do much up there, did it? Well, let's go out to the barn and get that cleared up.

The men go outside.

MRS. HALE: [*Resentfully.*] I don't know as there's anything so strange, our takin' up our time with little things while we're waiting for them to get the evidence. [*She sits down at the big table smoothing out a block with decision.*] I don't see as it's anything to laugh about.

MRS. PETERS: [*Apologetically.*] Of course they've got awful important things on their minds.

Pulls up a chair and joins MRS. HALE *at the table.*

MRS. HALE: [*Examining another block.*] Mrs. Peters, look at this one. Here, this is one she was working on, and look at the sewing! All the rest of it has been so nice and even. And look at this! It's all over the place! Why, it looks as if she didn't know what she was about!

After she has said this they look at each other, then start to glance back at the door. After an instant MRS. HALE *has pulled at a knot and ripped the sewing.*

MRS. PETERS: Oh, what are you doing, Mrs. Hale?

MRS. HALE: [*Mildly.*] Just pulling out a stitch or two that's not sewed very good. [*Threading a needle.*] Bad sewing always made me fidgety.

MRS. PETERS: [*Nervously.*] I don't think we ought to touch things.

MRS. HALE: I'll just finish up this end. [*Suddenly stopping and leaning forward.*] Mrs. Peters?

MRS. PETERS: Yes, Mrs. Hale?

MRS. HALE: What do you suppose she was so nervous about?

MRS. PETERS: Oh—I don't know. I don't know as she was nervous. I sometimes sew awful queer when I'm just tired. [MRS. HALE *starts to say something, looks at* MRS. PETERS, *then goes on sewing.*] Well, I must get these things wrapped up. They may be through sooner than we think. [*Putting apron and other things together.*] I wonder where I can find a piece of paper, and string.

MRS. HALE: In that cupboard, maybe.

MRS. PETERS: [*Looking in cupboard.*] Why, here's a bird-cage. [*Holds it up.*] Did she have a bird, Mrs. Hale?

MRS. HALE: Why, I don't know whether she did or not—I've not been here for so long. There was a man around last year selling canaries cheap, but I don't know as she took one; maybe she did. She used to sing real pretty herself.

MRS. PETERS: [*Glancing around.*] Seems funny to think of a bird here. But she must have had one, or why would she have a cage? I wonder what happened to it.

MRS. HALE: I s'pose maybe the cat got it.

MRS. PETERS: No, she didn't have a cat. She's got that feeling some people have about cats—being afraid of them. My cat got in her room and she was real upset and asked me to take it out.

MRS. HALE: My sister Bessie was like that. Queer, ain't it?

MRS. PETERS: [*Examining the cage.*] Why, look at this door. It's broke. One hinge is pulled apart.

MRS. HALE: [*Looking too.*] Looks as if someone must have been rough with it.

MRS. PETERS: Why, yes.

She brings the cage forward and puts it on the table.

MRS. HALE: I wish if they're going to find any evidence they'd be about it. I don't like this place.

MRS. PETERS: But I'm awful glad you came with me, Mrs. Hale. It would be lonesome for me sitting here alone.

MRS. HALE: It would, wouldn't it? [*Dropping her sewing.*] But I tell you what I do wish, Mrs. Peters. I wish I had come over sometimes when *she* was here. I—[*Looking around the room*]—wish I had.

MRS. PETERS: But of course you were awful busy, Mrs. Hale—your house and your children.

MRS. HALE: I could've come. I stayed away because it weren't cheerful—and that's why I ought to have come. I—I've never liked this place. Maybe because it's down in a hollow and you don't see the road. I dunno what it is but it's a lonesome place and always was. I wish I had come over to see Minnie Foster sometimes. I can see now—

Shakes her head.

MRS. PETERS: Well, you mustn't reproach yourself, Mrs. Hale. Somehow we just don't see how it is with other folks until—something comes up.

MRS. HALE: Not having children makes less work—but it makes a quiet house, and Wright out to work all day, and no company when he did come in. Did you know John Wright, Mrs. Peters?

MRS. PETERS: Not to know him; I've seen him in town. They say he was a good man.

MRS. HALE: Yes—good; he didn't drink, and kept his word as well as most, I guess, and paid his debts. But he was a hard man, Mrs. Peters. Just to pass the time of day with him—[*Shivers.*] Like a raw wind that gets to the bone. [*Pauses, her eye falling on the cage.*] I should think she would 'a wanted a bird. But what do you suppose went with it?

MRS. PETERS   I don't know, unless it got sick and died.

She reaches over and swings the broken door, swings it again, both women watch it.

MRS. HALE: You weren't raised round here, were you? [MRS. PETERS *shakes her head.*] You didn't know—her?

MRS. PETERS: Not till they brought her yesterday.

MRS. HALE: She—come to think of it, she was kind of a like a bird her-self—real sweet and pretty, but kind of timid and—fluttery. How—she—did—change. [*Silence; then as if struck by a happy thought and relieved to get back to everyday things.*] Tell you what, Mrs. Peters, why don't you take the quilt in with you? It might take up her mind.

MRS. PETERS: Why, I think that's a real nice idea, Mrs. Hale. There could-n't possibly be any objection to it, could there? Now, just what would I take? I wonder if her patches are in here—and her things.

They look in the sewing basket.

MRS. HALE: Here's some red. I expect this has got sewing things in it. [*Brings out a fancy box.*] What a pretty box. Looks like something somebody would give you. Maybe her scissors are in here. [*Opens box. Suddenly puts her hand to her nose.*] Why— [Mrs. PETERS *bends nearer, then turns her face away.*] There's something wrapped up in this piece of silk.

MRS. PETERS: Why, this isn't her scissors.

MRS. HALE: [*Lifting the silk.*] Oh, Mrs. Peters—it's—

MRS. PETERS *bends closer.*

MRS. PETERS: It's the bird.

MRS. HALE: [*Jumping up.*] But, Mrs. Peters—look at it! Its neck! Look at its neck! It's all—other side *to.*

MRS. PETERS: Somebody—wrung—its—neck.

Their eyes meet. A look of growing comprehension, of horror. Steps are heard outside. MRS. HALE *slips box under quilt pieces, and sinks into her chair. Enter* SHERIFF *and* COUNTY ATTORNEY. MRS. PETERS *rises.*

COUNTY ATTORNEY: [*As one turning from serious things to little pleasantries.*] Well, ladies, have you decided whether she was going to quilt it or knot it?

MRS. PETERS: We think she was going to—knot it.

COUNTY ATTORNEY: Well, that's interesting, I'm sure. [*Seeing the birdcage.*] Has the bird flown?

MRS. HALE: [*Putting more quilt pieces over the box.*] We think the—cat got it.

COUNTY ATTORNEY: [*Preoccupied.*] Is there a cat?

MRS. HALE *glances in a quick covert way at* MRS. PETERS

MRS. PETERS: Well, not *now.* They're superstitious, you know. They leave.

COUNTY ATTORNEY: [*To* SHERIFF PETERS, *continuing an interrupted conversation.*] No sign at all of anyone having come from the outside. Their own rope. Now let's go up again and go over it piece by piece. [*They start upstairs.*] It would have to have been someone who knew just the—

MRS. PETERS *sits down. The two women sit there not looking at one another, but as if peering into something and at the same time holding back. When they talk now it is in the manner of feeling their way over strange ground, as if afraid of what they are saying, but as if they cannot help saying it.*

MRS. HALE: She liked the bird. She was going to bury it in that pretty box.

MRS. PETERS: [*In a whisper.*] When I was a girl—my kitten—there was a boy took a hatchet, and before my eyes—and before I could get there—[*Covers her face an instant.*] If they hadn't held me back I would have—[*Catches herself, looks upstairs where steps are heard, falters weakly*]—hurt him.

MRS. HALE: [*With a slow look around her.*] I wonder how it would seem never to have had any children around. [*Pause.*] No, Wright wouldn't like the bird—a thing that sang. She used to sing. He killed that, too.

MRS. PETERS: [*Moving uneasily.*] We don't know who killed the bird.

MRS. HALE: I knew John Wright.

MRS. PETERS: It was an awful thing was done in this house that night, Mrs. Hale. Killing a man while he slept, slipping a rope around his neck that choked the life out of him.

MRS. HALE: His neck. Choked the life out of him.

Her hand goes out and rests on the birdcage.

MRS. PETERS: [*With rising voice.*] We don't know who killed him. We don't know.

MRS. HALE: [*Her own feeling not interrupted.*] If there'd been years and years of nothing, then a bird to sing to you, it would be awful—still, after the bird was still.

MRS. PETERS: [*Something within her speaking.*] I know what stillness is. When we homesteaded in Dakota, and my first baby died— after he was two years old, and me with no other then—

MRS. HALE: [*Moving.*] How soon do you suppose they'll be through looking for the evidence?

MRS. PETERS: I know what stillness is. [*Pulling herself back.*] The law has got to punish crime, Mrs. Hale.

MRS. HALE: [*Not as if answering that.*] I wish you'd seen Minnie Foster when she wore a white dress with blue ribbons and stood up there in the choir and sang. [*A look around the room.*] Oh, I *wish* I'd come over here once in a while! That was a crime! That was a crime! Who's going to punish that?

MRS. PETERS: [*Looking upstairs.*] We mustn't—take on.

MRS. HALE: I might have known she needed help! I know how things can be—for women. I tell you, it's queer, Mrs. Peters. We live close together and we live far apart. We all go through the same things—it's all just a different kind of the same thing. [*Brushes her eyes, noticing the bottle of fruit, reaches out for it.*] If I was you I wouldn't tell her her fruit was gone. Tell her it *ain't*. Tell her it's all right. Take this in to prove it to her. She—she may never know whether it was broke or not.

MRS. PETERS: [*Takes the bottle, looks about for something to wrap it in; takes petticoat from the clothes brought from the other room, very nervously begins winding this around the bottle. In a false voice.*]   My, it's a good thing the men couldn't hear us. Wouldn't they just laugh! Getting all stirred up over a little thing like a—dead canary. As if that could have anything to do with—with—wouldn't they *laugh*!

The men are heard coming down stairs.

MRS. HALE: [*Under her breath.*] Maybe they would—maybe they wouldn't.

COUNTY ATTORNEY: No, Peters, it's all perfectly clear except a reason for doing it. But you know juries when it comes to women. If there was some definite thing. Something to show—something to make a story about—a thing that would connect up with this strange way of doing it—

The women's eyes meet for an instant. Enter HALE *from outer door.*

HALE: Well, I've got the team around. Pretty cold out there.

COUNTY ATTORNEY: I'm going to stay here a while by myself. [*To the* SHERIFF.] You can send Frank out for me, can't you? I want to go over everything. I'm not satisfied that we can't do better.

SHERIFF: Do you want to see what Mrs. Peters is going to take in?

The LAWYER *goes to the table, picks up the apron, laughs.*

COUNTY ATTORNEY: Oh, I guess they're not very dangerous things the ladies have picked out. [*Moves a few things about, disturbing the quilt pieces which cover the box. Steps back.*] No, Mrs. Peters doesn't need supervising. For that matter, a sheriff's wife is married to the law. Ever think of it that way, Mrs. Peters?

MRS. PETERS: Not—just that way.

SHERIFF: [*Chuckling.*] Married to the law. [*Moves toward the other room.*] I just want you to come in here a minute, George. We ought to take a look at these windows.

COUNTY ATTORNEY: [*Scoffingly.*] Oh, windows!

SHERIFF: We'll be right out, Mr. Hale.

HALE *goes outside. The* SHERIFF *follows the* COUNTY ATTORNEY *into the other room. Then* MRS. HALE *rises, hands tight together, looking intensely at* MRS. PETERS, *whose eyes make a slow turn, finally meeting* MRS. HALE*'s. A moment* MRS. HALE *holds her, then her own eyes point the way to where the box is concealed. Suddenly* MRS. PETERS *throws back quilt pieces and tries to put the box in the bag she is wearing. It is too big. She opens box, starts to take bird out, cannot touch it, goes to pieces, stands there helpless. Sound of a knob turning in the other room.* MRS. HALE *snatches the box and puts it in the pocket of her big coat. Enter* COUNTY ATTORNEY *and* SHERIFF.

COUNTY ATTORNEY: [*Facetiously.*] Well, Henry, at least we found out that she was not going to quilt it. She was going to—what is it you call it, ladies?

MRS. HALE: [*Her hand against her pocket.*] We call it—knot it, Mr. Henderson.

Questions and Ideas for Journaling and Discussion

1. Discuss the relationship between the title of the play and the events in the play.
2. How do the women both sympathize and identify with Minnie?
3. How would you explain the women's silence?

Writing to Explore and Learn

1. Using the evidence in *Trifles*, explain what Glaspell suggests about the nature of women and men.
2. How do those constructions affect gender relations?

Open Question for Writing

1. Choose two or three works in any section, and discuss the ways in which each poet and/or writer represents gender and the changing roles of women and/or men.

CREDITS

INDEX